HIGH-PERFORMANCE ORACLE DATABASE APPLICATIONS

HIGH-PERFORMANCE
ORACLE DATABASE
APPLICATIONS

Donald K. Burleson

CORIOLIS GROUP BOOKS

Publisher	Keith Weiskamp
Project Editor	Toni Zuccarini
Copy Editor	Maggy Miskell
Cover Artist	Gary Smith
Cover Design	Anthony Stock
Interior Design	Michelle Stroup
Layout Production	Dorothy Bungert
Proofreader	Shelly Crossen
Indexer	Mary Millhollon

The Coriolis Group, Inc.
7339 E. Acoma Drive, Suite 7
Scottsdale, AZ 85260
Phone: (602) 483-0192
Fax: (602) 483-0193
Web address: http://www.coriolis.com

ISBN 1-57610-100-2: $39.99

Printed in the United States of America

10 9 8 7 6 5 4 3 2 1

To my children, Andy and Jenny, and to Patti, whose love and support made this book possible.

Contents

Chapter 5   Tuning Oracle Locking   161

Chapter 6   Oracle DBA Performance And Tuning   189

Chapter 7   Performance And Tuning For Distributed Oracle Databases   203

Chapter 8   Performance And Tuning For Oracle Database Connectivity Tools   249

Chapter 9   Linking Oracle And Non-Oracle Databases   283

Chapter 10 Tuning Oracle Data Warehouse And OLAP Applications 295

Chapter 11 Oracle Application Monitoring 333

Introduction

This book was written because I felt there was a need for a comprehensive text for the application developer and DBA who must implement fast, efficient, and reliable client/server applications. Unlike other theoretical books on this subject, *Designing High-Performance Oracle Databases* provides tangible examples and easy-to-understand techniques for getting the most out of your database and client/server application. I have attempted to explain complex database interactions in plain English so developers can immediately begin tuning their Oracle applications. Throughout the book I use actual code examples from Oracle databases, and I guide the developer through all of the implementation steps, from initial planning to final rollout, drawing on my many years of real-world experience in tuning large applications, and focusing on the effective use of Oracle and client/server technology. The CD-ROM that is included with the text will allow the reader to immediately begin monitoring and tuning their Oracle databases.

The focus of this book is on the application of Oracle performance and tuning techniques to real-world systems. The text will explore how performance bottlenecks are identified and remedied. I also concentrate on specific components of Oracle performance and describe each in detail, using dozens of database examples. In addition to real-world examples, the text contains numerous code listings and other tools that can be immediately used to assist in the diagnosis and treatment of performance problems.

This book introduces the evolution and internals of database management and client/server technology and shows how proven techniques can be used to fully exploit Oracle—through the use of existing hardware and software resources. Furthermore, it will show the professional applications developer how he can intelligently use the client/server paradigm to implement fast and efficient systems.

Until this book, there has been nothing in the marketplace that addresses client/server as a whole and provides an overall strategy for tuning. *Designing High-Performance Oracle Databases* fills this void in the Oracle universe, and is designed to give you easy-to-understand, real-world advice to get your Oracle system working the way you want it to.

Logical Performance Design For Oracle Databases

Today's relational database environment offers a wide number of books with tips on the effective design of relational database systems. Unfortunately, many of these texts are purely theoretical and fail to take into account the real-world issues that are involved in designing a high-performance Oracle database. At the same time, dozens of Computer Aided Systems Engineering (CASE) vendors claim that their tools are indispensable for database design. In reality, taking a design through the performance stage is the only way to fully understand the issues. Real-world experience has no substitute in this realm.

Performance And Database Distribution

It is critical to remember that database distribution is a design issue—not an analysis issue. The structured specification for the systems analysis phase specifies the logical data stores, but has no reference to the physical placement or type for the data stores. In the analysis phase, it doesn't matter whether data storage is in a VSAM file on a mainframe, an Oracle database on a VAX, or on a Rolodex file on the user's desk. The concern is documenting the data flows between the logical processes and showing how data interacts with the logical data repositories. While it can be very tempting for some analysts to address physical design issues in the middle of an analysis, the disconnection of analysis and design is critical to the development of an effective Oracle system. In fact, this contamination of a logical analysis with a physical design issue is one of the main reasons that projects suffer from "analysis paralysis." Analysis paralysis usually occurs when tasks overwhelm the analysis team, shifting the focus from "How does it function?" to "How can we implement the function?"

If we accept the premise that creating a high-performance database is a physical design issue, it follows that any generally accepted analysis methodology will suffice for documenting the requirements of the system. Structured specifications with data flow diagrams (for example, the popular DeMarco style or Gane & Sarson methods of systems analysis), along with a data dictionary and process logic specifications, represent an excellent starting point for system design.

The Economics Of Database Design

One of the primary reasons that companies abandon centralized mainframes is the promise of running open systems with cheaper hardware and software. With the costs of an IBM mainframe data center approaching $500,000 per month, it is not surprising that many top IS managers force organizations to undertake the long march into open, distributed databases. In addition to hardware costs, database software costs are dramatically more for mainframe systems. A large mainframe DBMS package easily reaches the $250,000 price range, yet a good relational database for a Unix-based midrange computer costs as little as $10,000.

As attractive as these savings may sound, they still must be balanced against the costs of maintaining the distributed systems. As processors are added to remote locations, human functions—system administration, LAN management, and database administration—must also be replicated. And while the costs of a database server may be low, many companies lapse into shock when they are ready to attach 1,000 PC workstations to the server and find the cost for PC seats soaring up to $2,000 per database desktop client. PC workstations using a GUI with multiple database connections carry a price tag in excess of

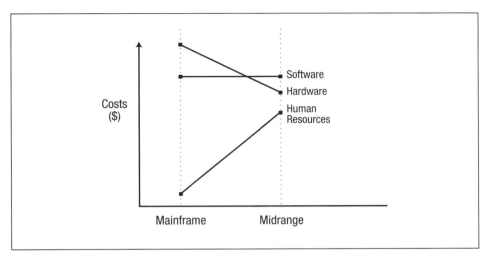

Figure 1.1   Downsizing cost-factor analysis for database systems.

$5,000 per PC, a figure that often prompts managers to question the economic justification for downsizing. Performing a valid cost-benefit analysis (see Figure 1.1) requires the identification and quantification of all of the potential costs and savings for hardware, software, and human resources.

Many IS managers do not realize that their staff sizes may more than double, depending upon the type of open systems database migration. The open system approach has a tremendous initial cost, and the savings accrue several years after implementation. When a mainframe database is partitioned into 20 remote Oracle servers, the database administration and system administration support staff may actually triple in size.

Saving money is not the only reason for downsizing, however. Companies relying on competitive information are often forced to the new midrange platforms in order to use the most advanced software. For example, the advanced object-oriented databases are found almost exclusively on midrange Unix systems. Consequently, no company can capitalize on object-oriented technology while using mainframe technology.

Location Transparency And Database Design

Location transparency refers to the distributed database's ability to function as a unified whole, appearing to end users as a single unified system. Where the database resides, what type of database is used, or the required database access method are all unimportant to the end user. With Oracle, this type of transparency is definitely possible—but not without expense. Even a distributed system composed entirely of relational databases must deal with different dialects of SQL (see Figure 1.2).

Managing the various dialects of SQL is one of the most pressing problems with distributed databases. Each major database vendor (ostensibly to improve its implementation of SQL) adds its own features and extensions. Oracle is one of the most prolific at adding SQL extensions. It is true that Oracle implements some outstanding and useful extensions such as the **DECODE** function, but queries to non-Oracle databases using these features can mean failure.

These SQL dialect problems are even more aggravating when the distributed database is composed of databases from nonrelational architectures. In order to achieve transparency, sophisticated techniques are necessary to interrogate the distributed query, identifying which data components reside in what architecture and decomposing the subqueries into the appropriate access language (see Figure 1.3).

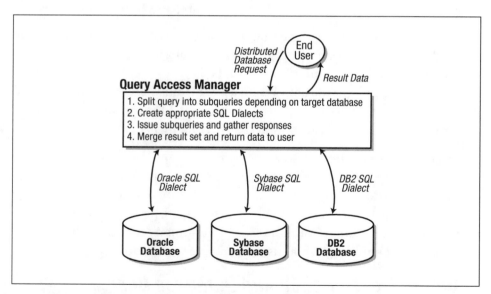

Figure 1.2   An example of single-architecture database queries.

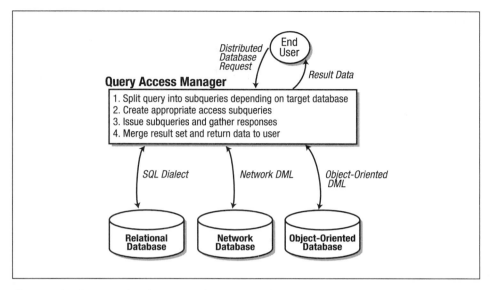

Figure 1.3 An example of multi-architecture database queries.

To understand the concept of location transparency, consider this example: Assume a part inventory system with separate databases in Washington, Boise, New York, and Albuquerque. The manager needs the number of widgets in stock at all the locations. The manager issues the following SQL command to the distributed database manager:

```
SELECT count(*)
FROM INVENTORY
WHERE partname = 'widget';
```

In the above example of **count(*)** with location transparency, the end user has no interest in any individual databases when servicing this request, defining it as a *global transaction*. The transaction manager has the responsibility to query all of the distributed **INVENTORY** tables and collect the counts from each table, merging them into a single result set.

In many relational databases, such as Oracle with SQL*Net, creating "database links" to the remote database and assigning a global synonym to the remote tables achieves transparency. Later in this chapter, all examples showing distributed database requests will use the Oracle database link approach to illustrate connecting remote databases.

A location suffix associated with a Telnet name creates database links in Oracle. At the lowest level, computers are assigned an internal address, or IP address, which gives the computer a distinct number. An example would be 150.223.90.27. The Telnet name translates into the IP (Internal Protocol) address for the computer. In the following example, **london_unix** translates into the IP address 143.32.142.3:1:

```
CREATE PUBLIC DATABASE LINK london.com
    CONNECT TO london_unix USING oracle_user_profile;
```

You can now include any tables from the London sites by qualifying the remote site name in the SQL query, as in the following:

```
SELECT     CUSTOMER.customer_name,
           ORDER.order_date
    FROM   customer@london.com,
           ORDER
    WHERE
    CUSTOMER.cust_number = ORDER.customer_number;
```

But where is the location transparency? To make the location of the **CUSTOMER** table transparent, the DBA assigns synonyms for the **CUSTOMER** table in London, giving the query the appearance of being local:

```
CREATE SYNONYM CUSTOMER for customer@london.com;
```

The query can now run with complete location transparency, since the SQL has no need to reference either the IP address of the computer or the name of the database on that computer:

```
SELECT     CUSTOMER.customer_name,
           ORDER.order_date
    FROM   CUSTOMER,
           ORDER
    WHERE
    CUSTOMER.cust_number = ORDER.customer_number;
```

Oracle stored procedures can also be defined for the remote table without any reference to its physical location. For example, this procedure can be called with the following statement:

```
add_customer("Burleson")

CREATE PROCEDURE add_customer (cust_name char(8)) AS
    BEGIN
        INSERT INTO CUSTOMER VALUES(cust_name);
    END;
```

Many sites recognize the need to track the locations of their remote database while still providing location transparency to the users and programmers. The concept of database domains and hierarchies of physical locations are especially important in situations of horizontal partitioning where tables with identical names are kept at numerous locations. Domains establish a logical hierarchy of physical locations for the enterprise. This sample database establishes a domain hierarchy for its remote databases (see Figure 1.4).

The DBA at each node in the network assigns synonyms for all unique tables within the distributed network, creating abbreviated domain names for the duplicate table structures that exist at remote locations. For example, assume both Japan and Ohio have a **CUSTOMER** table that is identical in structure but contains different rows. Assign Oracle synonyms as follows:

```
CREATE SYNONYM japan_customer FOR      customer@hq.sales.asia.japan;

CREATE SYNONYM ohio_customer  FOR      customer@hq.mtfg.ohio;
```

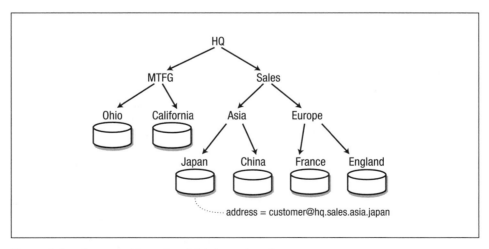

Figure 1.4   A sample hierarchy of database domains.

Distributed Database Performance And Tuning Methods

The ability to identify and correct performance problems has plagued distributed database systems since their genesis. Even within the context of a single transaction, distributed query optimization can be a formidable challenge. On a single database, SQL query tuning takes place by running an SQL **EXPLAIN** and performing the appropriate tuning. However, when a single query is split into distributed databases, the overall query tuning becomes far more complex. When a query spans hosts, several distributed database managers are required to take the distributed query and partition it into subqueries, which are then independently optimized and run (sometimes simultaneously) on the distributed databases. The query is considered complete when the last subquery has completed successfully and results are returned to the user. This approach is sometimes dubbed "the weakest link" architecture. The longest running of any number of partitioned subqueries determines the overall performance of the entire query. This is true despite the execution speed of any other partitioned subqueries involved. An excellent example of this approach is Oracle's parallel query facility in version 7.3.

Tuning a distributed query requires the user to consider the following:

- The physical location of the database

- The availability of multiple CPUs

Today, tools are available to perform *load balancing*, whereby a processor may borrow CPU cycles from underutilized processors to balance the query and achieve maximum throughput.

Distributed databases need to be able to address information regardless of the hardware platform or the architecture of the database, especially in volatile environments where hardware and network configurations may change frequently. The two types of interoperability that emerge with distributed databases fall into the general categories of database and hardware:

- *Database Interoperability*—The ability of a database to function autonomously, allowing the distributed database to access numerous types of databases within the domain of a unified environment. The UniFace and PowerBuilder tools attempt to serve this market, automatically providing mechanisms for subtasking database queries and merging result sets. Chapter 2, Physical Performance Design For Oracle Databases, discusses how Oracle parallel query techniques partition a single Oracle query into multiple processes.

- *Hardware Interoperability*—The ability of the distributed system to address resources at many locations on an as-needed basis. At the hardware level, a single subquery of a distributed query runs on numerous processors, and load balancing tools assign multiple processors to a single database.

An Example Of A Distributed Database Design

The key to success with distributed servers is very simple. Start small and phase in new servers only after communications with the existing servers have been debugged. Companies choosing a very large or mission-critical system often get mired in technical problems, unable to deliver a finished system.

The mastery of distributed databases is achieved by doing, not by reading. To understand the issues fully and first hand, do the following exercise. This exercise requires:

- A small, well-tested Oracle system that resides on a midrange computer or mainframe
- A PC with Oracle's SQL*Net connectivity software
- Another database on the same platform as the source system

Begin with a small existing system which is not mission critical and remove part of the centralized data onto another platform. Assume that we are dealing with a customer-order system running on an Oracle database on a Unix platform. This system is very old and needs replacement, but all components have been fully tested and operational for several years. See from the sample E/R model in Figure 1.5 that the database has five tables:

1. A **CUSTOMER** table to store information about the customer

2. An **ORDER** table with order information

3. An **ITEM** table for product information

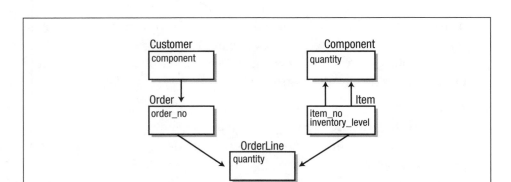

Figure 1.5   A sample customer-order database.

4. A **COMPONENT** table

5. An **ORDERLINE** table to store the quantity for each item that participates in an order

A huge difference exists in the amount of effort that will be required to migrate the data depending on the architecture of the target system (see Figure 1.6). With a relational target system, extracting the data and reformatting the data for import into other relational tables is relatively simple. Other architectures, such as object or network databases, are far more complicated and require sophisticated load programs.

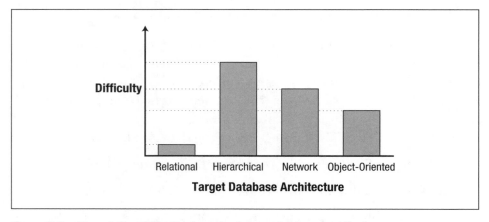

Figure 1.6   The relative difficulty of moving to new database architectures.

For this example, we simply take the existing **CUSTOMER** table and export the table from Oracle. Next, we add the table to the new database on another platform using Oracle's Import utility. In sum, we have extracted data from a centralized source and created a distributed relational environment. While this exercise may seem trivial and artificial, the industry is moving toward architectures where the data will reside on a multitude of hardware platforms.

Using Referential Integrity

Oracle databases allow for the control of business rules with "constraints." These Referential Integrity (RI) rules ensure that one-to-many and many-to-many relationships are enforced within the relational schema.

Several types of "constraints" can be applied to Oracle tables to enforce referential integrity, which include:

- **CHECK CONSTRAINT**—This constraint validates incoming columns at row insert time. For example, rather than having an application verify that all occurrences of **REGION** are North, South, East, or West, a check constraint can be added to the table definition to ensure the validity of the region column.

- **NOT NULL CONSTRAINT**—This constraint is used to specify that a column may never contain a NULL value. This is enforced at SQL **INSERT** and **UPDATE** time.

- **PRIMARY KEY CONSTRAINT**—This constraint is used to identify the primary key for a table. This operation requires that the primary column(s) are unique, and Oracle will create a unique index on the target primary key.

- **REFERENCES CONSTRAINT**—This is the foreign-key constraint as implemented by Oracle. A references constraint is only applied at SQL **INSERT** and **DELETE** times. For example, assume a one-to-many relationship between the **CUSTOMER** and **ORDER** tables such that each **CUSTOMER** may place many **ORDER**s, yet each **ORDER** belongs to only one **CUSTOMER**. The references constraint tells Oracle at **INSERT** time that the value in **ORDER.cust_num** must match the

CUSTOMER.cust_num in the customer row, thereby ensuring that a valid customer exists before the order row is added. At SQL **DELETE** time, the references constraint can be used to ensure that a **CUSTOMER** is not deleted if rows still exist in the **ORDER** table.

- **UNIQUE CONSTRAINT**—This constraint is used to ensure that all column values within a table never contain a duplicate entry.

Note the distinction between **UNIQUE** and **PRIMARY KEY**. While both of these constraints create a unique index, a table may only contain one **PRIMARY KEY** constraint column—but it may have many **UNIQUE** constraints on other columns.

 Referential integrity usually needs to be double coded, once for the database and again within the application. For example, in a multipart SQL*Form, you may not become aware of an RI violation until you are many pages into the form and your form attempts to commit.

As previously explained, referential integrity maintains business rules. Relational systems allow control of business rules with constraints, and RI rules form the backbone of relational tables. For example, RI ensures that a row in the **CUSTOMER** table is not deleted if the **ORDER** table contains orders for that customer (Figure 1.7).

It is clear that enforcing this business rule in our new distributed environment is a real challenge. While it is relatively simple to tell an Oracle system not to delete a row from its **CUSTOMER** table if rows for that customer exist in the **ORDER** table, it is not simple to enforce this rule when the **CUSTOMER** table resides in a Sybase database and the order table resides within Oracle. The solution is to remove the database RI rules from each database, remembering to manually replicate the RI rules using procedural code within the application. This essentially creates your own customized RI within the application.

The next step is to import the data into the newly defined table in one of two ways. The easiest method uses Oracle's import/export utility to import the customer table into SQL **INSERT** statements. The second, and

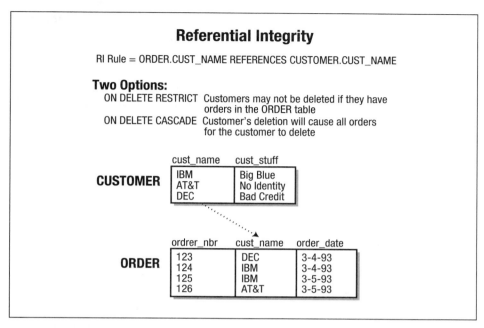

Figure 1.7   An example of referential integrity.

more complicated way, extracts the table into a flat file, adds column de-
limiters, and then uses Oracle's SQL*Loader to add the data into the new
database. Of course, Oracle's import utility can only be used when the
import file is formatted according to the format required by Oracle's import facility.

For example, a flat-file data extract could be manipulated to state the
following:

```
INSERT INTO CUSTOMER VALUES ('Burleson','343 State St','Rochester','NY');
INSERT INTO CUSTOMER VALUES ('Joe Chelko','123 4th st.','New York','NY');
```

Let's assume that a **CUSTOMER** table has been added to an instance
called Triton, and that an **ORDERS** table resides in an instance called
Phobos. How does the user make these tables function as if they resided
in a unified database? When a distributed request is made to tables within
different architectures, the query is partitioned into separate subqueries
and executed against each database engine. The processor governing the

distributed request acts as the consolidator, merging the result sets and performing any postretrieval processes such as **ORDER BY** or **GROUP BY** clauses that must manipulate all of the returned data.

In our example, we join the tables for a customer, pulling the customer information from Sybase and the order information from Oracle. Directly addressing SQL across different database products generates the following sample query:

```
SELECT          cust_name,
                customer_street_address,
                order_date
FROM
     CUSTOMER@triton,
     ORDERS@phobos
WHERE
     ORDERS.cust_number=CUSTOMER.cust_number        AND
     CUSTOMER.cust_name like 'Burleson';
```

NOTE *This SQL uses node names to identify the physical location of the tables. This is not standard SQL syntax, but it illustrates the need to join diverse tables.*

For a more realistic test, let's retrieve information from all of the four tables. Listing 1.1 joins the **CUSTOMER** table with the **ORDERS** table where **cust_name = 'Burleson'** and then joins the **ORDERS** table entries with the **ORDER_LINE** table. Finally, the SQL joins **ORDER_LINE** with the **PRODUCT** table, retrieving product information.

Listing 1.1   A sample distributed query.

```
SELECT    CUSTOMER.cust_name,
          CUSTOMER.customer_street_address,
          ORDERS.order_date,
          PRODUCT.product_cost,
          PRODUCT.product_name
FROM
     CUSTOMER@triton,
     ORDERS@phobos,
```

```
     ORDER_LINE@phobos,
     PRODUCT@phobos
WHERE
     CUSTOMER.cust_number = ORDERS.cust_number
     AND
     ORDERS.order_number = ORDER_LINE.order_number
     AND
     ORDER_LINE.prod_number = PRODUCT.prod_number
     AND
     CUSTOMER.cust_name like 'Burleson';
```

This query can be easily issued from a remote PC using the SQL*Net software. Another access route to these tables is an already-defined tool that accesses protocols for each database, such as the popular UniFace tool.

Accessing a remote database node from a PC platform uses similar steps. Simply punch the relational table into a flat file, and transfer this file to the PC using either FTP or some other file transfer utility. At this point, the flat file can be loaded into a PC-based database for local reference.

The steps to populate a relational table on a PC platform differ from the steps for a midrange database. Most PC databases do not support **CREATE TABLE** SQL. The table is defined using the online GUI screens. To define the table to FoxPro, choose File|New, and define the tables using the GUI interface. Now we can manually define a **PRODUCT** table with identical column names and field sizes. Fortunately, adding rows to a FoxPro table is very simple. Using the PC's text editor, insert a delimiter character between each field in the flat file in the PC text editor.

Choose a character that does not exist in the data, such as the caret (^) or at sign (@). If your database support adding literals to queries, characters can be added at extraction time:

```
SELECT cust_name||"^"||cust_city||"^"||cust_state from CUSTOMER;
```

The massaged file appears as follows:

```
Burleson^343 State St^Rochester^NY
Joe Chelko^123 4th st.^New York^ NY
```

This flat file can now be easily imported into FoxPro. From the FoxPro command prompt, enter the following commands:

```
CLOSE DATA
USE PRODUCT
APPEND from c:\myfile.dat TYPE SDF DELIMITED with '^'
```

This **APPEND** command takes the data from the flat file and moves it into the FoxPro table. Incidentally, even though FoxPro does not support SQL **INSERT** statements, it is one of the easiest databases for data migration. Also, because FoxPro's "Rushmore" technology is so fast, many sites move systems directly from mainframes into FoxPro. Systems can move directly from mainframes onto FoxPro data servers and gain improved response-time. I have proven this point from personal experience: I migrated from an IBM 3090 to FoxPro, each one performed faster (on a stand-alone PC) than its counterpart on the mainframe.

Database Design For Performance

This section focuses on database server techniques for creating high-performance, client/server Oracle applications. Without an effective database design, no amount of tuning allows the system to achieve optimal performance. Hence, it is critical to a database design that we derive the most from all of the available servers.

Normalization And Modeling Theory

As we know, five types of data relationships must be considered when designing any Oracle database:

1. One-to-one relationship

2. One-to-many relationship

3. Many-to-many relationship

4. Recursive many-to-many relationship

5. The ISA relationship

The effective client/server designer's role represents these types of relationships in a sensible way and ensures acceptable server performance.

In a hierarchical, or CODASYL (Network), database, it is possible to define and implement a database design that contains absolutely no redundant information (such as pure Third Normal Form or 3NF). Hierarchical and network databases can be truly free of redundant information because all data relationships are represented through pointers and not through duplicated foreign keys. Because object-oriented systems use pointers to establish data relationships, many object-oriented systems can also be designed totally free of redundant data. Since the elimination of redundancy requires embedded pointers to establish the data relationships, no relational database can ever be totally free of redundant data.

An Oracle database with either one-to-many or many-to-many relationships has redundant "foreign keys" embedded in the tables to establish the logical relationships. Redundant duplication of foreign keys in the subordinate tables creates the data relationships, making it possible to join tables together and relate the contents of the data items in the tables.

As the size of the database increases, redundancy can become a major problem. Today, many users create very large databases, many of which contain trillions of bytes. For databases of this size, a single table can contain more than a billion rows, and the introduction of a single new column to a table can represent thousands of dollars in additional disk expense. Data redundancy is detrimental for two reasons. First and foremost, duplicating the redundant material consumes disk storage space. The second and most ominous reason is that updating redundant data requires extra processing. Redundant duplication of very large and highly volatile data items can cause huge processing bottlenecks.

However, this does not imply that redundancy is always undesirable. Performance is still an overriding factor in most systems. Proper control of redundant information implies that redundant information may be introduced into any structure so long as the performance improvements outweigh the additional disk costs and update problems.

Since the first publication of Dr. E. F. Codd's 1993 research paper "Providing OLAP (Online Analytical Processing) to User-Analysts: An IT Mandate," database designers have attempted to find an optimum way of structuring tables for low data redundancy. Codd's rules of normalization guide the designer to create a logically correct table structure with no redundancy, but performance rules often dictate the introduction of duplicated data to improve performance.

This is especially true for distributed Oracle databases. Any node in a distributed database may want to browse a list of customers at other nodes without establishing a connection to that node. The technological problems inherent in the two-phase commit necessitate widespread replication of entire tables or selected columns from tables. However, the distributed database designer does not have free reign to introduce redundancy anywhere in the enterprise. Redundancy always has a price tag, whether it is the cost of the disk storage or the cost of maintaining a parallel update scheme. Figure 1.8 shows a strategy for analyzing the consequences of data redundancy.

In Figure 1.8, a boundary line lies within a range between the size of a redundant data item and the frequency of update of the data item. The size of the data item relates to the disk costs associated with storing the item and the frequency of update is associated with the cost of keeping the redundant data current, whether by replication techniques or by two-phase commit updates. Because the relative costs are different for each

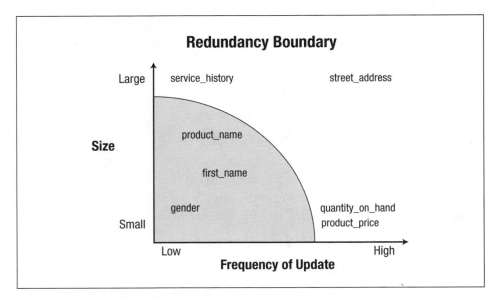

Figure 1.8   A comparison of size versus volatility for redundant data.

hardware configuration and for each application, this boundary may be quite different depending on the type of application. The rapid decrease in the disk storage costs designates that the size boundary is only important for very large-scale redundancy. A large, frequently changing item (for example, **street_address**) is not a good candidate for redundancy. But large static items (for example, **service_history**) or small, frequently changing items (for example, **product_price**) are acceptable for redundancy. Small static items (for example, **gender**) represent ideal candidates for redundant duplication.

DENORMALIZING ONE-TO-MANY DATA RELATIONSHIPS

One-to-many relationships exist in many real-world situations. Many entities that possess one-to-many relationships can be removed from the data model, eliminating some join operations. The basic principle here is simple: Redundant information avoids expensive SQL joins and yields faster processing. But remember, we must deal with the issue of additional disk storage and the problems associated with updating the redundant data. For example, consider the entity/relation (E/R) model shown in Figure 1.9, where we see that the structure is in pure Third Normal Form. Note that the **CITY** and **STATE** tables exist because each state has many cities and each city has many customers. This model works for most transactions on an online transaction processing (OLTP) system. However, this high degree of normalization would require the joining of the **CITY** and **STATE** tables each time that address information is requested, forcing some SQL requests to perform very slowly.

Consider a query to display the **state_bird** for all orders that have been placed for **BIRDSEED**. This is a cumbersome query that requires the joining of six tables:

```
SELECT state_bird
FROM STATE, CITY, CUSTOMER, ORDER, QUANTITY, ITEM
WHERE
item_name = 'BIRDSEED'
AND
ITEM.item.nbr = QUANTITY.item.nbr
AND
QUANTITY.order_nbr = ORDER.order_nbr
AND
```

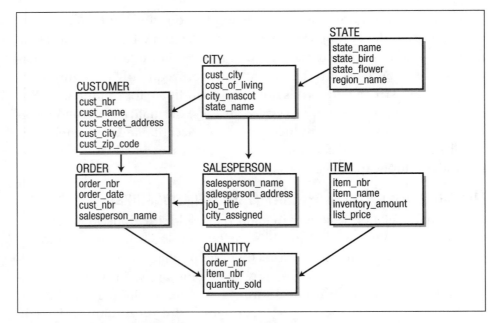

Figure 1.9　A fully normalized E/R model sales database.

```
ORDER.cust_nbr = CUSTOMER.cust_nbr
AND
CUSTOMER.cust_city = CITY.cust_city
AND
CITY.state_name = STATE.state_name;
```

With Oracle and the rule-based optimizer, this type of complex join guarantees that at least one table is read front to back using a full-table scan. This is a shortcoming of Oracle's rule-based optimizer, since an SQL optimizer should always avoid a full-table scan whenever indexes are present—and full-table scans are very expensive. This situation might be avoided by using Oracle "hints" with the cost-based optimizer to determine the optimal path to this data. A "hint" is an extension of Oracle's SQL that directs the SQL optimizer to change its normal access path. For more detailed information on optimizing full-table scans, see Chapter 6, Oracle DBA Performance And Tuning. For more information on hints, refer to Chapter 4, Tuning Oracle SQL.

What if your goal is to simplify the data structure by removing several of the one-to-many relationships? Adding redundancy poses two problems: You need additional space for the redundant item, as well as a technique to update the redundant item if it changes. One solution is to build a table of columns that roll the **CITY** and **STATE** tables into the **CUSTOMER** table. For the example in Table 1.1, assume that the **STATE** table contains 50 rows, the **CITY** table has 2,000 rows, and the **CUSTOMER** table has 10,000 rows.

From Table 1.1, you can see that the **CITY** and **STATE** tables can be removed entirely for a total savings of 400,000 bytes (refer to Figure 1.10). What about the **cost_of_living** field? If we choose to eliminate the **CITY** table, and duplicate **cost_of_living** in every **CUSTOMER** row, it would be necessary to visit each and every **CUSTOMER** row—which means changing the cost of living 10,000 times. Before this change, the following SQL was used to update each **CITY** table:

```
UPDATE CITY SET cost_of_living = :var1
WHERE CITY = :var2;
2000 ROWS UPDATED
```

While the management of redundancy seems a formidable challenge, the following SQL **UPDATE** statement makes this change easily, and we can make the change to all affected rows:

```
UPDATE CUSTOMER SET cost_of_living = :var1
WHERE CITY = :var2;
100,000 ROWS UPDATED
```

Table 1.1 Redundancy matrix to determine optimal normalization.

Column	Size	Duplication	Total Space	Change
state_bird	10	10,000	100,000	Rare
state_flower	10	10,000	100,000	Rare
region_name	2	10,000	20,000	Never
cost_of_living	8	10,000	80,000	Quarterly
city_mascot	10	10,000	100,000	Rare

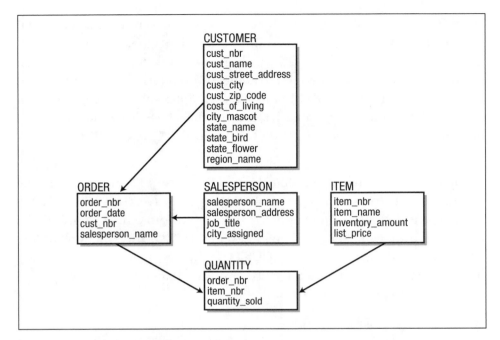

Figure 1.10　A denormalized E/R model sales database.

Using this same **state_bird** query as before, we see how it is simplified by removing the extra tables:

```
SELECT state_bird
FROM  CUSTOMER, ORDER, QUANTITY, ITEM
WHERE
item_name = 'BIRDSEED'
AND
ITEM.item_nbr = QUANTITY.item_nbr
AND
QUANTITY.order_nbr = ORDER.order_nbr
AND
ORDER.cust_nbr = CUSTOMER.cust_nbr;
```

It is still necessary to join three tables together, but this results in a much faster, simpler query than the original five-way table join. You can carry this concept to the point where this model is condensed into a single, highly redundant table.

Misleading Data Relationships

When creating an E/R model, it is often tempting to look at the data model from a purely logical perspective without any regard for the physical implications of the model. The designer strives to recognize and establish all of the logical relationships in the model while sometimes finding that the relationships are misleading. A relationship can be misleading when the relationship actually exists, but the application may have no need to reference this relationship. Consider the E/R model for a university shown in Figure 1.11.

Consider the association of the **hair_color** attribute to the **student** entity. Does a many-to-many data relationship really exist between **hair_color** and **student**? Many students have blonde hair, and blonde hair is common to many students. Why not create a many-to-many relationship between **student** and **hair_color**? The solution depends upon whether any other non-key data items exist within the **hair_color** entity.

If many other data items relating to hair color are present, then it is perfectly appropriate to create another entity called **hair_color**. But in this case, even though a many-to-many relationship exists between **hair_color** and **student**, **hair_color** is a stand-alone data attribute, so it is unnecessary to create an additional data structure.

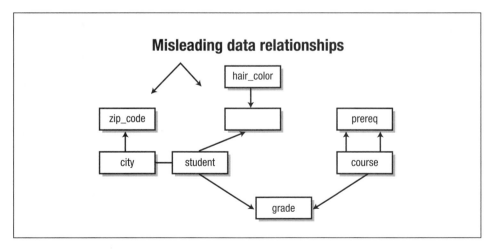

Figure 1.11 An example of misleading data relationships.

Another example is the **zip_code** attribute in the **student** entity. At first glance, it appears that a violation of Third Normal Form (that is, a transitive dependency) has occurred between **city** and **zip_code**. In other words, it appears that a **zip_code** is paired with the city of residence for the student. If each **city** has many **zip_code**s, while each **zip_code** refers only to one **city**, it makes sense to model this as a one-to-many data relationship (see Figure 1.11). The presence of this data relationship requires creating a separate entity called **zip** with attached **student** entities. However, this is another case where the **zip** entity lacks key attributes, making it impractical to create the **zip** entity. In other words, **zip_code** has no associated data items. Creating a database table with only one data column would be nonsense.

This example demonstrates that it is not enough to group together "like" items and then identify the data relationships. A practical test must be made regarding the presence of no-key attributes within an entity class. If an entity has no attributes (that is, the table has only one field), the presence of the entity is nothing more than an index to the foreign key in the member entity. It can be removed from the E/R model. This technique not only simplifies the number of entities, but it creates a better environment for a client/server architecture. More data is logically grouped together, resulting in less data access effort. Figure 1.12 shows an example of correct relationships.

Denormalizing Many-To-Many Data Relationships

In many cases, a many-to-many relationship can be condensed into a more efficient structure to improve the speed to data retrieval. After all, less

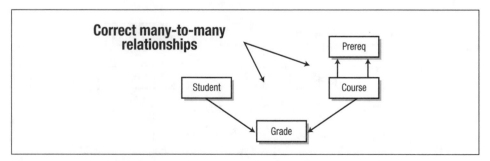

Figure 1.12   An example of correct many-to-many relationships.

tables need to be joined to get the desired information. To understand how a many-to-many relationship can be collapsed into a more compact structure by considering the relationship between a course and a student, refer to Figure 1.13.

A student takes many courses, and each course has many students. This is a classical many-to-many relationship and requires that we define a junction table between the base entities to establish the foreign keys necessary in joining them together. Note that the junction table is called **GRADE** with the following contents: **course_nbr**, the primary key for the **COURSE** table; **student_nbr**, the primary key for the **STUDENT** table; and **grade**, which is a no-key attribute to both foreign keys. Next, consider the question, "In what context does a grade have meaning?" Stating "The grade was A in CS-101" is insufficient, and stating "Joe earned an A" makes no sense. Only when both the student number and the course number are associated does the grade column have meaning. Stating "Joe earned an A in CS-101" does make sense.

Dealing With Recursive Data Relationships

Recursive many-to-many relationships contain an object that also has a many-to-many relationship with other occurrences of the same object. These relationships are often termed *Bill-of-Materials* (BOM) *relationships*, and the graphical representation of the recursive relationship is sometimes termed a *Bill-of-Materials explosion*. These relationships are termed recursive

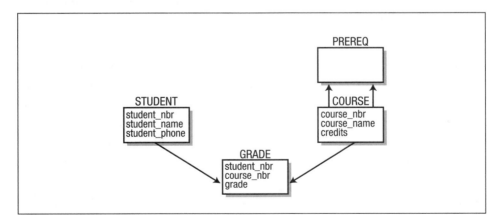

Figure 1.13 An example university database.

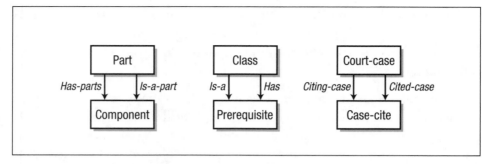

Figure 1.14 An example of recursive many-to-many relationships.

because a single query makes many subpasses through the tables to arrive at the solution (see Figure 1.14).

Bill-of-Materials relationships denote an object with a many-to-many relationship with another object in the same class. For example, a part may consist of other parts, but at the same time it is a component in a larger assembly. A class at a university may have many prerequisites, but at the same time it is a prerequisite for another class. In the legal arena, a court case may cite other cases—but at the same time it is being cited by later cases.

For example, a BOM request for components of a Big Meal shows that it consists of a hamburger, fries, and soda. Yet a hamburger consists of a meat patty, bun, and pickle—and a meat patty consists of meat and filler, and so on. Another example of a BOM relationship would be the division of a carburetor into subparts, although the carburetor itself is a subassembly in a still larger unit, such as an engine.

Figure 1.15 describes course-prerequisite hierarchy for a university. Note that the Is-a prerequisite relationships are relatively straightforward, indicating which courses are required before taking another course. For example, the prerequisites for Linear Equations 445 are Business 400, Accounting 305, and Multivariate Statistics 450. These courses all have prerequisites of their own, which may also have prerequisites, and so on.

Each occurrence of a **COURSE** object has different topics, and a complete implementation must iterate through all courses until reaching *terminus,* the point where the course has no further prerequisites.

Unfortunately, the recursive many-to-many relationship is very confusing and almost impossible to understand without the aid of a graphical

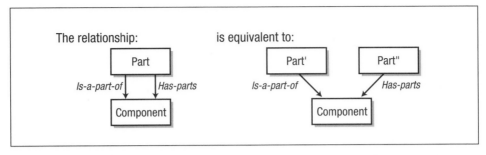

Figure 1.15   Viewing a recursive many-to-many relationship as an ordinary many-to-many relationship.

representation. Visualize the recursive many-to-many relationship as an ordinary many-to-many relationship with the owner entity "pulled apart" into **owner1** and **owner2**. Figure 1.15 shows how the junction entity establishes the relationship.

Only graphical representations conceptualize a recursive many-to-many relationship. In the CODASYL model, these are called "set occurrence" diagrams, and they show the pointer chains that link the relationships (see Figure 1.16). Table sketches show that the junction table contains both an implosion and an explosion column in relational databases. Use the set occurrence diagram to understand data relationships.

In Figure 1.16, we can navigate the database, determining the components for a **Big_Meal**. To navigate this diagram, start at the object **Big_Meal** and follow the **Has_parts** link to the bubble containing the number 1. This is the quantity for the item. We now follow these bubbles to the **Is_a_part** link, which shows that one order of fries is included in a **Big_Meal**. We return to the **Has_parts** link for **Big_Meal** and find the next bubble. The **Is_a_part** link shows that one soda is included in a **Big_Meal**. We then continue this process until no further entities can be found in the **Has_parts** relationship. In sum, the **Has_parts** relationships indicate that a **Big_Meal** consists of one order of fries, one soda, and one hamburger. In addition, the hamburger consists of two meat patties and one bun.

Here we can see how the database is navigated to determine which parts use a specific component. For example, if you start at the **Hamburger** bubble and navigate the **Is_a_part** relationships, you see that one hamburger participates in the **Value_Meal** and also in the **Big_Meal**.

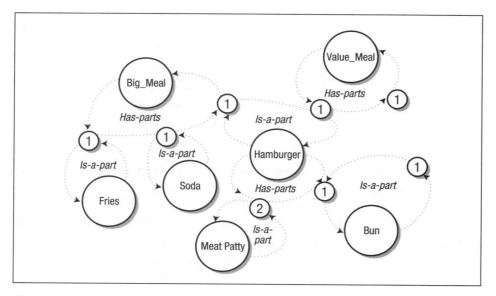

Figure 1.16   A set occurrence diagram for a recursive relationship.

Recursive relationships can now be generated from the structure. For example, when listing the components of a **Big_Meal**, all components appear as in Table 1.2.

Conversely, the recursive association can be applied to any item to see its participation in other items. For example, the uses of grease can be seen by running an implosive query, as shown in Table 1.3.

These examples may seem simplistic, but many database systems have items with numerous subassemblies. Recursions may cascade dozens of levels down in a hierarchy. Consider the design of a database that manages fast food items (see Figure 1.17). All non-food items have a *class construct*, which hold all data and behaviors. This class construct is an example of an *abstract class*, with no object of **non_food_part** created. But **non_food_part** does include ordering behaviors and the names of suppliers. These data items cascade to lower-level classes, specifically the **toy_part** and **paper_part** objects. The **toy_part** class is not only next in the class hierarchy, it also has data and behaviors. Contrasted with the **non_food_part** abstract class, **toy_part** is a *concrete class*.

Clearly, we compound the problem of recursive relationships by adding this additional construct—namely, a class hierarchy. Unfortunately, these

Table 1.2 BOM explosion for Big_Meal.

Part1	Part2	Part3	Quantity
Hamburger			1
	Meat Patty		2
		Oatmeal	4 oz.
		Beef Lips	3 oz.
	Bun		1
Fries			1 order
	Potato		1
	Grease		1 cup
Soda			1
	Ice		1/2 cup
	Drink		1/3 cup

Table 1.3 BOM implosion for grease.

Part1	Part2	Part3
Fries		
		Big Meal
		Value Meal
Meat Patty		
	Hamburger	
		Big Meal
		Value Meal
	Cheeseburger	
	Big Mac	
Fried Pies		
		Value Meal

types of challenges are very common. While it is true that "parts are parts," the different parts have subtle variations, leading to different data items depending on part type. For example, a food-related part might have a **shelf_life** column, but that column does not apply to a non-food part.

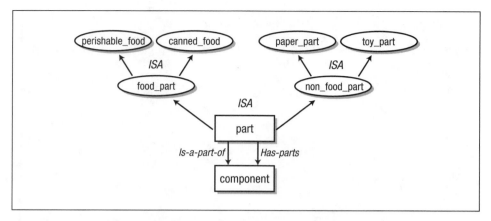

Figure 1.17 A recursive many-to-many relationships with the addition of an ISA Hierarchy.

With an understanding of the nature of recursive relationships, the question becomes one of implementation: What is the best way to represent a recursive relationship in Oracle and navigate the structure?

The following Oracle table definitions describe the tables for the part-component example:

```
CREATE table part(
part_nbr      number,
part_name     varchar2(10),
part_desc     varchar2(10),
qty_on_hand   number);

CREATE table component (
has_part      number,
is_a_part     number,
qty           number);
```

Look closely at the **component** example. Both the **has_part** and **is_a_part** fields are foreign keys for the **part_nbr** field in the **part** table. Therefore, the component table is all keyed except for the **qty** field, which tells how many parts belong in an assembly. Look at the following SQL code that is required to display all components in a **Big_Meal**:

```
SELECT part_name
FROM part, component
```

```
WHERE
has_part = 'HAPPY MEAL'
AND
part.part_nbr = COMPONENT.has_part;
```

This type of Oracle SQL query requires joining the table against itself. Unfortunately, since all items are of the same type (namely, **part**), no real substitute exists for this type of data relationship.

STAR Schema Design

The STAR schema design was first introduced by Dr. Ralph Kimball as an alternative database design for data warehouses. The name STAR comes directly from the design form, where a large FACT table resides at the center of the model surrounded by various "points" or reference tables. The basic principle behind the STAR query schema is the introduction of highly redundant data for high performance. A more exhaustive discussion of STAR schema design is included in Chapter 10, Tuning Oracle Data Warehouse And OLAP Applications.

Returning to the customer-order E/R model in Figure 1.9, we see an illustration of a standard Third Normal Form database used to represent the sales of items. Since redundant information is not an issue, salient data (such as the total for an order) is computed from the items comprising the order. In this Third Normal Form database, users need a list of line items to multiply the quantity ordered by the price for all items belonging in order 123. An intermediate table called TEMP holds the result list, shown in the following example:

```
CREATE table TEMP as
SELECT (QUANTITY.quantity_sold * ITEM.list_price) line_total
FROM QUANTITY, ITEM
WHERE
QUANTITY.order_nbr = 123
AND
QUANTITY.item_nbr = ITEM.item_nbr;
SELECT sum(line_total) from TEMP;
```

 The state-city-customer hierarchy in Figure 1.9 is very deliberate. To be truly in the Third Normal Form, no redundant information is possible. As such, a user's seemingly simple query is complex to

the system. For example, the SQL calculating the sum of all orders for the western region looks very complex and involves the five-way table join:

```
CREATE table TEMP as
SELECT (QUANTITY.quantity_sold * ITEM.list_price) line_total
FROM QUANTITY, ITEM, CUSTOMER, CITY, STATE
WHERE
QUANTITY.item_nbr = ITEM.item_nbr      /* join QUANTITY and ITEM */
AND
ITEM.item_nbr = CUSTOMER.cust_nbr      /* join ITEM and CUSTOMER */
AND
CUSTOMER.cust_city = CITY.cust_city /* join CUSTOMER and CITY */
AND
CITY.state_name = STATE.state_name   /* join CITY and STATE */
AND
STATE.region_name = 'WEST';
```

In reality, sufficient redundancy eliminates the city and state tables. The point is clear: A manager who is analyzing a series of complete order totals requires a huge amount of realtime computation. This process arrives at the basic tradeoff. For true freedom from redundant data, query time demands a price.

In practice, the Third Normal Form database generally evolves into a STAR schema as you create a **FACT** table to hold the quantity for each item sold (see Figure 1.18).

At first glance, it's hard to believe this is the same data as the normalized database. The new **FACT** table contains one row for each item on each order, resulting in a tremendous amount of redundant key information in the **FACT** table. It should be obvious that the STAR query schema requires far more disk space than a Third Normal Form database. Also, the STAR schema is most likely a read-only database because of the widespread redundancy introduced into the model. Finally, the widespread redundancy makes updating difficult (if not impossible) for the STAR schema.

Notice the dimension tables around the **FACT** table. Some of the dimension tables contain data that is added to queries with joins. Other dimensions, such as Region Dimension, contain no data. What purpose, then, does this STAR schema achieve with huge disk space consumption and a read-only restriction?

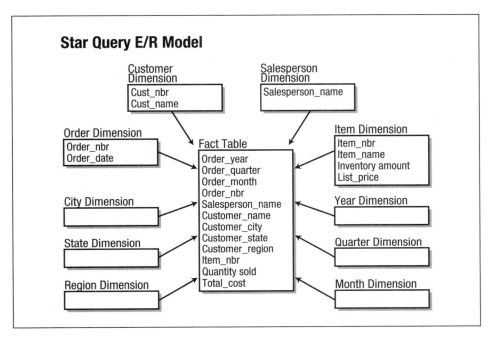

Figure 1.18　The STAR query E/R model.

Using the STAR schema in Figure 1.18, let's formulate SQL queries for rapid retrieval of desired information. For example, identifying the total cost for an order is simple, as seen in the following code:

```
SELECT sum(total_cost) order_total
FROM FACT
WHERE
FACT.order_nbr = 123;
```

It is clear that the new structure makes the realtime query faster and simpler. Consider the result if the goal is to analyze information by aggregate values using this schema. Suppose that the manager needs the breakdown of regional sales. The data by region is not available, but the **FACT** table supplies the answer. Obtaining the sum of all orders for the western region is now simple, as seen in the following code:

```
SELECT sum(total_cost)
FROM FACT
WHERE
REGION = 'WEST';
```

The merits of the STAR schema should now be apparent, but we need to note some other ways to represent time-oriented data suitable for Online Analytical Processing (OLAP) type systems; namely, the multidimensional database architecture as seen in Oracle Express.

Summary

This chapter has hopefully demonstrated how a proper design can be critical for good performance as the database is created. While far from being an exhaustive description of all of the relational design techniques, it has focused on the basic principles that will help to ensure that your Oracle database functions as quickly as possible.

I have come to believe that response time is one of the most critical factors to the success of any database. Regardless of how well the system was analyzed or implemented—no matter now flashy the GUI interface—if the system fails to deliver data in a timely fashion, the project is doomed. Now that we have reviewed logical database design, let's move on to the physical implementation of Oracle databases.

Of course, there is far more to performance and tuning than just design principles. The following chapter referral list should serve as a general guide for further exploration:

- For more information on distributed database tuning, see Chapter 7, Performance And Tuning For Distributed Oracle Databases.

- For more information on Database connectivity for client/server, see Chapter 8, Performance And Tuning For Database Connectivity Tools.

- For more information on SQL scripts, see Appendix A, Useful SQL Scripts.

- For more information on STAR schema design, see Chapter 10, Tuning Oracle Data Warehouse And OLAP Applications.

Physical Performance Design For Oracle Databases

Once a good logical model has been created, it is critical to translate the logical model into an Oracle implementation capable of performing at optimal speed. Because Oracle involves so many design issues, this chapter will take a detailed look at how specific physical design tools can be used to exploit client/server performance. Topics include:

- When to use an index

- Using multi-column indexes

- How Oracle chooses indexes

- Allocating Oracle tables

- Referential integrity and performance

- Enforcing business rules with RI

- Alternatives to RI for client/server systems

- Performance and stored procedures

- Using stored procedures to encapsulate processing logic

- Pinning Oracle stored procedures in the SGA

- Deciding when to use a trigger

- Oracle hash tables and clusters

- Using Oracle's parallel query

Indexes

In Oracle, an index is used to speed up the time that is required to access table information. Internally, Oracle indexes are B-tree data structures in which each tree node may contain many sets of key values and row-IDs.

In general, Oracle indexes exist for the purpose of preventing full-table scans. Full-table scans have two problems, the most important being the time lost in servicing the request as each and every row of the table is read into Oracle's buffer pool. In addition to causing the individual task performance to suffer, a full-table scan will also cause performance degradation at the system level and all other tasks on the system may have to incur additional I/O, because the buffer block held by competing tasks will have been flushed by the full-table scan. As blocks are flushed from the buffer pool, other tasks are required to incur additional I/Os to reread information that would have remained in the buffer pool if the full-table scan had not been invoked. More information on optimizing full-table scans can be found in Chapter 6, Oracle DBA Performance And Tuning.

In general, just about any Oracle table will benefit from the use of indexes. The only exception to this rule would be a very small table that can be read in less than two-block I/Os. Two-block I/Os are used as this guideline because Oracle will need to perform at least one I/O to access the root node of the index tree and another I/O to retrieve the requested data. For example, assume that a lookup table contains rows of 25 bytes each, and you have configured Oracle to use 4 K block sizes. Since each data block would hold about 150 rows, using an index for up to 300 rows would not make the processing any faster than a full-table scan.

If you plan to use the Oracle parallel query facility, all tables specified in the SQL query must be optimized for a full-table scan. If an index exists, the cost-based optimizer must be used with a hint to invalidate the index in order to use parallel query. For the rule-based optimizer, indexes can be turned off by using an Oracle function in the **WHERE** clause. Look for details on this in Chapter 4, Tuning Oracle SQL.

One important concept in indexing is the "selectivity" or the uniqueness of the values in a column. To be the most effective, an index column must have many unique values. Columns that have only a few values (e.g., sex = m/f, status = y/n) would not be good candidates for indexing. Similar to the index itself, the sparse distribution of values would be less efficient than a full-table scan. To see the selectivity for a column, compare the total number of rows in the table with the number of distinct values for the column:

```
SELECT count(*) FROM CUSTOMER;

SELECT DISTINCT STATUS FROM CUSTOMER;
```

Another concept used in indexing is called "distribution," which refers to the frequency that each unique value is distributed within the database. For example, we may have a **state_abbreviation** column that contains one of 50 possible values. This would be acceptable to use as an index column, provided that the state abbreviations are uniformly distributed across the rows. However, if 90 percent of the values are for New York, then the index will not be very effective. Oracle has addressed the index data distribution issue with the **ANALYZE TABLE** command. When using Oracle's cost-based SQL optimizer, **ANALYZE TABLE** will look at both the selectivity and distribution of the column values. If they are found to be out-of-bounds, Oracle may decide not to use the index.

Oracle recommends the following guidelines when considering whether to index on a column:

- Columns that are frequently referenced in SQL **WHERE** clauses are good candidates for an index.

- Columns that are used to join tables (primary and foreign keys) should be indexed.

- Do not use a **b**-tree index on columns with poor selectivity. Any column with less than 10 percent of unique values should be indexed as a bitmap index.

- Frequently modified columns are not good candidates for indexing, since excessive processing is necessary to maintain the structure of the index tree.

- Do not index on columns that are used in SQL **WHERE** clauses using Oracle functions or operators. For example, an index on **last_name** will not be effective if it is referred to in the SQL as **upper(last_name)**.

- When using referential integrity, always create an index on the foreign key.

Most programmers do not realize that database deadlocks occur frequently within the database indexes. It is important to note that a **SELECT** of a single row from the database may cause more than one lock entry to be placed in the storage pool as all affected index rows are also locked. In other words, the individual row receives a lock, but each index node that contains the value for that row will also have locks assigned (see Figure 2.1). If the "last" entry in a sorted index is retrieved, the database will lock all index nodes that reference the indexed value, in case the user changes that value. Since many indexing schemes always carry the high-order key in multiple index nodes, an entire branch of the index tree can be locked—all the way up to the root node of the index. While each database's indexing scheme is different, some relational database vendors recommend that tables with ascending keys be loaded in descending order, so that the rows are loaded from Z to A on an alphabetic key field. Other databases such as Oracle recommend that the indexes be dropped and re-created after the rows have been loaded into an empty table.

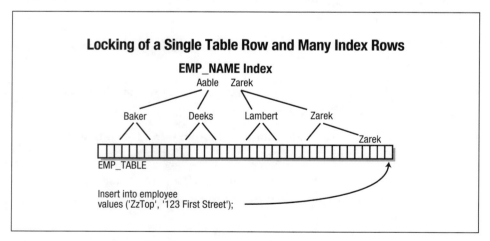

Figure 2.1 An overview of Oracle locking.

When an update or delete is issued against a row that participates in the index, the database will attempt an exclusive lock on the row, which requires the task to check if any shared locks are held against the row as well as any index nodes that will be affected. Many indexing algorithms allow for the index tree to dynamically change shape, spawning new levels as items are added and condensing levels as items are deleted.

However, for any table of consequential size, indexes are recommended to improve performance. Of course, indexes require additional disk space, and a table with an index on each column will have indexes that consume more space than the table that they support. Oracle will also update the indexes at runtime as columns are deleted, added, or modified—and this index updating can cause considerable performance degradation. For example, adding a row to the end of a table will cause Oracle to adjust the high-key value for each node in the table.

One guideline for determining when to use an index involves examination of the SQL that is issued against the tables. In general, the SQL can be collected, and each value supplied in each SQL **WHERE** clause could be a candidate for inclusion in an index.

Another common approach for determining where to create indexes is to run an explain plan for all SQL and carefully look for any full-table scans. The Oracle optimizers operate in such a fashion that Oracle will sometimes perform a full-table scan, even if an index has been defined for the table. This occurs most commonly when issuing complex n-way joins, and techniques for avoiding this problem are discussed in Chapter 4, Tuning Oracle SQL. If you are using rule-based optimization in Oracle, the structure of the SQL statement can be adjusted to force the use of an existing index. For Oracle's cost-based optimizer, adding "hints" to the structure will ensure that all indexes are used.

However, indexes do much more than speed up an individual query. When full-table scans are performed on a large Oracle table, the buffer pool begins to page out blocks from other queries. This causes additional I/O for the entire database and results in poor performance for all queries—not just the offending full-table scan.

Indexes are never a good idea for long descriptive columns. A column called **customer_description** would be a poor choice for an index because of its length and the inconsistency of the data within the column. If this column was 300 bytes, Oracle would be forced to do a huge amount of processing whenever the column is altered. Also a field such as **customer_description** would usually be referenced in SQL by using Oracle extensions such as **substr**, **like**, and **upper**. Remember, these Oracle extensions invalidate the index. Suppose that an index has been created on **customer_last_name**. The following query would use the index:

```
SELECT STATUS
FROM CUSTOMER
WHERE
customer_last_name = 'BURLESON';
```

The following queries would bypass the index, causing a full-table scan:

```
SELECT STATUS
FROM CUSTOMER
WHERE
customer_last_name = lower('burleson');

SELECT STATUS
FROM CUSTOMER
WHERE
customer_last_name like 'BURL%';
```

Unlike other relational databases such as DB2, we cannot physically load a table in key order. Consequently, we can never guarantee that the rows in the table will be in any particular order.

The use of an index can also help whenever the SQL **ORDER BY** clause is used. For example, even if there are no complex **WHERE** conditions, the presence of a **WHERE** clause will assist the performance of the query. Consider the following SQL:

```
SELECT customer_last_name, customer_first_name
FROM CUSTOMER
ORDER BY customer_last_name, customer_first_name;
```

Here, building a multi-valued index on **customer_last_name** and **customer_first_name** will alleviate the need for an internal sort of the data, significantly improving the performance of the query:

```
CREATE INDEX  cust_name
ON CUSTOMER
(customer_last_name, customer_first_name) ascending;
```

Constraints And Indexes

In Oracle, some constraints will create an index on your behalf. For example, creating a primary key constraint on the customer table for the **cust_id** will create an index on the field, and it is not necessary to manually build an index (see Listing 2.1).

Listing 2.1   Creating a primary key constraint.

```
CREATE TABLE CUSTOMER (
        cust_nbr                number
        CONSTRAINT cust_ukey
PRIMARY KEY (CUST_NBR)
USING INDEX
PCTFREE  10
INITRANS 2
MAXTRANS 255
TABLESPACE TS1
STORAGE  (
  INITIAL   256000
  NEXT    102400
  MINEXTENTS  1
  MAXEXTENTS  121
  PCTINCREASE  1 ),
        dept_name               char(10)
        CONSTRAINT dept_fk references DEPT ON DELETE CASCADE,

        organization_name       char(20)
        CONSTRAINT org_fk references ORG ON DELETE RESTRICT,

        region_name             char(2)
        CONSTRAINT state_check
        CHECK region_name in ('NORTH', SOUTH', 'EAST', 'WEST')
);
```

Note that you should always specify the location clause when declaring constraints. In the previous example, had the **cust_ukey** constraint been defined without the **STORAGE** clause, the index would have been placed in whatever tablespace is specified by the table owner's **DEFAULT** tablespace, with whatever default storage parameters are in effect for that tablespace.

Listing 2.1 shows us some examples of Oracle constraints. The first constraint is on the **cust_nbr** column, the primary key. When we use Oracle's RI to specify a primary key, Oracle automatically builds a unique index on the column to ensure that no duplicate values are entered.

The second constraint is on the **dept_name** column of the **DEPT** table. This constraint tells Oracle that it may not remove a department row if there are existing customer rows that reference that department. The **ON DELETE CASCADE** tells Oracle that when the department row is deleted, all customer rows that reference that department will also be deleted.

The next RI constraint on **organization_name** ensures that no organization is deleted if customers are participating in that organization. **ON DELETE RESTRICT** tells Oracle not to delete an organization row if any customer rows still reference the organization. Only after each and every customer has been set to another organization can the row be deleted from the organization table.

The last RI constraint is called a "check" constraint: The Oracle will verify that the column is one of the valid values before inserting the row, but it will not create an index on the column.

Using Multi-Column Indexes

When an SQL request is commonly issued using multiple columns, a concatenated or multi-column index can be used to improve performance. Oracle supports the use of multi-valued indexes, but there are some important limitations. Unlike other relational databases, Oracle requires that all columns in the index be sorted in the same order, either ascending or descending. For example, if we needed to index on **customer_last_name** ascending, followed immediately by **gross_pay** descending, we would not be able to use a multi-valued index.

Sometimes two columns—each with poor selectivity (i.e., the columns have few unique values)—can be combined into an index that has better selectivity. For example, we could combine a status field that has three values (good, neutral, bad) with another column such as **state_name** (only 50 unique values), thereby creating a multi-valued index that has far better selectivity than each column would have if indexed separately.

Another reason for creating concatenated indexes is to speed the execution of queries that reference all of the values in the index. For example, consider the following query:

```
SELECT      customer_last_name,
            customer_status,
            customer_zip_code
FROM CUSTOMER
ORDER BY customer_last_name;
```

Now, we create an index as follows:

```
CREATE INDEX last_status_zip
ON CUSTOMER
(customer_last_name, customer_status, customer_zip_code) ascending;
```

If this query were to be issued against the customer table, Oracle would never need to access any rows in the base table! Since all of the key values are contained in the index and the high-order key (**customer_last_name**) is in the **ORDER BY** clause, Oracle can scan the index, retrieving the data without ever touching the base table.

With the assistance of this feature, the savvy Oracle developer may also add columns to the end of the concatenated index so that the base table is never touched. For example, if the above query also returned the value of the **customer_address** column, this column could be added to the concatenated index, dramatically improving performance.

In summary, the following guidelines apply when creating a concatenated index:

- Use a composite index whenever two or more values are used in the SQL where the clause and the operators are **AND**ed together.

- Place the columns in the **WHERE** clause in the same order as in the index, with data items added at the end of the index.

How Oracle Chooses Indexes

It is interesting to note that the fastest execution for an individual task may not always be the best choice. For example, consider the following query against a customer table:

```
SELECT customer_name
FROM CUSTOMER
WHERE
    credit_rating = 'POOR'
AND
    amount_due > 1000
AND
    state = 'IOWA'
AND
    job_description like lower('%computer%');
```

Here we see a query where a full-table scan would be the most efficient processing method. Because of the complex conditions and the use of Oracle extensions in the SQL, it might be faster to perform a full-table scan. However, the fast execution of this task may be done at the expense of other tasks on the system as the buffer pool becomes flushed.

In general, the type of optimizer will determine how indexes are used. As we know, the Oracle optimizer can run as either rule-based or cost-based. As a general rule, Oracle is intelligent enough to use an index if it exists, but there are exceptions to this rule. The most notable exception is the n-way join with a complex **WHERE** clause. The rule-based optimizer will get "confused" and invoke a full-table scan on at least one of the tables, even if the appropriate foreign key indexes exist for all of the tables. The only remedy to this problem is to use the cost-based optimizer, which involves analyzing statistics for each table. This problem is discussed at length in Chapter 4, Tuning Oracle SQL.

We always need to remember that Oracle will only use an index when the index column is specified in its "pure" form. The use of the **substr**, **upper**, **lower**, and other functions will invalidate the index. However, we do have a few tricks to help us get around this obstacle. Consider the two equivalent SQL queries:

```
SELECT * FROM CUSTOMER
WHERE
total_purchases/10 > 5000;
```

```
SELECT * FROM CUSTOMER
WHERE
total_purchases > 5000*10;
```

The second query, by virtue of the fact that it does not alter the index column, would be able to use an index on the **total_purchases** column.

Allocating Oracle Tables

Several parameters can be used to ensure that all data stored within Oracle tables remains in an optimal configuration. Consider the following Oracle table definition:

```
CREATE TABLE ITEM (
        item_nbr                NUMBER,
        item_name               VARCHAR(30),
        item_description        VARCHAR(50))
STORAGE(         INITIAL 50K
                NEXT 50K
                PCTFREE 10
                PCTUSED 60
                FREELISTS 1);
```

PCTFREE tells Oracle how much space to reserve in each Oracle block for future updates and can have an important impact on the performance of an Oracle database if it is set too low. For example, if a row contains a lot of **VARCHAR** data types and the rows are initially inserted without values, later updates of values into the **VARCHAR** fields will cause the row to expand on the block. If the target block does not have enough room, Oracle must fragment the row and store some row information on the next physical block in the tablespace. If this block is also full, Oracle may create a very long chain until it finds a block with enough room to store the new column data. This condition can lead to many unnecessary I/Os when the row is retrieved, since many database blocks must be read to retrieve the row. The rule here is simple: Determine the average row length and predicted growth for each row, then use **PCTFREE** to reserve that amount of space on each block. For static read-only tables, it is acceptable to set **PCTFREE** to a very small number in order to fully occupy each database block. Again, the **PCTFREE** parameter is only useful for the SQL **UPDATE** statement—and only when the **UPDATE** will cause the row to grow in size. If this is not the case, then **PCTFREE** should be set to 5, reserving only 5 percent of each database block for updates.

PCTUSED tells Oracle when it is acceptable to insert rows onto a database block. For example, if **PCTUSED** is set to 80, Oracle will not allow rows to be added to any database blocks unless they are less than 80 percent full. Oracle will try to keep a database block at least **PCTUSED** full. As rows are deleted from a table, those database blocks that fall below **PCTUSED** will become eligible to receive new rows. Since the default is 40 percent, any database block that is less than 40 percent full may have rows added to that block. **PCTUSED** is a tradeoff between efficient table utilization and performance. If **PCTUSED** is set to a large value, Oracle will keep the database blocks more full, making more efficient use of storage. However, it does so at the expense of performance, especially for **INSERT** and **UPDATE** operations. For very high performance, **PCTUSED** could be set to a lower value, say 60. This will keep Oracle from constantly moving database blocks onto the **FREELIST** as rows are deleted, thereby improving performance. Again, **PCTUSED** plays an essential role for very volatile tables with many **DELETE** operations.

*Note that **PCTFREE** and **PCTUSED** work together. The sum of these values can never equal more than 100, and it is usually wise to sum the values at a limit of 90 because of the overhead that is found on each database block.*

INITTRANS specifies the initial number of transactions that are allocated within each block. **MAXTRANS** is a value that specifies the maximum number of concurrent transactions that can update a block.

FREELIST is the parameter used when more than one concurrent process is expected to access a table. Oracle keeps one **FREELIST** for each table in memory, and uses the **FREELIST** in order to determine what database block to use when an SQL **INSERT** occurs. As a row is added, the **FREELIST** is locked. If more than one concurrent process is attempting to insert into your table, one of the processes may need to wait until the **FREELIST** has been released by the previous task. To see if adding a **FREELIST** to a table will improve performance, you will need to evaluate how often Oracle had to wait for a **FREELIST**. Fortunately, Oracle keeps a **V$** table called **V$WAITSTAT** for this purpose. The following query example tells you how many times Oracle has waited for a **FREELIST** to become available. As you can see, it does not tell you which **FREELISTS** are experiencing the contention problems:

```
SELECT CLASS, COUNT
FROM V$WAITSTAT
WHERE CLASS = 'free list';

    CLASS                      COUNT
 - - - - - - - - - - - - - -    - - - - - - - - - - -
   free list                    83
```

Here we see that Oracle had to wait 83 times for a table **FREELIST** to become available. This could represent a wait of 83 times on the same table, or perhaps a single wait for 83 separate tables. We have no idea. While 83 may seem to be a large number, remember that Oracle may perform hundreds of I/Os each second, so 83 may be quite insignificant to the overall system. In any case, if you suspect that you know which table's **FREELIST** is having the contention, the table can be exported, dropped, and redefined to have more **FREELISTS**. While an extra **FREELIST** consumes more of Oracle's memory, additional **FREELISTS** can help the throughput on tables that have lots of inserts. Generally, you should define extra **FREELISTS** only on those tables that will have many concurrent update operations.

Now, let's take a look at some table definitions and see if we can infer the type of activity that will be taking place against the tables.

Example 1:

```
CREATE TABLE ORDER (
        order_nbr           number,
        order_date          date)
STORAGE ( PCTFREE  10 PCTUSED  40 FREELISTS 3);
```

Here we can infer the table has very few updates that cause the row length to increase since **PCTFREE** is only 10 percent. We can also infer that this table will have a great deal of delete activity, since **PCTUSED** is at 40 percent, thereby preventing immediate reuse of database blocks as rows are deleted. This table must also have a lot of insert activity, since **FREELISTS** is set to 3, indicating that up to 3 concurrent processes will be inserting into the table.

Example 2:

```
CREATE TABLE ITEM (
        item_nbr                    NUMBER,
        item_name                   VARCHAR(20),
        item_description            VARCHAR(50),
        current_item_status         VARCHAR(200) )
STORAGE ( PCTFREE  10 PCTUSED  90 FREELISTS 1);
```

Here we can infer that update operations are frequent and will probably increase the size of the **VARCHAR** columns, since **PCTFREE** is set to reserve 10 percent of each block for row expansion. We can also infer that this table has few deletes, because **PCTUSED** is set to 90, making efficient use of the database blocks. Assuming that there will not be very many deletes, these blocks would become constantly re-added to the **FREELISTS**.

Referential Integrity And Performance

Before most relational database-supported referential integrity, it was the responsibility of the programmer to guarantee the maintenance of data relationships and business rules. While this was fine for the applications, the risk came into play when ad hoc updated SQL commands were issued using Oracle's SQL*Plus. With these ad hoc update tools, the programmatic SQL could be easily bypassed, skipping the business rules and creating logical corruption.

Relational database systems such as Oracle allow for the control of business rules with "constraints." These RI rules are used to enforce one-to-

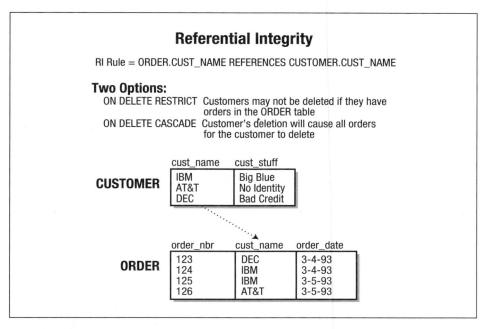

Figure 2.2 An overview of referential integrity.

many and many-to-many relationships within the relational tables. For example, RI would ensure that a row in the **CUSTOMER** table could not be deleted if orders for that customer exist in the **ORDER** table. (See Figure 2.2.)

Referential integrity has earned a bad reputation in Oracle because of the overhead that is created when enforcing the business rules. In almost every case, it will be faster and more efficient to write your own rules to enforce RI instead of having Oracle do it for you. Provided that your application does not allow ad hoc query, it is relatively easy to attach a trigger with a PL/SQL routine to enforce the RI on your behalf. In fact, this is one of the best uses of a trigger, since the DML **DELETE** event will not take place if the RI rules are invalid. For example, consider the foreign key constraint that protects a customer from being deleted if they have outstanding orders:

```
CREATE TABLE CUSTOMER (
    cust_id                 NUMBER
    CONSTRAINT cust_ukey UNIQUE (cust_id),
    cust_name               VARCHAR(30),
    cust_address            VARCHAR(30);)
```

```
CREATE TABLE ORDER (
    order_id              NUMBER,
    order_date            DATE,
    cust_id               NUMBER
    CONSTRAINT cust_fk REFERENCES CUSTOMER ON DELETE RESTRICT,
);
```

To ensure that SQL*Plus has no ad hoc updates, it can be configured to disallow update operations. This is accomplished with the **PRODUCT_USER_PROFILE** table. Issuing the following row into this table will disable any ad hoc updates with SQL*Plus:

```
INSERT INTO PRODUCT_USER_PROFILE (product, user_id, attribute)
VALUES (
        'SQL*Plus',
        '%',
        'UPDATE');
```

Are you now free to write your own procedural RI without fear of accidental corruption? Actually, there is another way that users can access ad hoc query, thereby bypassing your business rules. A user on a PC (with SQL*Net installed) can access Oracle using ODBC without ever entering SQL*Plus. So beware, and be sure that all ad hoc holes have been plugged before attempting to write your own RI rules.

Another problem with RI occurs when two tablespaces each contain tables that have foreign key rules into the other tablespace. The DBA must commonly drop and rebuild the tablespaces as a part of routine database compression. For example, when trying to drop a tablespace (say TS1) that has RI into another tablespace, the **DROP TABLESPACE CASCADE** will fail because foreign key references are contained in table B in tablespace TS2. Conversely, the DBA cannot drop tablespace TS2 because it has references into tablespace TS1. This turns DBA maintenance into a nightmare, since all constraints must be identified and disabled from TS2 in order to drop tablespace TS1.

Oracle Stored Procedures

As objects such as stored procedures and triggers become more popular, more application code will move away from external programs and into the database engine. Oracle has been encouraging this approach in anticipation of the object-oriented features of Oracle version 8. However, the Oracle DBA must be conscious of the increasing memory demands of stored procedures, and carefully plan for the days when all of the database access code resides within the database.

Today, most Oracle databases have only a small amount of code in stored procedures—but this is rapidly changing. Many compelling benefits can be derived by placing all Oracle SQL inside stored procedures. These include:

- *Better Performance*—Stored procedures are loaded once into the SGA and remain there unless they become paged out. Subsequent executions of the stored procedure are far faster than external code.

- *Coupling of Data with Behavior*—Relational tables can be coupled with the behaviors that are associated with them by using naming conventions. For example, if all behaviors associated with the employee table are prefixed with the table name (e.g., **EMPLOYEE.hire**, **EMPLOYEE. give_raise**), then the data dictionary can be queried to list all behaviors associated with a table (for instance, select * from **dba_objects** where owner = '**EMPLOYEE**'), and code can be readily identified and reused.

- *Isolation of Code*—Since all SQL is moved out of the external programs and into stored procedures, the application programs are nothing more than calls to stored procedures. As such, it becomes very simple to swap out one database and swap in another.

One of the foremost reasons why stored procedures and triggers function faster than traditional code is related to Oracle System Global Area (SGA). After a procedure has been loaded into the SGA, it will remain in the library cache until it is paged out of memory. Items are paged out of memory based upon a least-recently-used algorithm. Once loaded into the RAM memory of the shared pool, the procedure will execute very quickly. The trick is to prevent pool-thrashing during the period when many procedures are competing for a limited amount of library cache within the shared pool memory.

When tuning Oracle, two init.ora parameters emerge as more important than all of the other parameters combined. These are the **db_block_buffers** and the **shared_pool_size** parameters. These two parameters define the size of the in-memory region that Oracle consumes on startup and determines the amount of storage available to cache data blocks, SQL, and stored procedures.

Oracle also provides a construct called a *package*. Essentially, a package is a collection of functions and stored procedures, and can be organized in a variety of ways. For example, functions and stored procedures for employees can be logically grouped together in an employee package:

```
CREATE PACKAGE EMPLOYEE AS

    FUNCTION compute_raise_amount (percentage NUMBER);
    PROCEDURE hire_employee();
    PROCEDURE fire_employee();
    PROCEDURE list_employee_details();1

END employee;
```

Here we have encapsulated all employee "behaviors" into a single package that will be added into Oracle's data dictionary. If we force our programmers to use stored procedures, the SQL moves out of the external programs and into the database, reducing the application programs into nothing more than a series of calls to Oracle stored procedures.

As systems evolve and the majority of process code resides in stored procedures, Oracle's shared pool becomes very important. The shared pool consists of the following subpools:

1. Dictionary cache

2. Library cache

3. Shared SQL areas

4. Private SQL area (these exist during cursor open–cursor close)

    a) persistent area

    b) runtime area

As we have mentioned, the shared pool utilizes a "least-recently-used" algorithm to determine which objects are paged out of the shared pool. As this paging occurs, "fragments" or discontiguous chunks of memory are created within the shared pool.

This means that a large procedure that initially fits into memory may not fit into contiguous memory when it's reloaded after paging out. Consider a problem that occurs when the body of a package has been paged out of the instance's SGA because of other more recent/frequent activity. Fragmentation occurs, and the server cannot find enough contiguous memory to reload the package body, resulting in an ORA-4031 error.

Pinning Oracle Packages In The SGA

To prevent paging, packages can be marked as nonswappable, which tells the database that after their initial load they must always remain in memory. This is called *pinning* or *memory fencing*. Oracle provides a procedure called **dbms_shared_pool.keep** to pin a package. Packages can be unpinned with **dbms_shared_pool.unkeep**.

 Only packages can be pinned. Stored procedures cannot be pinned unless they are placed into a package.

The choice of whether to "pin" a package in memory is a function of the size of the object and the frequency of its use. Very large packages that are called frequently might benefit from pinning, but any difference may go unnoticed because the frequent calls to the procedure have kept it loaded into memory. Therefore, since the object never pages out, the pinning has no effect. Also, the way that procedures are grouped into packages may have some influence. Some Oracle DBAs identify high-impact procedures and group them into a single package, which is pinned in the library cache.

In an ideal world, the **shared_pool** parameter of the init.ora should be large enough to accept every package, stored procedure, and trigger that may be used by the applications. However, reality dictates that the shared pool cannot grow indefinitely, and wise choices must be made in terms of which packages are pinned.

Because of their frequent usage, Oracle recommends that the **standard**, **dbms_standard**, **dbms_utility**, **dbms_describe**, and **dbms_output** packages always be pinned in the shared pool. The following snippet demonstrates how a stored procedure called sys.standard can be pinned:

```
CONNECT INTERNAL;

@/usr/oracle/rdbms/admin/dbmspool.sql

EXECUTE dbms_shared_pool.keep('sys.standard');
```

A standard procedure can be written to pin all of the recommended Oracle packages into the shared pool. Here is the script:

```
EXECUTE dbms_shared_pool.keep('DBMS_ALERT');
EXECUTE dbms_shared_pool.keep('DBMS_DDL');
EXECUTE dbms_shared_pool.keep('DBMS_DESCRIBE');
EXECUTE dbms_shared_pool.keep('DBMS_LOCK');
EXECUTE dbms_shared_pool.keep('DBMS_OUTPUT');
EXECUTE dbms_shared_pool.keep('DBMS_PIPE');
EXECUTE dbms_shared_pool.keep('DBMS_SESSION');
EXECUTE dbms_shared_pool.keep('DBMS_SHARED_POOL');
EXECUTE dbms_shared_pool.keep('DBMS_STANDARD');
EXECUTE dbms_shared_pool.keep('DBMS_UTILITY');
EXECUTE dbms_shared_pool.keep('STANDARD');
```

AUTOMATIC RE-PINNING OF PACKAGES

Unix users may want to add code to the /etc/rc file to ensure that the packages are re-pinned after each database startup, which guarantees that all packages are re-pinned with each bounce of the box. A script might look like this:

```
[root]: more pin
ORACLE_SID=mydata
export ORACLE_SID
su oracle -c "/usr/oracle/bin/svrmgrl /<<!
connect internal;
select * from db;
   @/usr/local/dba/sql/pin.sql
exit;
!"
```

The Database Administrator also needs to remember to run pin.sql whenever he or she must restart a database. This is done by reissuing the pin command from inside SQL*DBA immediately after the database has been restarted.

HOW TO MEASURE PINNED PACKAGES

Listing 2.2 shows a handy script to look at pinned packages in the SGA.

Listing 2.2   Looking at pinned packages in the SGA.

```
memory.sql - Display used SGA memory for triggers, packages, & procedures

SET PAGESIZE 60;

COLUMN EXECUTIONS FORMAT 999,999,999;
COLUMN Mem_used    FORMAT 999,999,999;

SELECT SUBSTR(owner,1,10) Owner,
       SUBSTR(type,1,12)  Type,
       SUBSTR(name,1,20)  Name,
       executions,
       sharable_mem       Mem_used,
       SUBSTR(kept||' ',1,4)   "Kept?"
 FROM v$db_object_cache
 WHERE TYPE IN ('TRIGGER','PROCEDURE','PACKAGE BODY','PACKAGE')
 ORDER BY EXECUTIONS DESC;
```

Listing 2.3 shows the output of MEMORY.SQL.

Listing 2.3   The output of MEMORY.SQL.

```
SQL> @memory

OWNER   TYPE          NAME                  EXECUTIONS   MEM_USED   KEPT
----    ------        ------                ----------   --------   -----
SYS     PACKAGE       STANDARD                 867,600    151,963   YES
SYS     PACKAGE BODY  STANDARD                 867,275     30,739   YES
SYS     PACKAGE       DBMS_ALERT               502,126      3,637   NO
SYS     PACKAGE BODY  DBMS_ALERT               433,607     20,389   NO
SYS     PACKAGE       DBMS_LOCK                432,137      3,140   YES
SYS     PACKAGE BODY  DBMS_LOCK                432,137     10,780   YES
SYS     PACKAGE       DBMS_PIPE                397,466      3,412   NO
SYS     PACKAGE BODY  DBMS_PIPE                397,466      5,292   NO
HRIS    PACKAGE       S125_PACKAGE             285,700      3,776   NO
SYS     PACKAGE       DBMS_UTILITY             284,694      3,311   NO
SYS     PACKAGE BODY  DBMS_UTILITY             284,694      6,159   NO
HRIS    PACKAGE       HRS_COMMON_PACKAGE       258,657      3,382   NO
HRIS    PACKAGE BODY  S125_PACKAGE             248,857     30,928   NO
HRIS    PACKAGE BODY  HRS_COMMON_PACKAGE       242,155      8,638   NO
HRIS    PACKAGE       GTS_SNAPSHOT_UTILITY     168,978     11,056   NO
```

HRIS	PACKAGE BODY	GTS_SNAPSHOT_UTILITY	89,623	3,232	NO
SYS	PACKAGE	DBMS_STANDARD	18,953	14,696	NO
SYS	PACKAGE BODY	DBMS_STANDARD	18,872	3,432	NO
KIS	PROCEDURE	RKA_INSERT	7,067	4,949	NO
HRIS	PACKAGE	HRS_PACKAGE	5,175	3,831	NO
HRIS	PACKAGE BODY	HRS_PACKAGE	5,157	36,455	NO
SYS	PACKAGE	DBMS_DESCRIBE	718	12,800	NO
HRIS	PROCEDURE	CHECK_APP_ALERT	683	3,763	NO
SYS	PACKAGE BODY	DBMS_DESCRIBE	350	9,880	NO
SYS	PACKAGE	DBMS_SESSION	234	3,351	NO
SYS	PACKAGE BODY	DBMS_SESSION	65	4,543	NO
GIANT	PROCEDURE	CREATE_SESSION_RECOR	62	7,147	NO
HRIS	PROCEDURE	INIT_APP_ALERT	6	10,802	NO

Here is an easy way to tell the number of times that a non-pinned stored procedure was swapped out of memory and required a reload. To effectively measure memory, two methods are recommended. The first is to regularly run the estat-bstat utility (usually located in ~/rdbms/admin/utlbstat.sql and utlestat.sql) for measuring SGA consumption over a range of time. Another handy method would be writing a snapdump utility to interrogate the SGA and note any exceptional information relating to the library cache. This would include the following measurements:

- Data dictionary hit ratio

- Library cache miss ratio

- Individual hit ratios for all namespaces

Also, be aware that the relevant parameter, **shared_pool_size**, is used for other objects besides stored procedures. This means that one parameter fits all, and Oracle offers no method for isolating the amount of storage allocated to any subset of the shared pool.

Listing 2.4 is a sample report for gathering information relating to **shared_pool_size**. As you can see, the data dictionary hit ratio is above 95 percent and the library cache miss ratio is very low. However, we see over 125,000 reloads in the SQL area namespace, and we may want to increase the **shared_pool_size**. When running this type of report, always remember that statistics are gathered from startup, and the numbers may be skewed. For example, for a system that has been running for six months, the data dictionary hit ratio will be a running average over six months. Consequently, data from the **V$** structures is meaningless if you want to measure today's statistics.

Some DBAs will run utlbstat.sql, wait one hour, and run utlestat.sql. This produces a report, shown in Listing 2.4, that shows the statistics over the elapsed time interval.

Listing 2.4   The generated report showing statistics.

```
================================
DATA DICT HIT RATIO
================================
(should be higher than 90 else increase shared_pool_size in init.ora)
```

Data Dict. Gets	Data Dict. cache misses	DATA DICT CACHE HIT RATIO
41,750,549	407,609	99

```
================================
LIBRARY CACHE MISS RATIO
================================
(If > 1 then increase the shared_pool_size in init.ora)
```

executions	Cache misses while executing	LIBRARY CACHE MISS RATIO
22,909,643	171,127	.0075

```
================================
LIBRARY CACHE SECTION
================================
hit ratio should be > 70, and pin ratio > 70 ...
```

NAMESPACE	Hit ratio	pin hit ratio	reloads
SQL AREA	84	94	125,885
TABLE/PROCEDURE	98	99	43,559
BODY	98	84	486
TRIGGER	98	97	1,145
INDEX	0	0	
CLUSTER	31	33	
OBJECT	100	100	
PIPE	99	99	52

Let's take a look at the SQL*Plus script (Listing 2.5) that generated Listing 2.4.

Listing 2.5   The script that generated Listing 2.4.

```
PROMPT
PROMPT
PROMPT                ==========================
PROMPT                DATA DICT HIT RATIO
PROMPT                ==========================
PROMPT (should be higher than 90 else increase shared_pool_size in
init.ora)
PROMPT

COLUMN "Data Dict. Gets"            FORMAT 999,999,999
COLUMN "Data Dict. cache misses"    FORMAT 999,999,999
SELECT sum(gets) "Data Dict. Gets",
       sum(getmisses) "Data Dict. cache misses",
       trunc((1-(sum(getmisses)/sum(gets)))*100)
       "DATA DICT CACHE HIT RATIO"
FROM v$rowcache;

PROMPT
PROMPT                ==========================
PROMPT                LIBRARY CACHE MISS RATIO
PROMPT                ==========================
PROMPT (If > 1 then increase the shared_pool_size in init.ora)
PROMPT
COLUMN "LIBRARY CACHE MISS RATIO"        FORMAT 99.9999
COLUMN "executions"                      FORMAT 999,999,999
COLUMN "Cache misses while executing"    FORMAT 999,999,999
SELECT sum(pins) "executions", sum(reloads)
                "Cache misses while executing",
   (((sum(reloads)/sum(pins)))) "LIBRARY CACHE MISS RATIO"
FROM v$librarycache;

PROMPT
PROMPT                ==========================
PROMPT                LIBRARY CACHE SECTION
PROMPT                ==========================
PROMPT hit ratio should be > 70, and pin ratio > 70 ...
PROMPT

COLUMN "reloads" FORMAT 999,999,999
SELECT namespace, trunc(gethitratio * 100)
       "Hit ratio",
trunc(pinhitratio * 100) "pin hit ratio",
       reloads "reloads"
FROM v$librarycache;
```

Just as the wisdom of the 1980s dictated that data should be centralized, the 1990s have begun an era where SQL is also centralized and managed. With the centralization of SQL, many previously impossible tasks have become trivial:

- SQL can easily be identified and reused.

- SQL can be extracted by the DBA, allowing him or her to run EXPLAIN PLAN utilities to determine the proper placement of table indexes.

- SQL can be searched, allowing for fast identification of "where used" information. For example, when a column changes definition, all SQL referencing that column can be quickly identified.

As memory becomes less expensive, it will eventually become desirable to have all of the application's SQL and code loaded into the Oracle library cache, where the code will be quickly available for execution by any external applications regardless of its platform or host language. The most compelling reasons for putting all SQL within packages are portability and code management. If all applications become "SQL-less," with calls to stored procedures, then entire applications can be ported to other platforms without touching a single line of the application code.

As the cost of memory drops, 500 MB Oracle regions will not be uncommon. Until that time, however, the DBA must carefully consider the ramifications of pinning a package in the SGA.

Oracle Triggers

Many database systems now support the use of *triggers* that can be fired at specific events. The insert, modification, or deletion of a record may fire a trigger, or business events such as **place_order** may initiate a trigger action. Oracle Corporation claims that the design of its triggers closely follow the ANSI/ISO SQL3 draft standard (ANSI X3H6), but Oracle triggers are more robust in functionality than the ANSI standard. Triggers are defined at the schema level of the system, and will "fire" whenever an SQL **select**, **update**, **delete**, or **insert** command is issued. Remember that a trigger is always associated with a single DML event.

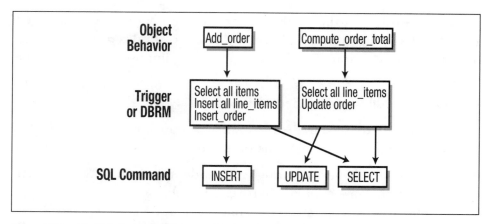

Figure 2.3 The relationship between objects, triggers, and SQL.

Deciding When To Use A Trigger

The choice of when to use a trigger and when to use a stored procedure can have a profound impact on the performance of the system. In general, triggers are used when additional processing is required as a row is inserted into a table. For example, assume that whenever a **customer** row is added, the system is required to look for the customer in the **bad_credit** table. If the customer appears in the **bad_credit** table, then its **shipping_status** column is set to '**COD**'. In this case, a trigger on **INSERT OF CUSTOMER** can fire the PL/SQL procedure to do the necessary lookup and set the **shipping_status** field to its appropriate value.

Oracle triggers have the ability to call procedures and a trigger may include SQL statements, thus providing the ability to "nest" SQL statements. Oracle triggers are stored as procedures that may be parameterized and used to simulate object-oriented behavior. For example, assume that we want to perform a behavior called **CHECK_TOTAL_INVENTORY** whenever an item is added to an order. (See Figure 2.3.)

The trigger definition would be:

```
CREATE TRIGGER CHECK_TOTAL_INVENTORY
            AFTER  SELECT OF ITEM
FOR EACH ROW
```

```
    SELECT COUNT(*) INTO :count
    FROM QUANTITY WHERE ITEM_# = :myitem:

IF :count < ITEM.TOTAL THEN
    ......
END IF;
```

Triggers could also be combined to handle multiple events, such as the reordering of an **ITEM** when the quantity-on-hand falls below a predefined level:

```
CREATE TRIGGER REORDER BEFORE UPDATE ON ITEM
    FOR EACH ROW WHEN (new.reorderable = 'Y')
        BEGIN
            IF new.qty_on_hand + old.qty_on_order < new.minimum_qty
            THEN
                INSERT INTO REORDER VALUES (item_nbr,
                reorder_qty);
                new.qty_on_order := old.qty_on_order +
                reorder_qty;
            END IF;
END;
```

Oracle Hash Tables

Oracle7 now supports the concepts of hash clusters. A hash cluster is a construct that works with Oracle clusters and uses the **HASHKEYS** command to allow fast access to the primary key for the cluster. Oracle relies upon a "hashing algorithm," which takes a symbolic key and converts it into a row ID (**ROWID**), as in Figure 2.4. The hashing function ensures that the cluster key is retrieved in a single I/O, which is faster than reading multiple blocks from an index tree. Because a hashing algorithm always produces the same key each time it reads an input value, duplicate keys have to be avoided. In Oracle, these "collisions" result when the value of **HASHKEYS** is less than the maximum number of cluster key values. For example, if a hash cluster uses the **customer_nbr** field as the key, and we know that there will be 50;000 unique **customer_nbr** values, then we must be sure that the value of **HASHKEYS** is set to at least 50,000. Also, you should always round up your value for **HASHKEYS** to the next highest prime number. Here is an example of a hash cluster:

```
CREATE CLUSTER my_cluster (customer_nbr      VARCHAR(10))
    TABLESPACE user1
        STORAGE (initial 50K next 50K pctincrease 1)
        SIZE 2K
        HASH IS customer_nbr HASHKEYS 50000;
```

Now a table is defined within the cluster:

```
CREATE TABLE CUSTOMER (
        customer_nbr   NUMBER PRIMARY KEY )
CLUSTER my_cluster (customer_nbr);
```

The **SIZE** parameter is usually set to the average row size for the table. Oracle recommends using a hash cluster when the following is true:

- Use hash clusters to store tables that are commonly accessed by **WHERE** clauses that specify equalities.

- Only use a hash clusters when you can afford to keep plenty of free space on each database block for updates. This value is set by the **PCTFREE** statement in the **CREATE TABLE** parameter.

- Only use hash cluster if you are absolutely sure that you will not need to create a new, larger cluster at a later time.

- Do not use a hash cluster if your table is commonly accessed by full-table scans, especially if a great deal of extra space from future growth has been allocated to the hash cluster. In a full-table scan, Oracle will

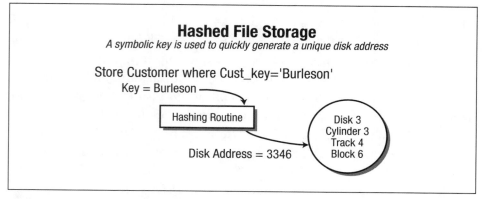

Figure 2.4 A sample hashing routine.

read all blocks of the hash cluster, regardless of whether or not they contain any data rows.

- Do not use a hash cluster if any of the hash cluster keys are frequently modified. Changing the value of a hash key causes the hashing algorithm to generate a new location, and the database will migrate the cluster to a new database block if the key value is changed. This is a very time-consuming operation.

Keep in mind that the total size of the index columns must fit inside a single Oracle block. If the index contains too many long values, additional I/O will be required and **UPDATE**s and **INSERT**s will cause serious performance problems. Note the sample hashing routine shown in Figure 2.4.

The database designer may choose to make the buffer blocks large to minimize I/O if the application "clusters" records on a database page. If a customer record is only 100 bytes, we will not gain by retrieving 32,000 bytes in order to get the 100 bytes that we need. However, if we cluster the orders physically near the customer (on the same database page), and if I/O usually proceeds from customer to order, then we will not need further I/O to retrieve orders for the customer. They will already reside in the initial read of 32,000 bytes. (See Figure 2.5.)

Oracle Clusters

Clustering is a very important concept for improving client-server performance. When traversing a database, reducing I/O always improves throughput. The concept of clustering is very similar to the use of the VIA set in the CODASYL Network database model, where member records are stored physically near their parent records. For Oracle, clusters can be used to define common one-to-many access paths, and the member rows can be stored on the same database block as their owner row. For example, assume that we have a one-to-many relationship between customers and orders. If our application commonly access the data from customer to order, we can cluster the order rows on the same database block as the customer row. In this way, we'll receive the list of all orders for a customer in a single I/O. (See Figure 2.5.) Of course, we will need to size the database blocks with **db_block_size** so that an entire order will fit onto a single database

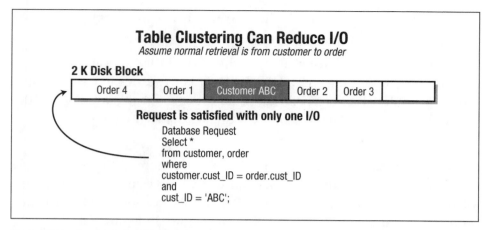

Figure 2.5 A sample Oracle cluster.

block. For more information on **db_block_size**, refer to Chapter 6, Oracle DBA Performance And Tuning.

We need to note one important issue, however: While a cluster will tremendously improve performance in one direction, queries in the other direction will suffer. For example, consider the many-to-many relationship between customers and orders. We have the junction table, **ORDER_LINE**, at the intersection of this many-to-many relationship and we need to decide which owner, **ORDER** or **ITEM**, will be the anchor for our cluster. If we commonly traverse from order to item (e.g., displaying an order form), it would make sense to cluster the **ORDER_LINE** records on the same database block as their **ORDER** owner. If, on the other hand, we commonly traversed from **ITEM** to **ORDER** (e.g., requesting the details for all orders containing widgets), we would cluster the **ORDER_LINE** rows near their **ITEM** owner. If we cluster on the **ORDER** owner, database queries that display order forms will be very fast, while queries in the other direction will have to do additional I/O.

Oracle Parallel Query

One of the most exciting performance features of Oracle version 7.3 and above is the ability to partition an SQL query into subqueries, and dedicate separate processors to concurrently service each subquery. At this time, parallel query is only useful for queries that perform full-table scans on long tables, but the performance improvements can be dramatic. Here's how it works.

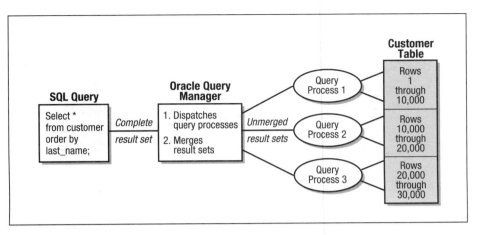

Figure 2.6   A sample parallel query.

Instead of having a single query server to manage the I/O against the table, parallel query allows the Oracle query server to dedicate many processors to simultaneously access the data, as shown in Figure 2.6.

In order to be most effective, the table should be partitioned onto separate disk devices, such that each process can do I/O against its segment of the table without interfering with the other simultaneous query processes. However, the client-server environment of the 1990s relies on RAID or a logical volume manager (LVM), which scrambles datafiles across disk packs in order to balance the I/O load. Consequently, full utilization of parallel query involves "striping" a table across numerous data files, each on a separate device.

Even if your system uses RAID or LVM, some performance gains are still available with parallel query. In addition to using multiple processes to retrieve the table, the query manager will also dedicate numerous processes to simultaneously sort the result set. (See Figure 2.7.)

However, parallel query works best with symmetric multiprocessor (SMP) boxes, which have more than one internal CPU. Also, it is important to configure the system to maximize the I/O bandwidth, either through disk striping or high-speed channels. Because of the parallel sorting feature, it is also a good idea to beef up the memory on the processor.

While sorting is no substitute for using a presorted index, the parallel query manager will service requests far faster than a single process. While the

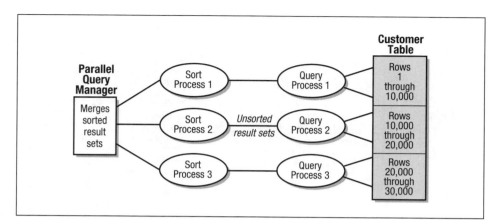

Figure 2.7 A sample parallel sort.

data retrieval will not be significantly faster because all of the retrieval processes are competing for a channel on the same disk, each sort process has its own sort area (as determined by the **sort_area_size** init.ora parameter)—which speeds along the sorting of the result set. In addition to full-table scans and sorting, the parallel query option also allows for parallel processes for merge joins and nested loops.

To invoke the parallel query option requires that all indexing is bypassed. The most important is that the execution plan for the query specifies a full-table scan. If the output of the explain plan does not indicate a full-table scan, the query can be forced to ignore the index by using query hints.

The number of processors that are dedicated to service an SQL request is ultimately determined by Oracle's query manager, but the programmer can specify the upper limit on the number of simultaneous processes. When using the cost-based optimizer, the **PARALLEL** hint can be embedded into the SQL to specify the number of processes. For example:

```
SELECT /*+ FULL(employee_table) PARALLEL(employee_table,  4) */
       employee_name
       FROM
       employee_table
       WHERE
       emp_type = 'SALARIED';
```

If you are using SMP with many CPUs, you can issue a parallel request and leave it up to each Oracle instance to use their default degree of parallelism:

```
SELECT /*+ FULL(employee_table) PARALLEL(employee_table,  DEFAULT,
DEFAULT) */
        employee_name
        FROM
        employee_table
        WHERE
        emp_type = 'SALARIED';
```

Several important init.ora parameters have a direct impact on parallel query:

- **sort_area_size**—The higher the value, the more memory available for individual sorts on each parallel process. Note that the **sort_area_size** parameter allocates memory for every query on the system that invokes a sort. For example, if a single query needs more memory and you increase the **sort_area_size**, all Oracle tasks will allocate the new amount of sort area, regardless of whether or not they will use all of the space.

- **parallel_min_servers**—The minimum number of query servers that will be active on the instance. System resources are involved in starting a query server, so having the query server started and waiting for requests will speed up processing. Note that if the actual number of required servers is less than the value of **parallel_min_servers**, the idle query servers will be consuming unnecessary overhead and the value should be decreased.

- **parallel_max_servers**—The maximum number of query servers allowed on the instance. This parameter will prevent Oracle from starting so many query servers that the instance is unable to service all of them properly.

To see how many parallel query servers are busy at any given time, the following query can be issued against the **v$pq_sysstat** table:

```
SELECT * FROM v$pq_sysstat
       WHERE STATISTIC = 'Servers Busy';

  STATISTIC                VALUE
  ----------           -----------
Servers Busy               30
```

In this case, we see that 30 parallel servers are busy at this moment in time. Do not be misled by this number. Parallel query servers are constantly accepting work or returning to idle status, so it is a good idea to issue the query many times over a one-hour period. Only then will you have a realistic measure of how many parallel query servers are being used.

Towards Oracle8

The next progression of database architectures is toward object-oriented databases. Just as early file managers stored data, network databases stored data and relationships—and object-oriented database store data, data relationships, and the behaviors of the data.

In general, the Oracle8 engine is remarkably similar to the relational engine found in Oracle 7.3, but with major extensions to the relational architecture. It is interesting to note that Oracle has not discarded the idea of creating a "universal" database engine. Oracle is calling Oracle8 the "Oracle Universal Server," adding text, multidimensional, and object capabilities to the relational engine. The most exciting enhancements involve the introduction of "Sedona," the incorporation of the Oracle Express MDDB, and the "object layer" that will be tightly coupled with the relational engine.

Oracle Sedona

Due to the secrecy around the development of Oracle8, many Oracle professionals assumed that Sedona was the code name for the Oracle8 product. However, Sedona is actually an extension to the Oracle8 product. Sedona has been billed as a "Universal Object Manager," and it appears that its basic function is to act as an "object consolidator" by allowing for Oracle methods to be indexed and quickly located across many databases and platforms. Sedona achieves this by placing an object wrapper around Oracle objects so they can be accessed by other distributed systems. While the details are still sketchy, Sedona will incorporate many of the features of an Object Request Broker (ORB) with a metadata dictionary for the distributed management of objects. With Sedona, object classes may be registered in a central repository so they will be available for use transparently across the enterprise. Oracle has made the interface specifications for Sedona to third-party software vendors, hoping that these vendors will create application products that utilize Sedona.

Oracle ConText

A text searching option called Oracle ConText has also been added to the relational engine of Oracle8. Oracle ConText allows thematic word searching capabilities against Oracle's relational database. Although the ConText option indexes on each word within the text, the real power of the text retrieval system is located in the front-end software. While this represents major improvement over Oracle Book (which is now obsolete), it remains to be seen how ConText will compete in the marketplace as a text search engine. There are two fundamental ways to measure the accuracy of text retrieval:

- *Precision*—The ability to retrieve only relevant documents (no false or "noisy" hits)

- *Recall*—The ability to retrieve all relevant documents in a given data collection

Together, precision and recall represent the overall accuracy of a text retrieval system. "Natural language" is a phrase frequently heard in conjunction with concept-based searching, and "morphology" is commonly used by the text databases to simulate natural language query. Morphology recognizes basic units of meaning and parts of speech. To understand morphology, consider the phrase "Please write to Mr. Wright right now." From the initial review, it is still unclear how well Oracle ConText will be able to compete with the other more established text engines such as ConQuest, Fulcrum and Folio.

Oracle Express

Unlike Oracle 7.3, where the Express multidimensional database was installed independently of Oracle, the Express product has been incorporated into the Oracle8 kernel. This implies yet another change for Oracle DBAs, who must now manage both the relational and multidimensional components of Oracle. Oracle Express will be offered for NT and PC, as well as Unix platforms. The basic reporting functions of Express have also been enhanced to provide forecasting and model building.

Unlike the Express product from IRI (IRI was the company that originally developed Express), Oracle Express has been enhanced so that it does not require data to be preloaded into its internal data structures. This enhancement allows Express to read relational data directly from relational Oracle, dynamically transforming and aggregating the data for multidimensional presentation. This means that Express will now compete against the other relational back-end products such as Holos and MetaCube.

The Object Layer

Rather than rebuild the Oracle engine as an object-oriented architecture, Oracle has decided to keep the base relational engine and add object functionality on top of the standard relational architecture. While claiming to be an active member in the Object Management Group (OMG), Oracle has departed from the OMG's standard for "pure" object databases as defined by the Object Data Management Group (ODMG). Oracle's intent is to provide a generic relational database while extending the architecture to allow for objects. The object layer of Oracle8 claims to have the following features:

ABSTRACT DATA TYPING (ADTs)

Rather than being constrained to the basic relational data types of **INT VARCHAR**, and **FLOAT**, Oracle8 will allow the definition of data types that may be composed of many subtypes. For example, the following data definition could be implemented in Oracle8 as an **ADDRESS** data type:

```
03 ADDRESS.

        05 STREET-ADDRESS              VARCHAR(30).
        05 CITY-ADDRESS                VARCHAR(30).
        05 ZIP-CODE                    NUMBER(5).
```

In this manner, aggregate data types can be defined and addressed in a table definition just like any other relational data type. In the example below, we see the **phone_nbr** and **address** data types being used in a table definition:

```
CREATE TABLE CUSTOMER (
        cust_name          VARCHAR(40),
        cust_phone         phone_nbr,
        cust_address       address);
```

Here we see that a single data "field" in a table may be a range of values or an entire table. This concept is called complex, or unstructured, data typing (Figure 2.8). The domain of values for a specific field in a relational

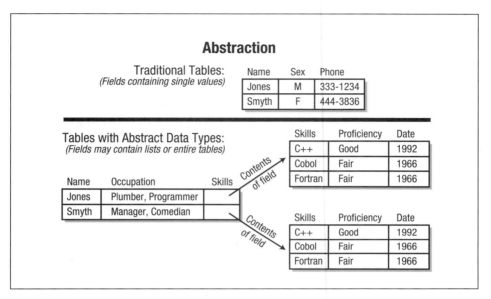

Figure 2.8   An example of abstract data types (ADTs).

database may be defined with this approach. This ability to "nest" data tables allows for relationship data to be incorporated directly into the table structure. For example, the **Occupation** field in the table establishes a one-to-many relationship between an employee and his or her valid occupations. Also note the ability to nest the entire **Skills** table within a single field. In this example, only valid skills may reside in the **Skills** field, and this implements the relational concept of "domain integrity."

DEFINITION OF AGGREGATE OBJECTS

In Oracle8, aggregate objects can be defined and preassembled for fast retrieval. For example, a **report_card** may be defined for a university database. The **report_card** object may be defined such that it is assembled at runtime from its atomic components (similar to an Oracle view), or the **report_card** may be preassembled and stored in the database. These aggregate objects may have methods (such as stored procedures) attached to them, such that an Oracle object couples data and behavior together.

COUPLING OF DATA AND BEHAVIOR

The Oracle8 engine allows for the direct coupling of a database entity (a table or object) with a set of predefined behaviors. In this fashion, calls to

Oracle will be made by specifying an object name and the method that is associated with the object. For example:

```
CUSTOMER.add_new('Jones', 123, 'other parms');
```

This call tells Oracle to invoke the **add_new** procedure that is attached to the **CUSTOMER** object, using the supplied parms. As you might expect, this new way of invoking database calls has important ramifications for the developers and DBA staff.

For developers, applications will become SQL-less and will consist of calls to stored procedures. Of course, this has the important benefit of making applications portable across platforms, while also making it very easy to find and reuse code. In addition, since each method is encapsulated and tested independently, the pretested methods can be assembled with other methods without worry of unintended side effects.

For DBAs, the coupling of data with behaviors will dramatically change the way that the DBA performs database administration tasks. Instead of only managing data and tables, the Oracle8 DBA will also be responsible for managing objects and the methods that are associated with each object. These new "object administrator" functions will need to be defined so that the developers know the functions of all methods and all parameters for each method.

ABSTRACTION

Abstraction within Oracle8 is defined as the conceptual (not concrete) existence of classes within the database. For example, a database may have a class hierarchy which includes classes without objects. A military database may contain the conceptual entities of **DIVISION**, **BATTALION**, **SQUADRON**, and **PLATOON**. The function of the database is to track the platoons, and the entity classes of **DIVISION**, **BATTALION**, and **SQUADRON** may not have any associated objects. This is not to say that abstract classes have no purpose. When a class is defined, it is associated with behaviors, which in turn will be inherited by each object in the **PLATOON** class. From a database perspective, there will be no instances of any objects except **PLATOON**, but higher levels in the class hierarchy will contain behaviors which the **PLATOON** objects inherit.

INHERITANCE

Inheritance is defined as the ability of a lower-level object to inherit or access the data structures and behaviors associated with all classes that are above it in the class hierarchy. Multiple inheritance refers to the ability of an object to inherit data structures and behaviors from more than one superclass.

To illustrate, let's look at an application of this system for a vehicle dealership. Occurrences of **ITEM**s to a dealership are **VEHICLE**s; beneath the vehicle class, we may find subclasses for cars and for boats. Within cars, the classes may be further partitioned into classes for **TRUCK**, **VAN**, and **SEDAN**. The **VEHICLE** class would contain the data items which are unique to vehicles, including the vehicle ID and the year of manufacture. The **CAR** class, because it ISA **VEHICLE**, would inherit the data items of the **VEHICLE** class. The **CAR** class might contain data items such as the number of axles and the gross weight of the vehicle. Because the **VAN** class ISA **CAR**, which in turn ISA **VEHICLE**, objects of the **VAN** class will inherit all data structures and behaviors relating to **CAR**s and **VEHICLE**s.

 It is critical to the understanding of inheritance to note that inheritance happens at different times during the life of an object.

- *Inheritance of Data Structures*—At object creation time, inheritance is the mechanism whereby the initial data structure for the object is created. It is critical to note that only data structures are inherited, never data. It is a common misconception that data is inherited, such that an order may inherit the data items for the customer who placed the order. We must understand that inheritance is only used to create the initial, empty data structures for the object. In our example, all vehicles would inherit data definitions in the **VEHICLE** class, while an object of a lower-level class (say, **SAILBOAT**) would inherit data structures that apply only to sailboats—as in **sail_size**.

- *Inheritance of Methods*—Inheritance also happens at runtime when a call to a method (stored procedure) is made. For example, assume that the following call is made to sailboat object:

```
SAILBOAT.compute_rental_charges();
```

The database will first search for the **compute_rental_charges** in the **SAILBOAT** class; if it is not found, the database will search *up the class hierarchy* until **compute_rental_charges** is located.

Not all classes within a generalization hierarchy will have objects associated with them. The object-oriented paradigm allows for abstraction, which means that a class may exist only for the purpose of passing inherited data and behaviors. The classes **VEHICLE** and **CAR** would probably not have any concrete objects, while objects within the **VAN** class would inherit from the abstract **VEHICLE** and **CAR** classes. Multiple inheritance is also demonstrated by the **AMPHIBIAN_CAR** class. Any instances of this class will inherit data and behaviors from both the **CAR** and the **BOAT** classes.

It is important to note the tremendous difference between one-to-many relationships and ISA relationships. In the above example, this entire class hierarchy describes vehicles that are associated with the **ITEM** entity in the overall database. Class hierarchies do not imply any data relationships between the classes. While one **CUSTOMER** may place many **ORDER**s, it is not true that one **CAR** may have many **SEDAN**s.

POLYMORPHISM

Polymorphism is the ability of different objects to receive the same message and behave in different ways. This concept has many parallels in the real world. An event, such as a volcanic eruption, may have many different effects on the living things in the area: The poisonous gases may kill all air-breathing animals, while at the same time nourish the small marine organisms nearby. The single behavior of **ERUPTION** has had different effects upon objects within the **ANIMAL** class. Another analogy can be found in the business world: For a personnel manager, the event of **PROMOTION** will cause different behaviors depending upon the class of **EMPLOYEE** that receives the **PROMOTION**. **MANAGEMENT** objects will receive stock options and country club memberships, which are not offered to **JANITOR** objects.

Ronald Popeil was a master of polymorphism. Many folks remember the heyday of Ronco and Popeil, where polymorphic products were advertised at the national level. Consider the statement "It's a hair cream AND a floor wax." If this is indeed true, the method **spread_it_on** would invoke very different processes depending upon whether we are applying the cream to a floor or a person's head.

The concept of polymorphism originally came from the programming concept of "overloading." Overloading refers to the ability of a programming function to perform more than one type of operation depending upon the context in which the function is used. For example, consider the following Basic program:

```
REM    Sample Basic program to show polymorphism

REM    Increment the counter

COUNTER = COUNTER + 1

REM Concatenate the String

N$ = "Mr. Burleson"
S$ = "Hello there, " + N$

END
```

In this example, the operator "+" is used to indicate addition in one context and concatenation in another context. But what determines the way that the operator will function? Clearly, the Basic compiler knows that the "+" operator means addition when it is used in the context where a number is passed as an argument, and it knows that concatenation is required when character strings are passed as an argument to the operator.

The implications of polymorphism are that a standard interface may be created for a related group of objects. The specific action performed by the object will depend upon the message that is passed to the interface. Because the programmer is no longer concerned with the internal constructs of the object, extremely complex programs can be created. The programmer only needs to understand the interface to use the object.

In the real world, polymorphism can be described by looking at standard interfaces. In most PC-based software, the F1 key has a special meaning. Pressing F1 will invoke a context-sensitive help function and explain the function to the user. These help functions have vastly different methods and different data storage techniques, but the standard interface (F1) is polymorphic and invokes different internal mechanisms depending upon the software.

Another example is the controls on an automobile. While the internal workings of automobiles are vastly different, the steering wheels are always round and the gas petal is always to the right of the brake. These polymorphic interfaces make it possible for any person to drive a car without being concerned with the underlying structures of the vehicle.

All communication between objects and their behaviors is accomplished with "messages" that are passed as behaviors. For example, consider the two objects of **rush_order** and **cod_order** belonging to the **ORDER** class.

When a message such as **prepare_invoice** is called, it may contain sub-behaviors such as **prepare_invoice** and **compute_charges** (see Figure 2.9). The message **prepare_invoice** directs the system to compute the shipping changes. Different procedures will then be invoked depending upon whether the receiving object is a **rush_order** object or a **cod_order** object—even they are both objects within the **ORDER** class. A rush order would include overnight mail calculations, while the COD order would contain additional computations for the total amount due. This is equivalent to the following procedural language code.

Here we see an illustration of the differences between an object-oriented procedure call (a message) and the procedural language equivalent:

- Object-oriented call:

```
place_order(prepare_invoice(compute_charges))
```

- Procedural language equivalent:

```
IF (rush_order)
        COMPUTE SHIPPING = TOT_AMNT * .25
```

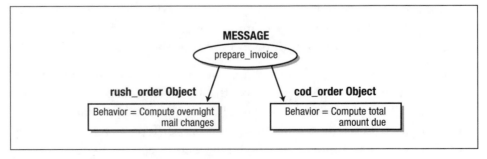

Figure 2.9　An example of polymorphism.

```
ELSE
        COMPUTE SHIPPING = TOT_AMNT * .10

IF (cod_order)
        COMPUTE TOT_DUE = TOT_AMNT + SHIPPING
ELSE
        COMPUTE TOT_DUE = 0
```

ENCAPSULATION

Encapsulation means that each object within the system has a well-defined interface with distinct borders. In plain English, encapsulation refers to the "localized" variables that may be used within an object behavior, and cannot be referenced outside of that behavior. This closely parallels the concept of information hiding. Encapsulation also ensures that all updates to the database are performed by using (or by way of) the behaviors associated with the database objects.

Code and data can be enclosed together into a "black box," and these "boxes" may then function totally independent of all other objects within the system. (See Figure 2.10.) From a programming perspective, an object is an encapsulated routine of data and behaviors. Objects may contain "public" variables, which are used to handle the interfaces to the object, and "private" variables, which are known only to the object. Once created, an object is treated as a variable of its own type. For example, an object of class **CAR** is created as a routine with a data type called **CAR**, and is treated as a compound variable by the program.

Encapsulation is used in nondatabase object-oriented applications to ensure that all operations are performed through the programmer-defined interface, and that data will never be modified outside of the application shell. But what about ad hoc query and update? It appears that any declarative database language such as SQL that allows "external" retrieval and update does not follow the dictates of encapsulation, and is therefore inconsistent with object-oriented database management.

For example, a relational database could be defined to have a behavior called **add_line_item,** which serves to check inventory levels for an item, and add an item to an order only if sufficient stock is available. This behavior ensures that orders are not entered for out-of-stock items. However, with a language

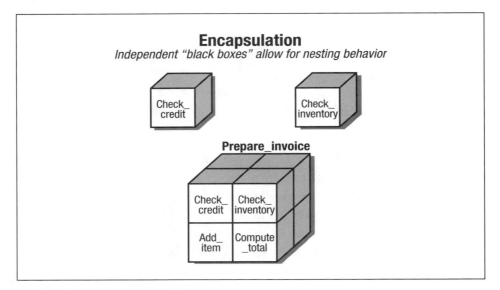

Figure 2.10 An example of encapsulation.

such as SQL, the object-oriented behavior could be bypassed, and **line_item** records could be added without any regard for inventory levels.

Because encapsulation and SQL are clearly incompatible, the only conclusion that can be reached is that encapsulation may be violated in Oracle8 by using ad hoc tools such as SQL*Plus.

EXTENSIBILITY

Extensibility is the ability of the Oracle8 engine to add new behaviors to an existing application without affecting the existing application shell. This is an especially powerful concept and will allow Oracle8 to extend existing classes, guaranteeing that no unintended side effects from the introduction of a new object class will occur.

For example, consider a company that provides payroll services for businesses in many states. Some payroll computations are global (for example **Gross_pay** = **hours_worked** * **payrate**), while others are specific to a municipality or state. Using Oracle8, an existing object class definition can be extended, such that the new object behaves exactly like its superclass definition, with whatever exceptions are specified. For example, if New York City instituted a new payroll rule for New York City residents, then the general definition for New York payroll customers could be extended with a new class definition for New York

City payroll customers. The only method that would be attached to this class definition would be the code that is specific to New York City; all other methods would be inherited from the existing superclasses.

THE "ISA" CONSTRUCT

Oracle is planning to introduce an extension to its Designer/2000 product to allow for the modeling of class hierarchies. This new extension, tentatively dubbed Designer/2001, should allow for object-oriented constructs to be described and modeled.

Here is a vision of how it might work. After establishing a class hierarchy with the Entity/Relation model, the principle of generalization is used to identify the class hierarchy and the level of abstraction associated with each class. Generalization implies a successive refinement of the class, allowing the superclasses of objects to inherit the data attributes and behaviors that apply to the lower levels of the class. Generalization establishes "taxonomy hierarchies," organizing the classes according to their characteristics—usually in increasing levels of detail. Generalization begins at a very general level and proceeds to a specific level, with each sublevel having its own unique data attributes and behaviors.

The ISA relationship is used to create a hierarchy within the object class, and all of the lower-level classes will inherit the behaviors. The ISA relationship is used to model the hierarchy that is created as the class entity is decomposed into its logical subcomponents. Customers may be **preferred_customers** or **new_customers**, and orders may be **cod_orders** or **prepaid_orders**—each with their own data items and behaviors.

SQL For Object-Orientation

The object-oriented approach borrows heavily from the C++ and Smalltalk languages. Both of these languages allow for the storing of behaviors with the data, such that data and business rules also share a common repository.

With the properties of encapsulation, abstraction, and polymorphism, object technology systems are moving toward a unified data model that models the real world far more effectively than previous modeling techniques. Furthermore, a properly designed object-oriented model promises to be maintenance-free, because all changes to data attributes and behaviors become a database task—not a programming task.

Let's take a look at a human analogy to the object-oriented approach. It is very natural for humans to recognize objects, and to associate objects with their classes. It is also a very natural concept to associate an object with its expected behaviors.

Even as very young children, we learned to associate behaviors with certain characteristics of objects. For example, it is not uncommon to visit the zoo and hear a three-year-old call all four-legged animals "doggies." The child has learned to associate an object class (dog) with a data attribute (four legs). Later a child will refine his/her object-oriented paradigm, associating other data attributes with animal objects. A child also learns to associate behaviors (such as playing, having fun, feeling pain) with different visual and auditory stimuli. Many young children learn to associate unpleasant sensations (pain) with a visit to the man who wears a white lab coat (the doctor). McDonald's corporation has spent millions of dollars exploiting this principle (much to the consternation of many parents), associating pleasant behavior with objects such as golden arches, Happy Meals, and Ronald McDonald.

Behaviors must be dynamic, and human experience shows that human associations of behaviors with attributes also change with time. In the 1930s, people with tattoos were usually categorized as belonging to the **sailor** class. In the 1980s, tattoos were generally categorized as belonging to the **criminal** class, while today, tattoos are also indicative of the **college_student** class of humans. The ODMG object model partially addressed this issue, whereby objects are assigned lifetimes by the object-oriented database system. Unfortunately, the concept of object lifetimes has not been included in Oracle8.

Humans are also familiar with the concept of abstraction. Intangible objects such as time are easily understood, and the conceptual, nonconcrete existence of time has meaning to most individuals.

The distinguishing characteristic of the object-oriented database is its ability to store data behavior, but how is the behavior of the data incorporated into the database? At first glance, this may seem to be a method for moving application code from a program into a database. While it is true that an object-oriented database stores "behaviors," these databases must also have the ability to manage many different objects—each with different data items.

THE "ISA" RELATIONSHIP

The ISA relationship (pronounced "is a") is a data relationship that indicates a type/subtype data relationship. While traditional E/R modeling deals only with single entities, the ISA approach recognizes that many "types" or classes of an individual entity may exist. In fact, the ISA relationship is the foundation of object-oriented programming, which allows the designer to create hierarchies of related classes and then use inheritance and polymorphism to control which data items will participate in the low-level objects.

After establishing a class hierarchy with the Entity/Relation model, the object-oriented principle of generalization is used to identify the class hierarchy and the level of abstraction associated with each class. Generalization implies a successive refinement of the class, allowing the superclasses of objects to inherit the data attributes and behaviors that apply to the lower levels of the class. Generalization establishes "taxonomy hierarchies," which organize the classes according to their characteristics in increasing levels of detail. These hierarchies begin at a very general level, proceeding to a specific level, with each sublevel having its own unique data attributes and behaviors.

In Figure 2.11, the ISA relationship is used to create a hierarchy within the **CUSTOMER** and **ORDER** entities, and all of the lower-level classes will inherit the data items and behaviors from the "base" classes. The ISA relationship is used to model the hierarchy, which is created as the class entity is decomposed into its logical subcomponents. Customers may be **preferred_customers** or **new_customers**, and orders may be **cod_orders** or **prepaid_orders**, each with their own data items and behaviors. Those data items that are generic to customers and orders would reside in the **CUSTOMER** and **ORDER** entities, while the data items that are unique to **preferred_customers** (such as **percent_discount**) would reside in the lower-level entities.

Let's look at an application of the ISA relationship for a vehicle dealership as shown in Figure 2.12.

As you can see, the highest level in the hierarchy is **VEHICLE**s; and beneath the **VEHICLE** class, we may find subclasses for **CAR**s and for **BOAT**s. Within **CAR**s, the classes may be further partitioned into classes for **TRUCK**,

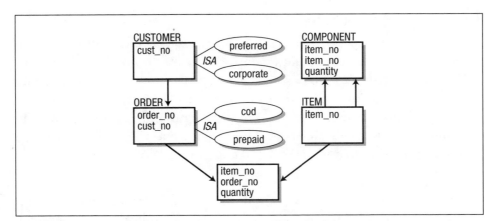

Figure 2.11   An entity/relation model with added "ISA" relationships.

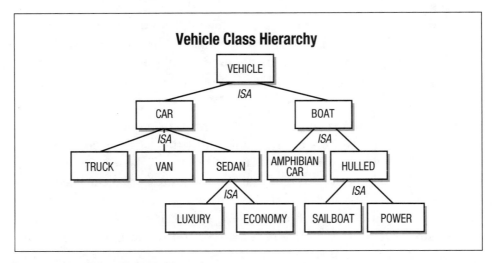

Figure 2.12   A sample class hierarchy.

VAN, and **SEDAN**. The **VEHICLE** class would contain the data items that are unique to vehicles, including the vehicle ID and the year of manufacture. The **CAR** class, because it ISA **VEHICLE**, would inherit the data items of the **VEHICLE** class. The **CAR** class might contain data items such as the number of axles and the gross weight of the vehicle. Because the **VAN** class ISA **CAR**, which in turn ISA **VEHICLE**, objects of the **VAN** class will inherit all data items and behaviors relating to **CAR**s and **VEHICLE**s.

These types of ISA relationships, while valid from a data modeling viewpoint, do not have a simple implementation in Oracle. Since Oracle does not support hierarchical relationships, it is impossible to directly represent the fact that a database entity has subentities. However, we can model this type of relationship in a relational database in two ways.

The first technique is to create subtables for car, boat, sedan, and so on. This encapsulates the data items within their respective tables, but it also creates the complication of doing unnecessary joins when retrieving a high-level item in the hierarchy. For example, the following SQL would be required to retrieve all of the data items for a luxury sedan:

```
SELECT
        VEHICLE.vehicle_number,
        CAR.registration_number,
        SEDAN.number_of_doors,
        LUXURY.type_of_leather_upholstery
FROM
        VEHICLE,
        CAR,
        SEDAN,
        LUXURY
WHERE
VEHICLE.key = CAR.key
AND
CAR.key = SEDAN.key
AND
SEDAN.key = LUXURY.key;
```

The second approach is to create a megatable in Oracle with each data item represented as a column, regardless of whether or not it is needed by the individual row. A "type" column would be used to identify if the row represents a car, a van, or a sailboat; and the application must have intelligence to access only those columns that are applicable to the row. For example, the sail-size column may have meaning for a sailboat row, but would be irrelevant to a sedan row.

The ISA relationship is best suited to the object-oriented data model, where each level in the hierarchy has associated data items and methods, and inheritance and polymorphism can be used to complete the picture. It is important to note that not all classes within a generalization hierarchy will be associated with objects. These "non-instantiated" classes only serve the purpose of passing data definition to the lower-level classes. The object-oriented paradigm allows for abstraction, which means that a class may exist only for the purpose of passing inherited data and behaviors to the lower-level entities. The classes **VEHICLE** and **CAR** would probably not have any concrete objects, while objects within the **VAN** class would inherit from the abstract **VEHICLE** and **CAR** classes.

Multiple inheritance is also shown by the **AMPHIBIAN_CAR** class. Any instances of this class will inherit data and behaviors from both the **CAR** and the **BOAT** classes.

It is important to note one very big difference between one-to-many relationships and ISA relationships. The ISA construct does not imply any type of recurring association, while the one-to-many and many-to-many relationships imply multiple occurrences of the subclasses. In the previous example, the entire class hierarchy describes vehicles that are associated with the **ITEM** entity in the overall database. The fact that a class hierarchy exists *does not* imply any data relationships between the classes. While one **CUSTOMER** may place many **ORDER**s, it is not true that one **CAR** may have many **SEDAN**s.

Summary

Now that we have completed the physical design issues, we can begin to look at tuning for the entire Oracle instance. Tuning is much more than guaranteeing that your application will have a good design. We must also ensure that Oracle has enough system resources to properly service our requests.

Tuning The Oracle Architecture

A holistic approach to the tuning of the overall Oracle architecture is paramount to the development of effective client/server systems. Regardless of how slick and well-tuned the client performs, poor response time at the server level will cause the entire development effort to fail. Whether your server is private to your application or shared between many client applications, the optimal usage of Oracle resources can ensure that the system performs at an acceptable level. Topics in this chapter include:

- The Oracle architecture

- Oracle's internal structures

- Oracle metadata—the **V$** tables

- Tuning Oracle memory

- Simulating the pinning of database rows

- Interoperability features

- Creating a batch-oriented Oracle instance

- I/O-based tuning

The Oracle Architecture

Oracle is the world's leading relational database, continuing to dominate the marketplace for midrange computer platforms. Since Oracle's inception in 1971, it has evolved to the point where Oracle7 bears little resemblance to the original offering. While Oracle has many extensions, the base product consists of the following components:

- *The Oracle SGA*—This is the region in RAM memory that is created when Oracle is started.

- *SQL*Plus*—This is the online interface to the Oracle database. Like SPUFI on DB2 and IDD for CA-IDMS, SQL*Plus is used to allow ad hoc queries and updates to be issued against the database.

- *SQL*DBA*—This is the interface to Oracle for the database administrator. It allows the DBA to create databases, tablespaces, tables, clusters, indexes, and sundry other Oracle constructs.

- *Server Manager and Enterprise Manager*—This is the visual reporting component to Oracle. Server Manager provides a graphical interface to online reports that give fast, visual access to the database. Server Manager can be run with Windows using Oracle SQL*Net for communications to the database, or it can be run on the individual server using Motif.

- *SQL*Net*—This is the communications protocol that allows remote database servers to communicate with each other. SQL*Net is described extensively in Chapter 8.

- *PL/SQL*—This is Oracle's proprietary implementation of the ANSI SQL standard. PL/SQL can be used within Oracle applications tools called SQL*Forms or embedded into remote tools, such as C programs or PC GUIs. A fully functional programming language by itself, PL/SQL adds extensions to the SQL to allow sophisticated processing.

- *SQL*Menu*—This is the menu builder for Oracle that allows individual SQL*Forms screens to be linked together.

The following list represents related Oracle products that also may be of interest, including some utilities:

- *Oracle Express*—Formerly called Express by IRI Software, Oracle MultiDimension is a multidimensional database for supporting data warehouse and online analytical processing (OLAP). This product has yet to be integrated with the standard Oracle engine, and communications with the relational database are usually accomplished by extracting data from Oracle7 and loading it into Oracle MultiDimension.

- *Oracle Book*—A text database, Oracle Book is used primarily for creating hypertext documents.

- *Import/Export*—These are the utilities allowing the developer to dump the contents of tables into a flat file, and allowing the flat file to be restored to the database.

- *SQL*Loader*—A utility that allows delimited flat files to be loaded into Oracle tables. For example, an extract from a DB2 database could be created with commas delimiting each table column. SQL*Loader would be used to import this flat file into an Oracle table.

- *Designer/2000*—This utility is part of the Oracle family of CASE tools. Designer/2000 allows the developer to maintain logical table definitions and create a physical model from the logical structure.

Oracle's Internal Structures

When Oracle is started, a region of memory is configured according to initial parameters that are defined in two files, the init.ora and the config.ora. These files tell the database software how to configure the system global area (SGA), which is the term used to describe a running Oracle.

Since the SGA resides within an operating system, it is dependent upon the operating environment (see Figure 3.1). In Unix, Oracle must share space with many other memory regions, competing for the limited memory and processing resources (as shown in Figure 3.2).

The SGA consists of several main components, each of which is configured at database startup time:

- Buffer cache
- Log buffer

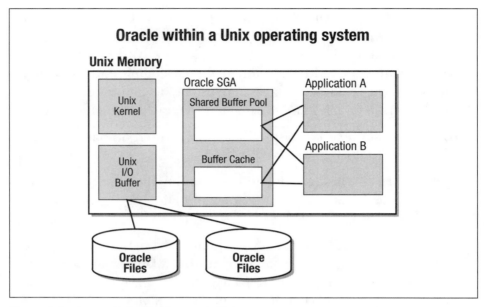

Figure 3.1 A sample Oracle instance in Unix.

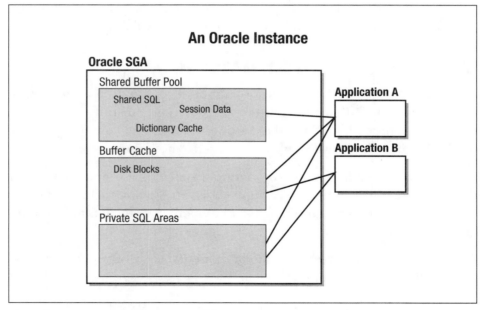

Figure 3.2 The relationships between Oracle and applications.

- Shared pool

- Private SQL areas

At the internal level, each Oracle instance has predefined interfaces to the hardware to allow it to communicate with the physical devices. Being a database software product, Oracle must be able to communicate with disk devices and CD-ROMs, retrieving and storing information from these devices. When the DBA defines a tablespace, a physical data file is associated with the tablespace, and Oracle will manage the addressability to this file. In other words, Oracle manages all of the mapping of the logical tablespaces to the physical data files.

The configuration of the SGA is critical to designing high performance client/server applications. The sizes allocated to the program pool and the buffer pools have a direct impact on the speed at with Oracle retrieves information. Remember, most business applications are I/O bound—the single greatest delay being the time required to access data from disk. As such, tuning for I/O becomes a critical consideration.

The single most important component for tuning an Oracle database is the size of the database buffer. The database buffer is where Oracle holds blocks that have already been retrieved by a prior database request. Whenever a new request for data is made, Oracle will first check this buffer. If the block already is in memory, Oracle can deliver the block to the user ten thousand times faster than if Oracle had to perform an I/O to go to the external disk for information. Access time on disks now reaches an impressive speed—between 10 and 25 milliseconds. However, data that already resides in the RAM area of Oracle SGA can be retrieved in nanoseconds. The parameter controlling the size of the buffer is called **db_block_buffers**, and is one of the parameters in the init.ora file. For more information on **db_block_size**, see Chapter 6, Oracle DBA Performance And Tuning.

The other important region of the SGA is the shared pool, which keeps a number of subareas. One of the confounding problems with Oracle is that all of these areas are sized by only one parameter, **shared_pool_size**. It is impossible to dedicate separate regions of memory for the components within the shared pool.

However, the SGA is not the only memory structure used by Oracle. Each application that accesses Oracle receives a program global area, or PGA. The PGA contains private SQL areas that are used by individual programs and keep application-specific database information. The private SQL area keeps the current values of cursors, and other program-dependent information.

The second largest memory component with the SGA is the shared pool. The shared pool holds memory for the following purposes:

- *Library Cache*—An area that holds the plan information for SQL that is currently being executed. This area also holds stored procedure and trigger code.

- *Dictionary Cache*—Keeps environmental information, including referential integrity, table definitions, indexing information, and other metadata that is stored within Oracle's internal tables.

- *Session Information*—Session information is only kept for systems that are using SQL*Net version 2 with Oracle's multithreaded server. See Chapter 8 for details on using the multithreaded server.

Oracle Metadata—The V$ Tables

The **V$** tables are internal structures built into memory when an Oracle instance is started. Although they appear to be tables, they are really internal memory structures implemented in the C language. Therefore, the **V$** tables only exist during the execution of the instance and are destroyed at shutdown time. The **V$** tables are used by Oracle to capture information about the overall status of the database, and the information from the **V$** tables can provide tremendous insight into the internal operations. While dozens of **V$** tables exist, only a handful can be used for Oracle performance and tuning.

The **V$** tables have limited use for measuring time-dependent information, since they accumulate information from the moment that the Oracle instance is started up until the present time. As such, measures such as the buffer hit ratio are normalized, presenting only the average for the entire time that the instance has been running. Instead of offering an exhaustive list of all the Oracle **V$** tables, I included only relevant queries against the **V$** tables throughout this text.

Tuning Oracle Memory

The memory size of the SGA is commonly called the Oracle region. The way that the Oracle memory is managed can have a huge impact on performance, and each SGA can be tuned according to the needs of the application. However, one must remember that the SGA faces dynamic forces, and one transaction can cause problems for other transactions that are accessing Oracle. Hundreds of transactions may be serviced concurrently, each requesting different data. Tuning the memory for the activity at one point in time may not be suitable for another time. Because of the dynamic nature of the Oracle database, only general tuning is possible.

This general approach works out well because of the high level of sophistication: Oracle has only three parameters that affect the size of the parts of the SGA: **db_block_buffers**, **shared_pool_size**, and **log_buffer**.

Sizing The SGA

The init.ora file and the config.ora file not only determine the overall size of the SGA, but also determine which Oracle constructs get a specified amount of memory. init.ora parameters rank in the dozens. To see all of the init.ora parameters, enter SQL*DBA and issue this command:

```
SQLDBA> show parameters
```

The results are shown in Listing 3.1.

Listing 3.1   The results of the show parameters command.

NAME	TYPE	VALUE
async_read	boolean	TRUE
async_write	boolean	TRUE
audit_file_dest	string	/opt/oracle/admin/my_sid/audit
audit_trail	string	TRUE
background_core_dump	string	full
background_dump_dest	string	/opt/oracle/admin/my_sid/bdump
blank_trimming	boolean	FALSE
cache_size_threshold	integer	40
ccf_io_size	integer	134217728
checkpoint_process	boolean	FALSE
cleanup_rollback_entries	integer	20
close_cached_open_cursors	boolean	FALSE

commit_point_strength	integer	1
compatibl	string	
compatible_no_recovery	string	

control_files	string	/Datadisks/d09/ORACLE/mysid/
		   control1.dbf,
		/Datadisks/d10/ORACLE/my_sid/
		   control2.dbf,
		/Datadisks/d01/ORACLE/mysid/
		   control3.dbf

core_dump_dest	string	/opt/oracle/admin/mysid/cdump
cursor_space_for_time	boolean	FALSE
db_block_buffers	integer	400
db_block_checkpoint_batch	integer	8
db_block_lru_extended_ statistics	integer	0
db_block_lru_statistics	boolean	FALSE
db_block_size	integer	4096
db_domain	string	WORLD
db_file_multiblock_read_ count	integer	16
db_file_simultaneous_writes	integer	4
db_files	integer	30
db_name	string	my_sid
db_writers	integer	1
dblink_encrypt_login	boolean	FALSE
discrete_transactions_ enabled	boolean	FALSE
distributed_lock_timeout	integer	60
distributed_recovery_ connection_hol	integer	200
distributed_transactions	integer	19
dml_locks	integer	100
enqueue_resources	integer	177
event	string	
fixed_date	string	
gc_db_locks	integer	400
gc_files_to_locks	string	
gc_lck_procs	integer	1
gc_rollback_locks	integer	20
gc_rollback_segments	integer	20
gc_save_rollback_locks	integer	20
gc_segments	integer	10
gc_tablespaces	integer	5
global_names	boolean	FALSE
ifile	file	/opt/oracle/admin/my_sid/ pfile/configmptp.ora

```
instance_number                integer    0
job_queue_interval             integer    60
job_queue_keep_connections     boolean    FALSE
job_queue_processes            integer    0
license_max_sessions           integer    0
license_max_users              integer    0
license_sessions_warning       integer    0
log_archive_buffer_size        integer    64
log_archive_buffers            integer    4
log_archive_dest               string     /opt/oracle/admin/my_sid/arch/
                                             my_sid
log_archive_format             string     %t_%s.dbf
log_archive_start              boolean    TRUE
log_buffer                     integer    32768
log_checkpoint_interval        integer    10000
log_checkpoint_timeout         integer    0
log_checkpoints_to_alert       boolean    FALSE
log_files                      integer    255
log_simultaneous_copies        integer    2
log_small_entry_max_size       integer    800
max_commit_propagation_        integer    90000
   delay
max_dump_file_size             integer    500
max_enabled_roles              integer    20
max_rollback_segments          integer    30
max_transaction_branches       integer    8
mts_dispatchers                string
mts_listener_address           string     (address=(protocol=ipc)
                                             (key=%s))
mts_max_dispatchers            integer    0
mts_max_servers                integer    0
mts_servers                    integer    0
mts_service                    string     my_sid
nls_currency                   string
nls_date_format                string
nls_date_language              string
nls_iso_currency               string
nls_language                   string     AMERICAN
nls_numeric_characters         string
nls_sort                       string
nls_territory                  string     AMERICA
open_cursors                   integer    100
open_links                     integer    4
optimizer_comp_weight          integer    0
optimizer_mode                 string     CHOOSE
os_authent_prefix              string
```

```
os_roles                        boolean      FALSE
parallel_default_max_           integer      0
    instances
parallel_default_max_scans      integer      0
parallel_default_scansize       integer      100
parallel_max_servers            integer      5
parallel_min_servers            integer      0
parallel_server_idle_time       integer      5
post_wait_device                string       /devices/pseudo/pw@0:pw
pre_page_sga                    boolean      FALSE
processes                       integer      60
recovery_parallelism            integer      0
reduce_alarm                    boolean      FALSE
remote_login_passwordfile       string       NONE
remote_os_authent               boolean      FALSE
remote_os_roles                 boolean      FALSE
resource_limit                  boolean      FALSE
rollback_segments               string       rolb1, rolb2, rolb3, rolb4
row_cache_cursors               integer      10
row_locking                     string       default
sequence_cache_entries          integer      10
sequence_cache_hash_buckets     integer      7
serializable                    boolean      FALSE
session_cached_cursors          integer      0
sessions                        integer      71
shadow_core_dump                string       full
shared_pool_reserved_min_       integer      5000
    alloc
shared_pool_reserved_size       integer      0
shared_pool_size                integer      6000000
single_process                  boolean      FALSE
snapshot_refresh_interval       integer      60
snapshot_refresh_keep_          boolean      FALSE
    connections
snapshot_refresh_processes      integer      0
sort_area_retained_size         integer      65536
sort_area_size                  integer      65536
sort_mts_buffer_for_fetch_      integer      0
    size
sort_read_fac                   integer      5
sort_spacemap_size              integer      512
spin_count                      integer      2000
sql92_security                  boolean      FALSE
sql_trace                       boolean      FALSE
temporary_table_locks           integer      71
```

```
thread                          integer     0
timed_statistics                boolean     FALSE
transactions                    integer     78
transactions_per_rollback_      integer     34
    segment
use_ism                         boolean     TRUE
use_post_wait_driver            boolean     FALSE
use_readv                       boolean     FALSE
user_dump_dest                  string      /opt/oracle/admin/mysid/udump
```

 *The SQL*DBA **show parameters** command does not display some of the specialized Oracle parameters that begin with an underscore such as _offline_rollback_segments and _db_block_write_batch.*

To see the size of the SGA, you can issue the **show SGA** command from SQL*DBA:

```
SQLDBA> show sga

Total System Global Area        8252756 bytes
Fixed Size                        48260 bytes
Variable Size                   6533328 bytes
Database Buffers                1638400 bytes
Redo Buffers                      32768 bytes
```

Fortunately, only a few parameters are really important to the overall performance of Oracle:

- **db_block_buffers**—This parameter determines the number of database block buffers in the Oracle SGA and represents the single most important parameter to Oracle memory.

- **db_block_size**—The size of the database blocks can make a huge improvement in performance. While the default value is 2,048 bytes, databases that have large tables with full-table scans will see a tremendous improvement in performance by increasing **db_block_size** to a larger value.

- **log_buffer**—This parameter determines the amount of memory to allocate for Oracle's redo log buffers. The higher the amount of update activity, the more space needs to be allocated to the **log_buffer**.

- **shared_pool_size**—This parameter defines the pool that is shared by all users in the system, including SQL areas and data dictionary caching.

NOTE *For more information on init.ora parameters, see Chapter 6, Oracle DBA Performance And Tuning.*

Using The db_block_size Parameter With db_file_multiblock_read_count

As I'll discuss in Chapter 6, the **db_block_size** parameters can have a dramatic impact on system performance. Minimizing I/O is essential to performance, so the less physical I/O incurred by Oracle, the faster the database will run.

In general, **db_block_size** should never be set to less than 8 K, regardless of the type of application. Even online transaction processing systems (OLTP) will benefit from using 8 K blocks, while systems that perform many full-table scans may benefit from even larger block sizes. Depending upon the operating system, Oracle can support 16 K block sizes. Systems that perform full-table scans may benefit from this approach.

Also, note the relationship between **db_block_size** and the **multi_block_read_count** parameter. At the physical level in Unix, Oracle always reads in a minimum of 64 K blocks. Therefore, the values of **multi_block_read_count** and **db_block_size** should be set such that their product is 64 K. For example:

8 K blocks　　　**db_block_size**=8192　**db_file_multiblock_read_count**=8

16 K blocks　　**db_block_size**=16384 **db_file_multiblock_read_count**=4

Note that the block size for Oracle is not immutable. Eventually, all Oracle databases should be compressed (export/import) to reduce fragmentation, and it becomes trivial at this time to alter the value of **db_block_size**.

Remember that increasing the size of **db_block_size** will increase the size of the Oracle SGA. The values of **db_block_size** are multiplied by the value of **db_block_buffers** to determine the total amount of memory to allocate for Oracle's I/O buffers.

Tuning Oracle Sorting

As a small but very important component of SQL syntax, sorting is a frequently overlooked aspect of Oracle tuning. In general, the Oracle database will automatically perform sorting operations on row data as requested by a **CREATE INDEX** or an SQL **ORDER BY** or **GROUP BY** statement. In Oracle, sorting occurs under the following circumstances:

- Using the **ORDER BY** clause in SQL

- Using the **GROUP BY** clause in SQL

- When an index is created

- When a **MERGE SORT** is invoked by the SQL optimizer because inadequate indexes exist for a table join

At the time a session is established with Oracle, a private sort area is allocated in memory for use by the session for sorting. Unfortunately, the amount of memory must be the same for all sessions—it is not possible to add additional sort area for tasks that are sort intensive. Therefore, the designer must strike a balance between allocating enough sort area to avoid disk sorts for the large sorting tasks, keeping in mind that the extra sort area will be allocated and not used by tasks that do not require intensive sorting.

The size of the private sort area is determined by the **sort_area_size** init.ora parameter. The size for each individual sort is specified by the **sort_area_retained_size** init.ora parameter. Whenever a sort cannot be completed with this assigned space, a disk sort is invoked using the temporary tablespace for the Oracle instance. As a general rule, only index creation and **ORDER BY** clauses using functions should be allowed to use a disk sort.

Disk sorts are expensive for several reasons. First, they consume resources in the temporary tablespaces. Oracle must also allocate buffer pool blocks to hold the blocks in the temporary tablespace. In-memory sorts are always preferable to disk sorts, and disk sorts will surely slow down the individual task, as well as impacting other concurrent tasks on the Oracle instance. Also, excessive disk sorting will also cause a high value for free buffer waits, paging other tasks' data blocks out of the buffer. To see the amount of disk and in-memory sorts, issue the following query against the **v$sysstat** table:

```
sorts.sql - displays in-memory and disk sorts
SPOOL /tmp/sorts
COLUMN VALUE FORMAT 999,999,999
SELECT NAME, VALUE FROM v$sysstat
  WHERE NAME LIKE 'sort%';
SPOOL OFF;
```

Here is the output:

```
SQL> @sorts

NAME                          VALUE
--------                 ------------
sorts (memory)                7,019
sorts (disk)                     49
sorts (rows)              3,288,608
```

Here we see that there were 49 sorts to disk. Out of a total of 3.2 million sorts, this is well below 1 percent and is probably acceptable for the system.

 For tips on avoiding disk sorts, see Chapter 4, Tuning Oracle SQL, where we'll take a look at specific techniques for ensuring in-memory sorts.

With Oracle version 7.2, several new parameters were added for the init.ora file to allocate a new in-memory sort area. The **sort_write_buffer_size** parameter defines the size of this new buffer, and the **sort_write_buffers** defines the number of buffer blocks. You must also set the parameter **sort_direct_writes=true** to use this feature. Writing sorts to this buffer bypasses the need for the sort to contend for free blocks in the buffer cache, thereby improving sorting performance by up to 50 percent. Of course, this is done at the expense of additional memory with the SGA. This move towards segmenting the buffer into individual components can dramatically improve response time in Oracle.

The Oracle PGA

Please note that the SGA is not the only memory area available to programs. The PGA is a private memory area that is allocated to external tasks. The PGA is used for keeping application-specific information, such as the values of cursors, and also allocates memory for internal sorting of result sets from SQL queries. Two init.ora parameters influence the size of the PGA:

- **open_links**—This parameter defines the maximum number for concurrent remote sessions that a process may initiate. Oracle's default is 4, meaning that a single SQL statement may reference up to four remote databases within the query.

- **sort_area_size**—This defines the maximum amount of PGA memory that can be used for disk sorts. For very large sorts, Oracle will sort the data in its temporary tablespace, and the **sort_area_size** memory is used to manage the sorting process.

Tuning The shared_pool_size

The shared pool component of the Oracle SGA is primarily used to store shared SQL cursors, stored procedures, and the cache for data from the data dictionary cache. The library and dictionary cache are the two components of the shared pool. The shared SQL areas and the PL/SQL areas are called the library cache, which is a subcomponent of the shared pool. The other main component of the shared pool is the dictionary cache.

TUNING THE LIBRARY CACHE

The library cache miss ratio tells the DBA whether or not to add space to the shared pool, and represents the ratio of the sum of library cache reloads to the sum of pins. In general, if this ratio is over 1, you may want to consider adding to the **shared_pool_size**. Library cache misses occur during the compilation of SQL statements. The compilation of an SQL statement consists of two phases: the parse phase and the execute phase. When the time comes to parse an SQL statement, Oracle first checks to see if the parsed representation of the statement already exists in the library cache. If not, Oracle will allocate a shared SQL area within the library cache and then parse the SQL statement. At execution time, Oracle checks to see if a parsed representation of the SQL statement already exists in the library cache. If not, Oracle will reparse and execute the statement.

Within the library cache, the hit ratios can be determined for all dictionary objects that are loaded. These include table/procedures, triggers, indexes, package bodies, and clusters. If any of the hit ratios fall below 75 percent, you might be well advised to add to the **shared_pool_size**.

The table **V$librarycache** is the **V$** table that keeps information about library cache activity. The table has three relevant columns. The first is the **namespace**, which says whether the measurement is for the SQL area, a table or procedure, a package body, or a trigger. The second value in this table is **pins**, which counts the number of times that an item in the library cache was executed. The **reloads** column counts the number of times that the parsed representation did not exist in the library cache, forcing Oracle to allocate the private SQL areas in order to parse and execute the statement.

Listing 3.2 shows an example of a SQL*Plus query to interrogate the **V$librarycache** table to retrieve the necessary performance information.

Listing 3.2   An example of an SQL*Plus query.

```
library.sql - lists the library cache
PROMPT
PROMPT           ===========================
PROMPT           LIBRARY CACHE MISS RATIO
PROMPT           ===========================
PROMPT (If > 1 then increase the shared_pool_size in init.ora)
PROMPT
COLUMN "LIBRARY CACHE MISS RATIO"        FORMAT 99.9999
COLUMN "executions"                      FORMAT 999,999,999
COLUMN "Cache misses while executing"    FORMAT 999,999,999
SELECT sum(pins) "executions", sum(reloads)
       "Cache misses while executing",
       (((sum(reloads)/sum(pins)))) "LIBRARY CACHE MISS RATIO"
FROM v$librarycache;

PROMPT
PROMPT           ===========================
PROMPT           LIBRARY CACHE SECTION
PROMPT           ===========================
```

```
PROMPT hit ratio should be > 70, and pin ratio > 70 ...
PROMPT

COLUMN "reloads" FORMAT 999,999,999
SELECT namespace, trunc(gethitratio * 100) "Hit ratio",
TRUNC(pinhitratio * 100) "pin hit ratio", RELOADS "reloads"
FROM v$librarycache;
```

Listing 3.3 shows the output.

Listing 3.3   The output of the query.

```
SQL> @temp


============================
LIBRARY CACHE MISS RATIO
============================
(If > 1 then increase the shared_pool_size in init.ora)


  executions Cache misses while executing LIBRARY CACHE MISS RATIO
------------ ------------------------------ ------------------------
   251,272                           2,409                    .0096



============================
LIBRARY CACHE SECTION
============================
hit ratio should be > 70, and pin ratio > 70 ...


NAMESPACE           Hit ratio   pin hit ratio     reloads
--------------      ----------  -------------   ------------
SQL AREA                   90              94         1,083
TABLE/PROCEDURE            93              94         1,316
BODY                       96              95             9
TRIGGER                    89              86             1
INDEX                       0              31             0
CLUSTER                    44              33             0
OBJECT                    100             100             0
PIPE                      100             100             0

8 rows selected.
```

One of the most important things that a developer can do to reduce usage of the library cache is to ensure that all SQL is written within stored procedures. For example, Oracle library cache will examine the following SQL statements and conclude that they are not identical:

```
SELECT * FROM customer;

SELECT * FROM Customer;
```

While capitalizing a single letter, adding an extra space between verbs, or using a different variable name may seem trivial, the Oracle software is not sufficiently intelligent to recognize that the statements are identical. Consequently, Oracle will reparse and execute the second SQL statement, even though it is functionally identical to the first SQL statement.

Another problem occurs when values are hard coded into SQL statements. For example, Oracle considers the following statements to be different:

```
SELECT COUNT(*) FROM CUSTOMER WHERE STATUS = 'NEW';

SELECT COUNT(*) FROM CUSTOMER WHERE STATUS = 'PREFERRED';
```

This problem is easily alleviated by using an identical bind variable:

```
SELECT COUNT(*) FROM CUSTOMER WHERE STATUS = :var1;
```

The best way to prevent reloads from happening is to encapsulate all SQL into stored procedures, bundling the stored procedures into packages. This removes all SQL from application programs and moves them into Oracle's data dictionary. This method also has the nice side effect of making all database calls appear as functions. As such, we have created a layer of independence between the application and the database. Again, by efficiently reusing identical SQL, the number of reloads will be kept at a minimum and the library cache will function at optimal speed.

The **cursor_space_for_time** parameter can be used to speed executions within the library cache. Setting **cursor_space_for_time** to **FALSE** tells Oracle that a shared SQL area may be deallocated from the library cache to make room for a new SQL statement. Setting **cursor_space_for_time** to **TRUE** means that all shared SQL areas are pinned in the cache until all application cursors are closed. When set to **TRUE**, Oracle will not bother to check the library cache on subsequent execution calls because it has already pinned the SQL in the cache. This technique can improve the performance for some queries, but **cursor_space_for_time** should not be set to **TRUE** if there are cache misses on execution calls. Cache misses indicate that the **shared_pool_size** is already too small, and forcing the pinning of shared SQL areas will only aggravate the problem.

Another way to improve performance on the library cache is to use the init.ora **session_cached_cursors** parameter. As we know, Oracle checks the library cache for parsed SQL statements, but **session_cached_cursors** can be used to cache the cursors for a query. This is especially useful for tasks that repeatedly issue parse calls for the same SQL statement—for instance, where an SQL statement is repeatedly executed with a different variable value. An example would be an SQL request that performs the same query 50 times, once for each state:

```
SELECT SUM(sale_amount)
FROM SALES
WHERE
state_code = :var1;
```

Tuning The Dictionary Cache

The data dictionary cache is used to hold rows from the internal Oracle metadata tables, including SQL that is stored in packages. Based on my experience, I highly recommend that all SQL should be stored in packages, so let's take a look at how packages interact with the dictionary cache.

When a package is invoked, Oracle will first check the dictionary cache to see if the package is already in memory. Of course, a package will not be in memory the first time it is requested, and Oracle will register a "dictionary cache miss." Consequently, it is virtually impossible to have an instance with no dictionary cache misses, since each item must be loaded once.

The **V$rowcache** table is used to measure dictionary cache activity. Three columns are of interest. The first column, **Data Dict.**, describes the type of dictionary object that has been requested. The second parameter, **gets**, provides the total number of requests for objects of that type. The last column, **getmisses**, counts the number of times that Oracle had to perform a disk I/O to retrieve a row from its dictionary tables.

The data dictionary cache hit ratio is used to measure the ratio of dictionary hits to misses. Bear in mind, however, that this ratio is only good for measuring the average hit ratio for the life of the instance.

The data dictionary cache hit ratio can be measured with the script in Listing 3.4.

Listing 3.4　The script that measures the cache hit ratio.

```
dict.sql - displays the dictionary cache hit ratio
PROMPT
PROMPT
PROMPT          ==========================
PROMPT          DATA DICT HIT RATIO
PROMPT          ==========================
PROMPT (should be higher than 90 else increase shared_pool_size in
       init.ora)
PROMPT

COLUMN "Data Dict. Gets"          FORMAT 999,999,999
COLUMN "Data Dict. cache misses"    FORMAT 999,999,999
SELECT sum(gets) "Data Dict. Gets",
       sum(getmisses) "Data Dict. cache misses",
       trunc((1-(sum(getmisses)/sum(gets)))*100)
       "DATA DICT CACHE HIT RATIO"
FROM v$rowcache;

SQL> @t2
```

This is the output of the script:

```
==========================
DATA DICT HIT RATIO
==========================

(should be higher than 90 else increase shared_pool_size in init.ora)


Fri Feb 23                                                 page    1
                        dbname Database
                     Data Dictionary Hit Ratios

Data Dict. Gets Data Dict. cache misses DATA DICT CACHE HIT RATIO
---------------------------------------------------------------
409,288         11,639                          97

1 row selected.
```

Listing 3.5 measures the contention for each dictionary object type.

Listing 3.5   The script that measures the contention.

```
ddcache.sql - Lists all data dictionary contention
REM SQLX SCRIPT
SET PAUSE OFF;
SET ECHO OFF;
SET TERMOUT OFF;
SET LINESIZE 78;
SET PAGESIZE 60;
SET NEWPAGE 0;
TTITLE "dbname Database|Data Dictionary Hit Ratios";
SPOOL /tmp/ddcache
SELECT    SUBSTR(PARAMETER,1,20) PARAMETER,
          gets,getmisses,count,usage,
          ROUND((1 - getmisses / decode(gets,0,1,gets))*100,1) HITRATE
FROM      v$rowcache
ORDER BY 6,1;
SPOOL OFF;
```

Here is the output of the script:

```
SQL> @t1
```

Fri Feb 23   page   1

                             dbname Database
                       Data Dictionary Hit Ratios

PARAMETER	GETS	GETMISSES	COUNT	USAGE	HITRATE
dc_object_ids	136	136	12	0	0
dc_free_extents	1978	1013	67	48	48.8
dc_used_extents	1930	970	63	5	49.7
dc_database_links	4	2	3	2	50
dc_sequence_grants	101	18	121	18	82.2
dc_synonyms	527	33	34	33	93.7
dc_objects	18999	947	389	387	95
dc_columns	163520	6576	2261	2247	96
dc_segments	8548	314	127	117	96.3
dc_constraint_defs	7842	250	218	210	96.8
dc_table_grants	26718	792	772	763	97
dc_sequences	4179	75	11	7	98.2
dc_users	1067	14	20	14	98.7
dc_tables	49497	261	272	271	99.5
dc_tablespace_quotas	957	4	5	4	99.6

dc_indexes	59548	172	329	328	99.7
dc_tablespaces	1162	3	7	3	99.7
dc_tablespaces	1201	4	27	4	99.7
dc_user_grants	9900	14	24	14	99.9
dc_usernames	18452	18	20	18	99.9
dc_users	14418	17	18	17	99.9
dc_column_grants	0	0	1	0	100
dc_constraint_defs	0	0	1	0	100
dc_constraints	0	0	1	0	100
dc_files	0	0	1	0	100
dc_histogram_defs	0	0	1	0	100
dc_profiles	0	0	1	0	100
dc_rollback_segments	18560	6	17	7	100

```
28 rows selected.
```

Multithreaded Server Tuning

Remember, if you are using SQL*Net version 2 with the multithreaded server, Oracle will allocate storage in the library cache to hold session information. As new connections are established through the MTS, Oracle will allocate memory, and the amount of memory can be measured with the **v$sessstat** table. Listing 3.6 shows a sample query.

Listing 3.6   A sample query.

```
SELECT (sum(value) || ' bytes' "Total memory for all sessions"
   FROM v$sessstat, v$statname
WHERE
NAME = 'session memory'
AND
v$sessstat.statistics# = v$statname.statistic#;


SELECT (sum(value) || ' bytes' "Total maximum memory for all sessions"
   FROM v$sessstat, v$statname
WHERE
NAME = 'max session memory'
AND
v$sessstat.statistics# = v$statname.statistic#;
```

The output might look as follows:

```
Total memory for all sessions
-------------------------------------------
203460 bytes

Total maximum memory for all sessions
-------------------------------------------
712473 bytes
```

Based on this instant in time, this report shows that 204 K is allocated to sessions, while the maximum memory for all sessions is 712 K. When deciding whether or not to increase the **shared_pool_size** parameter, the total memory for all sessions is the best guideline, since it is unlikely that all sessions will reach maximum memory allocation at the same moment in time.

Tuning The db_block_buffers Parameter

When a request is made to Oracle to retrieve data, Oracle will first check the internal memory structures to see if the data is already in the buffer. In this fashion, Oracle avoids doing unnecessary I/O. It would be ideal if we could create one buffer for each database page, ensuring that Oracle would read each block only once. However, the costs of memory in the real world make this prohibitive.

At best, we can only allocate a small number of real-memory buffers, and Oracle will manage this memory for us. Oracle utilizes a least-recently-used algorithm to determine which database pages are to be flushed from memory. Another related memory issue emerges that deals with the size of the database blocks. In most Unix environments, database blocks are sized to only 2 K. Unlike the mainframe ancestors that allowed blocks of up to 16,000 bytes, large blocks are not possible because of the way Unix handles its page I/O. Remember, I/O is the single most important slow-down in a client-server system, and the more relevant the data that can be grabbed in a single I/O, the better the performance. The cost of reading a 2 K block is not significantly higher than the cost of reading an 8 K block. However, the 8 K block read will be of no benefit if we only want a small row in a single table. On the other hand, if the tables are commonly read front-to-back, or if you make appropriate use of Oracle clusters (as described in Chapter 2), you can reap dramatic performance improvements by switching to large block sizes.

For batch-oriented reporting databases, very large block sizes are always recommended. However, many databases are used for online transaction processing during the day, while the batch reports are run in the evenings. Nevertheless, as a general rule, 8 K block sizes will benefit most systems.

Fortunately, Oracle does allow for large block sizes, and the **db_block_size** parameter is used to control the physical block size of the data files. Unlike other relational databases, Oracle allocates the data files on your behalf when the **CREATE TABLESPACE** command is issued. One of the worst things that can happen to a buffer cache is the running of a full-table scan on a large table.

Predicting The Benefit Of Additional Block Buffers

As database blocks are retrieved from disk into the database, they are stored in RAM memory in an area called a buffer. The block remains in the buffer until it is overwritten by another database request. At read time, the database first checks to see if the data already resides in the buffer before incurring the overhead of a disk I/O (see Figure 3.3).

The size of the buffer is determined by the database administrator—and for some databases, separate buffers may be created for different tables.

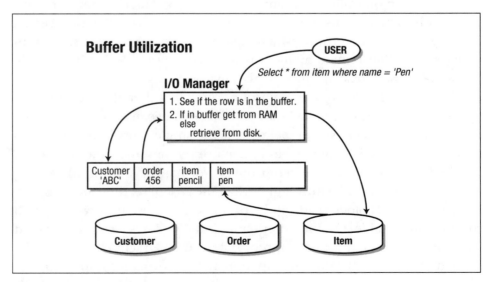

Figure 3.3   Oracle's data buffer operation.

The method for maximizing the use of buffers is to perform a check on the "buffer hit ratio." The buffer hit ratio is the ratio of logical requests to physical disk reads. A logical read is a request from a program for a record, while a physical read is real I/O against a database. A 1:1 correspondence does not always exist between logical and physical reads, since some records may have been fetched by a previous task and still reside in the buffer. In other words, the buffer hit ratio is the probability of finding the desired record in the memory buffer. The equation for finding the buffer hit ratio is:

Hit Ratio = Logical Reads - Physical Reads / Logical Reads

Listings 3.7 and 3.8 show two scripts for calculating the buffer hit ratio.

Listing 3.7   Method 1 for the script.

```
buffer1.sql - displays the buffer hit ratio
PROMPT ***********************************************************
PROMPT  HIT RATIO SECTION
PROMPT ***********************************************************
PROMPT
PROMPT           ============================
PROMPT           BUFFER HIT RATIO
PROMPT           ============================
PROMPT (should be > 70, else increase db_block_buffers in init.ora)

SELECT TRUNC((1-(sum(decode(name,'physical reads',value,0))/
               (sum(decode(name,'db block gets',value,0))+
               (sum(decode(name,'consistent gets',value,0))))))
            )* 100) "Buffer Hit Ratio"
FROM v$sysstat;
```

Listing 3.8   Method 2 for the script.

```
buffer2.sql - displays the buffer hit ratio

PROMPT ***********************************************************
PROMPT  HIT RATIO SECTION
PROMPT ***********************************************************
PROMPT
PROMPT           ============================
PROMPT           BUFFER HIT RATIO
PROMPT           ============================
PROMPT (should be > 70, else increase db_block_buffers in init.ora)
```

```
COLUMN "logical_reads" FORMAT 99,999,999,999
COLUMN "phys_reads"    FORMAT 999,999,999
COLUMN "phy_writes"    FORMAT 999,999,999
SELECT a.value + b.value  "logical_reads",
       c.value            "phys_reads",
       d.value            "phy_writes",
       ROUND(100 * ((a.value+b.value)-c.value) / (a.value+b.value))
         "BUFFER HIT RATIO"
FROM v$sysstat a, v$sysstat b, v$sysstat c, v$sysstat d
WHERE
    a.statistic# = 37
AND
    b.statistic# = 38
AND
    c.statistic# = 39
AND
    d.statistic# = 40;
```

Listing 3.9 shows the output from the second method.

Listing 3.9   The second method's output.

```
SQL> @t3
*************************************************************
HIT RATIO SECTION
*************************************************************


=========================
BUFFER HIT RATIO
=========================
(should be > 70, else increase db_block_buffers in init.ora)

Fri Feb 23                                              page    1
                        dbname Database
                   Data Dictionary Hit Ratios

   logical_reads    phys_reads      phy_writes    BUFFER HIT RATIO
   -------------   ------------    ------------    ----------------
     18,987,002       656,805          87,281            97

1 row selected.
```

Be aware that the buffer hit ratio (as gathered from the **V$** tables), measures the overall buffer hit ratio of the system since the Oracle instance was started. Since the **V$** tables keep their information forever, our current buffer hit ratio may be far worse than the 97 percent we see in Listing 3.9. To get a measure of the buffer hit ratio over a specific time period, use Oracle's bstat-estat utility, as described in Chapter 9.

While some of the mainframe databases allow for individual buffers for each record type, midrange databases such as Oracle provide only one database-wide buffer for all of the database I/O. In general, the buffer hit ratio is a function of the application and of the size of the buffer pool. For example, an application with a very large customer table is not likely to benefit from an increase in buffers, since the I/O is widely distributed across the tables. However, smaller applications will often see an improvement as the buffer size is increased, since this also increases the probability that frequently requested data remains in the buffer. For example, the high level nodes of an index are generally used by all applications, and response time can be improved if these blocks can be kept in the buffers at all times.

Databases that allow segmented buffer pools (such as the CA-IDMS) can be configured such that small indexes will be kept in the buffer at all times. This is accomplished by allocating an index to a separate area, and assigning the area to a separate buffer in the Device Media Control Language (DMCL).

If the hit ratio is less then 70 percent (i.e., two-thirds of data requests require a physical disk I/O), you may want to increase the number of blocks in the buffer. In Oracle, a single buffer pool exists and is controlled by a parameter called **db_block_buffers** in the init.ora process.

To estimate statistics, the following init.ora parameters must be set, and the database must be bounced:

db_block_lru_statistics = true

db_block_lru_extended_statistics = #buffers

 *Where **#buffers** is the number of buffers to add, be aware that the SGA will increase in size by this amount, such that a value of 10,000 would increase an SGA by 40 megabytes (assuming a 4 K block size). Make sure that your host has enough memory before trying this. Also, note that performance will be degraded while these statistics are running, and it is a good idea to choose a non-critical time for this test.*

Oracle uses two system tables called **sys.x$kcbrbh** (to track buffer hits) and **sys.x$kcbcbh** (to track buffer misses). Note that these are temporary tables and must be interrogated before stopping Oracle. An SQL query can be formulated against this table to create a chart showing the size of the buffer pool and the expected buffer hits:

```
REM morebuff.sql - predicts benefit from added blocks to the buffer

SET LINESIZE 100;
SET PAGES 999;

COLUMN "Additional Cache Hits" FORMAT 999,999,999;
COLUMN "Interval"              FORMAT a20;

SELECT 250*TRUNC(indx/250)+1
               ||' to '||250*(TRUNC(indx/250)+1) "Interval",
               SUM(count) "Additional Cache Hits"
FROM sys.x$kcbrbh
GROUP BY TRUNC(indx/250);
```

This SQL creates a result that shows the range of additional buffers blocks that may be added to the cache and the expected increase in cache hits:

```
SQL> @morebuff

Interval                Additional Cache Hits
------------------      ---------------------
1 to 250                           60
251 to 500                         46
501 to 750                         52
751 to 1000                       162
1001 to 1250                      191
1251 to 1500                      232
1501 to 1750                      120
1751 to 2000                       95
2001 to 2250                       51
2251 to 2500                       37
2501 to 2750                       42
```

Here, we see that the number of cache hits peaks at 232 with the addition of 1,500 buffer blocks. We then see a decreasing marginal benefit from adding more buffers. This is very typical of online transaction processing databases that have common information that is frequently referenced by all end users.

The following sample is from a database that primarily performs reports that invoke full-table scans:

```
SQL> @morebuff

Interval                     Additional Cache Hits
--------------------         --------------------
1 to 250                              60
251 to 500                            46
501 to 750                            52
751 to 1000                           62
1001 to 1250                          51
1251 to 1500                          24
1501 to 1750                          28
1751 to 2000                          35
2001 to 2250                          31
2251 to 2500                          37
2501 to 2750                          42
```

Here we see no peak and no marginal trends with the addition of buffers. This is very typical of databases that read large tables front-to-back. Doing a full-table scan on a table that is larger than the buffer will cause the first table blocks to eventually page out as the last table rows are read. Consequently, we will see no specific "optimal" setting for the **db_block_buffers** parameter.

As a general rule, all available memory on the host should be tuned, and Oracle should be given **db_block_buffers** up to a point of diminishing returns. There is a point where the addition of buffer blocks will not significantly improve the buffer hit ratio, and these tools give the Oracle DBA the ability to find the optimal amount of buffers.

The general rule is simple: As long as marginal gains can be achieved from adding buffers and you have the memory to spare, you should increase the value of **db_block_buffers**. Increases in buffer blocks increase the amount of required RAM memory for the database, and it is not always possible to "hog" all of the memory on a processor for the database management system. Therefore, the DBA will carefully review the amount of available memory and determine an optimal amount of buffer blocks.

> **NOTE** *If you overallocate SGA memory on a Unix system, such as with Oracle user's sign-on, the Unix kernel will begin to swap out chunks of active memory in order to accommodate the new users and cause a huge performance problem.*

Today, many databases reside alone on a host. When this is the case, you can predict the amount of "spare" memory and run your Oracle SGA up to that amount. For example, assume that your host machine has 350 megabytes of available memory. The Unix kernel consumes 50 megabytes, leaving 300 megabytes available for your Oracle database. We know that each online user will need to allocate a PGA when accessing the application, and the largest share of the PGA is determined by the value of the **sort_area_size** init.ora parameter. Therefore, assuming that we have a **sort_area_size** of 20 megabytes and 10 online users, we can assume that about 200 megabytes of real memory must be reserved for end-user sessions, leaving 100 megabytes for the Oracle SGA.

In many cases, we will see conditions where memory may be subtracted from the SGA without causing any serious performance hits. Oracle provides the **x$kcbcbh** table for this purpose, and we can query this table to track the number of buffer misses that would occur if the SGA was decreased in size:

```
REM lessbuff.sql - predicts losses from subtracting db_block_buffer
values

SET LINESIZE 100;
SET PAGES 999;

COLUMN "Additional Cache Misses" FORMAT 999,999,999;
COLUMN "Interval"                FORMAT a20;

SELECT 250*TRUNC(indx/250)+1
     ||' To '||250*(TRUNC(indx/250)+1) "Interval",
     SUM(count) "Additional Cache Misses"
FROM x$kcbcbh
WHERE indx > 0
GROUP BY TRUNC(indx/250);
```

Here is an example of how the output might appear:

```
SQL>@lessbuff

Interval                     Additional Cache Misses
--------------------         -----------------------
1 To 250                         3,895,959
251 To 500                          35,317
501 To 750                          19,254
751 To 1000                         12,159
1001 To 1250                         9,853
1251 To 1500                         8,624
1501 To 1750                         7,035
1751 To 2000                         6,857
2001 To 2250                         6,308
2251 To 2500                         5,625
2501 To 2750                         5,516
2751 To 3000                         5,343
3001 To 3250                         5,230
3251 To 3500                         5,394
3501 To 3750                         4,965
```

We can clearly see that this database has some shared information, with nearly 4 million cache hits in the first 250 buffer blocks. From 250 on up, we see a slowly decreasing downward trend, indicating that this application is doing some full-table scans or is not referencing a lot of common information.

For more sophisticated databases, we can control not only the number of buffer blocks—we can also control the block size for each buffer. For example, on an IBM mainframe, we might want to make the buffer blocks very large so that we can minimize I/O contention. For example, an I/O for 32,000 bytes is not a great deal more expensive than an I/O for 12,000 bytes; and the database designer may choose to make the buffer blocks large to minimize I/O if the application "clusters" records on a database page. If a customer record is only 100 bytes, we will not gain by retrieving 32,000 bytes to get the 100 bytes that we need. However, if we cluster the orders physically near the customer (i.e., on the same database page), and if I/O usually proceeds from customer to order, we won't need further I/O to retrieve orders for the customer. They will already reside in the initial read of 32,000 bytes, as shown in Figure 3.4.

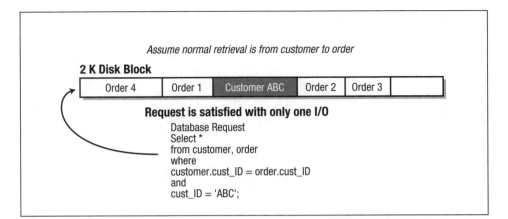

Figure 3.4   Using table clusters to reduce I/O.

Memory Cache Tuning

When I/O contention causes a performance problem, we have alternatives to disk striping. For very small and high-impact data tables, it is possible to make these tables reside in RAM memory. The access time against RAM is 10,000 times faster than disk I/O, and this solution can often make a huge performance difference. Two approaches to caching are possible. The first is caching, a hardware solution that uses extra RAM memory to hold the data table (table caching). The other alternative uses software mechanisms to reserve buffer memory for the exclusive use of the data table. While not all databases support this feature, some allow the memory buffer to be "fenced" or partitioned for the exclusive use of specific tables.

Simulating The Pinning Of Database Rows

Unfortunately, Oracle does not yet support the pinning of database blocks within its buffer cache. If it were possible to keep specific data blocks from swapping out, commonly used blocks such as common reference tables and the high-level nodes of indexes could be kept in memory. However, tricks can be used to simulate this type of buffer pinning. Introduced in Oracle's 7.2, read-only tablespaces allow for the creation of separate instances that concurrently access the same tablespace. For example, assume that your application had a common set of lookup tables, commonly referenced by every user. This table could be placed inside a separate instance, sized only for the lookup tables. Since the instance has its private buffer pool, you can ensure that the reference tables will always reside in memory. This type of architecture is also beneficial for systems that must do full-table scans. This alleviates the buffer flushing that occurs when an online transactions system is slowed by a single task that is required to do a full-table scan on a large table. But what if the table is read both by the online transaction processing and by the full-table scan request? Oracle version 7.2 offers read-only tablespaces.

With read-only tablespaces, the tablespace can be in update mode for the online transactions processing instance, while a separate instance handles read-only full-table scans (see Figure 3.5). The Oracle DBA should make every possible effort to identify and isolate read-only tables into a read-only tablespace, since performance is dramatically faster in read-only processing mode.

NOTE *For details on read-only tablespaces, refer to Chapter 6, Oracle DBA Performance And Tuning.*

The ability to identify and correct performance problems has plagued distributed systems from their genesis. Even within the context of a single transaction, distributed query optimization can be a formidable challenge.

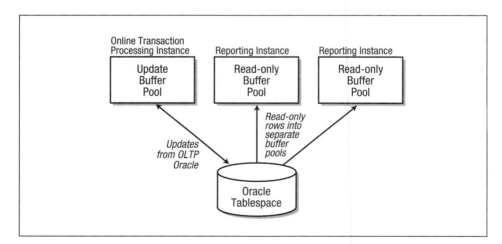

Figure 3.5   Oracle's read-only tablespaces.

On a single database, query tuning takes place by running an SQL **EXPLAIN** and performing the appropriate tuning. However, when a query is "spilt" into distributed databases, the overall query tuning becomes much more complex. Many distributed database managers take a distributed query and partition it into subqueries, which are then independently optimized and run (sometimes simultaneously) on the distributed databases. The query is considered complete when the last subquery has completed successfully and the results are returned to the user. This approach is sometimes called "the weakest link" architecture: If a distributed query partitions into four subqueries, for example, the longest running of the four subqueries determines the overall performance for the entire query, regardless of how fast the other three subqueries execute.

Clearly, tuning a distributed query is going to need to take into consideration the load on the network, the physical location of the database, and the availability of multiple CPUs. Today, tools are available to perform "load balancing," whereby a processor may borrow CPU cycles in order to balance the query and achieve maximum throughput.

Interoperability Facilities

It is very important for a distributed database to have the ability to address information regardless of the hardware platform or the architecture of the database; especially in volatile environments where hardware and network configurations may change frequently. Three types of interoperability come into play with distributed databases: hardware, operating systems, and network factors.

Database interoperability refers to the ability of a database to function autonomously to allow the distributed database to access many different types of databases within the domain of a unified environment. Tools such as UniFace and PowerBuilder attempt to serve this market, providing mechanisms for subtasking database queries and merging result sets automatically.

Hardware interoperability refers to the ability of the distributed system to address resources at many locations on an as-needed basis. At the hardware level, it is possible for a single subquery of a distributed query to run on numerous processors, and load balancing tools are available for assigning multiple processors to a single database.

Creating Batch-Oriented Oracle Instances

In some cases, widely differing applications may access the same tables. An excellent example of this scenario would be a banking application that processes fast, online transactions during the day, and is updated with long-running background tasks in the evening.

A fundamental difference exists between the database resources required for transaction processing and "batch" processing. Online transactions are usually small and require few resources from the database lock manager. Batch processes are generally lock intensive, sweeping a table in a linear fashion.

Oracle's buffer pool offers a finite amount of RAM storage within the region. This storage may be allocated to lock pools or buffer pools, but it is impossible to reallocate these resources as the applications change, unless the system is brought down and then restarted with a new configuration (called "bouncing"). For online transaction systems with hundreds of concurrent users, the demands upon the database buffer pool are much more intensive than with system-wide updates. Conversely, batch updates make very little use of large buffers, but require a lot of room in the lock pools to hold row locks between commit checkpoints.

One simple solution to these application-specific requirements is to create two database configurations, each with a different configuration of buffers and lock pools. At the end of the online transaction day, the online system may be brought down and a "batch" version of the database may be started with a different memory configuration.

I/O-Based Tuning

In a distributed database environment, it is important to understand that the overall distributed system is only going to perform as well as the weakest link. Therefore, most distributed database tuning treats each remote node as an independent database, individually tuning each one and thereby improving overall distributed system requests.

Input/Output is the single most important factor in database tuning. Business systems, by their very nature, are relatively light on processing and heavy on their demands from the disks that comprise the database. Several tricks are available to reduce I/O time from disk, including cache memory, buffer expansion, file placement, and file striping.

Disk Striping

Striping involves taking a very large or very busy data table and distributing it across many disks. When a performance problem occurs on a regular basis, it is most often the result of disks waiting on I/O. By distributing the file across many physical devices, the overall system response time will improve. Disk striping is generally done for tables that are larger than the size of a disk device, but striping can be equally effective for small, heavily accessed tables (see Figure 3.6).

Note that the data file appears to the database management system as a single logical file, which avoids any I/O problems from within the database when doing table striping. As rows are requested from the table, the SQL I/O module will request physical data blocks from the disk—one at a time—unaware that the logically continuous table is actually comprised of many physical data files.

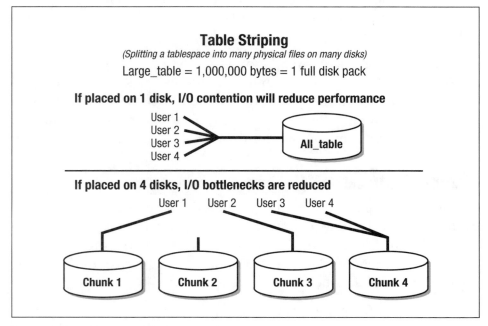

Figure 3.6 Striping a table across many disks.

In an Oracle database, disk striping is done in a similar fashion. Consider the following Oracle syntax:

```
CREATE TABLESPACE TS1
  DATA FILE "/usr/disk1/bigfile1.dbf"  SIZE30M
  DATA FILE "/usr/disk2/bigfile2.dbf"  SIZE30M;


CREATE TABLE BIG_TABLE (
  big_field1    CHAR(8)
  big_field2    VARCHAR(2000))
TABLESPACE TS1
STORAGE (INITIAL 25M   NEXT 25M   MINEXTENTS 2   PCTINCREASE 1);
```

Here we see that a tablespace is created with two data files—bigfile1 and bigfile2—each with a size of 30 megabytes. When we are ready to create a table within the tablespace, we size the extents of the table such that the database is forced to allocate the table's initial extents into each data file. As the table is created in the empty tablespace, the **MINEXTENTS** parameter tells the database to allocate two extents, and the **INITIAL** parameter tells the database that each extent is to be 25 megabytes each. The database then goes to bigfile1 on disk1 and allocates an extent of 25 megabytes. It then tries to allocate another extent of 25 megabytes on bigfile1, but only 5 megabytes of free space are available. The database must move to bigfile2 to allocate the final extent of 25 megabytes, as shown in Figure 3.7.

After the table has been initially created, the value for the **NEXT** extent should be changed to a smaller value than the **INITIAL** extent:

```
ALTER TABLE BIG_TABLE
STORAGE (NEXT 1M);
```

Some database administrators recommend striping all tables across each and every physical disk. If a system has 10 tables and the CPU is configured for 2 disks, then each of the 10 tables would be striped into each disk device.

It is unfortunate that the relational databases require the DBA to "trick" the database allocation software into striping the files rather than allowing direct control over the file placement process. This lack of control can be a real problem when tables are "compressed."

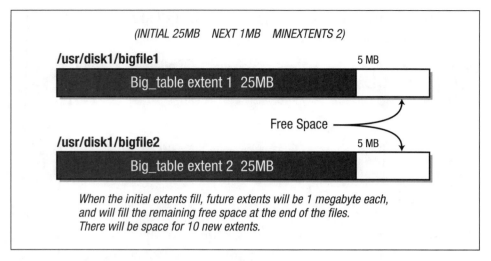

Figure 3.7   Allocating an Oracle table with striped extents.

Several methods will ensure that the tables are striped across the disks. Many databases with a sophisticated data dictionary allow queries that reveal the striping of the files. Oracle relies upon the following script:

```
striping.sql - displays striped file names
SELECT DISTINCT file_name,
FROM    dba_data_files a, dba_extents b
WHERE
        a.file_id = b.file_id
AND
        segment_name = :striped_table_name;

(WHERE :striped_table_name = 'BIG_TABLE')
```

Other databases offer utilities that report on the physical file utilization for a specific table or database record type.

Tuning Data Fragmentation

Fragmentation occurs when the preallocated space for a data area or table has been exceeded. In relational databases, tables are allocated into tablespaces, and each table is given several storage parameters. The storage parameters include **INITIAL**, **NEXT**, **PCTINCREASE**, and **MAXEXTENTS**.

As tables grow, they automatically allocate "extents," or extra storage at a size determined by the **NEXT** parameter. If a table reaches its maximum number of extents, all processing against that table will stop, causing major performance interruptions. In Oracle, the maximum number of extents can range from 121 extents for a 2 K blocksize to 505 for an 8 K block size, and increases according to the value of the **db_block_size** init.ora parameter. See your Oracle installation and configuration guide for the exact values for max extents on your operating system. If you are using Oracle 7.3 and above, you may want to consider using **MAXEXTENTS UNLIMITED**.

Even before the data tables fill, performance against the table may degrade as the amount of extents increases. An operating system such as Unix is forced to chase the "inode" chains to scan the entire table, and the increased I/O translates into performance delays (see Figure 3.8).

Several SQL queries can be used to detect table fragmentation. These queries are unique to the database system tables, but most databases allow for table fragmentation to be measured. These reports are generally incorporated into a periodic report, and those files that are fragmenting are then scheduled for export-import to unfragment the tables.

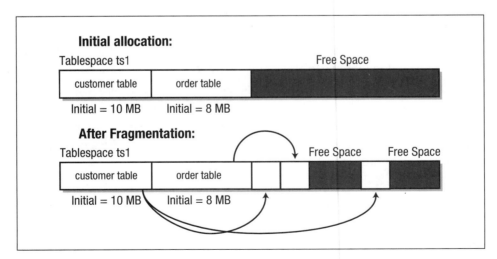

Figure 3.8 Free space allocation in an Oracle tablespace.

As the initial extents of a table fill, the database manager allocates additional spaces on the disk to allow the table to expand. These fragments eventually create a performance problem, and the tables need to be compressed to remove these extents.

Table compression is achieved in the following manner:

1. Determine the level of fragmentation and determine the new table sizes.

2. Offload all table data using an export utility.

3. Drop the old tables.

4. Reallocate the new tables at their new sizes.

5. Import the data to repopulate the tables.

Disk Issues With Other System Resources

Most databases have other high-impact resources such as the recovery logs and transaction logs. Most systems have several recovery logs, and it is a good idea to locate these logs on different disk devices as well as devices that do not have any other high-impact data tables.

Summary

Now that we have discussed how Oracle functions at the system level, we are ready to take a closer look at how individual SQL can be tuned to get the most from the available database resources. As we have already learned, myriad factors can degrade performance. Fortunately, many techniques are available for diagnosing and correcting performance problems, from tuning Oracle locks and/or the client application, to performance and tuning for distributed servers.

4

Tuning Oracle SQL

While several books have been devoted to the efficient use of Oracle SQL, only a few general rules and guidelines are actually effective in guaranteeing the most effective performance from your Oracle systems. This chapter will focus on the basic techniques for quickly achieving the maximum SQL performance with the least amount of effort. Topics include:

- Tips for efficient SQL

- Index predicates

- Concatenated indexes

- Using temporary tables to improve performance

- Tuning with the rule-based optimizer

- Using hints with the cost-based optimizer

Tuning Oracle SQL Syntax

Because SQL is a declarative language, we can write a query many ways. And although each query will return identical results, the execution time can be dramatically different. To illustrate this concept, let's consider a small employee table with only 15 rows and an index on **sex** and **hiredate**.

We issue the following query to retrieve all female employees who have been hired within the last 90 days. Here we are assuming that we are using Oracle's rule-based optimizer:

```
SELECT emp_name
FROM EMPLOYEE
WHERE
sex = 'F'
AND
hiredate BETWEEN sysdate-90 AND sysdate;
```

Since the table has only 15 rows, the most efficient way to service this request would be to use a full-table scan. However, Oracle will walk the index that exists, performing extra I/Os as it reads the index tree to access the rows in the table. While this is a simplistic example, it serves to illustrate the concept that the execution time of SQL is heavily dependent upon the way that the query is stated as well as the internal index structures within Oracle.

Entire books are devoted to some of the subtle nuances of SQL behavior, most notably Joe Celko's best selling book *SQL for Smarties*. For our purposes, we will omit discussion of tuning some of the more obscure queries such as outer joins and nullable foreign key queries. Instead, we will concentrate on tuning some of the common SQL queries that rely on Oracle's cost-based and rule-based optimizer.

It is true that each dialect of SQL is different, but general rules apply that can be used to keep database queries running efficiently. And while these guidelines are no substitute for the SQL **EXPLAIN PLAN** facility, they can reduce the chances that a database query will consume large amounts of system resources.

The first step is to look at the relative costs for each type of SQL access. Oracle has published the cost list shown in Table 4.1 that describes the relative cost of each type of row access.

As we can see, the fastest way to retrieve a row is by knowing its row ID. A row ID (called a **ROWID** in Oracle) is the number of the database block followed by the "displacement" or position of the row on the block. For example, 1221:3 refers to a row on block number 1221, the row being the third on the page. Many savvy programmers capture the **ROWID** for a row

Table 4.1   Costs for SQL access.

Cost	Type of Operation
1	Single row by row ID (**ROWID**)
2	Single row by cluster join
3	Single row by hash cluster key with unique or primary key
4	Single row by unique or primary key
5	Cluster join
6	Hash cluster key
7	Indexed cluster key
8	Use of a multi-column index
9	Use of a single-column index
10	Bounded range search on indexed columns
11	Unbounded range search on unindexed columns
12	Sort-merge join
13	**MAX** or **MIN** search of an indexed column
14	Use of **ORDER BY** on an indexed column
15	Full-table scan

if they plan to retrieve it again. In Oracle, **ROWID** is a valid column statement, such that we can select the **ROWID** along with our data in a single statement:

```
SELECT ROWID FROM EMPLOYEE INTO :myvar;
```

On the other end of the cost spectrum we see the full-table scan. As I have noted earlier in this book, a full-table scan is acceptable for small tables, but it can wreak havoc on Oracle when a full-table scan is invoked against a large table. Therefore, more than any other SQL tuning technique, avoiding full-table scans is a primary consideration. In short, full-table scans can *always* be avoided by using indexes and index hints. However, another issue must be considered. While a full-table scan may be the fastest for an individual query with many complex **WHERE** conditions, the full-table scan is done at the expense of other SQL on the system. The question then becomes: Do we tune an individual query for performance, or do we tune the database as a whole?

General Tips For Efficient SQL

Fortunately, some general rules are available for writing efficient SQL in Oracle. These rules may seem simplistic, but following them in a diligent manner will relieve more than half of the SQL tuning problems:

- Never do a calculation on an indexed column (e.g., **WHERE salary*5 > :myvalue**).

- Whenever possible, use the **UNION** statement instead of **OR**.

- Avoid the use of **NOT IN** or **HAVING** in the **WHERE** clause. Instead use the **NOT EXISTS** clause.

- Always specify numeric values in numeric form, and character values in character form (e.g., **WHERE emp_number = 565, WHERE emp_name = 'Jones'**).

- Avoid specifying **NULL** in an indexed column.

- Avoid the **LIKE** parameter if = will suffice. Using any Oracle function will invalidate the index, causing a full-table scan.

- Never mix data types in Oracle queries, as it will invalidate the index. If the column is numeric, remember not to use quotes (e.g., **salary = 50000**). For **char** index columns, always use quotes (e.g., **name = 'BURLESON'**).

- Remember that Oracle's rule-based optimizer looks at the order of table name in the **FROM** clause to determine the driving table. Always make sure that the last table specified in the **FROM** clause is the table that will return the smallest number of rows. In other words, specify multiple tables with the largest result set table specified first in the **WHERE** clause.

- Avoid using subqueries when a **JOIN** will do the job.

- Use the Oracle decode function to minimize the number of times that a table has to be selected.

- To turn off an index that you do not want to use (only with cost-based), concatenate a null string to the index column name (e.g., **name||'**), or add zero to a numeric column name (e.g., **salary+0**).

- If your query will return more than 20 percent of the rows in the table, use a full-table scan rather than an index scan.

- Always use table aliases when referencing columns.

One of the historic problems with SQL involves queries. Simple queries can be written in many different ways, each variant of the query producing the same result—but with widely different access methods and query speeds.

For example, a simple query such as "What students received an A last semester?" can be written in three ways, as shown in Listings 4.1, 4.2, and 4.3, each returning an identical result.

Listing 4.1   A standard join.

```
SELECT *
FROM STUDENT, REGISTRATION
WHERE
    STUDENT.student_id = REGISTRATION.student_id
AND
    REGISTRATION.grade = 'A';
```

Listing 4.2   A nested query.

```
SELECT *
FROM STUDENT
WHERE
    student_id =
    (SELECT student_id
        FROM REGISTRATION
        WHERE
        grade = 'A'
    );
```

Listing 4.3   A correlated subquery.

```
SELECT *
FROM STUDENT
WHERE
    0 <
    (SELECT count(*)
        FROM REGISTRATION
        WHERE
        grade = 'A'
        AND
        student_id = STUDENT.student_id
    );
```

Each of these queries will return identical results. The following discussion will review the basic components of an SQL query, showing how to optimize a query for remote execution.

It is important to note that several steps are required to understand how SQL is used in a distributed database. Distributed SQL queries function in the same way as queries within a single database, with the exception that cross-database joins and updates may utilize indexes that reside on different databases. Regardless, a basic understanding of the behavior of SQL can lead to dramatic performance improvements.

Tuning SQL With Indexes

As a general rule, indexes will always increase the performance of a database query. In some databases, such as DB2, in situations where a query intends to "sweep" a table in the same sequence that the rows are physically stored, the indexes may actually hinder performance. For Oracle, indexes are recommended for two reasons: to speed the retrieval of a small set of rows from a table, and to "presort" result sets so that the SQL **ORDER BY** clause does not cause an internal sort.

In order to use an index, the SQL optimizer must recognize that the column has a valid value for index use. This is called a sargeable predicate, and is used to determine the index access. Listing 4.4 shows some valid predicates, and Listing 4.5 shows invalid predicates.

Listing 4.4   Valid predicates.

```
SELECT * FROM EMPLOYEE WHERE emp_no = 123;

SELECT * FROM EMPLOYEE WHERE dept_no = 10;
```

Listing 4.5   Invalid predicates.

```
SELECT * FROM EMPLOYEE WHERE emp_no = "123";

SELECT * FROM EMPLOYEE WHERE salary * 2 < 50000;

SELECT * FROM EMPLOYEE WHERE dept_no != 10;
```

Whenever a transformation to a field value takes place, the Oracle database will not be able to use the index for that column.

Some databases, such as DB2, will recognize a linear search and invoke a "sequential prefetch" to look ahead, reading the next data block while the previous data block is being fetched by the application. As a general rule, an SQL query that retrieves more than 15 percent of the table rows in a table will run faster if the optimizer chooses a full-table scan than if it chooses to use an index.

For example, assume that a student table has 1,000 rows, representing 900 undergraduate students and 100 graduate students. A non-unique index has been built on the **student_level** field that indicates **UNDERGRAD** or **GRAD**. The same query will benefit from different access methods depending upon the value of the literal in the **WHERE** clause. The following query will retrieve 90 percent of the rows in the table, and will run faster with a full-table scan than it will if the SQL optimizer chooses to use an index:

```
SELECT * FROM STUDENT WHERE student_level = 'UNDERGRAD';
```

This next query will only access 10 percent of the table rows, and will run faster by using the index on the **student_level** field:

```
SELECT * FROM STUDENT WHERE student_level = 'GRAD';
```

Unfortunately, the Oracle database cannot predict in advance the number of rows that will be returned from a query. Many SQL optimizers will invoke an index access even though it may not always be the fastest access method.

To remedy this problem, some dialects of SQL allow the user to control the index access. This is a gross violation of the declarative nature of theoretical SQL: The user does not control access paths. But in practice, these extensions can improve performance. Oracle, for example, allows the concatenation of a null string to the field name in the **WHERE** clause to suppress index access. The previous query could be rewritten in Oracle SQL to bypass the **student_level** index as follows:

```
SELECT * FROM STUDENT WHERE student_level||'' = 'UNDERGRAD';
```

The concatenation (||) of a null string to the field tells the Oracle SQL optimizer to bypass index processing for this field, instead invoking a faster-running full-table scan.

This a very important point. While SQL optimizers are becoming more intelligent about their databases, they still cannot understand the structure of the data and will not always choose the best access path.

Concatenated Indexes

A concatenated index is created on multiple columns. This type of index can greatly speed up queries where all of the index columns are specified in the queries' SQL **WHERE** clause. For example, assume the following index on the **STUDENT** table:

```
CREATE INDEX idx1
ON STUDENT
(student_level, major, last_name) ASCENDING;
```

The following concatenated index could be used to speed up queries that reference both **student_level** and **major** in the **WHERE** clause:

```
SELECT student_last_name FROM STUDENT
WHERE
    student_level = 'UNDERGRAD'
AND
    major = 'computer science';
```

However, some queries using **major** or **student_level** will not be able to use this concatenated index. In this example, only the **major** field is referenced in the query:

```
SELECT * FROM STUDENT
WHERE
    major = 'computer science';
```

In this example, even though **student_level** is the high-order index key, it will not be used since there are other index keys following **student_level**. Since **major** is the second column in the index, Oracle will conclude that the index cannot be used:

```
SELECT last_name FROM STUDENT
WHERE
    student_level = 'PLEBE'
ORDER BY last_name;
```

Since **student_level** is the first item in the index, the leading portion of the index can be read and the SQL optimizer will invoke an index scan. Why have we chosen to add the **last_name** to the index, even though it is not referenced in the **WHERE** clause? Because Oracle will be able to service the request by reading only the index, and the rows of the **STUDENT** table will never be accessed. Also, since the **ORDER BY** clause asks to sort by **last_name**, Oracle will not need to perform a sort on this data.

The **NOT** (!) operator will cause an index to be bypassed and the query "show all undergrads who are **NOT** computer science majors" will cause a full-table scan:

```
SELECT * FROM STUDENT
WHERE
    student_level = 'UNDERGRAD'
AND
    major != 'computer science';
```

Here, the **NOT** condition isn't a sargeable predicate and will cause a full-table scan.

Using Oracle's Explain Plan Facility

Tools exist within most implementations of SQL that allow the access path to be interrogated.

To see the output of an **EXPLAIN PLAN**, you must first create a plan table. Oracle provides a script in $ORACLE_HOME/rdbms/admin with a script called utlxplan.sql. Execute utlxplan.sql and create a public synonym for the **plan_table**:

```
sqlplus > @utlxplan
table created.

sqlplus > create public synonym plan_table for sys.plan_table;
synonym created.
```

Most relational databases use an explain utility that takes the SQL statement as input, runs the SQL optimizer, and outputs the access path information into a **plan_table**, which can then be interrogated to see the access methods. Listing 4.6 runs a complex query against a database.

Listing 4.6 A sample database query.

```
EXPLAIN PLAN SET STATEMENT_ID = 'test1' FOR
SET STATEMENT_ID = 'RUN1'
INTO plan_table
FOR
SELECT   'T'||salesnet.terr_code, 'P'||detsale.pac1 || detsale.pac2 ||
detsale.pac3, 'P1', sum(salesnet.ytd_d_ly_tm),
 sum(salesnet.ytd_d_ty_tm),
 sum(salesnet.jan_d_ly),
 sum(salesnet.jan_d_ty),
FROM salesnet, detsale
WHERE
    salesnet.mgc = detsale.mktgpm
AND
    detsale.pac1 in ('N33','192','195','201','BAI',
    'P51','Q27','180','181','183','184','186','188',
    '198','204','207','209','211')
GROUP BY 'T'||salesnet.terr_code, 'P'||detsale.pac1 || detsale.pac2 ||
detsale.pac3;
```

This syntax is piped into the SQL optimizer, which will analyze the query and store the plan information in a row in the plan table identified by **RUN1**. Please note that the query will not execute; it will only create the internal access information in the plan table. The plan tables contains the following fields:

- **operation**—The type of access being performed. Usually table access, table merge, sort, or index operation.

- **options**—Modifiers to the operation, specifying a full table, a range table, or a join.

- **object_name**—The name of the table being used by the query component.

- **Process ID**—The identifier for the query component.

- **Parent_ID**—The parent of the query component. Note that several query components may have the same parent.

Now that the **plan_table** has been created and populated, you may interrogate it to see your output by running the following query:

```
plan.sql - displays contents of the explain plan table
SET PAGES 9999;
SELECT  lpad(' ',2*(level-1))||operation operation,
        options,
        object_name,
        position
FROM plan_table
START WITH id=0
AND
statement_id = 'RUN1'
CONNECT BY prior id = parent_id
AND
statement_id = 'RUN1';
```

Listing 4.7 shows the output from the plan table shown in Listing 4.6.

Listing 4.7   The plan table's output.

```
SQL> @list_explain_plan

OPERATION
-----------------------------------------------------------------
OPTIONS                          OBJECT_NAME                    POSITION
-----------------------------    ----------------------------   -----------
SELECT STATEMENT


  SORT
GROUP BY                                                            1

    CONCATENATION                                                   1

      NESTED LOOPS                                                  1

        TABLE ACCESS FULL        SALESNET                          1

        TABLE ACCESS BY ROWID    DETSALE                           2

          INDEX RANGE SCAN       DETSALE_INDEX5                    1

      NESTED LOOPS
```

From this output, we can see the dreaded **TABLE ACCESS FULL** on the **SALESNET** table. To diagnose the reason, we return to the SQL and look for any salesnet columns in the **WHERE** clause. There we see that the salesnet column called "**mgc**" is being used as a join column in the query, indicating that an index is necessary on **salesnet.mgc** to alleviate the full-table scan.

While the plan table is useful for determining the access path to the data, it does not tell the entire story. The configuration of the data is also a consideration. While the SQL optimizer is aware of the number of rows in each table (the cardinality), and the presence of indexes on fields, the SQL optimizer is not aware of data distribution factors such as the number of expected rows returned from each query component.

The other tool that is used with the plan table is an SQL trace facility. Most database management systems provide a trace facility that shows all of the resources consumed within each query component. The trace table will show the number of I/Os that were required to perform the SQL, as well as the processor time for each query component.

Some other relational databases such as DB2 allow the DBA to specify the physical sequence for storing the rows. Generally, this sequence will correspond to the column value that is most commonly used when the table is read sequentially by an application. If a customer table is frequently accessed in customer ID order, then the rows should be physically stored in customer ID sequence.

The explain plan output will display many database access methods. The major access techniques include:

- **AND-EQUAL**—This means that tables are being joined and that Oracle will be able to use the values from the indexes to join the rows.

- **CONCATENATION**—This indicates an SQL **UNION** operation.

- **COUNTING**—This indicates the use of the SQL **COUNT** function.

- **FILTER**—This indicates that the **WHERE** clause is removing unwanted rows from the result set.

- **FIRST ROW**—This indicates that a cursor has been declared for the query.

- **FOR UPDATE**—This indicates that returned rows were write locked (usually by using the **SELECT . . . FOR UPDATE OF . . .**).

- **INDEX** (**UNIQUE**)—This indicates that an index was scanned for a value specified in the **WHERE** clause.

- **INDEX** (**RANGE SCAN**)—This indicates that a numeric index was scanned for a range of values (usually with the **BETWEEN LESS_THAN** or **GREATER_THAN** specified).

- **INTERSECTION**—This indicates a solution set from two joined tables.

- **MERGE JOIN**—This indicates that two result sets were used to resolve the query.

- **NESTED LOOPS**—This indicates that the last operation will be performed n times, once for each preceding operation. For example, below the **INDEX** (**UNIQUE**), these operations will be performed for each row returned by **TABLE ACCESS** (**FULL**): **NESTED LOOPS**, **TABLE ACCESS** (**FULL**) **OF 'CUSTOMER'**, and **INDEX** (**UNIQUE**) **OF SY_01_IDX**.

- **PROJECTION**—This indicates that only certain columns from a selected row are to be returned.

- **SORT**—This indicates a sort, either into memory or the **TEMP** tablespace.

- **TABLE ACCESS** (**ROWID**)—This indicates a row access by **ROWID** that is very fast.

- **TABLE ACCESS** (**FULL**)—This is a full-table scan and is usually cause for concern unless the table is very small.

- **UNION**—This indicates that the **DISTINCT** SQL clause was probably used.

- **VIEW**—This indicates that a SQL view was involved in the query.

Database statistics packages can be made to capture this information, but they tend to be very resource intensive. Turning on SQL trace statistics for a very short period of time during processing is a good practice to follow in order to gather a representative sample of the SQL access.

Using Temporary Tables

The prudent use of temporary tables can dramatically improve Oracle performance. Consider the following example: We want to identify all users who exist within Oracle, but have not been granted a role. We could formulate the following query:

```
SELECT USERNAME FROM dba_users
WHERE USERNAME NOT IN
(SELECT GRANTEE FROM dba_role_privs);
```

This query runs in 18 seconds. Now, we rewrite the same query to utilize temporary tables:

```
CREATE TABLE temp1 AS
  SELECT DISTINCT USERNAME FROM dba_users;

CREATE TABLE temp2 AS
  SELECT DISTINCT GRANTEE FROM dba_role_privs;

SELECT USERNAME FROM temp1
WHERE USERNAME NOT in
(SELECT GRANTEE FROM temp2);
```

This query runs in less than three seconds.

Tuning With The Rule-Based Optimizer

In Oracle's rule-based optimizer, the ordering of the table names in the **FROM** clause determines the driving table. The driving table is important because it is retrieved first, and the rows from the second table are then merged into the result set from the first table. Therefore, it is essential that the second table return the least amount of rows based on the **WHERE** clause. *This is not always the table with the least amount of rows* (i.e., the smallest cardinality).

For example, consider two **emp_tables**—one in London and another in New York, as shown in Table 4.2.

In this example, a total select from the **emp_table** should specify the New York table first, since London has the least amount of returned rows:

```
SELECT *
FROM emp@new_york, emp@london;
```

Table 4.2   New York and London emp_tables.

	Rows	Dept 100	Dept 200
New York	1,000	100	900
London	200	150	50

If the SQL specifies a **WHERE** condition to include only Department 100, the order of table names should be reversed:

```
SELECT *
FROM emp@london, emp@new_york
WHERE
    dept = 100;
```

Since it is not always known what table will return the least amount of rows, procedural code could be used to interrogate the tables and specify the tables in their proper order. This type of SQL generation can be very useful for ensuring optimal database performance, as shown in Listing 4.8.

Listing 4.8   Automatic generation of optimal rule-based SQL.

```
SELECT count(*) INTO :my_london_dept
    FROM emp@london
    WHERE dept = :my_dept;

SELECT count(*) INTO :my_ny_dept
    FROM emp@new_york
    WHERE dept = :my_dept;

IF my_london_dept >= my_ny_dept
{
    table_1 = emp@london
    table_2 = emp@new_york
ELSE
    table_1 = emp@new_york
    table_2 = emp@london
};

/* Now we construct the SQL */

SELECT *
FROM :table_1, :table_2
WHERE
    dept = :my_dept;
```

As we know, Oracle version 7 offers two methods of tuning SQL. If you are running version 7.2 or above, you can use the cost-based optimizer; releases of Oracle 7.1 and below recommend the rule-based optimizer. The rule-based method was the only method available in version 6. With the rule-based optimizer, the indexing of tables and order of clauses within the SQL statement control the access path in rule-based optimization. The cost-based optimizer automatically determines the most efficient execution path, and the programmer is given "hints" that can be added to the query to alter the access path. The cost-based optimizer or the rule-based optimizer is set in the init.ora file by setting the **optimizer_mode** to **RULE**, **CHOOSE**, **FIRST_ROWS**, or **ALL_ROWS**. Be careful when using the **CHOOSE** option. When you give Oracle the ability to choose the optimizer mode, Oracle will favor the cost-based approach if *any* of the tables in the query have statistics. (Statistics are created with the **ANALYZE TABLE** command.) For example, if a three-table join is specified in **CHOOSE** mode and statistics exist for one of the three tables, Oracle will decide to use the cost-based optimizer and will issue an **ANALYZE TABLE ESTIMATE STATISTICS** at runtime. This will dramatically slow down the query.

The optimizer option (rule versus cost) can be controlled at the database level or at the program level. Prior to version 7.0.16, the cost-based analyzer had significant problems, and Oracle recommended the use of the rule-based optimizer.

Here are some tips for effective use of Oracle's rule-based optimizer:

1. Try changing the order of the tables listed in the **FROM** clause. Page 19-15 in *Oracle RDBMS Database Administrator's Guide* states that "Joins should be driven from tables returning fewer rows rather than tables returning more rows." In other words, the table that returns the fewest rows should be listed *last*. This *usually* means that the table with the most rows is listed *first*. If the tables in the statement have indexes, the driving table is determined by the indexes. One Oracle developer recently slashed processing in half by changing the order of the tables in the **FROM** clause. Another developer had a process shift from running for 12 hours to running in 30 minutes by changing the **FROM** clause.

2. Try changing the order of the statements in the **WHERE** clause. Here's the idea: Assume that an SQL query contains an **IF** statement with several Boolean expressions separated by **AND**s. Oracle parses the SQL from the bottom of the SQL statement, in reverse order. Therefore, the most restrictive Boolean expression should be on the bottom. For example, consider the following query:

```
SELECT last_name
FROM STUDENT
WHERE
eye_color = 'BLUE'
AND
national_origin = 'SWEDEN';
```

Here, we assume that the number of students from Sweden will be smaller than the number of students with blue eyes. To further confound matters, if an SQL statement contains a compound **IF** separated by **OR**s, the rule-based optimizer parses from the top of the **WHERE** clause. Therefore, the most restrictive clause should be the first Boolean item in the **IF** statement.

3. Analyze the existence/non-existence of indexes. Understand your data. Again, unlike the cost-based optimizer, the rule-based optimizer only recognizes the existence of indexes and does not know about the selectivity or the distribution of the index column. Consequently, use care when creating indexes, especially when using rule-based optimization. Consider *all* programs that use a field in a **WHERE** clause of a **SELECT**. A field should only be indexed when a very small subset (less than 5-10 percent) of the data will be returned.

4. Is the target table fragmented? For example, a table could be fragmented if it constantly has a large number of rows inserted and deleted. This is especially true in **PCTFREE**, since the table has been set to a low number. Regular compression of the table with the Oracle utilities export/import will restore the table rows and remove the fragmentation.

5. Always run questionable SQL through **EXPLAIN PLAN** to examine the access path.

6. Understand which "query paths" are the fastest. For example, accessing a table by **ROWID** is the fastest access method available where a full-table scan is 17 out of 18 for the ranking of query paths. (Reference Table 4.1 for the complete list of relative costs.)

7. Avoid joins that use database links into Oracle version 6 tables.

8. Make effective use of arrays, since array processing significantly reduces database I/O. Consider the following example: A table has 1,000 rows to be selected. The records are manipulated and then updated in the database. Without using array processing, the database receives 1,000 reads and 1,000 updates. With array processing (assuming an array size of 100), the database receives 10 reads (1,000/100) and 10 updates. According to Oracle, increasing the array size to more than 100 has little benefit.

Beware of an Oracle rule-based "feature" whereby a join of numerous large tables will always result in a full-table scan on one of the tables, even if all of the tables have indexes and the join could be achieved with an index scan. Of course, full-table scans are costly, and SQL hints can be used to force the query to use the indexes. You can use hints with the rule-based optimizer.

Using Hints With The Cost-Based Optimizer

The rule-based optimizer is supposed to be obsolete with the introduction of Oracle version 8 in 1997, but its replacement—the cost-based optimizer—is available today. Unlike the rule-based optimizer, which uses heuristics to determine the access path, the cost-based optimizer uses data statistics to determine the most efficient way to service the request.

Here is a summary of the most common hints that can be added to SQL:

- **ALL_ROWS**—This is the cost-based approach designed to provide the best overall throughput.

- **CLUSTER**—Requests a cluster scan of the table(s).

- **FIRST_ROWS**—This is the cost-based approach designed to provide the best response time.

- **FULL**—Requests the bypassing of indexes, doing a full-table scan.

- **INDEX**—Requests the use of the specified index. If no index is specified, Oracle will choose the best index.

- **ROWID**—Requests a **ROWID** scan of the specified table.

- **RULE**—Indicates that the rule-based optimizer has been invoked (sometimes to the absence of table statistics).

- **ORDERED**—Requests that the tables should be joined in the order that they are specified. For example, if you know that a **STATE** table has only 50 rows, you may want to use this hint to make **STATE** the driving table.

- **USE_NL**—Requests a nested loop operation with the specified table as the driving table.

- **USE_MERGE**—Requests a sort merge operation.

Remember, the cost-based optimizer will only be as accurate as the statistics that are computed from the tables. Your DBA will need to create a periodic cron (a Unix-based job scheduling utility) job to re-estimate statistics for all tables that are volatile and change columns frequently. While a full **ANALYZE TABLE xxx ESTIMATE STATISTICS** will interrogate every row of the table, a faster method can be used by issuing **ANALYZE TABLE ESTIMATE STATISTICS SAMPLE nn ROWS**. By taking a sample of the rows within the table, the statistics generation will run much faster. Keep in mind that one of the things that the **ANALYZE** command reviews is the selectivity and distribution of values within an index. As such, care should be taken to sample at least 100 rows from each table.

Here is a test that created a set of three tables, **dept**, **dept1**, **dept2**, each with an index on **deptno** and set **optimizer_goal** as **RULE** in the init.ora. Listing 4.9 shows the results of the query.

Listing 4.9 The results of the query.

```
SELECT /*+ INDEX(dept DEPT_PRIMARY_KEY) INDEX(dept2 i_dept2)
INDEX(dept1 i_dept1)*/
dept.deptno, dept1.dname, dept2.loc
FROM dept, dept1, dept2
```

```
WHERE dept.deptno=dept1.deptno AND
dept1.deptno=dept2.deptno

Misses in library cache during parse: 1
Optimizer hint: RULE
Parsing user id: 48   (DON)


Rows      Execution Plan
------    -------------------------------------------------------
    0  SELECT STATEMENT    OPTIMIZER HINT: RULE
    4    MERGE JOIN
    4      SORT (JOIN)
    4        NESTED LOOPS
    5          INDEX (RANGE SCAN) OF 'DEPT_PRIMARY_KEY' (UNIQUE)
    4          TABLE ACCESS (BY ROWID) OF 'DEPT1'
    8            INDEX (RANGE SCAN) OF 'I_DEPT1' (NON-UNIQUE)
    4      SORT (JOIN)
    4        TABLE ACCESS (BY ROWID) OF 'DEPT2'
    5          INDEX (RANGE SCAN) OF 'I_DEPT2' (NON-UNIQUE)
```

Listing 4.10 shows what we receive without any hints.

Listing 4.10   The query results for no hints.

```
SELECT dept.deptno, dept1.dname, dept2.loc
FROM dept, dept1, dept2
WHERE dept.deptno=dept1.deptno AND
dept1.deptno=dept2.deptno

Misses in library cache during parse: 1
Optimizer hint: RULE
Parsing user id: 48   (JACK)


Rows      Execution Plan
------    -------------------------------------------------------
    0  SELECT STATEMENT    OPTIMIZER HINT: RULE
    4    NESTED LOOPS
    4      NESTED LOOPS
    4        TABLE ACCESS (FULL) OF 'DEPT2'
    4        TABLE ACCESS (BY ROWID) OF 'DEPT1'
    8          INDEX (RANGE SCAN) OF 'I_DEPT1' (NON-UNIQUE)
    4      INDEX (UNIQUE SCAN) OF 'DEPT_PRIMARY_KEY' (UNIQUE)
```

If we add a hint for the **dept2** index, the full-table scan would be on **dept1**, and so on.

Tuning PL/SQL

PL/SQL is the acronym for Procedure Language/SQL, the standard procedural language for online Oracle applications. PL/SQL is commonly used within Oracle's SQL*Forms application framework, but the popularity of PL/SQL for non-SQL*Forms applications has re-emerged because of the benefits of using Oracle stored procedures, which must be written with PL/SQL. PL/SQL offers the standard language constricts, including looping, **IF** statement structures, assignment statements, and error handling.

There are several problems with PL/SQL, each of which warrant special attention.

PL/SQL offers two types of SQL cursors, the "explicit" cursor and the "implicit" cursor. Explicit cursors are manually declared in the PL/SQL:

```
DECLARE
CURSOR C1 IS
SELECT last_name
FROM CUSTOMER
WHERE
cust_id = 1234;
```

However, it is possible to issue the SQL statement directly in PL/SQL without specifying the cursor name. When this happens, Oracle opens an implicit cursor to handle the request. Implicit cursors create a tremendous burden for Oracle, as the implicit cursor must always reissue a fetch command to be sure that only a single row was returned by the query. This will double the amount of fetch statements for the query. The moral is simple: Always declare all cursors in your PL/SQL.

PL/SQL allows certain types of correlated subqueries to run much faster than a traditional Oracle SQL query. Consider a situation where a bank maintains a general ledger table and a transaction table. At the end of the banking day, the check transaction table is applied to the **GENERAL_LEDGER** table, making the requisite deductions from the **account_balance** column. Let's assume that the **GENERAL_LEDGER** table contains 100,000 rows and 5,000 daily checks need to be processed.

A traditional SQL query (shown in Listing 4.11) to accomplish the updating of **account_balance** would involve a correlated subquery.

Listing 4.11   Using a traditional SQL query.

```
UPDATE GENERAL_LEDGER
SET account_balance = account_balance -
   (SELECT check_amount FROM TRANSACTION
      WHERE
      TRANSACTION.account_number = GENERAL_LEDGER.account_number)
WHERE
EXISTS
(SELECT 'x' FROM TRANSACTION
 WHERE
 TRANSACTION.account_number = GENERAL_LEDGER.account_number);
```

As we recall, a correlated subquery involves executing the subquery first, and then applying the result to the entire outer query. In this case, the inner query will execute 5,000 times, and the outer query is executed once for each row returned from the inner query. This Cartesian product problem has always been a problem for correlated subqueries.

Now consider the identical query as written in PL/SQL (Listing 4.12).

Listing 4.12   The PL/SQL query.

```
DECLARE
  CURSOR c1 is
  SELECT account_number,
    check_amount
  FROM TRANSACTION;

    keep_account_number        number;
    keep_check_amount          number;

BEGIN

    OPEN C1;
    LOOP
            fetch c1 into keep_account_number, KEEP check_amount;
    EXIT WHEN C1%NOTFOUND;

    UPDATE GENERAL_LEDGER
    SET account_balance = account_balance - keep_check_amount
    WHERE account_number = keep_account_number;
    END LOOP;
END;
```

Here we see that each check amount is retrieved in a separate transaction, and fetched into cursor **C1**. For each **check_amount**, the balance is applied to the **GENERAL_LEDGER** row, one at a time.

Using Oracle Stored Procedures And Triggers

Many excellent benefits can be derived from using stored procedures and triggers for all database access code. These enhancements include:

- *Encapsulation*—The code resides in the database instead of in external programs. With the proper use of Oracle packages, stored procedures can be logically grouped together into a cohesive framework of SQL statements.

- *Performance*—Stored procedures and triggers are cached into the shared pool, making repeated calls to the procedure very fast.

- *Flexibility*—By keeping all database access inside Oracle packages, the applications contain no SQL, becoming little more than a set of calls to the stored procedures. As such, the application is insulated from the database and becomes very easy to migrate to another platform or database product.

Certain rules apply in deciding when to use a trigger and when to use a stored procedure. The choice revolves around the nature of the desired SQL, and whether it is specific to a DML event or is global in nature. In general, the validation of input data is ideally suited to an **INSERT** trigger, especially when it involves accessing another Oracle table. If you are writing your own referential integrity, **DELETE** triggers are appropriate. Triggers are generally associated with SQL that is closely tied to a single DML event, such as the insertion, deletion, or updating of a row. In practice, **SELECT** triggers are used only in situations where hand-rolled auditing is used to keep a log of those who are viewing secure rows.

Stored procedures are generally used when an SQL query creates an aggregate object, which accesses rows from many tables to create a single result set. The creation of an invoice, an order form, or a student's schedule are examples of these types of queries.

One of the problems with utilizing Oracle stored procedures and triggers is keeping track of the SQL once it has been entered into the database. Unlike the object database products, Oracle does not yet provide a mechanism for directly associating a stored procedure with the tables that it touches.

Oracle version 8 promises to make this less of a problem, but client/server programmers must be able to identify and reuse queries that have already been written and tested. To achieve reusability, you can use naming conventions to ensure that all SQL is logically associated with the tables against which it operates. For example, the action of the SQL inserting a row into the customer table could be given a meaningful name, say **customer_insert()**. This way, the data dictionary can be interrogated to identify all existing SQL that touched a table. The use of naming conventions is tricky when a single SQL statement joins many tables, but prudent use of naming conventions can also help ensure that the SQL can be easily located.

Oracle triggers have the ability to call stored procedures, and a trigger may include many SQL statements, thus providing the ability to "nest" SQL statements. Oracle triggers are stored as procedures that can be parameterized and used to simulate object-oriented behavior. For example, assume that we want to perform a behavior called **CHECK_TOTAL_INVENTORY** whenever an item is added to an order. The trigger definition would be:

```
CREATE TRIGGER CHECK_TOTAL_INVENTORY
           AFTER  SELECT OF ITEM
FOR EACH ROW

    SELECT COUNT(*) INTO :count
    FROM QUANTITY WHERE ITEM_# = :myitem:

IF :count < item.total THEN
      ......
END IF;
```

Triggers could also be combined to handle combined events, such as the reordering of an **ITEM** when the quantity on hand falls below a predefined level:

```
CREATE TRIGGER REORDER BEFORE UPDATE ON ITEM
    FOR EACH ROW WHEN (new.reorderable = 'Y')
      BEGIN
        IF new.qty_on_hand + old.qty_on_order < new.minimum_qty
```

```
THEN
    INSERT INTO REORDER VALUES (item_nbr, reorder_qty);
    new.qty_on_order := old.qty_on_order + reorder_qty;
END IF;
END
```

Simulating Object-Orientation

The latest movement in the trendy database marketplace is to offer products that use object technology and also offer the popular SQL access language. On one side of this market we see the "pure" ODBMSs developing SQL interfaces to their object architectures, while the relational vendors are creating object layers for their table structures. While neither of these approaches is ideal from the perspective of the MIS manager, great progress has been made in both directions. The time has arrived when programmers who have mastered SQL also need to understand its object-oriented dialects. These products include SQL++ by Objectivity Inc., Object SQL by Ontos, and SQL/X[1] by UniSQL. Many proponents of the relational model state that the ad hoc query capability of SQL is inconsistent with the object oriented principle of encapsulation, but the sheer popularity of these tools has led to many attempts to reconcile SQL with object-oriented databases.

The object/relational hybrids promise to allow users to keep their existing relational technology while gaining object features. Unlike traditional relational databases, these hybrids allow cells within a table to contain multiple values or even another entire table. This "nesting" of tables within tables allows far more flexibility than with traditional database systems, even though it appears to toss away even the most fundamental principles of normalization. Codd's definition of First Normal Form (1NF) does not allow for repeating data items within a field, much less a nested table.

Using SQL to access nonrelational architectures is not limited to the object databases. In the early 1980s when SQL became popular, many database vendors wrote SQL "umbrellas" over their hierarchical and network database products. Some products such as CA's CA-IDMS were even renamed to IDMS/R, proudly proclaiming that they were "relational" because they supported SQL queries. Of course, it takes much more than SQL to make a database relational, and a great debate rages today about how relational an object database becomes when it allows SQL access.

The basic operators for SQL are **Select**, **Insert**, **Update**, and **Delete**. Mapping these to an object database requires first matching the context of the data involved, then the semantics of the operation. The SQL engine maps relational tables to object classes, rows to objects, row identifiers to object identifiers, and columns to object data members. Table and attribute information to identify accessible table and column names are also available through SQL select operations.

While originally specified in the ANSI X3H2 SQL syntax, SQL3 included object extensions for invoking object methods, navigating relationships between objects, and accessing nested structures. Furthermore, extents and virtual object identifiers were supported. Since SQL3 has failed to create a usable standard, the community will have to come up with a de facto standard for accessing object databases with SQL.

This section will explore how client/server developers can adapt their SQL programming to deal with objects. It will include comments from actual users of SQL++, and discuss how programmers can prepare for this new SQL paradigm.

 For details about Oracle's object layer, refer to the section in Chapter 2, Towards Oracle8.

If you make a careful comparison of the relational model and the object model, you will find several constructs within object technology for which SQL must be extended to address:

- *Inheritance*—Some or all objects within a class hierarchy can be selected.

- *Abstraction*—Selecting from "composite" objects.

- *Pointer-Based Navigation*—Non-key-based data retrieval.

- *Invoking Methods in SQL*—Addressing data behaviors and functions.

Inheritance

In an inheritance hierarchy, objects are "typed" with general objects and data items high in the hierarchy, while more specific objects

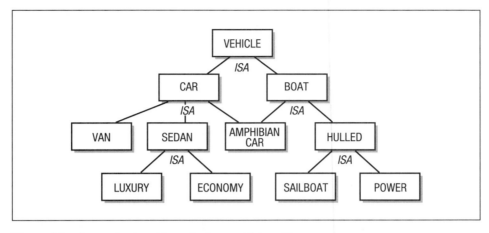

Figure 4.1 A sample class hierarchy for a vehicle entity.

appear lower in the tree. While subtyping is found very commonly in the real world, it is surprising that it was not addressed in the relational model. The idea of "class hierarchies" and inheritance is a very useful concept, and one that can be relatively easily incorporated into SQL, as illustrated in Figure 4.1.

Note that not all classes within a generalization hierarchy have objects associated with them. The object-oriented paradigm allows for abstraction, which means that a class may exist only for the purpose of passing inherited data and behaviors. The classes **VEHICLE** and **CAR** would probably not have any concrete objects, while objects within the **VAN** class would inherit from the abstract **VEHICLE** and **CAR** classes.

Now, let's assume that we have built this vehicle hierarchy in our database. How will we be able to traverse the inheritance hierarchy using SQL? One suggestion is to add an **ALL** operator to the SQL, such that all objects beneath the specified object will be included in the query. For example, we could state:

```
SELECT
vehicle_name, vehicle_ID, date_of_sale
FROM
ALL VEHICLE;
```

Here is the output:

```
name               ID      date
van                1234    01/01/95
van                5643    01/01/95
luxury sedan       6453    03/03/95
economy sedan      7342    03/01/95
economy sedan      9822    03/01/95
economy sedan      7254    03/01/95
amphibian car      5334    03/04/95
sailboat           4353    03/04/95
power boat         6452    03/01/95
```

Here we are saying that **ALL VEHICLE** includes all subclasses—starting at **VEHICLE** and working down the hierarchy. To limit the query to only boats, the query could state:

```
SELECT
vehicle_name, vehicle_ID, date_of_sale
FROM
ALL BOAT;
```

The result might look like this:

```
name               ID      date
amphibian car      5334    03/04/95
sailboat           4353    03/04/95
power boat         6452    03/01/95
```

Here we see that the **ALL BOAT** limited the results to only those objects beneath the **BOAT** class. Note that the **AMPHIBIAN CAR** appears in both queries. This is an example of multiple inheritance.

Abstraction

Unlike the Oracle server, in which every data item is required to be atomic, object databases allow for abstract data types to be represented. In a relational database, information is "assembled" from independent tables at the time of the query. Object-oriented advocates state that this atomic approach does not properly represent the real world—analogous to assembling your automobile when you want to travel and then disassembling the car after you have completed your trip. If the goal of the database is to model the real

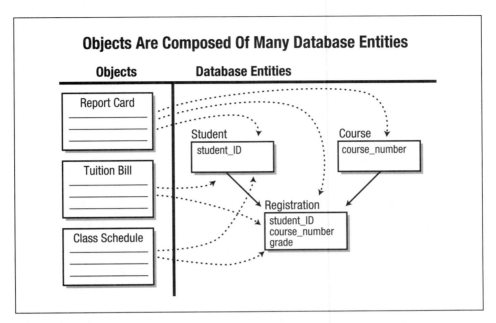

Figure 4.2   The relationships between database objects and aggregate entities.

world, then a mechanism should be in place to allow aggregate objects to exist independently from their components. (See Figure 4.2.)

In simple terms, an aggregate object contains "references" to atomic data that resides in other object classes—in addition to its own unique data. As seen below, a report card consists of its own data (date of report) and subobjects that have their own unique identity within the database.

If the aggregate object will have its own identity within the database, how can we represent these identities? In an object database, a student object (table) might have the following fields. Note that the **report_card_list** field is a pointer to an array of pointers to report cards:

```
first_name          char(20);
last_name           char(20);
age                 number;
report_card_list    pointer to an array of report cards
```

The concept of a pointer to an array of pointers is extremely confounding, but it is a very common type of data structure within an object database.

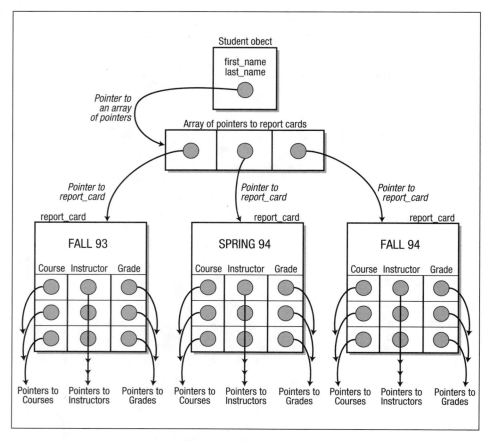

Figure 4.3 How pointers are used to build aggregate objects.

Pictorially, it is represented in Figure 4.3. What we see is a condition where a single value in an object contains a structure, or a pointer to another object. At first glance this seems very strange, since we are used to seeing single, "atomic" data items in a definition. While this violates First Normal Form, Chris Date has stated in his "third manifesto" that repeating groups and aggregate data items can be viewed as a "set," and are therefore compliant with relational theory.

As you can see, we have managed to represent the "real world" through a very sophisticated network of internal pointers. The question now becomes one of data access. How can we address the data in these report cards using SQL? Let's assume that the grade field is a numeric field, with 4 for an A, 3 for a B, and so on. We would like to query our object database to gather the names of all students that are qualified for the dean's list. The SQL query might appear like this:

```
SELECT last_name
FROM STUDENT
WHERE
semester = 'Fall 94'
AND
avg(report_card.grade) > 3.5;
```

Here we see that the pointer structures are simply referenced by prefacing the data name with the name of the structure in which they participate. The object engine will take care of the pointer navigation on our behalf, returning the proper list of students.

Pointer-Based Navigation

This sample query is written using the dialect of SQL that supports object constructs, and will not function within Oracle at this time. However, these are the concepts that are being discussed for Oracle version 8, where object extensions will be added to the base relational engine. This query returns the names of employees in the marketing department with an expertise in SQL.

For example, let's review a query to see a list of all employees in the Marketing department. To run this query against relational tables we would perform a relational join as in the following example. This SQL statement could also execute correctly against an object model database if the foreign key field (**dept_id**) was introduced into the employee record to indicate that the relationship with the department table was available:

```
SELECT last_name
FROM EMPLOYEE
WHERE
EMPLOYEE.dept_id = DEPARTMENT.dept_id
AND
department_name = 'marketing';
```

The SQL code example below uses object extensions to directly navigate the relationship to a department object and tests its value. There is no need to join two tables, since the employee object contains a pointer that takes the query directly to the department name:

```
SELECT last_name FROM employee WHERE
    TRAVERSE(oid, "employee", "DEPARTMENT.Dept_name") = 'marketing'
    AND
    Expertise_area = 'SQL';
```

The traversal operation uses the relationship between employees and departments to test the value of the department to which the employee belongs. In this case, the query directly navigates the relationship to acquire this value, without requiring any join operations. Since the employee object contains a pointer to the department in which it participates, the **TRAVERSE** operator can be used to chase the up-level pointer to get the name of the department object. The example demonstrates the natural use of an object model to capture information about relationships. These can be modeled directly, without requiring the developer to define keys and additional tables. Secondly, standard SQL can be used against the object model, returning the same results we would expect from a relational model.

In the case of relationships captured by the object model, this is accomplished without requiring costly join operations at runtime. This is an important principle of the object databases. By taking the time up front to establish a pointer chain to precreate the relationship, the database will be able to traverse the relationship far faster than with a relational join.

Of course, the precreation of data relationships has a downside—they are simply not as flexible as relational databases. Whereas a new table can be immediately joined with other tables, a new object cannot become associated with other objects until the database has been restructured to precreate the relationship.

Invoking Methods In SQL

As we know, the object data model coupled data with behavior in the class definition, and a data access language should be able to access any methods that are available to the object. For example, consider a table that contains **employee_name** and **birth_date**. We could create a method that would accept the **birth_date** and compute the age of the employee:

```
age(birth_date date) return int;
```

This method should be addressable as a data item from within the SQL. For example:

```
SELECT employee_name, age
FROM EMPLOYEE
WHERE
    age > 30;
```

To be fully functional, methods should be able to be called from SQL just as if they were native to the language. For example, assume that we create a method that computes the total amount for an order based on the individual prices of the items in the order. But take a close look at the sample method: It selects data from three tables and returns data from two tables. Given that no one-to-one correspondence exists between the tables and the method, where does this method belong? Should we associate it with the **ORDER**, **LINE_ITEM**, or **ITEM** class? For the moment, let's assume that the method is defined as a **ORDER** method, namely **ORDER.total_price()**:

```
example ORDER.total_price method

    SELECT sum(ITEM.price*LINE_ITEM.quantity)
    FROM ORDER, LINE_ITEM, ITEM
    WHERE
    order_number = :invar
    AND
    ORDER.order_number = LINE_ITEM.order_number
    AND
    LINE_ITEM.item_number = ITEM.item_number;
```

Now we should be able to reference **total_price** just as we would reference any other data item within the order object. For example, we could state:

```
SELECT    order_number,
    total_price
FROM ORDER
WHERE
    total_price > 300;
```

While access to object databases via SQL is a lofty goal, it remains to be seen if the SQL language will allow itself to become extended for object-orientation. It is possible that a totally new access method such as Object

Query Language (OQL) will evolve from the vendors. For the time being, the answer resides in the marketplace, and the major relational database vendors will exert a strong influence in the future direction of SQL. For now, we can only speculate on the future and direction of objects and SQL.

In summary, the following examples of SQL are used to illustrate each of the object-oriented concepts.

INHERITANCE

This code is used to include related rows *down* a class hierarchy:

```
SELECT * from ALL vehicle;
/*  all vehicles  */

SELECT * from ALL car;
/*  everything from car downward by class */
```

AGGREGATION

These commands will retrieve components of aggregate objects:

```
SELECT reportCard.grade
WHERE
    report_card.class = 'C++';
```

At this time, these extensions are only implemented in the object/relational databases such as Sybase/Illustra and UniSQL. However, they will become a reality in 1997 with the widespread acceptance of the SQL3 standard, as well as the commitment of every major relational database vendor to add object extensions to their engines.

Using ODBC As A Server Interface

The Open Database Connectivity (ODBC) product was initially developed by Microsoft as a generic database driver. Its architecture has now been generalized and many different vendors are offering open database connectivity products that are based on ODBC. ODBC is the predominant common-interface approach to database connectivity and is a part of Microsoft's Windows Open Service Architecture (WOSA). ODBC and WOSA define a standard set of data access services that can be used by a variety of other products when interfacing with MS-Windows applications.

ODBC consists of more than 50 functions that are invoked from an application using a call-level API. The ODBC API does not communicate with a database directly. Instead, it serves as a link between the application and a generic interface routine. The interface routine, in turn, communicates with the database drivers via a Service Provider Interface (SPI), as illustrated in Figure 4.4.

Each custom application within Windows will have call-level API calls to the ODBC database driver, which then directs the request to the appropriate database driver for execution. The database driver manages the communication between the databases and handles all returning data and messages, passing them back to the ODBC driver—which passes them back to the invoking application.

As ODBC becomes more popular, database vendors are creating new ODBC drivers that will allow ODBC to be used as a gateway into their database products. It needs to be noted that most programmers are successful with

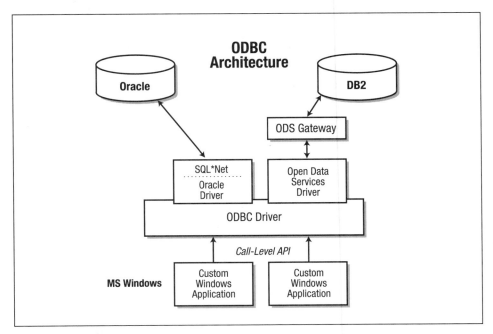

Figure 4.4   A look at the ODBC architecture.

ODBC in a simple application, but effective use of ODBC in multidatabase environments is a very difficult task. Programmers are not only faced with all the different dialects of SQL, they must also be aware of the native API to the database engines. However, despite the steep learning curve, a few tips can ease the effort with ODBC.

Essentially, ODBC serves as the "traffic cop" for all data within the client/server system. When a client requests a service from a database, ODBC receives the request and manages the connection to the target database. ODBC manages all of the database drivers, checking all of the status information as it arrives from the database drivers.

It is noteworthy that the database drivers should be able to handle more than just SQL. Many databases have a native API that requires ODBC to map the request into a library of functions—for example, an SQL-Server driver that maps ODBC functions to database library function calls. Databases without a native API (i.e., non-SQL databases) can also be used with ODBC, but they go through a much greater transformation than the native API calls.

When accessing multiple databases with ODBC, the API programmer has to manage the multiple database connections and the multiple SQL requests that are being directed to the connections. In ODBC, "handles" are used to point to each database connection. Handles are usually pointers into the database, and the value of the handle is a record key, a row ID, or an object ID.

Most people associate ODBC with SQL. While SQL is now the single most common access method for databases, many important non-SQL databases are widely used. Popular non-SQL databases include IMS, CA-IDMS, Basis Plus—and almost all of the new object-oriented databases. It is a misconception that a database that does not support SQL cannot use ODBC.

Summary

Now that we understand how individual SQL queries can be tuned to make efficient use of the database resources, we can move on to look at the other considerations for effective client/server implementation. Among the topics covered will be lock management, database connectivity issues, and tuning a distributed server environment.

Tuning
Oracle Locking

While most commercial database products provide mechanisms for locking and concurrency control, new issues emerge when using a relational database such as Oracle. This problem is especially prevalent when a single Oracle task updates multiple remote servers, which is becoming increasingly common with distributed Oracle systems. The real nightmare begins when the remote servers are of differing architectures—for example, a distributed update to a relational and a network database. In these cases, the concurrency control is generally turned off for each database and is provided for inside the application program, since neither of the databases can be expected to manage the internals of the other database.

In addition to the technical issues, the popularity of client/server interfaces has also changed the ways in which concurrency is handled. Many client/server systems disable their Oracle database locking and rely upon procedural tricks to maintain data integrity at the server level. Oracle is one of these products, and we will discuss how to avoid contention by disabling Oracle locks.

This chapter explains the basic features of Oracle access control and describes the issues involved when concurrency and database integrity must be maintained in a distributed Oracle server environment. Topics include:

- The problem of cohesive updating

- Database locking and granularity

- Oracle locking

- Database deadlocks

- Escalation of locks with non-Oracle servers

- Alternative locking mechanisms for Oracle

- Locking and distributed databases

- Understanding the two-phase commit

The Problem Of Cohesive Updating

To ensure that an Oracle transaction properly retrieves and updates information, it is important to understand the differences between two processing modes: conversational and pseudoconversational. In a conversational scenario, the unit of work is extended to include the entire wall-clock time that the user spends in the transaction. In pseudoconversational mode, the unit of work is partitioned. The duration of the task begins when the user requests a database service, and ends when the database delivers the response to the user. The system then stands idle, releasing any locks that may have been held by the previous transaction. (See Figure 5.1.)

As a point of illustration, consider a user who displays a customer's information, waits five minutes, and then issues an update of the customer information. If we process in fully conversational mode, a problem of database corruption never arises because "exclusive" record locks are held for the entire duration of the terminal session. However, the resources required to hold the locks may cause a burden on the database, and the lock will impede other transactions that desire to retrieve (and possibly update) the information that is being held by the session.

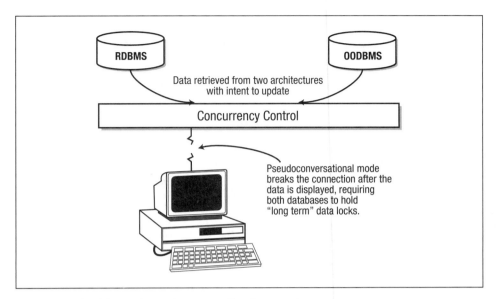

Figure 5.1   Locking and pseudoconversational processing.

The solution to the locking problem is to create your application structure in the pseudoconversational mode, releasing the row locks after the screen has mapped out to the user. In fact, for Oracle client/server, we highly recommend this approach. However, this processing mode can lead to a variety of problems. Releasing locks in the client/server environment can be very desirable from a performance perspective, but there are many side effects that must be addressed by the application.

Dirty Reads

A dirty read is a situation where a row has been retrieved while the row is held by another transaction with intent to update the row. Assume that a transaction begins, grabbing customer ABC with intent to update. The information for ABC is displayed on the screen, and the user changes the value of the **CUSTOMER_STATUS** field. At this time, the change has been written to the database, but the information is not made permanent until either a **COMMIT** or **ABORT** statement is issued. During the original transaction, the change may be nullified with an **ABORT** statement. Unfortunately, a transaction may have read the value of **CUSTOMER_STATUS** for ABC before the transaction was aborted, thereby reading incorrect information.

Nonreproducible Results

This situation most commonly occurs when a report is being run against an Oracle database that is actively being updated. The report may be run in "local mode," a processing mode using read-only tablespaces that bypasses the services of the database manager and ignores all database locks, reading the database files directly from the disk. The local mode report sweeps the database pages to obtain the requested information, but it also reports on information that is in the process of being changed. This can result in "phantom rows," since rows are read that are in the process of being deleted or added.

Database Corruption (Bad Foreign Keys)

This situation can occur when local mode reports are run against a system that is being updated. The report attempts to retrieve a row (usually via an index) while the index nodes are readjusting after an insert or delete. This results in the report terminating with a message that indicates a bad pointer. Many DBAs have gone into a panic over this scenario until they realize that the "bad" pointer was not really corrupt and their database is intact. Because Oracle maintains read consistency, this is not an issue. Oracle will read any changed data from its rollback segments, guaranteeing that the report receives a picture of the database as it existed at the time that the report started execution.

Conversational processing is usually associated with a pessimistic locking scheme—that is, the transaction manager assumes that the transaction is going to be "interfered with" during the duration of the session, and the locks are held for the entire time that the record is being viewed. Pseudo-conversational processing mode is associated with an optimistic locking scheme, whereby the system hopes that the transaction will remain isolated.

Database Locking And Granularity

Database locking can take place at many levels. For some relational databases, the locks can be set for the entire database: a tablespace within the database, a table within the tablespace, or a row within the table, as shown in Figure 5.2. Some relational databases also offer "page"-level locking. A database page is a unit of storage, usually associated with a physical block,

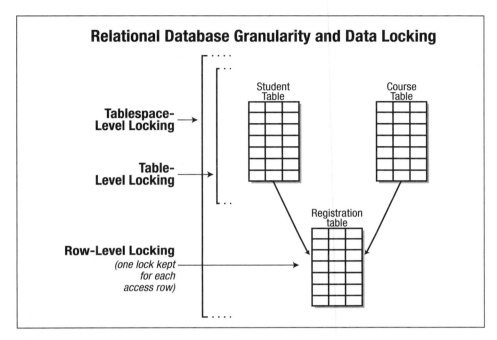

Figure 5.2   The different levels of database locking.

upon which rows are stored. For example, a page in the Oracle database defaults to 4 K, and the CA-IDMS database allows page sizes to range from 2 K up to 32 K, depending on the size of the records.

In object-oriented databases, locking can take place at the database level, the "container" within the database, or the object within the container. The concept of a container is new to the object-oriented databases. A container is defined as a partition of disk memory of arbitrary size that is used to hold objects. A container can be thought of as analogous to the "pages" that are used within CA-IDMS and DB2. In commercial object-oriented databases, most vendors only support locking at the container level, although most of the vendors recognize the necessity of providing object level locking mechanisms. As a general rule, as the locking level becomes finer, the demands on resources on the lock manager increase while the potential for database deadlocks decreases.

In some databases, the programmer has some control over whether a database lock is issued. In CODASYL databases such as CA-IDMS, the programmer may issue a **GET EXCLUSIVE** command to expressly hold a record lock for the duration of the transaction, and some relational databases allow for locks to be controlled with the SQL. Most relational databases offer commands that can allow an application to hold shared or exclusive locks on database rows.

Most commercial relational databases such as Oracle offer two types of locks: shared and exclusive. The most common type of locks are shared locks that are issued with SQL **SELECT** statements, and exclusive locks that are issued with **DELETE** and **UPDATE** statements. In shared locking, whenever a unit of data is retrieved from the database, an entry is placed in the database storage pool. This entry records the unit ID (usually a row or database page number). The usual size of a lock ranges from 4 to 16 bytes, depending on the database. This lock will be held by the database until a **COMMIT**, **END**, or **ABORT** message releases the lock. Most locking schemes use a "coexistence" method. For example, many clients may have shared locks against the same resource, but shared locks cannot coexist with exclusive locks. Whenever an update event occurs, the database attempts to post an exclusive lock against the target row. The exclusive lock will wait if any other tasks hold a shared lock against the target row (Figure 5.3).

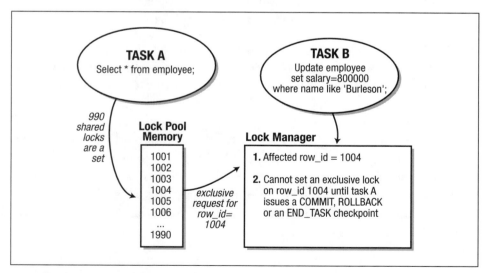

Figure 5.3   Exclusive vs. shared locks.

Oracle Locking

Oracle maintains locks at either the row level or the table level. Unlike other databases, such as DB2, Oracle will never "escalate" locks to the table level if the database detects that a majority of the rows in a table are being locked. Consequently, the Oracle programmer must decide in advance whether to lock the entire table or allow each row of the table to be locked individually.

Two init.ora parameters control locking: **serializable=false** and **row_locking=always**. These default values should never be changed except in very rare cases.

Oracle supports two types of locks: row locks and table locks. These locks can be subdivided into several categories:

- *Row Share Table Locks (RS)*—These locks are issued when an SQL transaction has declared its intent to update the table in row share mode. This type of lock will allow other queries to update rows in the customer table. For example:

```
lock table customer in row share mode;

SELECT customer_name
FROM CUSTOMER
FOR UPDATE OF CUSTOMER;
```

- *Row Exclusive Table Locks (RX)*—These locks are issued automatically against a table when an **UPDATE**, **DELETE**, or **INSERT** statement is issued against the table.

- *Table Share Locks (S)*—This type of lock is issued when the **LOCK TABLE** command is issued against the table. This indicates that the transaction intends to perform updates against some rows in the table, and prevents any other tasks from execution until the **LOCK TABLE xxx IN SHARE MODE** has completed.

- *Share Row Exclusive Table Locks (SRX)*—These locks are issued with the **LOCK TABLE xxx IN SHARE ROW EXCLUSIVE MODE** command. This prevents any other tasks from issuing any explicit **LOCK TABLE** commands until the task has completed, and also prevents any row-level locking on the target table.

- *Exclusive Table Locks (X)*—This is the most restrictive of the table locks and prevents everything except queries against the affected table. Exclusive locks are used when the programmer desired exclusive control over a set of rows until their operation has completed. The following command is used to lock the **CUSTOMER** table for the duration of the task:

```
LOCK TABLE CUSTOMER IN ROW EXCLUSIVE MODE NOWAIT;
```

In order to understand how the different types of locks interact with one another, we can reference Table 5.1, which describes how each lock type interacts with other locks. The NO values indicate those locks that cannot be simultaneously held.

Database Deadlocks

This locking scenario insures that all database integrity is maintained and that updates do not inadvertently overlay prior updates to the database. However, a penalty has to be paid for maintaining shared locks. In Oracle, each lock requires 4 bytes of RAM storage within the Oracle instance storage pool, and large SQL **SELECT** statements can create S.O.S. (Short On Storage) conditions that can cripple the entire database. For example, a **SELECT** statement that retrieves 1,000 rows into the buffer will require 4,000 bytes of lock space. This condition can also cause the "deadly embrace," or a database deadlock. A deadlock condition occurs when two tasks are waiting on resources that the other task has locked, as depicted in Figure 5.4.

Table 5.1	Lock mode compatibility.					
	NULL	**SS**	**SX**	**S**	**SSX**	**X**
NULL	YES	YES	YES	YES	YES	YES
RS	YES	YES	YES	YES	YES	NO
RX	YES	YES	YES	NO	NO	NO
S	YES	YES	NO	YES	NO	NO
SRX	YES	YES	NO	NO	NO	NO
X	YES	NO	NO	NO	NO	NO

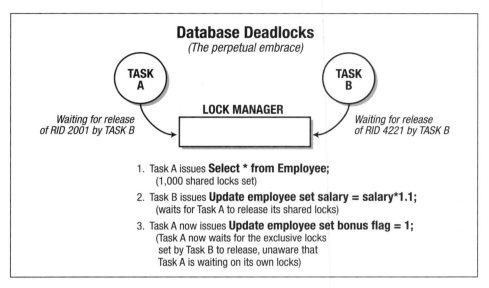

Figure 5.4   A database deadlock.

The majority of Oracle programmers do not realize that database dead-locks occur most commonly within a table index. It is important to note that a **SELECT** of a single row from the database may cause more than one lock entry to be placed in the storage pool. The individual row receives a lock, but each index node that contains the value for that row will also have locks assigned.

When an update or delete is issued against a row that participates in the index, the database will attempt to secure an exclusive lock on the row. This requires the task to check if any shared locks are held against the row, as well as check on any index nodes that will be affected. Many indexing algorithms allow for the index tree to dynamically change shape, spawning new levels as items are added and condensing levels as items are deleted.

Because most commercial databases only issue automatic locks against a row when they need to lock a row, programmatic solutions can be used to minimize the amount of locking that is used for very large update tasks. For example, in Oracle SQL, a programmer can use the **SELECT...FOR UPDATE** clause to explicitly lock a row or a set of rows prior to issuing the **UPDATE** operation. This will cause the database to issue exclusive locks (sometimes called pre-emptive locks) at the time of retrieval, and hold these exclusive locks until the task has committed or ended. In the following SQL, an exclusive lock is placed upon the target row, and no other task will be able to retrieve that row until the update operation has completed:

```
SELECT *
    FROM EMPLOYEE
    WHERE emp_name = 'Burleson'
    FOR UPDATE OF SALARY;
```

For large updates, statements can be issued to lock an entire table for the duration of the operation. This is useful when all rows in the table are going to be affected, as in the following salary adjustment routine:

```
LOCK TABLE emp_table IN EXCLUSIVE MODE NOWAIT;

UPDATE emp_table
    SET salary = salary * 1.1;
```

Sometimes the application will want to update all of the rows in a table, but it is not practical to lock the entire table. An alternative to the exclusive update is to use the Oracle's SQL **FETCH** statement to lock a small segment of the table, perform the update, and then release the locks with a **COMMIT** statement, as shown in Listing 5.1.

Listing 5.1   Using the FETCH statement.

```
DECLARE    CURSOR total_cursor IS
    SELECT emp_name FROM emp_table;

DECLARE CURSOR update_cursor IS
    SELECT ROWID
    FROM emp_table
    WHERE emp_name = :my_emp_name
    FOR UPDATE OF SALARY;

BEGIN
    count = 0;
    OPEN total_cursor;

    begin_loop;

        OPEN update_cursor;
```

```
FETCH total_cursor INTO :my_emp_name;

FETCH update_cursor INTO :my_rowid;

IF (update_cursor%found) THEN
{
    UPDATE emp_table
        SET salary = salary * 1.1
    WHERE
        ROWID = :my_rowid;

    COUNT++;

    IF (COUNT = 20) THEN
    {
        COMMIT;
        COUNT = 0;
    }
}
}
CLOSE update_cursor;
CLOSE total_cursor;
END;
```

As we see from the Listing 5.1, the locks are set as the rows are fetched, 20 at a time, and then released with a **COMMIT**. This technique consumes less memory in the lock pool and also allows other SQL statements to access other rows in the table while the update is in progress. Of course, if this code should fail, it would need to be restarted from the point of the last **COMMIT** statement. This would require additional logic to be inserted into the update program to record the row ID of the last **COMMIT**ted row, and to restart the program from that row.

Escalation Of Locks With Non-Oracle Servers

Some databases attempt to alleviate locking problems by performing "lock escalation." Lock escalation increases the granularity of the lock in an attempt to minimize the impact on the database lock manager. In a relational database, the level of locking is directly proportional to the type of update that is being executed. Remember, for row-level locking, a lock must be placed in the lock storage pool for every row that the SQL statement addresses. This can lead to very heavy resource consumption, especially for SQL statements that update numerous records in many tables. For example, an SQL query that selects many (but not all) of the records in the registration table might state:

```
SELECT *
FROM REGISTRATION
    WHERE
    REGISTRATION.grade = 'A';
```

Depending on the number of students affected, this type of query will begin to hold row locks until the task has successfully completed—or until the SQL statement terminates because of a lack of space in the lock pool. However, if the database supports lock escalation, the database will set a single lock for the entire table, even if only a portion of the rows in registration are affected.

In databases such as DB2, a statement such as **SELECT * FROM REGISTRATION**, to return all rows in the registration table, will cause DB2 to escalate from row-level locking to page-level locking. If the **REGISTRATION** table resides in a single tablespace, some database engines will escalate to tablespace-level locking. This strategy can greatly reduce strain on the lock pool; but some lock mechanisms will escalate locks, even if it means that some rows will be locked although they are not used by the large task. For example,

```
SELECT * FROM EMPLOYEE WHERE DEPARTMENT = 'MARKETING'
```

may cause the entire **EMPLOYEE** table to lock, preventing updates against employees in other departments.

Whenever possible, large SQL updates could be run using table-level locks, thereby reducing resource consumption and improving the overall speed of the query. Some implementations of SQL provide extensions that allow for the explicit specification of the locking level and granularity. This mechanism could allow exclusive locks to be placed on a result set if the user intends to update the rows, or to turn off shared locks if the rows will never be updated.

In all relational databases, the engine must be sure that a row is "free" before altering any values within the row. The database accomplishes this by issuing an exclusive lock on the target row. The exclusive lock mechanism will then sweep the internal "lock chain" to see if shared locks are held by any other tasks for any rows in the database. If shared locks are detected, the update task will wait for the release of the shared locks until they are freed or until the maximum wait time has been exceeded. While the task is waiting for the other tasks to release their locks, it is possible that one of these tasks may issue an update. If this update affects the original task's resources, a database deadlock will occur, and the database will abort the task that is holding the least amount of resources.

Unlike object, network, or hierarchical databases that update a single entity at a time, a relational database may update hundreds of rows in a single statement. For example:

```
UPDATE REGISTRATION
SET REGISTRATION.grade = 'A'
WHERE
course_id = 'CS101'
    AND
    COURSE.instructor_id = 'BURLESON';
```

This single statement may update many rows, and the concurrency manager must check for contention (i.e., shared locks). If any other tasks are viewing any other rows in the database, the engine will set as many exclusive locks as possible, and put the statement into a wait state until the shared locks from other tasks have been released. Only after all the desired rows are free will the transaction be completed.

Alternative Locking Mechanisms For Oracle

The problems of lock pool resources and database deadlocks have lead to some creative alternatives to Oracle's shared and exclusive locks. Locking can be turned off in Oracle by issuing a **COMMIT** statement immediately after the **SELECT**. Without long-term shared locks, lock pool utilization is reduced and the potential for database deadlocks is eliminated. But we

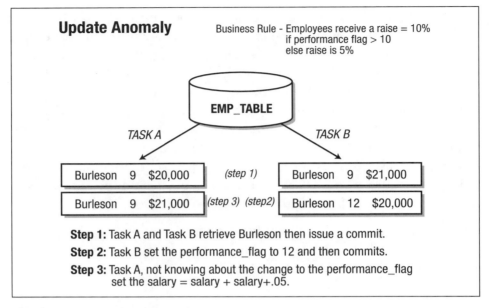

Figure 5.5   Accidental overlaying of data.

still must deal with the problem of ensuring that updates are not overlaid. Consider Figure 5.5, which is an example of updates without locking.

Both tasks have selected Burleson's employee record and issued **COMMIT** statements to release the locks. Task B now changes Burleson's performance rating to a 12 and issues an **UPDATE** that writes the column back to the database. Task B, which is now looking at an obsolete copy of Burleson's **performance_flag**, changes the salary to $21,000, improperly assigning Burleson's raise. This is a type of "logical" corruption, whereby a user may rely on outdated values in other rows, updating the target column based upon the obsolete information.

Some databases such as SQL/DS and Oracle allow **SELECT FOR UPDATE** commands. With **SELECT FOR UPDATE**, the before image of the row is compared with the current image of the row before the update is allowed.

If you must communicate with non-Oracle databases that do not support **SELECT FOR UPDATE**, several clever techniques are available to release locks while still maintaining database integrity.

The WHERE Clause

For example, if Burleson's row contains the fields in Figure 5.6, each of the fields will be specified in the update command, even if the user has not changed the item. If any of the values have changed since the row was initially retrieved, the database will reject the transaction with a "not found" SQL code. The application could interpret this code, re-retrieving the updated record and presenting it to the user with its new value.

 *It is very important to run the EXPLAIN utility with this type of update statement to be sure that the SQL optimizer uses the employee index to locate the row. With more than two items in the **WHERE** clause, some optimizers may become confused and service the request by using a full-table scan, causing significant performance delays. With Oracle SQL, the programmer can specify the index that will be used to service the query, although other implementations of SQL require that the indexed field be specified first in the **WHERE** clause. Regardless, it is important to run an **EXPLAIN PLAN** on the SQL to be sure that the additions to the **WHERE** clause do not impede performance.*

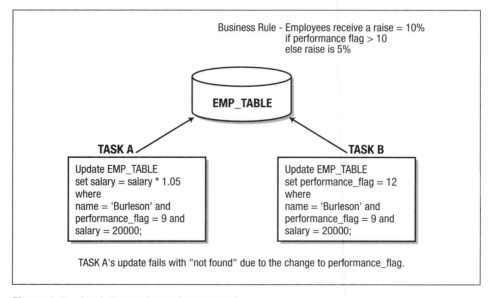

Figure 5.6 A solution to the update anomaly.

As demonstrated earlier, Oracle has SQL extensions that can explicitly "turn off" unwanted indexes. For example, indexes can be turned off by altering the key field that is used in the **WHERE** clause.

Assume that the **emp_table** has the following definition:

```
CREATE TABLE emp_table (
    emp_name              char(20),
    sex                   char(1),
    performance_flag      number,
    salary                decimal(8,2) );
```

Let's further assume that **emp_name** has a unique index—and that the field's **sex**, **performance_flag**, and **salary** have nonunique indexes. To ensure that the index on **emp_name** is used, the index key fields will be "altered" by concatenating a null string to the end of the **char** columns and adding a 0 to the end of each numeric column.

Hence, the following SQL update would read:

```
UPDATE emp_table
    SET salary            = salary*1.05
WHERE
    emp_name              = 'Burleson'
AND
    performance_flag+0    = 9
AND
    sex || ''             = 'M'
AND
    salary+0              = 20000;
```

Another method can guarantee the use of the **emp_name** index. We could alter the **emp_name** index to include the nonunique fields of **performance_flag**, **sex**, and **salary**, creating a large concatenated index on every column in the table. A slight index overhead will occur, but you can be assured that all index updates perform efficiently without relying on the SQL programmers to alter their SQL.

The Date-Time Stamp Solution

This solution requires that a date-time stamp column be added to each table that may be updated. All applications are required to select this column and include it in the **WHERE** clause when issuing any **UPDATE** SQL.

Of course, if the row has changed, the date-time stamps will not match, and the transaction will fail with a "not found" SQL code.

Locking And Distributed Databases

Whether the manager chooses to purchase an Application Programming Interface (API) or to create a custom API, it is very important to realize that the nature of the data access can tremendously impact the complexity of the processing. For read-only databases, API processing is relatively simple. However, processing problems increase exponentially for systems that require cohesive updating. In fact, it is impossible to implement any cohesive updating scheme with 100 percent reliability.

Distributed databases have an inherent updating problem that is common to all systems. This exposure occurs when a federated database attempts to simultaneously update two distributed databases. Commonly known as the *two-phase commit* (2PC), the procedure is illustrated in the following example:

```
APPLY UPDATE A
APPLY UPDATE B
IF A-OK And B-OK
    COMMIT A
            < ====   "Here is the deadly exposure"
    COMMIT B
  ELSE
    ROLLBACK A
    ROLLBACK B
```

As you can see, updates A and B get posted to the database. If the SQL code indicates that the transactions have completed successfully, the system will issue **COMMIT** statements to A and B. The point of exposure occurs when a failure happens after the **COMMIT** of A and before the **COMMIT** of B. Of course, the exposure can only happen when the failure occurs exactly between the commit of A and the commit of B. However, it is an exposure that has the potential to cause a major loss of integrity within the federation, and an exposure for which there is no automated recovery. The only remedy is to notify the DBA that the transaction has terminated, and manually roll back the updates to A and B. This type of corruption has a *very* small probability, and most databases do not worry about this exposure.

Understanding The Two-Phase Commit

Following the receipt of a message from each remote server stating that the transaction was successful, the initiating Oracle instance begins the two-phase commit. The commit itself consists of several steps: the prepare phase, the commit phase, and the forget phase.

To demonstrate, here is an SQL query that simultaneously updates all rows in a horizontally partitioned table residing in London and Paris. Assume that the SQL originates from a remote database in Denver, and that the Denver database will manage the two-phase commit:

```
UPDATE  employee@london,
        employee@paris
SET salary = salary * 1.1;
```

The initiating database in Denver is elected to manage the transaction, and will direct all stages of the two-phase commit. Most two-phase commit mechanisms have three phases:

1. Prepare phase—The prepare phase ensures that none of the remote databases will inadvertently issue a **COMMIT** or a **ROLLBACK** unless the initiating transaction directs the remote database to do so. In Oracle, the remote databases "promise" to allow the initiating request to govern the transaction at the remote database. The initiating request then converts its own locks to "in-doubt" locks that prevent either read or write operations against the data in question.

2. Commit phase—The initiating database commits and then instructs each remote database to commit. Each remote database then informs the initiating database that its commit transaction has been executed.

3. Forget phase—After all remote databases have committed, the initiating database "forgets" about the transaction, releasing all in-doubt locks. Each remote database then, in turn, releases its transaction locks.

Some of the more sophisticated databases allow the database administrator to manually recover any in-doubt transactions that remain after a failure in a distributed database network. For example, a common reason that distributed database transactions fail is from problems with the communications lines. These failures may cause an update against several remote databases to fail during any point of the prepare, commit, or forget phases. The database will detect the lost connection, and depending upon the state of the transaction, it will direct the online component to either **COMMIT** or **ROLLBACK** its part of the update. The remaining transaction piece, since it cannot be accessed due to the line failure, will be posted to an in-doubt system table. When the remote database returns online, the database will direct the failed node to either **COMMIT** or **ROLLBACK**. In the meantime, the DBA may wish to manually direct the operation of the in-doubt transactions.

Measuring Oracle Locks

While Oracle locking mechanisms appear to be very complex on the surface, some useful scripts are available that can be quickly run to identify lock resources. In Oracle, once a lock has been issued, only one of the following can be used to release the lock:

- Ask the **HOLDER** to commit or rollback.

- Kill the session which holds the lock.

- **ALTER SESSION KILL SESSION** sid, serial#.

- Use **KILL USER SESSION** menu found in the sqldba form.

- Kill the Unix shadow process, which is not recommended. When killing the Unix shadow process, please be careful of shared servers in a multithreaded environment.

- **ROLLBACK FORCE** or **COMMIT FORCE** if it is a two-phase commit transaction.

While many tools can be used to measure Oracle locks, Listing 5.2 will show all locking activity.

Listing 5.2   A locking script.

```
locks.sql - shows all locks in the database.
SET LINESIZE 132
SET PAGESIZE 60
COLUMN OBJECT HEADING 'Database|Object' FORMAT a15 truncate
COLUMN lock_type HEADING 'Lock|Type'    FORMAT a4 truncate
COLUMN mode_held HEADING 'Mode|Held'    FORMAT a15 truncate
```

```
COLUMN mode_requested HEADING 'Mode|Requested' FORMAT a15 truncate
COLUMN sid HEADING 'Session|ID'
COLUMN username HEADING 'Username'                FORMAT a20 truncate
COLUMN image HEADING 'Active Image'              FORMAT a20 truncate

SPOOL /tmp/locks
SELECT
        c.sid,
        substr(object_name,1,20) OBJECT,
        c.username,
        substr(c.program,length(c.program)-20,length(c.program)) image,
        DECODE(b.type,
                'MR', 'Media Recovery',
                'RT', 'Redo Thread',
                'UN', 'User Name',
                'TX', 'Transaction',
                'TM', 'DML',
                'UL', 'PL/SQL User Lock',
                'DX', 'Distributed Xaction',
                'CF', 'Control File',
                'IS', 'Instance State',
                'FS', 'File Set',
                'IR', 'Instance Recovery',
                'ST', 'Disk Space Transaction',
                'TS', 'Temp Segment',
                'IV', 'Library Cache Invalidation',
                'LS', 'Log Start or Switch',
                'RW', 'Row Wait',
                'SQ', 'Sequence Number',
                'TE', 'Extend Table',
                'TT', 'Temp Table',
                b.type) lock_type,
        DECODE(b.lmode,
                0, 'None',                /* Mon Lock equivalent */
                1, 'Null',                /* NOT */
                2, 'Row-SELECT (SS)',     /* LIKE */
                3, 'Row-X (SX)',          /* R */
                4, 'Share',               /* SELECT */
                5, 'SELECT/Row-X (SSX)',  /* C */
                6, 'Exclusive',           /* X */
                to_char(b.lmode)) mode_held,
        DECODE(b.request,
                0, 'None',                /* Mon Lock equivalent */
                1, 'Null',                /* NOT */
```

```
        2, 'Row-SELECT (SS)',      /* LIKE */
        3, 'Row-X (SX)',           /* R */
        4, 'Share',                /* SELECT */
        5, 'SELECT/Row-X (SSX)',   /* C */
        6, 'Exclusive',            /* X */
        to_char(b.request)) mode_requested
FROM sys.dba_objects a, sys.v_$lock b, sys.v_$session c WHERE
a.object_id = b.id1 AND b.sid = c.sid AND OWNER NOT IN ('SYS','SYSTEM');
```

Listing 5.3 shows the output of this script.

Listing 5.3 The output of the locking script.

```
Database        Lock          Mode   Mode                       Session          Active
Object          Type          Held   Requested                  ID    Username   Image
----------------------------------------------------------------------------------------
102 BANK        OPS$MCACIAT   @xdc (Pipe Two-Task DML Row-SELECT (SS)   None
57 INVOICE      OPS$DMAHTROB  @xdc (Pipe Two-Task DML Row-X     (SX)    None
57 LINE_ITEM    OPS$DMAHTROB  @xdc (Pipe Two-Task DML Row-X     (SX)    None
70 LINE_ITEM    OPS$JCONVICK  @xdc (Pipe Two-Task DML Row-X     (SX)    None
29 LINE_ITEM    OPS$NUMNUTS   @xdc (Pipe Two-Task DML Row-X     (SX)    None
70 LINE_ITEM    OPS$JKONV     @xdc (Pipe Two-Task DML Row-X     (SX)    None
57 LINE_ITEM    OPS$DMAHTROB  @xdc (Pipe Two-Task DML Row-X
```

You can also use Oracle Monitor within SQL*DBA to look at locks. Listings 5.4 and 5.5 show some sample screens.

Listing 5.4 SQL*DBA—monitor session.

Session ID	Serial Number	Process ID	Status	Username	Lock Waited	Current Statement
6	35	28	ACTIVE	BURLESON	C4D2B7A4	UPDATE
8	70	19	INACTIVE	TYTLER		SELECT
12	15	25	INACTIVE	JONES		INSERT
14	17	27	ACTIVE	PAPAJ	C3D2B638	DELETE
15	30	26	ACTIVE	ODELL		UNKNOWN

In Listing 5.4, the **Lock Waited** column is the one that tells us the address of the lock that is being waited for. In this example, we can see that Burleson and Gaston are waiting on a lock held by Tytler.

Listing 5.5   SQL*DBA—monitor lock.

Username	Session ID	Serial Number	Lock Type	Res ID 1	Res ID 2	Mode Held	Mode Requested
BURLESON	5	23	TM	23294	0	RX	NONE
BURLESON	5	23	TM	22295	0	RX	NONE
BURLESON	5	23	TX	266654	87	NONE	X
BURLESON	5	23	TX	3276482	97	X	NONE
TYTLER	14	13	TM	2211	0	RX	NONE
TYTLER	14	13	TM	2223	0	RX	NONE
TYTLER	14	13	TX	266654	87	X	NONE
GASTON	19	47	TM	2334	0	RX	NONE
GASTON	19	47	TM	2233	0	R	
GASTON	19	47	TX	266654	87	NONE	X
GASTON	19	47	TX	193446	87	X	NONE

Under the "type" column are four types of locks:

- *TX (Transaction)*—Decimal representation of rollback segment number "wrap" number (number and slot number times the rollback slot has been reused).

- *TM (Table Locks)*—Object ID of table being modified (always 0).

- *RW (Row Wait)*—Decimal representation of file number and decimal representation of row within block.

- *UL (User Defined Locks)*—Complete list is found in Chapter 10 of the Oracle7 Concepts Manual or in Appendix B-81 in the Oracle7 Admin Guide.

The users with an "X" in the **Mode Requested** column are waiting for a lock release. The following users are waiting for lock 266654:

BURLESON   5   23   TX   266654   87 NONE   X

GASTON   19   47   TX   266654   87 NONE   X

We can look for this lock ID, and see that the following resource is holding the lock:

TYTLER   14   13   TX   266654   87   X   NONE

Often, the user(s) may be modifying many tables within the same transaction. At times, this will make it difficult to find out which resource the "waiter" is contending from the "holder". This is easily resolved by looking at a combination of two monitors. **MONITOR SESSION** will tell you which user is waiting on a lock, and **MONITOR LOCK** will tell you the table that the user is currently trying to modify.

Identifying Conflicts

If you suspect a situation where one task is stopping another task from completing, Listing 5.6 shows a query you can run to find the objects that are involved in the locking conflict.

Listing 5.6   Finding the locking conflict.

```
waiters.sql - shows waiting tasks
COLUMN username        FORMAT a10
COLUMN lockwait        FORMAT a10
COLUMN sql_text        FORMAT a80
COLUMN object_owner    FORMAT a14
COLUMN object          FORMAT a15

SELECT   b.username username,
         c.sid sid,
         c.owner object_owner,
         c.object object,
         b.lockwait,
         a.sql_text SQL
FROM v$sqltext a, v$session b, v$access c
WHERE
     a.address=b.sql_address
     AND
     a.hash_value=b.sql_hash_value
     AND
     b.sid = c.sid
     AND
     c.owner != 'SYS';
```

Listing 5.7 shows the sample output.

Listing 5.7   The query's output.

```
USERNAME SID OBJECT_OWNER OBJECT      LOCKWAIT SQL
-------- --  ------------ ------      ------------------------------------
BURLESON 36  EMP EMPLOYEE C4D450F9    update employee set status = 'Fired'
                                      where emp_nbr=16152


PAPAJ    15  EMP EMPLOYEE C3D320C8    delete from employee where
                                      emp_nbr=16152
```

```
TYTLER    11  EMP EMPLOYEE D3D4F9E0   update employee set salary =
                                      salary*.01 lock table customer in
                                      exclusive mode
```

Here we see a situation where Burleson and Papaj are waiting for Tytler's update on the employee table to complete.

Using catblock.sql And utllockt.sql

Several locks scripts within $ORACLE_HOME/rdbms/admin can be used to see locks. To install the scripts, first enter SQL*DBA and then run catblock.sql followed by utllockt.sql.

catblock.sql creates the following views:

- **dba_waiters**
- **dba_blockers**
- **dba_dml_locks**
- **dba_ddl_locks**
- **dba_locks**

Listing 5.8 can be used whenever you suspect that locks are impeding performance. This script interrogates all of the views that were created in catblock.sql:

Listing 5.8　alllocks.sql.

```
REM alllocks.sql - shows all locks in the database.
REM written by Don Burleson

SET linesize 132
SET pagesize 60

SPOOL /tmp/alllocks

COLUMN owner          FORMAT a10;
COLUMN name           FORMAT a15;
COLUMN mode_held      FORMAT a10;
COLUMN mode_requested FORMAT a10;
COLUMN type           FORMAT a15;
```

```
COLUMN lock_id1        FORMAT a10;
COLUMN lock_id2        FORMAT a10;

PROMPT Note that $ORACLE_HOME/rdbma/admin/catblock.sql
PROMPT must be run before this script functions . . .

PROMPT Querying dba_waiters . . .
SELECT
 waiting_session,
 holding_session,
 lock_type,
 mode_held,
 mode_requested,
 lock_id1,
 lock_id2
FROM sys.dba_waiters;

PROMPT Querying dba_blockers . . .
SELECT
 holding_session
FROM sys.dba_blockers;

PROMPT Querying dba_dml_locks . . .
SELECT
 session_id,
 owner,
 name,
 mode_held,
 mode_requested
FROM sys.dba_dml_locks;

PROMPT Querying dba_ddl_locks . . .
SELECT
 session_id,
 owner,
 name,
 type,
 mode_held,
 mode_requested
FROM sys.dba_ddl_locks;


PROMPT Querying dba_locks . . .
SELECT
```

```
 session_id,
 lock_type,
 mode_held,
 mode_requested,
 lock_id1,
 lock_id2
FROM sys.dba_locks;
```

Listing 5.9 shows the output.

Listing 5.9   The output of alllocks.sql.

```
SQL> @alllocks
Note that $ORACLE_HOME/rdbma/admin/catblock.sql
must be run before this script functions . . .
Querying dba_waiters . . .

no rows selected

Querying dba_blockers . . .

no rows selected

Querying dba_dml_locks . . .

SESSION_ID OWNER       NAME           MODE_HELD  MODE_REQUE
---------- ----------  -------------- ---------- ----------
        19 RPT         RPT_EXCEPTIONS Row-X (SX) None

Querying dba_ddl_locks . . .

SESSION                                        MODE_    MODE_
   _ID  OWNER  NAME            TYPE            HELD     REQUE
-------  -----  --------------- -------------------- --------  -------
    13  RPT    SHP_PRE_INS_UPD Table/Procedure      Null     None
               _PROC
    13  SYS    STANDARD        Body                 Null     None
    14  SYS    STANDARD        Body                 Null     None
    13  SYS    DBMS_STANDARD   Table/Procedure      Null     None
    14  SYS    DBMS_STANDARD   Table/Procedure      Null     None
    13  SYS    DBMS_STANDARD   Body                 Null     None
    14  SYS    DBMS_STANDARD   Body                 Null     None
    13  SYS    STANDARD        Table/Procedure      Null     None
    14  SYS    STANDARD        Table/Procedure      Null     None

9 rows selected.
```

```
Querying dba_locks . . .

SESSION_ID LOCK_TYPE          MODE_HELD  MODE_REQUE LOCK_ID1   LOCK_ID2
---------- ----------------   ---------  ---------- ---------- ---------
         2 Media Recovery     Share      None       32         0
         2 Media Recovery     Share      None       31         0
         2 Media Recovery     Share      None       30         0
         2 Media Recovery     Share      None       29         0
         2 Media Recovery     Share      None       28         0
         2 Media Recovery     Share      None       27         0
         2 Media Recovery     Share      None       26         0
         2 Media Recovery     Share      None       25         0
         2 Media Recovery     Share      None       24         0
         2 Media Recovery     Share      None       23         0
         2 Media Recovery     Share      None       22         0
         2 Media Recovery     Share      None       21         0
         2 Media Recovery     Share      None       20         0
         2 Media Recovery     Share      None       19         0
         2 Media Recovery     Share      None       18         0
         2 Media Recovery     Share      None       17         0
         2 Media Recovery     Share      None       16         0
         2 Media Recovery     Share      None       15         0
         2 Media Recovery     Share      None       14         0
         2 Media Recovery     Share      None       13         0
         2 Media Recovery     Share      None       12         0
         2 Media Recovery     Share      None       11         0
         2 Media Recovery     Share      None       10         0
         2 Media Recovery     Share      None       9          0
         2 Media Recovery     Share      None       8          0
         2 Media Recovery     Share      None       7          0
         2 Media Recovery     Share      None       6          0
         2 Media Recovery     Share      None       5          0
         2 Media Recovery     Share      None       4          0
         2 Media Recovery     Share      None       3          0
         2 Media Recovery     Share      None       2          0
         2 Media Recovery     Share      None       1          0
         3 Redo Thread        Exclusive  None       1          0
        14 PS                 Null       None       0          0
        14 PS                 Null       None       0          1
        19 DML                Row-X (SX) None       1457       0

36 rows selected.
```

The utilockt.sql script creates a view called **lock_holders** that can then be queried to see the locked sessions. Beware, however—this view creates a temporary table and can run slowly. Listing 5.10 is an example query.

Listing 5.10   waitsess.sql displays waiting session information.

```
COLUMN waiting_session FORMAT a8

SELECT lpad(' ',3*(level-1)) || waiting_session waiting_session,
   lock_type,
   mode_requested,
   mode_held,
   lock_id1,
   lock_id2
FROM lock_holders
CONNECT BY  PRIOR waiting_session = holding_session
START WITH holding_session IS NULL;
```

Listing 5.11 shows the output.

Listing 5.11 Sample output.

```
WAITING_ LOCK_TYPE       MODE_REQUE MODE_HELD  LOCK_ID1   LOCK_ID2
-------- --------------- ---------- ---------- ---------- ----------
    34   None
    65   Transaction     Exclusive  Exclusive  662534     11291
    44   Transaction     Exclusive  Exclusive  662534     11291
```

Here, we can quickly see that sessions 65 and 44 are waiting on session 34 to complete and release its locks.

Summary

Concurrency control has become a pressing issue because of the increasing popularity of the client/server system. As client/server matures, we will begin to see concurrency methods that can automatically manage updates to distributed databases. In the meantime, the developer must decide which of the updated control mechanisms is best suited to the operation of their distributed database.

It's time now to look at tuning the client side of the application and see just how a distributed server environment will impact performance.

6

Oracle DBA Performance And Tuning

Aside from the basic features for applications programmers, the Oracle database administrator can benefit immensely benefit from an understanding of the Oracle performance features. These features can be especially useful for routine database administration tasks, such as exports/imports, index creation, and table replication. Topics will include:

- Unrecoverable option

- Read-only tablespaces

- Implementing parallelism

- init.ora parameters

Using The Unrecoverable Option

At specific times, Oracle allows its internal transaction logging mechanism to be turned off. With Oracle, the software maintains a read-consistent image of the data for long-running queries, while at the same time providing rollback capability for each update transaction. Of course, this level of recoverability carries a price tag, and significant performance improvements can be achieved with the prudent use of the "unrecoverable" option. In practice, use of the unrecoverable clause will improve response time from 40 to 60 percent. Care needs to be taken, of course, to synchronize the use of the *unrecoverable* clause with the traditional procedures used when taking backups of the archived redo logs.

Unrecoverable can be used for any of the following operations:

- **Create table . . . as select . . . unrecoverable**—This type of operation is generally performed when a table is "cloned" or replicated from a master table, usually with a subset of columns and rows. For example, we would use this command to create a subset of a customer table, containing only those customers in a specific region. Of course, a failure during the creation of the table would leave a half-built table in the destination tablespace, and the table would need to be manually dropped.

- **Create index . . . unrecoverable**—This is the most common use of the unrecoverable clause, and certainly the one that makes the most sense from an Oracle perspective. Regardless of any transaction failures, an index can always be re-created by dropping and redefining the index, so having an incomplete or corrupt index would never be a problem.

- **Alter table . . . add constraint . . . unrecoverable**—As we know, when a referential integrity constraint is added to a table, the Oracle software will sometimes create an index to enforce the constraint. Primary key, foreign key, and unique constraints may cause Oracle to create an index, that is built in unrecoverable mode.

- **SQL*Loader**—SQL*Loader is generally used when initially populating Oracle tables from external flat files. For very large numbers of inserts, it is best to leave the default. We already know that in the unlikely event of an abnormal termination, the incomplete tables must be dropped and SQL*Loader run again.

Using Read-Only Tablespaces

In a busy environment where many different applications require access to a tablespace, it is sometimes desirable to use the read-only tablespace feature of Oracle 7.3. With read-only tablespaces, separate instances can be mapped to the same tablespaces, each accessing the tablespace in

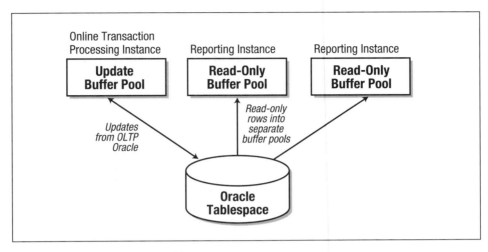

Figure 6.1   Oracle read-only tablespaces.

read-only mode. Of course, sharing a tablespace across Oracle instances increases the risk that I/O against the shared tablespaces may become excessive. As we can see in Figure 6.1, a read-only tablespace does not have the same overhead as an updatable tablespace.

This approach has several advantages:

- *Buffer pool isolation*—The foremost advantage is the isolation of the buffer pools for each instance that is accessing the tablespace. If user A on instance A flushes his buffer by doing a full-table scan, user B on instance B will still have the blocks needed in memory.

- *Easy sharing of table data*—Read-only tablespaces offer an alternative to table replication and the update problems associated with replicated tables. Since a read-only tablespace may only be defined as updatable by one instance, updates are controlled at the system level.

Determining Where To Place Indexes

One of the primary responsibilities of the Oracle DBA is ensuring that Oracle indexes are present when they are needed to avoid full-table scans. In order to achieve this goal, the Oracle DBA needs to understand the types of indexes that Oracle provides as well as the proper time to create a table index.

Unfortunately, the Oracle dictionary does not gather statistics about how many times an index is used, so the DBA must rely upon the application developers to provide guidance regarding index placement. As Oracle moves toward Oracle8, this reliance may change, since most of the SQL will be stored within the Oracle dictionary, where the DBA can analyze the explain plan output. However, until that time, the best that an Oracle DBA can hope for is to keep the existing indexes clean and functioning optimally.

Listing 6.1 is a script that can be run to view SQL that has been loaded into the SGA shared pool.

Listing 6.1   The sqltext.sql shows all SQL in the SGA shared pool.

```
REM Written by Don Burleson

SET PAGESIZE 9999;
SET LINESIZE 79;
SET NEWPAGE 0;
SET VERIFY OFF;

BREAK ON ADDRESS SKIP 2;

COLUMN ADDRESS FORMAT 9;

SELECT
        ADDRESS,
        sql_text
FROM
        v$sqltext
ORDER BY
ADDRESS, PIECE;
```

Listing 6.2 shows the output from sqltext.sql.

Listing 6.2   The output for sqltext.sql.

```
D09AFC4C    SELECT DECODE(object_type, 'TABLE', 2,  'VIEW', 2, 'PACKAGE',
            3, 'PACKAGE BODY', 3, 'PROCEDURE', 4, 'FUNCTION', 5, 0) from
            all_objects where object_name = upper('V_$SQLTEXT')  and
            object_type in ('TABLE', 'VIEW', 'PACKAGE', 'PACKAGE BODY',
            'PROCEDURE', 'FUNCTION') AND owner = upper('SYS')
```

```
D09B653C    SELECT OWNER, table_name, table_owner, db_link FROM
            all_synonyms where synonym_name = upper('V_$SQLTEXT') AND
            owner = upper('SYS')


D09BC5AC    SELECT OWNER, table_name, table_owner, db_link from
            all_synonyms where synonym_name = upper('v$sqltext') AND
            (owner = 'PUBLIC' or owner = USER)


D09C2D58    SELECT DECODE(object_type, 'TABLE', 2,  'VIEW', 2, 'PACKAGE',
            3,'PACKAGE BODY', 3, 'PROCEDURE', 4, 'FUNCTION', 5,  0)
            from user_objects where object_name = upper('v$sqltext')
            AND  object_type in ('TABLE', 'VIEW', 'PACKAGE', 'PACKAGE
            BODY',  'PROCEDURE', 'FUNCTION')

D09CFF4C    UPDATE SHPMT SET
            amt_sum_ili=:b1,pmt_wght_sum_ili=:b2,cust_pmt_wght_sum_ili=
            :b3 WHERE shpmt_id = :b4  AND shpmt_sys_src_cd = :b5
```

Of course, this script could be extended to feed the SQL statements into Oracle's explain plan utility, where long-table full-table scans could be detected and indexes created for these queries.

 Oracle's bstat/estat utility also provides information on the number of full-table scans incurred by the database as a whole. Please see Chapter 11 for more information.

Part of the job of the Oracle DBA is to detect badly out-of-balance indexes and schedule their reconstruction. Unfortunately, very dynamic tables (i.e., those with high **INSERT** and **UPDATE** activity) may always have some issues with out-of-balance indexes. As Oracle indexes grow, two things happen. The first is called a split, where a new node is created at the same index level as the existing node. As each level becomes full, the index may spawn, or create a new level to accommodate the new rows.

There are six Oracle dictionary values that are used to describe indexes:

- **BLEVEL**—This is the number of levels that the index has spawned. Even for very large indexes, there should never be more than four levels. Each **BLEVEL** represents an additional I/O that must be performed against the index tree.

- **LEAF_BLOCKS**—This is a reference to the total number of leaf blocks.

- **DISTINCT_KEYS**—This is a reference to the cardinality of the index. If this value is less than 10, you may want to consider redefining the index as a bitmapped index.

- **AVG_DATA_BLOCKS_PER_KEY**—This is a measure of the size of the index and the cardinality of the index. A low cardinality index (e.g., sex or region) will have high values, as will very large indexes.

- **CLUSTERING_FACTOR**—This is the most important measure in this report, since it measures how balanced the index is. If the clustering factor is greater than the number of blocks in the index, then the index has become out of balance due to a large volume of insert or delete operations. If the clustering factor is more than 50 percent of the number of rows in the table that it is indexing, you may want to consider dropping and re-creating the index.

- **AVG_LEAF_BLOCKS_PER_KEY**—This is always one, with the exception of non-unique indexes.

Now that we understand the basic constructs of indexes, let's look at a dictionary query (Listing 6.3) that will tell us the structure of our indexes. Note that this query assumes that your Oracle database is using the cost-based optimizer, and that your tables have been analyzed with the **ANALYZE TABLE** command.

Listing 6.3   index.sql shows the details for indexes.

```
SET PAGESIZE 999;
SET LINESIZE 100;

COLUMN c1 HEADING 'Index'      FORMAT a19;
COLUMN c3 HEADING 'S'          FORMAT a1;
COLUMN c4 HEADING 'Level'      FORMAT 999;
COLUMN c5 HEADING 'leaf blks'  FORMAT 999,999;
COLUMN c6 HEADING 'dist. Keys' FORMAT 99,999,999;
COLUMN c7 HEADING 'Bks/Key'    FORMAT 99,999;
COLUMN c8 HEADING 'Clust Ftr'  FORMAT 9,999,999;
COLUMN c9 HEADING 'Lf/Key'     FORMAT 99,999;
```

```
SPOOL index.lst;

SELECT
  owner||'.'||index_name       c1,
  substr(status,1,1)           c3,
  blevel                       c4,
  leaf_blocks                  c5,
  distinct_keys                c6,
  avg_data_blocks_per_key      c7,
  clustering_factor            c8,
  avg_leaf_blocks_per_key      c9
FROM dba_indexes
WHERE
OWNER NOT IN ('SYS','SYSTEM')
ORDER BY blevel desc, leaf_blocks desc;

SPOOL OFF;
```

Listing 6.4 shows the output of index.sql.

Listing 6.4   The output of index.sql.

Index	S	Level	Leaf Blks	dist. Keys	Bks/ Key	Clust Ftr	Lf/ Key
-------------------	-	-----	------	----------	------	--------	-----
RPT.LOB_SHPMT_PK	V	2	25,816	3,511,938	1	455,343	1
RPT.SHP_EK_CUST_INV	V	2	23,977	2,544,132	1	1,764,915	1
RPT.SHP_FK_GLO_DEST	V	2	23,944	22,186	112	2,493,095	1
RPT.LSH_FK_SHP	V	2	22,650	1,661,576	1	339,031	1
RPT.SHP_FK_ORL_ORIG	V	2	21,449	404	806	325,675	53
RPT.LSA_FK_LSH	V	2	21,181	2,347,812	1	996,641	1
RPT.LSH_FK_LOB	V	2	19,989	187	4,796	896,870	106
RPT.SHPMT_PK	V	2	19,716	3,098,063	1	1,674,264	1
RPT.SHP_FK_CAR	V	2	18,513	689	390	268,859	26
RPT.SHP_EK_ROLE_TY_	V	2	17,847	10	24,613	246,134	1,784

RPT.SHP_FK_SPT	V	2	16,442	4	46,872	187,489	4,110
RPT.INV_EK_INV_NUM	V	2	16,407	2,014,268	1	518,206	1
RPT.SHP_FK_ORL_DEST	V	2	15,863	385	692	266,656	41
RPT.SHP_FK_SRC	V	2	15,827	10	17,469	174,694	1,582
RPT.INV_LINE_ITEM_P	V	2	14,731	2,362,216	1	102,226	1

Here we see that we have no indexes that are more than two levels deep. Note also that we have two indexes with a clustering factor of more than 1 million. Should either of these tables have less than 3 million rows (clustering factor greater than 50 percent of rows), we will want to schedule a time to drop and re-create the index.

Bitmapped Indexes

Prior to release 7.3 of Oracle, it was never recommended that the DBA create an index on any fields that were not "selective" and had less than 50 unique values. Imagine, for example, how a traditional B-tree index would appear if a column such as **REGION** were indexed. With only four distinct values in the index, the SQL optimizer would rarely determine that an index scan would speed up a query; consequently, the index would never be accessed. Of course, the only alternative would be to invoke a costly full-table scan of the table. Today, we are able to use bitmapped indexes for low cardinality indexes.

It is interesting to note that bitmapped indexes have been used in commercial databases since Model 204 was introduced in the late 1960s. However, their usefulness had been ignored until the data warehouse explosion of 1994 made it evident that a new approach to indexing was needed to resolve complex queries against very large tables.

Bitmapped indexes are a new feature of Oracle 7.3 that allow for very fast boolean operations against low cardinality indexes. Complex **AND** and **OR** logic is performed entirely within the index—the base table need never be accessed. Without a bitmapped index, some decision support queries would be impossible to service without a full-table scan.

Bitmaps are especially important for data warehouse/decision support systems, where ad-hoc, unanticipated queries make it impractical for the Oracle DBA to index on all possible combinations of columns. Assume that a manager wants to know the average income for all college-educated customers who drive red or blue cars in Wyoming or Nevada. Furthermore, assume that there are 1 million rows in the customer table. The following query would be very hard to service using traditional indexing:

```
SELECT avg(yearly_income)
FROM CUSTOMER
WHERE
    education IN ('B','M','D')
AND
    car_color IN ('RED','BLUE')
AND
    state_residence IN ('WY','NV')
ORDER BY AVG(yearly_income);
```

In a bitmapped index, it is not necessary to read all 1 million rows in the customer table. Instead, the query manager will build row ID lists for all "1" values for **education**, **car_color**, and **state_residence**, and then match up the row IDs for those that appear in all three columns. When the query is ready to access the rows, it already has a list of row IDs for all rows that meet the selection criteria.

To understand bitmapped indexes, imagine a very wide, fat table with only a few rows. In a bitmapped index, each unique value has one row, such that our **REGION** index contains only four rows. Across the bitmap, each row in the base table is represented by a column, with a "1" in the bitmap array if the value is true, and a "0" if it is false. Because of the high amount of repeating ones and zeros, bitmapped indexes can be very effectively compressed and expanded at runtime. In fact, the lower the cardinality, the better the compression, such that we can expect a higher compression of a **GENDER** index with two distinct values than with a **STATE** index with 50 distinct values. Uncompressed, the **STATE** index would be 48 times larger than the **GENDER** bitmap, because one row in the bitmap array is required for each unique value.

Oracle bitmapped indexes can consume far less space than a traditional B-tree Oracle index. In fact, their size can easily be computed as follows:

bitmap size = (**cardinality_of_column** * **rows_in_table**)/8

For example, suppose that the **REGION** index would have four distinct values with 800,000 rows. The entire index would only consume 100,000 bytes uncompressed—and with Oracle's compression, this index would be far smaller than 100,000 bytes. In fact, it could probably be read entirely into the Oracle buffer with a few I/Os.

As we can see from the diagram in Figure 6.2, Oracle bitmapped indexes can dramatically reduce I/O for certain types of operations. For example, assume that we are interested in knowing the number of corporations in the western region. Because all of this information is contained entirely within the bitmapped indexes, we have no need to access the table. In other words, the query can be resolved entirely within the index.

How do we identify candidates for bitmapped indexes? Your existing data-base is the starting place. Listing 6.5 will check all of your B-tree indexes and provide you with a list of candidates in ascending order of cardinality.

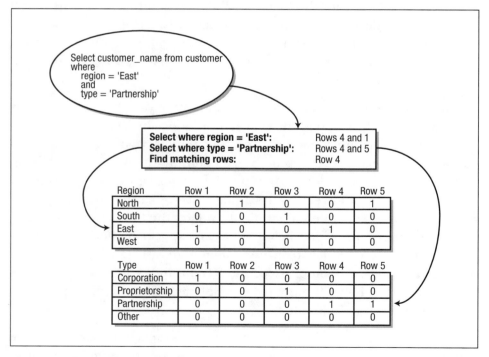

Figure 6.2　Oracle bitmapped indexes.

Listing 6.5   bitmap.sql identifies low cardinality indexes for bitmapped indexes.

```
REM  Written by Don Burleson

PROMPT Be patient. This can take awhile . . .

SET PAUSE OFF;
SET ECHO OFF;
SET TERMOUT OFF;
SET LINESIZE 300;
SET PAGESIZE 999;
SET NEWPAGE 0;
SET FEEDBACK OFF;
SET HEADING OFF;
SET VERIFY OFF;

REM  First create the syntax to determine the cardinality . . .


SPOOL idx1.sql;

SELECT 'set termout off;' FROM DUAL;
SELECT 'spool idx2.lst;' FROM DUAL;
SELECT 'column card format 9,999,999;' FROM DUAL;

SELECT 'select distinct count(distinct '
      ||a.column_name
      ||') card, '
      ||'''' is the cardinality of '
      ||'Index '
      ||a.index_name
      ||' on column '
      ||a.column_name
      ||' of table '
      ||a.table_owner
      ||'.'
      ||a.table_name
      ||'''' from '
      ||index_owner||'.'||a.table_name
      ||';'
 FROM dba_ind_columns a, dba_indexes b
 WHERE
  a.index_name = b.index_name
AND
```

```
  tablespace_name NOT IN ('SYS','SYSTEM')
;

SELECT 'spool off;' from dual;
SPOOL OFF;

SET TERMOUT ON;


@idx1

!SORT idx2.lst
```

Listing 6.6 shows the listing from bitmap.sql.

Listing 6.6   The results of bitmap.sql.

```
    3  is the cardinality of Index GEO_LOC_PK on column GEO_LOC_TY_CD of
       table RPT.GEM_LCC
    4  is the cardinality of Index REGION_IDX on column REHION of table
       RPT.CUSTOMER
    7  is the cardinality of Index GM_LCK on column GEO_LC_TCD of table
       RPT.GEM_LCC
    8  is the cardinality of Index USR_IDX on column USR_CD of table
       RPT.CUSTOMER
   50  is the cardinality of Index STATE_IDX on column STATE_ABBR of
       table RPT.CUSTOMER
 3117  is the cardinality of Index ZIP_IDX on column ZIP_CD of table
       RPT.GEM_LCC
71,513 is the cardinality of Index GEO_LOC_PK on column GEO_LOC_CD of
       table RPT.GEM_LCC
83,459 is the cardinality of Index GEO_KEY_PK on column GEO_LOC_TY_CD of
       table RPT.GEM_LCC
```

Of course, columns such as **GENDER** and **REGION** should be made into bitmaps—but what about **STATE** with 50 values, or **area_code** with a few hundred values? Intuition tells us that the benefits from bitmapped indexes are a function of the cardinality and the number of rows in the table, but no hard and fast rule exists for identifying what type of index is always best. An heuristic approach is called for, and it is relatively easy for the DBA to create a B-tree index, run a timed query, re-create the index with the **BITMAP** option, and re-execute the timed query.

Regardless, bitmapped indexes are critical to the performance of decision support system, especially those that are queried in an ad hoc fashion against hundreds of column values. See Chapter 10, Tuning Oracle Data Warehouse And OLAP Applications, for a discussion of the applications of bitmapped indexes.

Summary

While this chapter has been devoted to the obvious DBA issues relating to performance and tuning, it is imperative that the Oracle DBA become intimate with all of the various areas of Oracle tuning. The DBA, more than any other participant in the development of the system, has the ability to influence the system's overall performance.

Performance And Tuning For Distributed Oracle Databases

Performance and tuning of Oracle systems is anything but trivial with distributed database environments, since so many components within the database software contribute to the overall performance. The number of concurrent users, the availability of space within the buffer and lock pools, and the balancing of application access can all affect database performance. This chapter will review the following topics:

- The role of data replication—Oracle snapshots

- Replication with Oracle snapshots

- Asynchronous replication techniques

- Using Oracle's parallel facilities

- Planning for growth

- Designing expert systems for distributed database performance and tuning

- Disk I/O issues with distributed databases

When a client/server application must access several remote databases in a single transaction, another dimension of complexity is added to the system. The database administrator (DBA) must look at more than each individual database, and must consider transactions that span different servers. While accessing several servers in a distributed transaction may seem trivial, performance problems can be introduced by PC hardware, LAN and network bottlenecks, router overloads, and a plethora of other sources. Only by examining the relevant components of distributed databases can we gain a broad understanding of the issues.

Replication With Oracle Snapshots

Oracle snapshots are used to create read-only copies of tables in other Oracle databases. This is a highly effective way to avoid expensive cross-database joins of tables. As we know, an SQL join with a table at a remote server will be far slower than a join with a local table: SQL*Net overhead increases as it retrieves and transfers the data across the network.

It is interesting to note that the general attitude about data replication has shifted dramatically in the past 10 years. In the 1980s, replication was frowned upon. Database designers believed that there was no substitute for the Third Normal Form database. Today, the practical realities of distributed processing have made replication a cheap and viable alternative to expensive cross-database joins.

Table replication is so stable and has been so successful within Oracle version 7 that Oracle is now introducing the concept of updatable snapshots with Oracle version 7.3. However, replication is not to be used indiscriminately, and guidelines exist for using replicated tables to the best advantage:

- *The replicated table is read-only*—Obviously, a table snapshot cannot be updated since the master copy of the table is on another server.

- *The replicated table is relatively small*—Ideally, a replicated table is small enough that the table can be dropped and re-created each night, or the **REFRESH COMPLETE** option can be used. Of course, large tables can be replicated with the **REFRESH FAST** option, but this involves a complicated mechanism for holding table changes and propagating them to the replicated table.

- *The replicated table is frequently used*—It does not make sense to replicate a table if it is only referenced a few times per day, and the cost of the replication would outweigh the cost of the cross-database join.

Despite any claims by Oracle to the contrary, snapshots are not to be used indiscriminately. Only those tables that meet the above criteria should be placed in snapshots. In practice, snapshots are not maintenance-free, and many points of failure are possible—especially if the snapshot is created with the **REFRESH FAST** option. Problems can occur writing to the **snapshot_log** table, and SQL*Net errors can cause failures of updates to transfer to the replicated tables.

How Oracle Snapshots Work

A snapshot is created on the destination system with the **CREATE SNAPSHOT** command, and the remote table is immediately defined and populated from the master table.

After creation, a snapshot may be refreshed periodically. There are two types of refreshing: *complete* and *fast*. A complete refresh can be done in several ways, but most savvy Oracle developers drop and re-create the snapshots with a Unix cron job to achieve full refreshes, especially if the table is small and easily re-created. Optionally, tables can be refreshed with only the changes that are made to the master table. This requires additional work on the slave database to create an Oracle refresh process (in the init.ora), and the definition of a snapshot log on the master database (Figure 7.1).

Several steps need to be completed before your Oracle system is ready to use snapshots. First you need to run catsnap.sql, which can be found in your $ORACLE_HOME/rdbms/admin directory. This script will populate the Oracle dictionary with the necessary system tables to manage the snapshots. You'll also need to run dbmssnap.sql, which can be found in the $ORACLE_HOME/rdbms/admin directory. This script creates the stored procedures that can be used to manipulate the snapshots.

The following parameters must also be added to the init.ora file:

- **snapshot_refresh_interval=60**—This sets the interval (in minutes) for the refresh process to wake up.

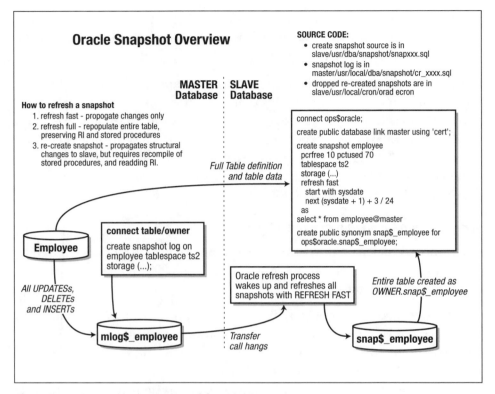

Figure 7.1　A high-level overview of Oracle snapshots.

- **snapshot_refresh_processes=1**—This is the number of refresh processes on the instance (minimum is 1).

- **snapshot_refresh_keep_connections=false**—This specifies whether the database should keep remote connections after refreshing the tables. Always use **FALSE**.

For snapshots that are small enough to be totally repopulated, the following steps are necessary. Note that it is possible to do a **REFRESH COMPLETE** or a **REFRESH FORCE** rather than a cron job, but using a cron is a simple way to guarantee that the replicated table will be fully repopulated. To avoid the **REFRESH FAST** option with a Unix cron, the following two steps are required:

1. Create the snapshot with the **REFRESH COMPLETE** option.

2. Alter **oracle.cron** to drop and re-create the snapshot.

For snapshots on large tables, you may want to use the **REFRESH FAST** option. For **REFRESH FAST**, the following steps are required:

1. **DESTINATION SYSTEM**—Create the snapshot with the **REFRESH FAST** option signed on as user SYS. (Be sure to define a database link with "**CONNECT TO XXX IDENTIFIED BY ZZZ**" and ensure that user XXX has "select" privileges against the master table.)

2. **MASTER SYSTEM**—Create a snapshot log on each master table.

3. Bounce the **DESTINATION SYSTEM** to begin the refreshes based on the interval specified in the **CREATE SNAPSHOT**.

Listing 7.1 shows an example of a snapshot that reads a table from an instance called **london**.

Listing 7.1   The london snapshot.

```
CONNECT sys/xxxx;
DROP PUBLIC DATABASE LINK london;
CREATE PUBLIC DATABASE LINK london
CONNECT TO db_link IDENTIFIED BY db_pass USING 'london';
- - - - - - - - - - - - - - - - - - - - - - - - - - - - - - - - - - - - - - - -
DROP SNAPSHOT my_replicated_table;
- - - - - - - - - - - - - - - - - - - - - - - - - - - - - - - - - - - - - - - -
CREATE SNAPSHOT my_replicated_table
      PCTFREE 10 PCTUSED 40
      TABLESPACE ts2
      STORAGE (initial 60k next 10k pctincrease 1)
      REFRESH FAST
            START WITH SYSDATE
            NEXT (sysdate+1) + 3/24
      AS SELECT * FROM ORACLE. my_master_table@london;

GRANT ALL ON my_replicated_table  TO PUBLIC;
*****************************************************
   Add the appropriate synonyms for the snapshots...
*****************************************************
CONNECT /;
CREATE PUBLIC SYNONYM snap$_my_replicated_table      FOR
ops$oracle.snap$_my_replicated_table;
```

Here we see that the **my_replicated_table** table is refreshed each morning at 3:00 AM, and the read-only name **snap$_my_replicated_table** has been replaced with synonym **my_replicated_table**. Here is an example of the snapshot log syntax that needs to be run on the master database:

```
CREATE SNAPSHOT LOG ON customer_table
TABLESPACE ts2
STORAGE (initial 20k next 20k);
```

The **dbms_snapshot.refresh_all** procedure can be run at any time on the destination system to refresh the snapshot tables. To force a refresh of an individual table, execute the following:

```
EXECUTE dbms_snapshot.refresh('office','f');
```

 Any refresh errors are written to the alert.log file.

The snapshot log is a table that resides in the same database as the master table, which can be seen in the **dba_tables** view as a table with the name **MLOG$_tablename**. In our example, the snapshot log would be called **MLOG$_customer**.

REAL-WORLD TIPS AND TECHNIQUES FOR ORACLE SNAPSHOTS

Even with Oracle's distributed features, it is still far faster to process a table on a local host than it is to process a remote table across SQL*Net's distributed communication lines. As such, table replication is a very desirable technique for improving processing speeds.

Several factors influence the decision about replicating tables. The foremost considerations are the size of the replicated table and the volatility of the tables. Large, highly active tables with many updates, deletes, and inserts will require a lot of system resources to replicate and keep synchronized with the master table. Smaller, less active tables would be ideal candidates for replication, since the creation and maintenance of the replicated table would not consume a high amount of system resources.

Oracle's snapshot facility is relatively mature and generally works as noted in the Oracle documentation. However, the flexibility of the snapshot tool gives the developer many choices in how the snapshot will be created and refreshed. We can refresh the replicated table in full, we can re-create the snapshot at will, we can choose periodic refreshes of the snapshot, and we can use database triggers to propagate changes from a master table to the snapshot table. Although the choice of techniques depends upon the individual application, some general rules apply.

If a replicated table is small and relatively static, it is usually easier to drop and re-create the snapshot than to use Oracle's **REFRESH COMPLETE** option. A crontab file can be set up to invoke the drop and re-creation at a predetermined time each day, completely refreshing the entire table.

Another popular alternative to the snapshot is using Oracle's distributed SQL to create a replicated table directly on the slave database. In the following example, the New York database creates a local table called **emp_ny,** which contains New York employee information from the master employee table at corporate headquarters:

```
CREATE TABLE emp_ny
AS
    SELECT
            emp_nbr,
            emp_name,
            emp_phone,
            emp_hire_date
    FROM emp@hq WHERE department = 'NY';
```

Very large replicated tables consume too much time in dropping and re-creating the snapshot or using the **REFRESH COMPLETE** option. For static tables, a snapshot log would not contain very many changes—we could direct Oracle to propagate the changes to the replicated table at frequent intervals. Let's take a look at the different refresh intervals that can be specified for a snapshot:

```
CREATE SNAPSHOT cust_snap1
REFRESH FAST
    START WITH SYSDATE
    NEXT SYSDATE+7
AS SELECT cust_nbr, cust_name FROM customer@hq WHERE department = 'NY';
```

Here we are saying that we want Oracle to take the snapshot log and apply it to the replicated table every seven days.

The next example shows a table that is refreshed each Tuesday at 6:00 AM:

```
CREATE SNAPSHOT cust_snap1
REFRESH FAST
    START WITH SYSDATE
    NEXT NEXT_DAY(trunc(sysdate),'TUESDAY')+6/24
AS SELECT cust_nbr, cust_name FROM customer@hq WHERE department = 'NY';
```

For very static tables, we can also specify refreshes to run quarterly. The example below refreshes a table completely on the first Tuesday of each quarter:

```
CREATE SNAPSHOT cust_snap1
REFRESH COMPLETE
    START WITH SYSDATE
    NEXT NEXT_DAY(ADD_MONTHS(trunc(sysdate,'Q'),3),'TUESDAY')
AS SELECT cust_nbr, cust_name FROM customer@hq WHERE department = 'NY';
```

For dynamic tables that require refreshing daily, we can specify that the table is refreshed at 11:00 AM each day:

```
CREATE SNAPSHOT cust_snap1
REFRESH FAST
    START WITH SYSDATE
    NEXT SYSDATE+11/24
AS SELECT cust_nbr, cust_name FROM customer@hq WHERE department = 'NY';
```

In addition to using the time range specified in the **CREATE SNAPSHOT** syntax, you can also use Oracle stored procedures to get the same result. If you have run the dbmssnap.sql script, you could also refresh a snapshot by issuing the following command:

```
EXECUTE dbms_snapshot.refresh('customer','c');  /* complete refresh */
EXECUTE dbms_snapshot.refresh('customer','f');  /* forced   refresh */
EXECUTE dbms_snapshot.refresh('customer','?');  /* fast     refresh */
```

Using Triggers To Update Snapshots

But what about replicated tables that require faster propagation? Oracle version 7.3 offers updatable snapshots, but users of previous releases of Oracle can also use database triggers to simulate the realtime propagation of changes from a master table to replicated tables. In the following example, an update trigger has been placed on the customer tables, and relevant changes will be propagated to the New York branch:

```
CREATE TRIGGER add_customer
    AFTER INSERT ON CUSTOMER
AS
IF :dept = 'NY' THEN
(INSERT INTO customer@NY
    VALUES(:parm1, :parm2,:parm3);
);
```

But what can we do about rows that are deleted from the customer table? Using the same technique, a delete trigger can be placed on the customer table to remove rows from the replicated tables:

```
CREATE TRIGGER delete_customer
    AFTER DELETE ON CUSTOMER
AS
IF :dept = 'NY' THEN
(DELETE FROM customer@NY
    WHERE
    cust_nbr = :customer_parm
);
```

USING SNAPSHOTS TO PROPAGATE SUBSETS OF MASTER TABLES

As we have seen, snapshot replication is very handy for taking a master and copying it to a remote location. But what if we only want to replicate a portion of the tables? Yes, Oracle provides a method for excluding certain rows and columns from the replicated table. For example, let's assume that we are replicating a central employee table for use by our New York branch. However, we only want to replicate employee records for those who work at the New York branch, and we want to exclude confidential columns such as the employee's salary. Here is how a snapshot would appear:

```
CREATE SNAPSHOT emp_ny
REFRESH FAST
    START WITH SYSDATE
    NEXT NEXT_DAY(trunc(sysdate),'TUESDAY')+6/24
```

```
AS
    SELECT
            emp_nbr,
            emp_name,
            emp_phone,
            emp_hire_date
    FROM emp@hq WHERE department = 'NY';
```

Asynchronous Updating Of Oracle Tables

The latest fad in the database marketplace is the widespread replication of data to mobile remote servers for updating purposes. The remote servers are completely disconnected from the central server, and the updates usually occur on laptop servers. At any time, the user of the laptop can dial in to the central server and transfer their updates (Figure 7.2).

This approach has been very popular with Oracle-based sales force automation (SFA) systems that strive to provide field salesmen with current information from the centralized host without requiring them to continually dial in to the server. Here is how they work.

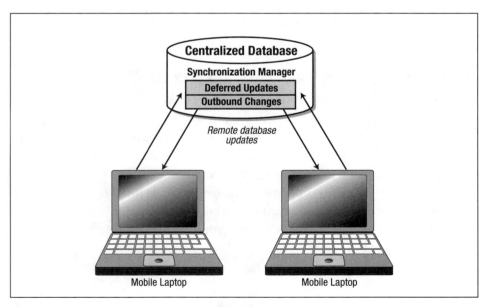

Figure 7.2   Asynchronous updating mechanisms.

Daily changes to the centralized host are collected and distributed to the remote laptop database whenever the salesmen dial in to the host and request a refresh. As the salesmen make changes on their laptops, they are able to feed these changes to the central host whenever they dial in. While this may seem like a sound idea on the surface, some very serious problems can occur with asynchronous updating:

- How are update anomalies handled?

- What happens when a change based on outdated information is made on a remote laptop?

- How do we develop a mechanism for synchronizing all of the remote laptops?

The asynchronous approach is used almost exclusively with distributed sales systems that require salespeople in the field to have current information without having to connect to a central server via modem.

The idea is to define a subset of the database for each mobile user, and then develop a mechanism that ensures that the disconnected laptop is updated each time the salesperson connects to the central database. In addition, the updates must occur quickly to minimize connect time. Most of these systems apply a date-time stamp to all relevant rows, using this date-time key to quickly retrieve the data from the master tables. It now becomes obvious that every laptop is going to be out of sync with the master database to some degree.

At connect time, the system must also upload all changes that have been made to the mobile database, updating the master tables on the central server. The absence of database locks leads to some interesting update anomalies. These anomalies take two forms. The first one happens when a row is updated by two mobile laptops, and the upload of one row overlays the changes that were made by the other mobile laptop. The second type of anomaly occurs when outdated information is used as the basis for making a change while on the mobile laptop.

Most of the SFA products have developed their own rules for dealing with anomalies. These rules include:

- Defer all update anomalies, writing them to a special area for manual resolution.

- The most recent update (as indicated at upload time) supersedes any prior updates.

- All end users are ranked, and the user with the highest rank supersedes all changes made by a lower-ranked employee.

Regardless of the method chosen, these tools are normally constructed using a relational database such as Oracle with a custom synchronization manager. The synchronization manager handles the downloading of information from the centralized server to the laptop and the uploading of changes to the main server.

For downloads, most of these tools prepackage the relevant information for the laptop user, keeping track of the last synchronization and writing changes to a special table. In this fashion, the laptop user does not have to wait while the server extracts the updates, and the updates can immediately be transferred and loaded into the laptop server.

For uploads, the laptop tracks all changes since the last upload—first extracting and then transferring them to the centralized server. The synchronization manager then inserts new information and carefully checks the date-time stamp on all rows that are marked for update. If a row has been updated since the laptop user's last time of synchronization, the data is handled according to the programmed rules in the synchronization manager. For most implementations, the safest method is to reject all potential anomalies, which triggers an exception report and requires manual resolution of the update. In practice, one of the largest problems is motivating the users of the mobile laptop to dial in frequently for their updates.

These types of systems recognize the problems that arise when trying to distribute data to mobile servers, and attempt to address the problem with custom rules and procedures. It is interesting to note that they have proven very successful in systems where up-to-the-minute information is not required for decision making, and the user required mobile access to information.

Parallelism And Client/Server

The widespread acceptance of distributed processing and multitasking operating systems has heralded a new mode of designing and implementing business systems. Instead of the traditional "linear" design of systems, tomorrow's system will incorporate massively parallel processing. The result? Many tasks may be concurrently assigned to service a database request. Indeed, the entire definition of data processing is changing. The corporate data resource has been expanded to include all sources of information, not just databases. Corporate information lies within email, Lotus Notes, and many other nontraditional sources. Many companies are collecting this information without fully exploiting its value, and multiprocessing is an ideal technique for searching these huge amounts of free-form corporate information.

Multitasking And Multithreading

Before we even tackle this subject, a distinction needs to be made between multitasking and multiprocessing. Multitasking refers to the ability of a software package to manage multiple concurrent processes, thereby allowing simultaneous processing. Although OS/2 and Windows NT are good examples of this technology, multitasking can be found within all midrange and mainframe databases. Multiprocessing refers to the use of multiple CPUs within a distributed environment where a master program directs parallel operations against numerous machines. Two areas of multiprocessing are possible. The first is at the hardware level, where arrays of CPUs are offered. The second is at the software level, where a single CPU can be partitioned into separate "logical" processors. The Prism software on the IBM mainframe environment is an example of this technology.

In any case, programming for multiprocessors is quite different from linear programming techniques. Multiprocessing programming falls into two areas: data parallel programming and control parallel programming. Data parallel programming partitions the data into discrete pieces, running the same program in parallel against each piece. Control parallel programming identifies independent functions that are simultaneously solved by independent CPUs (Figure 7.3).

One of the greatest problems with implementing parallel processing systems is the identification of *parallelism*. Parallelism refers to the ability of a computer system to perform processing on many data sources at the same instant in time. Whereas many of the traditional database applications were linear in nature, today's systems have many opportunities for parallel processing.

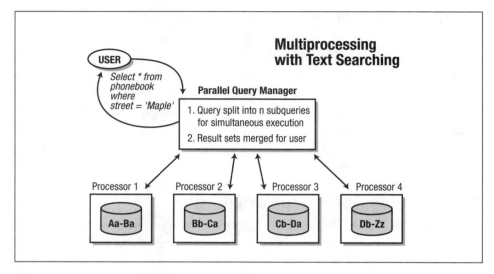

Figure 7.3   An example of a parallel query.

Parallelism is especially important to scientific applications that could benefit from the opportunity to have hundreds—or even thousands—of processors working together to solve a problem. But the same concept of parallelism applies to very large databases. If a query can be split into subqueries where each subquery is assigned to a processor, the response time for the query can reduce by a factor of thousands (Figure 7.4).

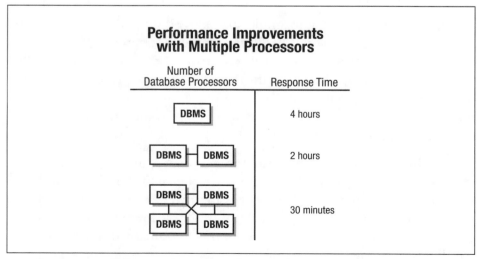

Figure 7.4   The performance benefits of adding processors.

A review of the past 30 years makes it clear that tremendous improvements have been made in the speed of processors. At the same time, the prices of processors have continued to decline. However, this trend cannot continue forever. The physical nature of silicon processors has been pushed to its limit and is now reaching a diminishing point of return. In order to continue to enjoy increases in performance, we either need to replace silicon as a medium or to devise ways to exploit parallelism in processing.

Parallelism is an issue of scale. Where a linear process may solve a problem in one hour, a parallel system with 60 processors *should* be able to solve the problem in 1 minute, as demonstrated in Figure 7.5. This is analogous to the statement that 1 woman takes nine months to have a baby, so nine women *should* be able to produce a baby in one month. Speed can only be improved in those situations where parallel processing is appropriate, which excludes traditional linear systems where one process may not begin until the preceding one ends.

Other facets to parallel processing can be extremely valuable. A query against a very large database can be dramatically improved if the data is partitioned. For example, if a query against a text database takes 1 minute to scan a terabyte, then partitioning the data and processing into 60 pieces will result in a retrieval time of 1 second. Another key issue is the balancing of the CPU processing with the I/O processing. In a traditional data processing environment, the systems are not computationally intensive, and

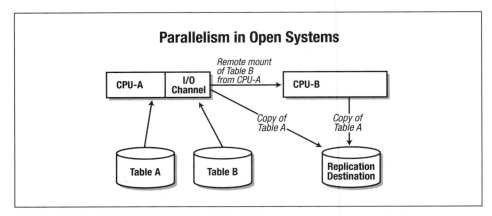

Figure 7.5 Parallelism across multiple CPUs.

most of the elapsed time is spent waiting on I/O. However, this does not automatically exclude business systems from taking advantage of multi-processing.

A continuum of processing architecture exists for parallel processing. On one end of the spectrum we find a few powerful CPUs that are loosely connected, while on the other end we see a large amount of small processors that are tightly coupled.

Parallelism can be easily identified in a distributed database environment. For the database administrator, routine maintenance tasks such as export/import operations can be run in parallel, reducing the overall time required for system maintenance.

In an open systems environment, parallelism may be easily simulated by using a remote mount facility. With a remote mount, a data file may be directly addressed from another processor, even though the data file physically resides on another machine. This can be an especially useful technique for speeding up table replication to remote sites, as shown in Figure 7.5.

To speed up the replication of two tables, a Unix shell script directs CPU-A to begin the copy of Table A as a background task. The script then directs CPU-B to issue a remote mount to Table B, making Table B addressable as if it were a local disk to CPU-B. The script then issues a copy of Table B, and the tables are copied simultaneously, reducing the overall processing time. (See Figure 7.6.)

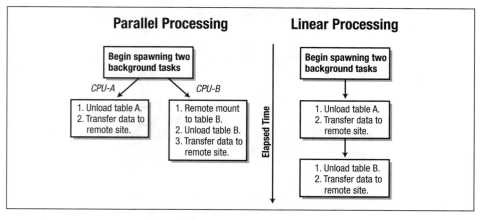

Figure 7.6 Linear versus parallel processing.

Of course, the overall elapsed time will not be half of the time required for a linear process—the remote mount still requires the database on CPU-A to manage the I/O against Table B. The benefit lies in having the second processor (CPU-B) handle all of the processing for the unload of Table B.

SMP Vs. MPP Processing

SMP, or symmetrical multiprocessing, describes an architecture where many CPUs share a common memory area and I/O buffer. This type of architecture is not scalable, as additional processors must compete for the shared memory and I/O resources. On the other hand, massively parallel processors (MPP) describes an architecture where many independent processors share nothing, operating via a common I/O bus. An MPP system can add processors without impeding performance, and performance will actually increase as processors are added.

Using Oracle's Parallel Query

With Oracle version 7.2, some powerful new features have been introduced to allow parallel processes to be used against the Oracle database. These features include:

- Parallel **CREATE TABLE** as **SELECT**

- Parallel query

- Parallel index building

Please note that the new features of Oracle 7.2 and Oracle 7.3 will not be activated unless the following init.ora parameter has been used:

```
COMPATIBILITY=7.3.0.0.0
```

Also, note that it is not necessary to have parallel processors (SMP or MPP) in order to use and benefit from parallel processing. Even on the same processor, multiple processes can be used to speed up queries. Oracle parallel query option can be used with any SQL **SELECT** statement—the only restriction being that the query performs a full-table scan on the target table.

Parallel queries are most useful in distributed databases where a single logical table has been partitioned into smaller tables at each remote node.

For example, a customer table that is ordered by customer name may be partitioned into a customer table at each remote database, such that we have a **phoenix_customer**, a **los_angeles_customer**, and so on. This approach is very common with distributed databases where local autonomy of processing is important. However, what about the needs of those in corporate headquarters? How can they query all of these remote tables as a single unit and treat the logical customer table as a single entity?

While this "splitting" of a table according to a key value violates normalization theory, it can dramatically improve performance for individual queries. For large queries that may span many logical tables, the isolated tables can be easily reassembled using Oracle's parallel query facility:

```
CREATE VIEW all_customer AS
    SELECT * FROM phoenix_customer@phoenix
    UNION ALL
    SELECT * FROM los_angeles_customer@los_angeles
    UNION ALL
    SELECT * FROM rochester_customer@rochester;
```

 The "@" references refer to SQL*Net service names for the remote hosts.

We can now query the **all_customer** view as if it were a single database table, and Oracle parallel query will automatically recognize the **UNION ALL** parameter, firing off simultaneous queries against each of the three base tables. It is important to note that the distributed database manager will direct each query to be processed at the remote location, while the query manager waits until each remote node has returned its result set. For example, the following query will assemble the requested data from the three tables in parallel, with each query optimized separately. The result set from each subquery is then merged by the query manager:

```
SELECT customer_name
FROM all_customer
WHERE
total_purchases > 5000;
```

 For more details on using Oracle's parallel query facility, refer to Chapter 2, Physical Performance Design For Oracle Databases.

Planning For Growth

One of the biggest problems in performance and tuning is the problem of planning for growth and ensuring that your distributed database continues to perform at an acceptable level. As we know, databases run within a well-defined domain of systems resources, and a shortage of these system resources can lead to performance degradation. The trick is to design a database system with the ability to add resources on an as-needed basis without interrupting processing.

Most databases have other high-impact resources, such as the recovery logs and transaction logs. Most systems have more than one recovery log. It is a good idea to locate these logs on different disk devices, as well as on devices that do not have any other high-impact data tables.

Growth of a database can occur in several areas. As the physical size of the database increases, so does the need for disk storage. As the volume of users increases, so does the need for increased buffer and lock pool storage. As network traffic increases, an increasing demand falls on the routers and bandwidth may need to be increased.

Unlike the CODASYL databases of the 1980s, today's relational databases allow for tables to grow according to specified rules and procedures. In the relational model, one or more tables may reside in a tablespace. A tablespace is a predefined container for the tables that map to fixed files of a finite size. Tables that are assigned to the tablespace may grow according to the growth rules that are specified, but the size of the tablespace supersedes the expansion rules. In other words, a table may, according to the table definition, have more extents available, but there may not be room in the tablespace to allocate those extents.

Several allocation parameters influence table growth:

- **DB_BLOCK_SIZE**—The size of each physical database block

- **INITIAL**—The initial size of each extent

- **NEXT**—The subsequent size of new extents

- **MINEXTENTS**—The minimum number of initial extents (used for striping)

- **MAXEXTENTS**—The maximum allowable number of extents (Note: Oracle 7.3 supports **MAXEXTENTS UNLIMITED**)

- **PCTINCREASE**—The percentage by which each subsequent extent grows (normally set to 1)

- **PCTFREE**—The percentage of space to be kept on each data block for future expansion

The **PCTFREE** parameter is used to reserve space on each data block for the future expansion of row values (via the SQL **UPDATE** command). Table columns may be defined as allowing **null** values that do not consume any space within the row, or with **varchar** data types. A **varchar** data type specifies the maximum allowable length for the column instance, but the acceptable range of values may be anywhere from 4 bytes (the size of the length holder) to the size of the field plus 4 bytes. Hence, a **varchar(2000)** may range in size from 4 bytes to 2,004 bytes.

If an application initially stores rows with empty values and later fills in the values, the **PCTFREE** parameter can dramatically reduce I/O contention. If a block of storage is filled by the addition of a row, subsequent updates to that row to fill in column values will cause the row to fragment—usually onto the next available contiguous block.

Block Sizing

It is very ironic that the Oracle developer must choose a block size when the database is initially created—a time when knowledge of system performance is so limited. While it is possible to use the Oracle import/export utilities to change block sizes, too little attention is given to the proper sizing of database blocks. The physical block size is set with the **DB_BLOCK_SIZE** parameter in the init.ora file. While the default is to have 4 K block sizes, many Oracle developers choose at least 8 K block sizes for large, distributed databases. Some DBAs believe that 16 K is the best block size, even for OLTP systems that seldom perform full-table scans. Depending upon the host platform and operating system, Oracle block sizes may be set from 2 K up to 32 K. The Oracle OS manual will provide the acceptable ranges for your operating system.

When determining the required space for your database, subtract the block header and **PCTFREE** from your calculations. Oracle block headers are a function of the **DB_BLOCK_SIZE** (in init.ora) and the value of **INITTRANS** (in tablespace definition).

The space (in bytes) required by the data block header is the result of the following formula:

Block Header size

$$= (\textbf{BLOCK\_SIZE} - \textbf{KCBH} - \textbf{UB4} - \textbf{KTBBH} - (\textbf{INITRANS} - 1)) * (\textbf{KTBIT} - \textbf{KDBH})$$

$$= (\textbf{DB\_BLOCK\_SIZE} - 20 - 4 - 48 - (\textbf{INITRANS} - 1)) * (24 - 14)$$

$$= (\textbf{DB\_BLOCK\_SIZE} - 72 - (\textbf{INITRANS} - 1)) * 10$$

Where

KCBH (block common header) = 20

UB4 (unsigned byte 4) = 4

KTBBH (transaction fixed header) = 48

INITRANS (initial number of transaction entries)

KTBIT (transaction variable header) = 24

KDBH (data header) = 14

The size (constants) of **KCBH**, **UB4**, **KTBBH**, **KTBIT**, and **KDBH** can also be found in the fixed view **V$TYPE_SIZE**.

The principle behind block sizing is simple. I/O is the single most expensive and time-consuming operation within a database. As such, the more data that can be read in a single I/O, the faster the performance of the Oracle database. This principle is especially true for databases that have many reports that read the entire contents of a table. For systems that read random single rows from the database, block size is not as important—especially with database clusters. An Oracle cluster is a mechanism whereby an owner row will reside on the same database block as its subordinate rows in other tables. For example, if we cluster **order** rows on the same block as their **customer** owners, Oracle will only need to perform a single I/O to retrieve the **customer** and all of the **order** rows. Of course, in a distributed database where joins take place across different Oracle instances, clustering cannot be used. The additional I/O will be required to read the rows individually.

Bear in mind that increasing the block size of an Oracle database will also affect the number of blocks that can be cached in the buffer pool. For example, if we set the **db_block_buffers** init.ora parameter to 8 MB, Oracle will be able to cache 1,000 4 K blocks, but only 500 8 K blocks.

Increasing the Oracle block size also increases the risk of concurrency bottlenecks, especially when the **INITTRANS** and **MAXTRANS** values are set too low. **INITTRANS** and **MAXTRANS** are Oracle tablespace creation parameters that determine the amount of space to be reserved on a block for concurrency locks. The maximum values for **INITTRANS** and **MAXTRANS** is 255, meaning that no more than 255 transactions may simultaneously access a specific database block.

If you suspect that your values are too low, a query of the **V$LOCK** table will reveal all tasks that are waiting for access to a page. Listing 7.2 shows an SQL script to check for lock contention.

Listing 7.2   locks.sql shows all locks in the database.

```
SET LINESIZE 132
SET PAGESIZE 60
COLUMN OBJECT HEADING 'Database|Object'        FORMAT a15 TRUNCATE
COLUMN lock_type HEADING 'Lock|Type'           FORMAT a4 TRUNCATE
COLUMN mode_held HEADING 'Mode|Held'           FORMAT a15 TRUNCATE
COLUMN mode_requested HEADING 'Mode|Requested' FORMAT a15 TRUNCATE
COLUMN sid heading 'Session|ID'
COLUMN username HEADING 'Username'             FORMAT a20 TRUNCATE
COLUMN IMAGE HEADING 'active image'            FORMAT a20 TRUNCATE


SPOOL /tmp/locks
SELECT
        c.sid,
        substr(object_name,1,20) OBJECT,
        c.username,
        substr(c.program,length(c.program)-20,length(c.program)) image,
        DECODE(b.type,
                'MR', 'Media Recovery',
                'RT', 'Redo Thread',
                'UN', 'User Name',
                'TX', 'Transaction',
                'TM', 'DML',
                'UL', 'PL/SQL User Lock',
                'DX', 'Distributed Xaction',
                'CF', 'Control File',
                'IS', 'Instance State',
                'FS', 'File Set',
```

```
                     'IR', 'Instance Recovery',
                     'ST', 'Disk Space Transaction',
                     'TS', 'Temp Segment',
                     'IV', 'Library Cache Invalidation',
                     'LS', 'Log Start or Switch',
                     'RW', 'Row Wait',
                     'SQ', 'Sequence Number',
                     'TE', 'Extend Table',
                     'TT', 'Temp Table',
                     b.type) lock_type,
          DECODE(b.lmode,
                 0, 'None',                 /* Mon Lock equivalent */
                 1, 'Null',                 /* NOT */
                 2, 'Row-SELECT (SS)',      /* LIKE */
                 3, 'Row-X (SX)',           /* R */
                 4, 'Share',                /* SELECT */
                 5, 'SELECT/Row-X (SSX)',   /* C */
                 6, 'Exclusive',            /* X */
                 to_char(b.lmode)) mode_held,
          DECODE(b.request,
                 0, 'None',                 /* Mon Lock equivalent */
                 1, 'Null',                 /* NOT */
                 2, 'Row-SELECT (SS)',      /* LIKE */
                 3, 'Row-X (SX)',           /* R */
                 4, 'Share',                /* SELECT */
                 5, 'SELECT/Row-X (SSX)',   /* C */
                 6, 'Exclusive',            /* X */
                 to_char(b.request)) mode_requested
FROM sys.dba_objects a, sys.v_$lock b, sys.v_$session c WHERE
a.object_id = b.id1 AND b.sid = c.sid AND OWNER NOT IN ('SYS','SYSTEM');
```

Listing 7.3 shows the output of locks.sql.

Listing 7.3   The results from locks.sql.

```
SQL> @locks
```

Session Database ID Object	Username	Active Ima	Lock Type	Mode Held	Mode Requested
2 DUAL		Media	Reco	Share	None
2 SYSTEM_PRIVI		Media	Reco	Share	None
2 TABLE_PRIVIL		Media	Reco	Share	None
2 STMT_AUDIT_O		Media	Reco	Share	None
2 V$CONTROLFIL		Media	Reco	Share	None
2 V$DATAFILE		Media	Reco	Share	None

2	V$LOG	Media	Reco	Share	None
2	V$THREAD	Media	Reco	Share	None
2	V$PROCESS	Media	Reco	Share	None
2	V$BGPROCESS	Media	Reco	Share	None
2	V$SESSION	Media	Reco	Share	None
2	V$LICENSE	Media	Reco	Share	None
2	V$TRANSACTIO	Media	Reco	Share	None
2	V$LATCH	Media	Reco	Share	None
2	V$LATCHNAME	Media	Reco	Share	None
2	V$LATCHHOLDE	Media	Reco	Share	None
2	V$RESOURCE	Media	Reco	Share	None
2	V$_LOCK	Media	Reco	Share	None
2	V$LOCK	Media	Reco	Share	None
2	V$SESSTAT	Media	Reco	Share	None

20 rows selected.

Tablespace Considerations

Choosing how to pair tables and indexes into tablespaces has a great impact on the performance of distributed databases. Since the designer has many choices, it is a good idea to explore the available options. In general, the following characteristics apply:

- Group tables with similar characteristics in a tablespace. For example, all tables that are read-only could be grouped into a single, read-only tablespace. Tables with random I/O patterns could also be grouped together, all small tables should be grouped together, and so on.

- Create at least two tablespaces for use by the **TEMP** tablespaces. This approach has the advantage of allowing the designer to dedicate numerous **TEMP** tablespaces to specific classes of users. As we know, the **TEMP** tablespace is used for large sorting operations, and assigning appropriately sized **TEMP** tablespaces to users depending upon their sorting requirements can enhance performance. Remember, in a distributed SQL query, the rows are fetched from the remote database and sorted on the Oracle that initiated the request. The use of multiple **TEMP** tablespaces has the added advantage of allowing the developer to switch **TEMP** tablespaces in case of disk failure.

- Use many small, manageable tablespaces. This approach makes it easier to take a single tablespace offline for maintenance without affecting the entire system. Oracle highly recommends that no tablespace should ever become greater than 10 GB, and placing all tables into a single tablespace also reduces recoverability in case of media failure. However, this approach does not advocate creating a single tablespace for each table in a system. For example, Oracle recommends that the system tablespace contain only systems tables, and that a separate tablespace be created for the exclusive use of the rollback segments.

- Place the rollback segments in a separate tablespace. This isolates the activity of the rollback segments (which tend to have a high I/O rate) from the data files belonging to the application.

Tablespace Fragmentation

As rows are added to tables, the table expands into unused space within the tablespace. Conversely, when rows are deleted, a table may coalesce extents, releasing unused space back into the tablespace. As this happens, it is possible for there to be discontiguous chunks, or fragments of unused space within the tablespace. Whenever the value for a table as specified by **STORAGE** (**INITIAL xx**) is exceeded, Oracle will create a new extent for the table. If the **PCTINCREASE** is set to 0, a new extent of the size specified in **STORAGE** (**NEXT xx**) will be added to the table. If **PCTINCREASE** is non-zero, the extent size will be equal to the value of the most recent extent size multiplied by **PCTINCREASE**.

 *PCTINCREASE for a tablespace should not be set to 0, since this will disable the automatic coalesce facility for Oracle tablespaces. In general, all tablespaces except the system tablespaces (**SYSTEM, RBS**) should have **PCTINCREASE** set to 1. The **PCTINCREASE** parameter for tablespaces is generally only used when a table is allocated without a **STORAGE** clause—although Oracle also uses it for coalescing.*

This allocation of new extents will be physically contiguous to the table's initial location, as long as the next physical data blocks are empty. Unfortunately, as many tables populate a tablespace, a table may not have contiguous data blocks for its next extent, which means that it must fragment the extents onto another spot in the datafile, as shown here:

```
CREATE TABLESPACE SALES
  DATAFILE '/Data/ORACLE/sales/sales.dbf'
  SIZE 500M REUSE
  DEFAULT STORAGE (INITIAL 500K  NEXT 50K  PCTINCREASE 1);
```

Here we see that the **SALES** tablespace has been allocated to a physical file called /Data/ORACLE/sales/sales.dbf, created at a size of 500 MB. Assuming that all tables within this tablespace use default storage, they will be initially allocated at 500 K and will extend in chunks of 50 K.

But what happens if the tablespace gets full? Processing will cease against the tablespace, and the Oracle DBA must intervene to add another data file to the tablespace with the **ALTER TABLESPACE** command:

```
ALTER TABLESPACE SALES
ADD DATAFILE '/Data/ORACLE/sales/sales1.dbf'
SIZE 200M REUSE;
```

Obviously, the DBA should carefully monitor tablespace usage so that tablespaces never fill, but Oracle version 7.2 and above offer an alternative. The **AUTOEXTEND** command can be used to allow a data file to grow automatically on an as-needed basis. Here are the different permutations of this command:

```
ALTER DATABASE DATAFILE '/Data/ORACLE/sales/sales.dbf' AUTOEXTEND ON;

ALTER DATABASE DATAFILE '/Data/ORACLE/sales/sales.dbf' AUTOEXTEND MAXSIZE
  UNLIMITED;

ALTER DATABASE DATAFILE '/Data/ORACLE/sales/sales.dbf' AUTOEXTEND MAXSIZE
  (500M);

ALTER DATABASE DATAFILE '/Data/ORACLE/sales/sales.dbf' RESIZE (600M);
```

When tables fragment, additional I/O will be required to access the table data, since the disk must access blocks on two noncontiguous spots on the datafile. The following script will detect all tablespaces whose tables have taken more than 10 extents:

```
tblsp_fr.sql - shows all tablespaces with more than 10 extents
SET PAGES 9999;
COLUMN c1 HEADING "Tablespace Name"
COLUMN c2 HEADING "Number of Extents"
TTITLE " Tablespaces with more than 10 extents"
```

```
SELECT tablespace_name c1,
       MAX(extent_id) c2
FROM dba_extents
WHERE
extent_id > 9
GROUP BY tablespace_name
;
```

Here is the output of this script:

```
SQL> @tblsp_fr

Fri Mar 15                                                   page    1
                    Tablespaces with more than 10 extents

Tablespace Name                      Number of Extents
------------------------------       -----------------
INDX                                          113
SALES                                          57
SYSTEM                                         56
```

Contrary to popular opinion, tables with noncontiguous extents do not cause performance problems. It is only the row fragmentation that sometimes accompanies discontiguous extents that negatively affect performance. In some studies, a table with discontiguous extents (and no row fragmentation) actually performed faster than a table that was in a single extent.

Tablespace Reorganization

Because they are dynamic, Oracle databases will always fragment over time and may require a periodic cleanup. In general, reorganization ensures that all tables and indexes do not have row fragmentation, and that they reside in a single extent, with all free space in a tablespace in a single, contiguous chunk. Reorganizing a tablespace can be accomplished in several ways. Rather than bring down the entire Oracle database to perform a full export/import, there are some other options.

Let's take a look at how a tablespace may become fragmented. At initial load time, all Oracle tables within the tablespace are contiguous—that is, only one chunk of free space resides at the end of the tablespace. As tables extend and new extents are added to the tablespace, the free space becomes smaller but it still remains contiguous.

Basically, a table can fragment in two ways:

- *A table extends (without row chaining)*—Contrary to popular belief, this is not a problem and performance will not suffer.

- *Rows fragment within the tablespace (due to SQL **UPDATES**)*—This causes a serious performance problem, and the offending tables must be exported, dropped, and reimported.

Tablespace fragmentation occurs when some "pockets" of free space exist within the tablespace. So, how do these pockets of free space appear? If tables are **DROPPED** and re-created, or if individual tables are exported and imported, space that was once reserved for a table's extent will now be vacant.

To see the fragmentation within a tablespace, you can run the script shown in Listing 7.4.

Listing 7.4   tsfrag.sql shows a tablespace map.

```
REM written by Don Burleson

SET LINESIZE 132;
SET PAGES 999;

REM SET FEEDBACK OFF;
REM SET VERIFY OFF;
REM SET HEADING OFF;
REM SET TERMOUT OFF;

BREAK ON file_id SKIP PAGE;
BREAK ON FREE SKIP 1;
COMPUTE SUM OF KB ON FREE;

SPOOL tsfrag;

COLUMN owner           FORMAT a10;
COLUMN segment_name    FORMAT a10;
COLUMN tablespace_name FORMAT a14;
COLUMN file_id         FORMAT 99 heading ID;
COLUMN end             FORMAT 999999;
COLUMN KB              FORMAT 9999999;
```

```
COLUMN begin              FORMAT 999999;
COLUMN blocks             FORMAT 999999;

SELECT
  tablespace_name,
   file_id,
   owner,
   segment_name,
   block_id begin,
   blocks,
   block_id+blocks-1 end,
   bytes/1024 KB,
   '' free
FROM sys.dba_extents
WHERE tablespace_name NOT IN ('RBS','SYSTEM','TEMP','TOOLS','USER')
UNION
SELECT
   tablespace_name,
   file_id,
   '' owner,
   '' segment_name,
   block_id begin,
   blocks,
   block_id+blocks+1 end,
   bytes/1023 KB,
   'F' free
FROM sys.dba_free_space
WHERE tablespace_name NOT IN ('RBS','SYSTEM','TEMP','TOOLS','USER')
ORDER BY 1, 2, 5
;

/

SPOOL OFF;

!cat tsfrag.lst
```

Listing 7.5 shows the the output of tsfrag.sql.

Listing 7.5   The results of the tsfrag.sql script.

TS_NAME	ID	OWNER	SEGMENT_NA	BEGIN	BLOCKS	END	KB	F
MASTER3_STAT_1	15	RPT	ZIP_UPS_ZO	2	5	6	20	

```
                           NE_XREF
MASTER3_STAT_1 15   RPT    ACHG_TY      7      2      8       8
MASTER3_STAT_1 15   RPT    BUSN_UNIT    9     35     43     140
MASTER3_STAT_1                         44      2     45       8  F
MASTER3_STAT_1 15   RPT    PLANT       46      3     48      12
MASTER3_STAT_1                         49     10     58      40  F
MASTER3_STAT_1  15 RPT     RPT_TABLES  59      4     62      16
MASTER3_STAT_1  15 RPT     ZONE        63      2     64       8
                                                    -------- *
                                                       252  s


MASTER3_STAT_1  15                     65   1216   1282    4869  F
                                                    -------- *
                                                      4869  s
```

In Listing 7.5, we see two discontiguous chunks of free space, as indicated by the "F" column on the far right-hand side of the report. Here, we see that blocks 44–45 are free, as are blocks 49–58.

Oracle version 7.3 will automatically detect and coalesce tablespaces—provided that all affected tablespaces' default storage clauses have **PCTINCREASE** set to 1. The coalesce mechanism for tablespace coalescing is the **SMON** process, which periodically wakes up to coalesce free space. Between **SMON** coalesces, any transaction that requires an extent that is larger than any available free extent, will trigger a coalesce on the tablespace to move all free space into a single chunk—hopefully making room for the required extent.

Also in Oracle 7.3 is a new dictionary view, **DBA_FREE_SPACE_COALESCED**, which provides details about the number of extents, bytes, and blocks that have been coalesced in each tablespace.

The following query will display coalesce information:

```
SELECT
    tablespace_name,
    bytes_coalesced,
    extents_coalesced,
    percent_extents_coalesced,
    blocks_coalesced,
    percent_blocks_coalesced
FROM
```

```
    sys.dba_free_space_coalesced
ORDER BY
    tablespace_name;
```

To change all tablespaces' **PCTINCREASE** from 0 to 1 so that tables will
automatically coalesce, run the script in Listing 7.6.

Listing 7.6 coalesce.sql changes all tablespaces with PCTINCREASE not equal to 1.

```
REM written by Don Burleson

SET LINESIZE 132;
SET PAGESIZE 999;
SET FEEDBACK OFF;
SET VERIFY OFF;
SET HEADING OFF;
SET TERMOUT OFF;

SPOOL COALESCE;

SELECT
    'alter tablespace '
    ||tablespace_name||
    ' storage ( pctincrease 1 );'
FROM dba_tablespaces
WHERE
 tablespace_name NOT IN ('RBS','SYSTEM','TEMP','TOOLS','USER')
AND
 pct_increase = 0;

SPOOL OFF;

SET FEEDBACK ON;
SET VERIFY ON;
SET HEADING ON;
SET TERMOUT ON;

@coalesce.lst
```

MANUAL TABLESPACE COALESCE

If you detect that a single tablespace has fragmented, you can quickly coalesce it with the following procedures:

1. Alter session by retrieving the tablespace number from sys.ts$:

    ```
    SELECT * FROM sys.ts$:
    ```

2. IN SQL*DBA, issue the following command:

    ```
    ALTER SESSION SET EVENTS immediate trace name coalesce level
    &tsnum;
    ```

    (where tsnum is the tablespace number from step 1)

3. Manual coalesce, from SQL*Plus enter:

    ```
    ALTER TABLESPACE <xxxx> COALESCE;
    ```

FULL EXPORT/IMPORT

While many vendor tools can aid in a database reorganization, many Oracle administrators will write a script that will export all tables within the tablespace, re-create the tablespace, and then import all of the tables and indexes to compress them into a single extent. However, be forewarned that referential integrity may make it difficult to drop a tablespace. This occurs when one tablespace contains a table that has a foreign-key constraint from a table within another tablespace.

Most often, the administrator will reorganize the entire database, performing the following steps:

1. Export the full database.

2. Generate the create database script.

3. Generate a list of data files to remove.

4. Remove the data files.

5. Create the database.

6. Import the full database.

7. Bounce the database and optionally turn on archive logging.

Table Fragmentation

Again, it needs to be emphasized that table fragmentation does not cause performance problems. Rather, the row chaining that often accompanies table fragmentation will seriously impede performance. In fact, some Oracle

DBAs have reported that extended tables (without row chaining) some-times outperform tables that reside in a single extent. For detecting row chaining, see the next section.

Listing 7.7 shows a simple script can be run to see the number of times that a table has extended.

Listing 7.7   tblexts.sql lists all tables with more than 10 extents.

```
SET PAUSE OFF;
SET ECHO OFF;
SET LINESIZE 150;
SET PAGESIZE 60;

COLUMN c1   HEADING "Tablespace";
COLUMN c2   HEADING "Owner";
COLUMN c3   HEADING "Table";
COLUMN c4   HEADING "Size (KB)";
COLUMN c5   HEADING "Alloc. Ext";
COLUMN c6   HEADING "Max Ext";
COLUMN c7   HEADING "Init Ext (KB)";
COLUMN c8   HEADING "Next Ext (KB)";
COLUMN c9   HEADING "Pct Inc";
COLUMN c10  HEADING "Pct Free";
COLUMN c11  HEADING "Pct Used";
BREAK ON c1 SKIP 2 ON c2 SKIP 2

TTITLE "Fragmented Tables";

SELECT  substr(seg.tablespace_name,1,10)  c1,
        substr(tab.owner,1,10)            c2,
        substr(tab.table_name,1,30)       c3,
        seg.bytes/1024                    c4,
        seg.extents                       c5,
        tab.max_extents                   c6,
        tab.initial_extent/1024           c7,
        tab.next_extent/1024              c8,
        tab.pct_increase                  c9,
        tab.pct_free                      c10,
        tab.pct_used                      c11
FROM    sys.dba_segments seg,
        sys.dba_tables    tab
WHERE   seg.tablespace_name = tab.tablespace_name
  AND   seg.owner = tab.owner
```

```
   AND    seg.segment_name = tab.table_name
   AND    seg.extents > 10
ORDER BY 1,2,3;
```

Listing 7.8 shows the listing from this script.

Listing 7.8   The results from the tblexts.sql script.

```
SQL> @tblexts

Thu Mar 14
                                                    page    1
                                              Fragmented Tables
```

Table space	Owner	Table Ext	Size (KB)	Alloc Ext	Max Ext	Init Ext(KB)	Next Ext(KB)	Pct Inc	Pct Free	Pct Used
MPTV	MPTVI	UST_CAT	5800	58	249	100	100	0	20	40
SYSTEM	SYS	AUD$	1724	11	249	12	840	50	10	40
		CHAINED_ROWS	684	57	249	12	12	0	10	40
		SOURCE$	1724	11	249	12	840	50	10	40

Row Fragmentation

Row fragmentation is one of the most problematic things that can happen to an Oracle system. This commonly occurs when an SQL **UPDATE** operation lacks sufficient room to expand the size of a row on its data block. When this happens, the row must extend onto the next available data block, causing an extra I/O when the row is accessed.

In Figure 7.7, the next five blocks are filled with rows. When an SQL update adds 1,500 bytes to row 1, the database chains to the next block. Finding no space, it chains to the next block, and the next block, before finding 1,500 bytes of free space on block 4. The fragment is stored in block 4, and a chain is established from the block header of block 1 to point to the next block header, and so on, until the fragment is located. Most databases have some type of "free list" at each block header to determine the total available space on each block.

Any subsequent retrieval of row 1 will require the database to perform four physical block I/Os in order to retrieve the entire row. Since I/O time is usually the largest component of overall response time, this type of row fragmentation can greatly reduce performance.

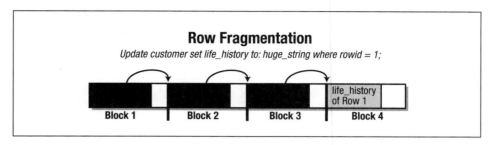

Figure 7.7 An example of Oracle row chaining.

Several preventative measures can be taken to avoid this situation. If the row will eventually contain all of its column values, and the values are of fixed length, the table could be defined with the parameter **NOT NULL**. This reserves space in the row when it is initially stored. If the row contains variable-length columns, then the **PCTFREE** parameter is increased to reserve space on each block for row expansion. By the way, this issue is not confined to Oracle. Most databases offer a utility that can be run periodically to check for row fragmentation. If fragments are found, the data must be exported to a flat file, the table redefined with different storage parameters, and the tables repopulated from a flat-file.

Listing 7.9 contains a script called chain.sql that will detect the number of chained rows for all Oracle tables. This script is a series of queries that acquire a list of all Oracle tables and write the **ANALYZE TABLE** syntax to an intermediate file, which is then executed to count the total number of chained rows for all tables. A chained row occurs when an SQL **UPDATE** operation has increased the size of a row, causing it to fragment onto another data block.

 *WARNING—Listing 7.9 creates table statistics that may force the use of the cost-based analyzer unless the database init.ora file parameter is set to **RULE** instead of **CHOOSE**.*

Listing 7.9   chain.sql shows all chained rows in the database tables.

```
SET ECHO OFF;
SET HEADING OFF;
```

```
SET FEEDBACK OFF;
SET VERIFY OFF;

DROP TABLE chained_rows;
@/opt/oracle/product/7.1.6/rdbms/admin/utlchain.sql

--define owner = &tableowner
SPOOL /opt/oracle/admin/adhoc/chainrun.sql;

SELECT 'analyze table ' || owner || '.' ||table_name ||
       ' list chained rows;'
FROM dba_tables
WHERE OWNER NOT IN ('SYS','SYSTEM');

SPOOL OFF;

--!more chainrun.sql
@chainrun.sql

SELECT 'There are ' || count(*) || ' chained rows in this database.'
FROM chained_rows;

SELECT DISTINCT owner_name, table_name, count(*)
FROM chained_rows
GROUP BY owner_name, table_name;

PROMPT
PROMPT You may now query the chained_rows table.
PROMPT This table contains one row for each row that has chained.
PROMPT
PROMPT suggested query:  select table_name, head_rowid, timestamp
PROMPT                          from chained_rows
PROMPT
PROMPT Refer to Oracle Administrators guide page 22-8 for directions
PROMPT regarding cleaning-up chained rows.

@chain

ANALYZE TABLE ORACLE.PUMPDATA LIST CHAINED ROWS;
ANALYZE TABLE ORACLE.SALESORG LIST CHAINED ROWS;
ANALYZE TABLE ORACLE.EMP LIST CHAINED ROWS;
ANALYZE TABLE ORACLE.LOB LIST CHAINED ROWS;
ANALYZE TABLE ORACLE.PRODUCT LIST CHAINED ROWS;
ANALYZE TABLE ORACLE.PAC1 LIST CHAINED ROWS;
```

```
ANALYZE TABLE ORACLE.PAC12 LIST CHAINED ROWS;
ANALYZE TABLE ORACLE.PAC23 LIST CHAINED ROWS;
ANALYZE TABLE ORACLE.MGC LIST CHAINED ROWS;
ANALYZE TABLE ORACLE.FILM_CODE LIST CHAINED ROWS;
ANALYZE TABLE ORACLE.CUST_CAT LIST CHAINED ROWS;
ANALYZE TABLE ORACLE.SALES_SUM LIST CHAINED ROWS;
ANALYZE TABLE ORACLE.DEPT LIST CHAINED ROWS;
ANALYZE TABLE ORACLE.BONUS LIST CHAINED ROWS;
ANALYZE TABLE ORACLE.SALGRADE LIST CHAINED ROWS;

ANALYZE TABLE ORACLE.DUMMY LIST CHAINED ROWS;
SQL>
SQL> SPOOL OFF;
SQL>
SQL> @chainrun.sql
SQL> SELECT 'analyze table ' || owner || '.' ||table_name ||
            ' list chained rows;'
SQL>   2   FROM dba_tables
SQL>   3   WHERE OWNER NOT IN ('SYS','SYSTEM');
SQL>

SQL> ANALYZE TABLE ORACLE.LOB LIST CHAINED ROWS;
SQL> ANALYZE TABLE ORACLE.PRODUCT LIST CHAINED ROWS;
SQL> ANALYZE TABLE ORACLE.PAC1 LIST CHAINED ROWS;
SQL> ANALYZE TABLE ORACLE.PAC12 LIST CHAINED ROWS;
SQL> ANALYZE TABLE ORACLE.PAC23 LIST CHAINED ROWS;
SQL> ANALYZE TABLE ORACLE.MGC LIST CHAINED ROWS;
SQL> ANALYZE TABLE ORACLE.FILM_CODE LIST CHAINED ROWS;
SQL> ANALYZE TABLE ORACLE.CUST_CAT LIST CHAINED ROWS;
SQL> ANALYZE TABLE ORACLE.SALES_SUM LIST CHAINED ROWS;
SQL> ANALYZE TABLE ORACLE.DEPT LIST CHAINED ROWS;
SQL> ANALYZE TABLE ORACLE.BONUS LIST CHAINED ROWS;
SQL> ANALYZE TABLE ORACLE.SALGRADE LIST CHAINED ROWS;
SQL> ANALYZE TABLE ORACLE.DUMMY LIST CHAINED ROWS;
```

Listing 7.10 shows the listing from this script.

Listing 7.10 The results from the chain.sql script.

```
There are 16784 chained rows in this database.

SQL>
SQL> select distinct owner_name, table_name, count(*)
  2     from chained_rows
```

```
3  group by owner_name, table_name;
```

ORACLE	SALESNET	16784
ORACLE	SALES	432
ORACLE	CUST	126744

Designing Expert Systems For Performance Measurement

When a centralized database is split into multiple distributed systems, the overall maintenance requirements for each database increases significantly. While the overall costs for the system hardware will decline as companies abandon their mainframes, human resources will increase as redundant personnel are added to perform system and database administration tasks at each node.

Many distributed database shops are responding to this challenge by creating systems that automate the common performance tracking for each remote database, alerting the DBA staff when predefined thresholds are exceeded. This type of automation can be extended with statistical trend analysis tools such as the SAS product to give forecasts of database maintenance and performance trends.

While these systems can become very sophisticated, this author recommends an evolutionary approach to the design of expert systems for performance and tuning. The work in 1981 by Robert Bonczeck into the theoretical structure of expert systems applies very well to performance and tuning applications. Bonczeck identifies a generalized framework for solving problems that consists of three components: states, operators, and goals. This approach assumes that the initial state is identified (namely a performance degradation), and a series of operators is applied to this state until the goal state is achieved (i.e., acceptable performance). This "state-space" approach to problem solving is especially useful for systems that collect and analyze performance and tuning information.

The idea is to create a knowledge system to store relevant statistical information, periodically feeding this knowledge system into a problem processing system as illustrated in Figure 7.8. The problem processing system contains the decision rules that are used to analyze trends in usage and alert the DBA if a parameter has been exceeded.

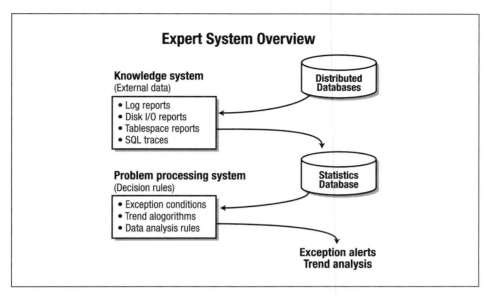

Figure 7.8 The architecture of expert systems.

This technique also relies on the knowledge that database performance and tuning do not require human intuition. While the decision rules applied to the problem are very complex, performance analysis is nothing more than the application of well-structured rules to problem data. Therefore, an automated system can be devised to replicate the DBA's expertise in performance analysis.

The following steps can be used to create an expert system for performance and tuning:

1. Identify the packaged utilities to be used, which may include:

    - SQL trace facility

    - Tablespace reports

    - Log analysis reports

    - Operating system specific reports

    - Performance monitor reports

2. Schedule the reports to run on a periodic basis and direct the output to a file.

3. Write a summary program to interpret the reports, and write summary statistics to a master file.

4. Create a problem processing system to read the knowledge system, generating trend reports and DBA alerts.

Many tools are available for performance analysis. Reports can be run against the database logs to produce reports containing statistics about every task in the database. The SQL trace utility can be turned on for a few minutes each day to attempt to identify inefficient SQL statements. Operating system reports can be generated containing information on disk contention and I/O bottlenecks. Performance monitors can also be used to detect information about database deadlocks and incomplete transactions.

Scheduling can be performed to fire the reports at specific time intervals. Unix utilities such as cron can be used for time-dependent scheduling, but it is convenient to have a gateway into the scheduler so that exception-based reporting can be conducted. For example, if a Unix monitor detects excessive hardware contention against a disk, it could trigger a user-exit to start an SQL trace to obtain detailed information.

Most database reports contain so much irrelevant information that a simple program written with C or even COBOL could be used to read the output from the reports, storing critical information into a table. This table would be used to feed the problem processing system, enabling the creation of exception reports and trend analysis reports. While this may sound complex, the data from the knowledge system can be fed directly into a canned statistical package such as SAS or SPSS to produce trend reports.

Table 7.1 shows a typical weekly exception report. All tasks for the day are analyzed and compared with a running average for their historical response time. If the response time for the task exceeds 15 percent of the historical average, the variance is noted in the right-hand column.

This type of report can provide very useful information about the overall operation of the distributed databases. Note, for example, the performance degradation on Wednesday (94308). We see that all of the tasks in the system were running below their historical average on that day, so we can assume that some external influence may have caused a system-wide response problem.

Table 7.1 Southern Meadows' weekly task exception report for the week ending 11/25/94.

Task Name	Day of Week							Times Invoked	Historical Response Variance
	94306	94307	94308	94309	94310	94311	94312		
PC01	.55	.54	.68	.56	.54	.57	.00	21932	.55
PC02	.05	.04	.08	.06	.04	.07	.00	3444	.01
PC03	.22	.23	.40	.21	.23	.21	.22	129342	.24
PC04	.05	.08	.09	.02	.04	.01	.00	3444	.01
PC05	.35	.33	.42	.33	.32	.40	.31	3444	.31

Other common reports can compare the buffer utilization for all of the distributed databases, comparing the ratio of **blocks_requested** to **blocks_in_buffer**. This can be used as a simple method of monitoring changes in buffer utilization over time.

DBAs who have implemented this type of system find that it removes the need for the tedious report analysis they once did by hand, providing a base for more sophisticated performance and tuning automation. For specific information about designing an Oracle system for performance monitoring, refer to Chapter 11, Oracle Application Monitoring.

Disk Issues With Distributed Database Performance

The placement of the database files on the DASD (disk) devices can have a significant impact on the system performance. On most disk devices, the volume table of contents (VTOC) can be placed anywhere on the disk device. While the VTOC placement is irrelevant if the database is not used for local mode processing (the database simply locates it once at startup time), the VTOC placement can become critical for local mode processing. A VTOC must be accessed each time a file is requested from disk storage, making it the most frequently accessed file on the disk. (See Figure 7.9.)

If one assumes an equal probability of the read-write heads being under any given track, it makes sense that all frequently accessed files (especially

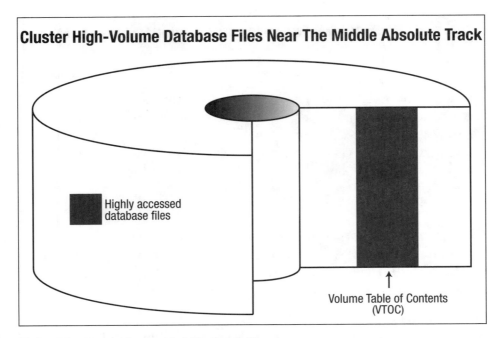

Cluster High-Volume Database Files Near The Middle Absolute Track

Highly accessed
database files

Volume Table of Contents
(VTOC)

Figure 7.9 Proper placement of Oracle data files.

the VTOC) should be placed near the "middle" track on the disk. Since seek time (the time it takes for the read-write head to relocate) is the greatest component of disk delay, this strategy will minimize overall disk access time.

Clearly, it follows that because I/O is the greatest contributor to database performance problems—and since seek time is the greatest component of disk response—whatever can be done to reduce seek delay will result in a performance improvement for the overall database.

Platform Computing's Load Sharing Facility

With all of the recent advances in symmetric multiprocessing (SMP), it is interesting to note that many companies are investigating tools that allow processors to be added and removed from a system on an as-needed basis. Load sharing, or the ability to dynamically add and remove processors, is the result of the shared memory cluster technology. By clustering multiple

SMP processors, the system administrators have the ability to easily scale-up a specific application, providing additional processing power on an as-needed basis.

The system administrators can link and unlink clusters of SMP hosts as they see fit, achieving the proper balance of processing power for an application. This new technology also relieves system planners from the chore of predetermining the full amount of CPU that an application will require. With multiple SMP clusters, the system can start small and new processors can be added as demands on the system grow.

While each vendor offers different tools to achieve CPU load sharing, the Load Sharing Facility (LSF) provides insight into the internal functioning of these types of tools. LSF is a distributed computing system that turns a cluster of Unix computers from several vendors into a "virtual supercomputer."

Platform's LSF supports fully transparent load sharing across Unix systems from different vendors, representing the enabling technology for the rapidly emerging cluster computing market. "There is a tremendous movement across the industries to downsize from mainframes and supercomputers to RISC-based open systems," said Songnian Zhou, President of Platform Computing. "Users' resources are transparently accessible to users. With LSF, we have seen interactive response time of key applications reduced by 30 to 40 percent and batch job throughput doubled at such large corporate sites."

The performance of low-cost workstations has been improving rapidly, and a cluster of workstations represents a tremendous amount of computing power. Up to now, however, such computing resources have been scattered over the network. Harnessing them to run user jobs has proved to be difficult.

Platform's LSF automates cluster computing by hiding the network and heterogeneous computers from users. Instead of running all compute jobs on the local computers like most Unix networks, LSF transparently distributes the jobs throughout the network—taking into consideration the architecture, the operating system, and the amount of resources required by the jobs, such as memory, disk space, and software licenses. LSF supports all types of applications—parallel and serial—submitted either interactively or in batch mode.

Distributed computing has been gaining importance over the last decade as a mode preferred over centralized computing. It has been widely observed that usage of computing resources in a distributed environment is usually "bursty" over time and uneven among the hosts. A user of a workstation may not use the machine all the time, but may require more than it can provide while actively working. Some hosts may be heavily loaded, whereas others remain idle. Along with the dramatic decrease in hardware costs, resource demands of applications have been increasing steadily, with new, resource-intensive applications being introduced rapidly. It is now (and will remain) too expensive to dedicate a sufficient amount of computing resource to each and every user.

Load sharing is the process of redistributing the system workload among the hosts to improve performance and accessibility to remote resources. Intuitively, avoiding the situation of load imbalances and exploiting powerful hosts may lead to better job response times and resource utilization. Numerous studies on load sharing in the 1980s have confirmed such an intuition. Most of the existing work, however, has been confined to the environment of a small cluster of homogeneous hosts, and has focused on the sharing of the processing power (CPU). With the proliferation of distributed systems supporting medium to large organizations, system scale has grown from a few time-sharing hosts to tens of workstations supported by a few server machines—and to hundreds and thousands of hosts. For effective load sharing, computing resources beyond the processing power of memory frames, disk storage, and I/O bandwidth should also be considered.

Heterogeneity

Another important development in distributed systems is heterogeneity, which may take a number of forms. In configurational heterogeneity, hosts may have different processing power, memory space, disk storage—or execute the same code on different hosts. Operating system heterogeneity occurs when the system facilities on different hosts vary and may be incompatible. Although heterogeneity imposes limitations on resource sharing, it also presents substantial opportunities. First, even if both a local workstation and a remote, more powerful host are idle, the performance of a job may still be improved if executed on the remote host rather than the local workstation. Secondly, by providing transparent resource locating and remote execution mechanisms, any job can be initiated from any host without considering the location of the resources needed by the task. Thus, a CAD package that can only be executed on a Sun host can now be initiated from an HP workstation.

Little research has been conducted regarding issues of large scale and heterogeneity in load sharing, yet they represent two of the most important research problems in load sharing in current and future distributed systems. As system scales for load sharing become inadequate, new research issues emerge.

Besides demonstrating the feasibility of a general purpose load-sharing system for large heterogeneous distributed systems by building a system that is usable in diverse system and application environments, the two main contributions of our research to the field of resource sharing in distributed systems are:

- The algorithms for distributing load information in systems with thousands of hosts, as well as task placements based on tasks' resource demands and hosts' load information.

- The collection of remote execution mechanisms that are highly flexible and efficient, thus enabling interactive tasks that require a high degree of transparency (as well as relatively fine-grained tasks of parallel applications) to be executed remotely and efficiently.

Summary

Considering the myriad factors that contribute to system performance, it is not surprising that we are missing the magic formula that can be applied to distributed databases to ensure acceptable performance. In a sense, performance and tuning for distributed systems is easier than centralized systems, since each remote site can be isolated and analyzed independently of the other remote sites. The complex nature of distributed processing ensures that performance and tuning will remain a complex endeavor, and it is only with a complete understanding of the nature of performance that effective measurement methods can be devised.

Performance And Tuning For Oracle Database Connectivity Tools

Database connectivity is much more than establishing communications with another database—it is the glue that holds the entire data federation together. Connectivity is achieved with many mechanisms, including application programming interfaces (APIs), remote procedure calls (RPCs), and a variety of vendor solutions. Each mechanism imposes strict rules for establishing database connections, and this chapter will review the most popular ways of making connectivity a reality. We'll be covering the following areas:

- Database APIs

- The internals of ODBC

- Programming for portability

- Intersystem connectivity

- The internals of Oracle's SQL*Net

- Cross-database connectivity with IBM mainframes

Database APIs

A great deal of confusion exists about the functions of APIs and how they communicate with connectivity tools and databases. In fact, some client/server architectures impose so many layers of interfaces that it is often very difficult to track the flow of information as it passes though all of the layers.

Ignoring the physical details, let's look at the logical methods for establishing connectivity. The most common type of logical connectivity is between remote databases of the same type. Oracle database software provides this type of mechanism with its SQL*Net software, allowing Oracle databases to connect with each other in a seamless fashion. Connectivity is established in Oracle by creating database links to the remote databases. Once defined by the DBA, these remote databases can participate in queries and updates from within any Oracle application. For example, a database in London and Paris can be defined to the Denver system with the following SQL extension:

```
CREATE PUBLIC DATABASE LINK london
    CONNECT TO london_unix;

CREATE PUBLIC DATABASE LINK paris
    CONNECT TO paris_vms;
```

We can now include any tables from these remote sites by qualifying their remote site name in the SQL query. This example joins three tables: a local **order** table in Denver, a **customer** table in Paris, and an **orderline** table in London.

```
SELECT customer.customer_name, order.order_date,
orderline.quantity_ordered
    FROM customer@london, order, orderline@paris
    WHERE
    customer.cust_number = order.customer_number
    AND
    order.order_number = orderline.order_number;
```

But what about remote databases that reside in other relational systems such as Sybase or FoxPro? And what about legacy data from a hierarchical database like IMS or a network database such as CA-IDMS? Here we enter a more complicated scenario—fortunately, we can choose from a variety of tools to accomplish this type of cross-architecture connectivity. The most popular connectivity gateway is Microsoft's Open Database Connectivity

(ODBC) product. However, many users have successfully implemented cross-architecture systems using custom-written RPCs and APIs.

An API is an interface that is generally embedded into an application program to interface with an external database. Database APIs come in two flavors: embedded and call-level. Embedded APIs are placed within an application program to interface with the database management system. Listing 8.1 shows a sample COBOL program that has embedded SQL commands.

Listing 8.1   A COBOL program.

```
WORKING-STORAGE SECTION.

01  CUST-RECORD.

    05  CUSTOMER_NAME        PIC X(80).
    05  CUSTOMER_ADDRESS     PIC X(100).
    05  CUSTOMER_PHONE       PIC 9(7).

EXEC-SQL    INCLUDE SQLCA    END-EXEC.

PROCEDURE DIVISION.

OPEN INPUT INPUT-FILE.
READ INPUT-FILE AT END MOVE 'Y' TO EOF-SWITCH.

EXEC-SQL

    CONNECT TO :REMOTE_SITE;

END-EXEC.

EXEC-SQL

    SELECT * FROM CUSTOMER
    WHERE
    DB_CUST_NAME = INPUT_CUSTOMER_NAME

END-EXEC.

IF SQLCODE <> 0 THEN PERFORM NOT-FOUND-ROUTINE.

NOT-FOUND-ROUTINE.
```

```
      DISPLAY "ERROR IN READING DATABASE"

CLOSE INPUT-FILE.
END RUN.
```

Here we see SQL that has been embedded in a COBOL program for access to a relational database. Unlike a regular COBOL program, special sections are embedded into the code that are foreign to the COBOL compiler. In this sample, the SQL commands are started with **EXEC-SQL** and ended with **END-EXEC**. An SQL precompiler is invoked to preprocess these statements, commenting them out and replacing them with native calls statements that the COBOL compiler will recognize. In Listing 8.2 we see that the "native" SQL has been replaced with calls to a routine called RDBINTC. The RDBINTC routine will place the SQL calls on behalf of the program.

Listing 8.2   The RDBINTC routine.

```
WORKING-STORAGE SECTION.

01  CUST-RECORD.

    05  CUSTOMER_NAME        PIC X(80).
    05  CUSTOMER_ADDRESS     PIC X(100).
    05  CUSTOMER_PHONE       PIC 9(7).

*  EXEC-SQL     INCLUDE SQLCA     END-EXEC.

01 SQLCA.
    05 SQL-FIELD1    PIC 99.
    05 SQL-FIELD2    PIC X(20).

PROCEDURE DIVISION.

OPEN INPUT INPUT-FILE.
READ INPUT-FILE AT END MOVE 'Y' TO EOF-SWITCH.

*    EXEC-SQL

*    CONNECT TO :REMOTE_SITE;

*    END-EXEC
```

```
CALL RDBINTC USING (SQLCA,45,:REMOTE_SITE);

*   EXEC-SQL
*   SELECT * FROM CUSTOMER
*   WHERE
*   DB_CUST_NAME = INPUT_CUSTOMER_NAME

*   END-EXEC


CALL RDBINTC USING (SQLCA,23,"CUSTOMER", DB-CUST-NAME,
    INPUT-CUSTOMER-NAME);

IF SQLCODE <> 0 THEN PERFORM NOT-FOUND-ROUTINE.

NOT-FOUND-ROUTINE.

    DISPLAY "ERROR IN READING DATABASE"

CLOSE INPUT-FILE.
END RUN.
```

At execution time, the COBOL program will interface with the database by making native calls to the database interface, called RDBINTC in this example. The interface will manage all of the I/O against the database on behalf of the COBOL program, and will pass the result set (or a cursor) back to the application program using the SQL Communications Area (SQLCA).

Notice how the COBOL program checks the value of the **SQLCODE** field. When the database is accessed from a remote program, the calling program must explicitly check the value of the **SQLCODE** to ensure successful execution of the intended statement.

The Internals Of ODBC

The Open Database Connectivity (ODBC) product was initially developed by Microsoft as a generic database driver. It's architecture has now been generalized and many different vendors are offering open database connectivity products that are based on ODBC. ODBC is the predominant common-interface approach to database connectivity and is a part of

Microsoft's Windows Open Service Architecture (WOSA). ODBC and WOSA define a standard set of data access services that can be used by a variety of other products when interfacing with an MS-Windows application.

ODBC consists of more than 50 functions that are invoked from an application using a call-level API. The ODBC API does not communicate with a database directly. Instead, it serves as a link between the application and a generic interface routine. The interface routine, in turn, communicates with the database drivers via a Service Provider Interface (SPI), as shown in Figure 8.1.

Each custom application within Windows will have call-level API calls to the ODBC database driver—which, in turn, directs the request to the appropriate database driver for execution. The database driver manages the communication between the database and the program, and handles all returning data and messages, passing then back to the ODBC driver—which, in turn, passes them back to the invoking application.

As ODBC becomes more popular, database vendors are creating new ODBC drivers that will allow ODBC to be used as a gateway into their database products. A word of caution is in order: Although most programmers can be successful with ODBC in a simple application, effective use of ODBC in

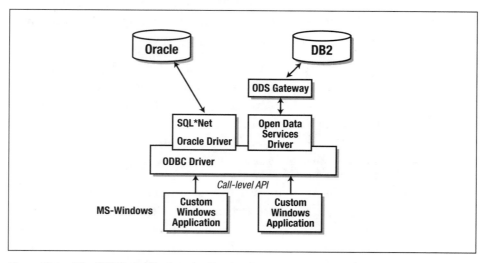

Figure 8.1   The ODBC architecture for Oracle.

multidatabase environments is a very difficult task. The programmers need to be aware of all of the different dialects of SQL, and they must also be aware of the native API to the database engines. However, a few tips can ease the effort, despite this steep learning curve.

Essentially, ODBC serves as the "traffic cop" for all data within the client/server system. When a client requests a service from a database, ODBC receives the request and manages the connection to the target database. ODBC manages all of the database drivers, checking all of the status information as it arrives from the database drivers.

It is noteworthy that the database drivers should be able to handle more than just SQL. Many databases have a native API that requires ODBC to map the request into a library of functions. An example would be an SQL-Server driver that maps ODBC functions to database library function calls. Databases without a native API (i.e., non-SQL databases) can also be used with ODBC, but they go through a much greater transformation than the native API calls.

When accessing multiple databases with ODBC, it is up to the API programmer to manage the multiple database connections and the multiple SQL requests that are being directed to the connections. In ODBC, *handles* are used to point to each database connection. A handle is usually a pointer into the database, and the value of the handle is a record key, a row ID, or an object ID.

Most people associate ODBC with SQL. While SQL is now the single most common access method for databases, there are many important non-SQL databases that are widely used. Popular non-SQL databases include IMS, CA-IDMS, Basis Plus, and almost all of the new object-oriented databases. It is a misconception that a database that does not support SQL cannot use ODBC.

Programming For Portability

The key to success with ODBC in a distributed relational database environment is to create the illusion of location transparency. This transparency is ideally maintained by requiring that all cross-database applications handle their queries with *vanilla* SQL. The term vanilla refers to the common features of SQL that are shared by all of the vendors. Determining which features are vanilla can often be a difficult task, since each major database vendor has implemented SQL with its own "enhancements" that are not shared by other vendors. Fortunately, most of these differences are found in the **CREATE TABLE** and referential integrity syntax, and are not germane to SQL queries. For queries, the most common extensions relate to syntax tricks that are used to force the SQL to use a specific index. For example, in Oracle SQL a null string can be concatenated into the query to force the transaction to use a specific index.

Please note that ODBC can also be used to interrogate the system tables of the target database. With additional programming effort, an ODBC routine can be written to interrogate the metadata in the target database and determine the SQL features that are supported by the database product.

For example, a database such as Oracle can be interrogated to see if it has stored procedures associated with a database event, and these procedures can be accessed by ODBC and displayed as a list. System users can then choose from the list if they want ODBC to utilize the stored procedure.

This approach can be very cumbersome, and most users of ODBC recommend the "generic SQL" approach. Unfortunately, the selection of the vanilla SQL must be done very carefully because of the differences in implementation of different vendors' SQL. Almost every implementation has vendor-supplied, nonstandard extensions called *features* that are not supported by other databases. These include support for stored procedures and built-in functions that the vendor adds to enhance programmer productivity.

Several problems arise when using non-ANSI SQL:

- The SQL is rejected as a syntax error. This is the simplest problem to correct and can be fixed in the testing phase, long before delivery of the completed system. The introduction of a new database into the federation may also cause problems if the existing SQL relies on non-standard extensions that are not supported by the new SQL dialect.

- Cross-database referential integrity is difficult to enforce. When business rules span physical databases, the enforcement of those rules can be very hard to accomplish. Since Oracle cannot enforce RI across servers, the developers must create procedural mechanisms to ensure that the rules are maintained. For example, a business rule that prohibits any rows in **tokyo.order** without parent entry in **cleveland.customer** will have to write an extended two-phase commit transaction to roll back the entire transaction if one piece of the distributed update fails.

- The SQL performance is different on each target database. This happens when the SQL optimizer uses different access paths for different implementations of SQL. For example, an identical SQL request that is valid for both Oracle and DB2 will return identical results sets, but may use different access methods to retrieve the data. For example, DB2 SQL uses the concept of sargeable predicates to determine the optimization of an SQL query. Depending on how the SQL request is phrased, the SQL optimizer may choose to invoke sequential prefetch, use a merge scan, or utilize other access techniques that can affect performance. Whenever possible, it is recommended that the programmer ignore this issue initially, because rewriting an SQL query for performance reasons can be very time-consuming. Of course, performance remains an issue, but the SQL tuning can be left to the final stages of the project.

Anyone who is considering ODBC as a connectivity tool should also be aware that ODBC does not support all of the SQL extensions that a database server may offer. In order to accommodate these nonstandard features, ODBC offers a back door that the programmer can use to send native API commands directly to the target database. Again, this procedure is not recommended unless the feature is absolutely necessary to the application. Mixing ODBC calls with native API calls creates a confusing jumble of access methods and makes the application much more difficult to support. Another obstacle with this approach to ODBC is maintaining the portability of the application. As new releases of the database add new extensions to the SQL, the ODBC component must be changed to accommodate these enhancements.

Some people argue that the "least common denominator" approach to ODBC SQL is too limiting. They state that learning the common syntax and facilities of SQL is too time consuming, and that a generalization of SQL would remove the most powerful features, making the system far less functional.

Intersystem Connectivity

In systems that allow cross-database access, a very common method of distribution uses the idea of horizontal partitioning. For example, customer service organizations commonly allow their remote sites to maintain customer information while still maintaining a location-transparent access mode to every customer, regardless of their physical location. The horizontal partitioning is achieved by taking a subset of each remote site's customer table, and populating a master lookup table that is accessible from any node in the distributed system, as shown in Figure 8.2.

In a Unix-based distributed system, the cron utility could be used to schedule a periodic refresh of the master table. The cron utility is a time-dependent task activation utility, and starts tasks at predetermined dates and times. An SQL script would automatically extract **customer_name** from the remote site and repopulate the master customer table, leaving the customer details at the remote site. The Oracle SQL might look like this:

```
/*  Delete remote rows in the master table... */

DELETE FROM customer@master
WHERE
LOCATION = :OUR_SITE;

/*  Repopulate the master table...  */

SELECT customer_name, ':our_site'
FROM customer@:OUR_SITE
AS
INSERT INTO customer@master
VALUES customer_name, site_name;
```

Once populated, the master look-up can be accessed by any node and used to redirect the database query to the appropriate remote database for customer detail, as shown in Figure 8.3.

Because of the dynamic substitution in the SQL, a common application can be made to access any customer in the federation regardless of the location—without any changes to the application code.

Dynamic transparency is especially useful for situations where remote locations have "ownership" of the data, while a corporate entity requires access to the data at a central location.

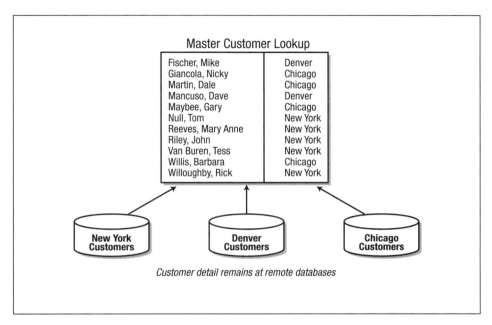

Figure 8.2   Horizontal data partitioning.

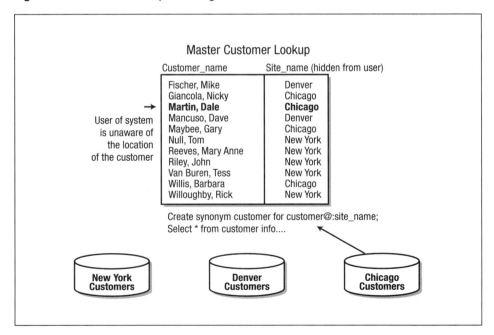

Figure 8.3   Dynamic location transparency.

The Internals Of Oracle's SQL*Net

In its most basic form, SQL*Net is a software tool that allows a network of Oracle clients and servers to communicate transparently on top of any underlying network topology or protocol using SQL. Although SQL*Net is a very robust and sophisticated tool, you must appreciate the inherent complexity that goes along with the flexibility of SQL*Net. This section provides a no-nonsense overview of the SQL*Net architecture. All of the examples are based on Unix.

Due to the sophisticated architecture of SQL*Net, it is not trivial to install on the client or the server. For Unix systems, the following files are necessary to operate SQL*Net 2.0:

- /etc/tnsnames.ora—Used for outgoing database requests, this file contains all of the database names (sids) running on the processor, as well as the domain name, protocol, host, and port information. When a new database is added to a box, you must update this file (changes to tnsnames.ora become effective instantly). Note: The SQL*Net version 1.0 equivalent is /etc/oratab.

- /etc/listener.ora—This file contains a list of local databases for use by incoming connections. When you add a new destination database to a Unix host, you must also add it to this file.

- /etc/hosts—This file lists all of your network addresses.

- /etc/services—This file lists all of the SQL*Net services.

In version 2.0, Oracle has added several important enhancements to SQL*Net. Aside from the badly needed bug fixes, SQL*Net now allows multiple community access. A community is a group of computers that share a common protocol (such as TCP/IP to LU6.2). In addition, the Oracle7 database engine now defines a multithreaded server (MTS) for servicing incoming data requests. In the MTS, all communication to the database is handled through a single dispatcher. In SQL*Net version 1, a separate process is spawned for each connection. These connections are easily viewed by using the Unix ps command.

When upgrading from SQL*Net 1.0 to SQL*Net 2.0, you should be aware of subtle differences between how the two versions handle communications. (See Figure 8.4.) SQL*Net version 1.0 uses an orasrv component on

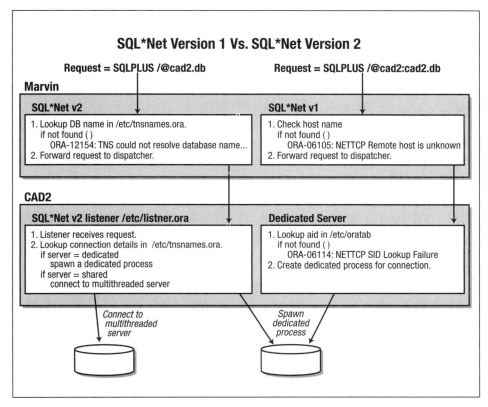

Figure 8.4 The two versions of SQL*Net.

the destination database to listen for incoming requests, while SQL*Net 2.0 uses a process called tnslsnr (TNS listener). In addition, SQL*Net 1.0 cannot use the multithreaded server.

When a connection is made to SQL*Net, it passes the request to its underlying layer, the transparent network substrate (TNS), where the request is transmitted to the appropriate server. At the server, SQL*Net receives the request from TNS and passes the SQL to the database. "Transparent network substrate" is a fancy term meaning a single, common interface to all protocols that allows you to connect to databases in physically separate networks. At the lowest level, TNS communicates to other databases with message-level send/receive commands.

On the client side, the User Programmatic Interface (UPI) converts SQL to associated **PARSE**, **EXECUTE**, and **FETCH** statements. The UPI parses the SQL, opens the SQL cursor, binds the client application, describes the contents of returned data fields, executes the SQL, fetches the rows, and closes the cursor. Oracle attempts to minimize messages to the server by combining UPI calls whenever possible. On the server side, the Oracle Programmatic Interface (OPI) responds to all possible messages from the UPI and returns requests.

No UPI exists for server-to-server communication. Instead, a Network Programmatic Interface (NPI) resides at the initiating server, and the responding server uses its OPI.

SQL*Net supports network transparency such that the network structure may be changed without affecting the SQL*Net application. Location transparency is achieved with database links and synonyms.

Let's trace a sample data request through SQL*Net. Essentially, SQL*Net will look for the link name in the database link table (**dba_db_links**) and extract the service name. The service name is then located in the tnsnames.ora file, and the host name is extracted. Once again, we have a three-stage process beginning with the link name, referencing the service name, which references the host name.

In Unix environments, the host name is found in a host file (/etc/hosts), and the Internal Protocol (IP) address is gathered. In the following example, **london_unix** might translate into an IP address of 143.32.142.3. These four steps illustrate how SQL*Net takes a remote request and translates it into the IP address of the destination database:

1. Issue a remote request—check the database link called **LONDON**:

   ```
   SELECT * FROM CUSTOMER@LONDON
   ```

2. Database link—get service name (**london_unix_d**) using the **link_name** (**LONDON**):

   ```
   CREATE PUBLIC DATABASE LINK LONDON
   CONNECT TO london_unix_d;
   ```

3. tnsnames.ora—get the sid name (**london_sid**) using service name (**london_unix_d**):

   ```
   london_unix_d = (description=(address=(protocol=tcp) (host=seagull)
   (port=1521) (connect_data=(sid=london_sid) (server=dedicated)))
   ```

4. /etc/hosts—get IP address (143.32.142.3) using sid name (**london_sid**):

```
143.32.142.3     london_sid        london_unix.corporate.com
```

As you can see, this translation occurs in a multistage process. The tnsnames.ora file specifies the name of the host containing the destination database. For Unix environments, this host name is then looked up in the /etc/hosts file to get the IP address of the destination box.

Note that the service name is looked up in tnsnames.ora—if the service exists, the IP address is found in the /etc/hosts file and a communications request is sent to the destination IP address. Note that both of the entries in this file connect to London, but **london_unix_d** directs SQL*Net to spawn a dedicated process, while **london_unix** uses the multithreaded server component because a shared server is specified.

Now that you have the tnsnames.ora and /etc/hosts files in place, you can include any tables from the London sites by qualifying the remote site name in the SQL query:

```
SELECT customer.customer_name, order.order_date
   FROM customer@london, ORDER
   WHERE customer.cust_number = order.customer_number;
```

Note that this query joins two tables at different locations, and the database link called **london** determines how the Oracle connection will be established on the destination system. Regardless of how the connection is made to the destination, however, the user ID must have **SELECT** privileges against the customer table, or this query will fail.

*Application Connection With SQL*Net*

Connections to remote databases can be made by specifying either *service names* or *connect strings*. Connect strings use the full connection. In the example below, the "t:" means a TCP/IP connection, "host:" is the name of the remote processor, and "database" is the name of the database on that processor:

1. Connect with a service name:

    ```
    emp@my_db
    ```

2. Connect with a server connect string:

    ```
    sqlplus /@t:host:database
    ```

Connect strings are stored in the **dba_dblinks** table, and are created with the **CREATE DATABASE LINK** command:

```
CREATE PUBLIC DATABASE LINK ny_emp FOR ny_emp@t:myhost:mydatabase
```

SQL*Net For Client/Server

SQL*Net can establish database communications in three ways: via a remote connection, a remote request, or a distributed request. A remote connection is the easiest way to make a database connection. The sending database simply makes a request by specifying a table name suffixed by "@". SQL*Net takes it from there, seamlessly accessing the remote database and returning the data to the initiating system. Communication is established simply by making a distributed request to a remote database. Within Oracle, @ specifies the remote database name, but the functionality of the @ operator depends on where it is used. Here's an example:

```
sqlplus scott/tiger@london

SELECT COUNT(*) FROM EMPLOYEE;

COUNT(*)
------------
        162
```

In this request, Scott is using SQL*Plus to connect to the London database, and **@london** is the service name, as defined in the tnsnames.ora file. SQL*Net recognizes this as a remote connection and determines the appropriate linkage to establish communications with London. Internally, Oracle will check the tnsnames.ora file to ensure that **london** is a valid destination.

Now, observe another way of connecting to London from the same database. This is called a remote request:

```
sqlplus scott/tiger
SELECT COUNT(*) FROM employee@london;

COUNT(*)
--------------
        162
```

Unlike a remote connection made directly from SQL*Plus, this remote request has Scott connecting to the local copy of SQL*Plus to specify the remote table (in this case, **employee@london**). In order for a remote request to work, a database link must define **london**. A database link is a connection pathway to a remote database that specifies the service name of the remote database. Without the database link, the following request would fail:

```
sqlplus scott/tiger

SELECT COUNT(*) FROM EMPLOYEE@LONDON;
```

This request will give you an error message that reads, "ORA-02019: connection description for remote database not found." The reason for this message is the way that Oracle defines the @ operator. When entering an Oracle service such as SQL*Plus, the @ operator will go directly to the tnsnames.ora file to manage the request, while the @ operator from within an Oracle program specifies the use of a database link.

To make the code functional, you must define a database link that specifies the service name used to establish the connection. Note that the database link name and the service name are the same in this example, but the database link and the connect descriptor are not related in any way:

```
CREATE DATABASE LINK LONDON USING 'london';
SELECT COUNT(*) FROM employee@london;

COUNT(*)
--------------
     162
```

Let's take a closer look at the database link. In this simple example, no mention is made of the user ID that is used to establish the connection on the remote database. Because Scott is the user connecting to SQL*Plus, Scott will be the user ID when the remote connection is established to the London database. Therefore, Scott must have **SELECT** privileges against the employee table in London in order for the query to work properly. Scott's privileges on the initiating Oracle have no bearing on the success of the query.

 *If you are using the Oracle Names facility, you must be sure that your database service names are the same as the **global_databases_names** and the **DOMAIN** init.ora parameter.*

In cases where **SELECT** security is not an issue, you can enhance the database link syntax to include a remote connect description:

```
CREATE DATABASE LINK LONDON USING 'LONDON'
CONNECT TO scott1 IDENTIFIED BY tiger1;
```

This way, all users who specify the **LONDON** database link will connect as **scott1** and will have whatever privileges that **scott1** has on the London system.

Once you establish a communications pathway to the remote database, it is often desirable to implement *location transparency*. In relational databases such as Oracle, you can obtain location transparency by creating database links to the remote database and then assigning a global synonym to the remote tables. The database link specifies a link name and an SQL*Net service name. You can create database links with a location suffix that is associated with a host name (in this example, **london_unix**).

You can use database links to allow applications to point to other databases without altering the application code. For data warehousing applications, you can replicate a table on another machine and establish links to enable the application to point transparently to the new box containing the replicated table.

To see the links for a database, query the Oracle dictionary:

```
SELECT DISTINCT db_link FROM dba_db_links;
```

Keep in mind that SQL*Net bypasses all operating system connections when it connects to a database. All user accounts that are identified externally (that is, without an Oracle password) will not be allowed in SQL*Net transactions unless the init.ora parameter is changed. The **IDENTIFIED EXTERNALLY** clause (OPS$) in Oracle version 6 allowed the operating system to manage passwords, but because SQL*Net bypasses the operating system, impostor accounts could be created from other platforms. The result? Security was bypassed. Consequently, Oracle now recommends that **IDENTIFIED EXTERNALLY** accounts be forbidden for distributed connections.

It is interesting to note that Oracle will allow you to create accounts with an OPS$ prefix. Therefore, the operating system can manage its passwords, while you also have passwords within Oracle. For example, assume the following user definition:

```
CREATE USER ops$scott IDENTIFIED BY tiger;
```

Assuming that Scott has logged onto the operating system, Scott could enter SQL*Plus either with or without a password:

```
sqlplus /
sqlplus scott/tiger
```

This ability to connect directly to Oracle presents a confounding issue with password management. Because two sets of passwords exist—one in the operating system and another in Oracle—you may need a third-party tool to keep the passwords synchronized. (See Figure 8.5.)

Understanding The SQL*Net Listener

To see what the Oracle listener is doing, Oracle provides a series of listener commands, which include:

- **LSNRCTL RELOAD**—Refreshes the listener

- **LSNRCTL START**—Starts the listener

- **LSNRCTL STOP**—Stops the listener

- **LSNRCTL STATUS**—Shows the status of the listener

Listing 8.3 shows the output of the **LSNRCTL** status command.

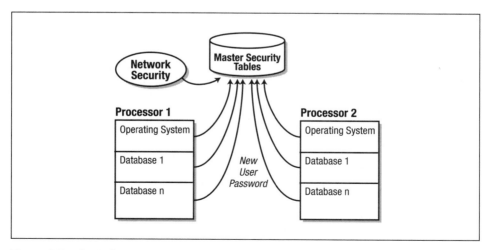

Figure 8.5   Centralized password management tool architecture.

Listing 8.3   Output of the LSNRCTL status command.

```
[oracle]ram2: lsnrctl stat

LSNRCTL for HPUX: Version 2.0.15.0.0 - Production on 16-SEP-94 15:38:00

Copyright (a)  Oracle Corporation 1993.  All rights reserved.

Connecting to (ADDRESS=(PROTOCOL=TCP)(HOST=ram2)(PORT=1521))
STATUS of the LISTENER
------------------------
Alias               LISTENER
Version             TNSLSNR for HPUX: Version 2.0.15.0.0 -
                    Production
Start Date          29-AUG-94 13:50:16
Uptime              18 days 1 hr. 47 min. 45 sec
Trace Level         off
Security            OFF
Listener Parameter File   /etc/listener.ora
Listener Log File         /usr/oracle/network/log/listener.log
Services Summary...
  dev7db              has 1 service handlers
  ram2db              has 1 service handlers
The command completed successfully

lsnrctl services     - lists all servers and dispatchers

[oracle]seagull: lsnrctl services

LSNRCTL for HPUX: Version 2.0.15.0.0 - Production on 16-SEP-94 15:36:47

Copyright (a)  Oracle Corporation 1993. All rights reserved.

Connecting to (ADDRESS=(PROTOCOL=TCP)(HOST=seagull)(PORT=1521))
Services Summary...
  tdb000              has 4 service handlers
    DISPATCHER established:1 refused:0 current:2 max:55 state:ready
      D001 (machine: seagull, pid: 4146)
      (ADDRESS=(PROTOCOL=tcp)(DEV=5)(HOST=141.123.224.38)(PORT=1323))
    DISPATCHER established:1 refused:0 current:2 max:55 state:ready
      D000 (machine: seagull, pid: 4145)
      (ADDRESS=(PROTOCOL=tcp)(DEV=5)(HOST=141.123.224.38)(PORT=1321))
    DISPATCHER established:0 refused:0 current:1 max:55 state:ready
      D002 (machine: seagull, pid: 4147)
      (ADDRESS=(PROTOCOL=tcp)(DEV=5)(HOST=141.123.224.38)(PORT=1325))
    DEDICATED SERVER established:0 refused:0
The command completed successfully
```

As a service request is intercepted by an Oracle server, the listener may direct the request via a dedicated server, an MTS, or an existing process (pre-spawned shadow). The key is whether the connection contacts the listener via a service name, or bypasses the listener with the **two_task** connect string. If the listener is contacted as part of the connection and the MTS parms are defined to init.ora, the client will use the MTS.

There are five basic listener commands: **RELOAD**, **START**, **STOP**, **STATUS**, and **SERVICES**. Based on the request, the listener decides whether to dispatch a connection to a dedicated-server process (which it spawns) or to use the MTS. The programmer has several options when deciding how Oracle will manage the process. Dedicated requests can be specified by a version 1.0 connect string, or by using a service name that specifies "**server=dedicated**" in the tnsnames.ora file.

 Local connections will use the listener if the MTSs are defined. Even internal invocations to Oracle (for example, sqlplus/) will add a connection to the MTS.

*Managing SQL*Net Connections*

Listing 8.4 describes some of the utilities you can use to manage SQL*Net sessions effectively. You should be aware that some of the examples in this section are operation system-independent, and may not apply to your environment.

Listing 8.4   Commit point strength.

```
commit.sql -  Reports the commit point strength for the database.

SET FEEDBACK OFF
COLUMN NAME   FORMAT a30 HEADING 'Name'
COLUMN TYPE   FORMAT a7  HEADING 'Type'
COLUMN VALUE FORMAT a60 HEADING 'Value'

PROMPT Commit Point-strength Report Output:
PROMPT
PROMPT
SELECT NAME,
       DECODE(type,1,'boolean',
```

```
                2,'string',
                3,'integer',
                4,'file') type,
      REPLACE(replace(value,'@','%{sid}'),'?','%{home}') VALUE
FROM    v$parameter
WHERE   NAME = 'commit_point_strength';
```

Showing And Killing SQL*Net Sessions

On systems running SQL*Net 2.0, you can use a session script to query the number of dedicated and shared servers on the system. For example, Listing 8.5, which appears later in this chapter, shows all connected users and their type of connection to the Oracle database.

Unlike dedicated SQL*Net sessions, you cannot kill multithreaded SQL*Net sessions directly from the Unix operating system. For example, you can identify a runaway session on a dedicated server by using the Unix **ps-ef|grep ora** command, and subsequently kill it using the **kill -9 nnn** command. With the multithreaded server, operating system processes no longer exist for each separate task, and you must use the Oracle SQL **ALTER SYSTEM KILL SESSION** command to kill the task at the Oracle subsystem level (using the **ALTER SYSTEM KILL SESSION 'sid, ser#';** command).

To kill a user in an MTS session, first enter SQL*Plus and type:

```
SELECT sid, serial#, USERNAME FROM v$session;

SID   SERIAL#    USERNAME
8     28         OPS$xxx
10    211        POS$yyy
13    8          dburleso
```

If **dburleso** is the session you want to kill, enter the **ALTER SYSTEM KILL SESSION '13, 8'** command.

This cumbersome method of clobbering runaway SQL*Net connections can be very annoying in development environments where dozens of programmers are testing programs, and they must call the DBA every time they want to kill a runaway task. The only alternative, however, is to grant the programmers **ALTER SYSTEM** authority on test platforms.

Managing The Multithreaded Server (MTS)

One of the problems with SQL*Net version 1.0 was that each incoming transaction was "spawned" by the listener as a separate operating system task. With SQL*Net version 2.0, Oracle now has a method for allowing the listener connection to dispatch numerous subprocesses. With the MTS, all communications to a database are handled through a single dispatcher instead of separate Unix process IDs (PIDs) on each database. This translates into faster performance for most online tasks. Even local transactions will be directed through the MTS, and you will no longer see a PID for your local task when you issue **ps-ef|grep oracle**.

However, be aware that the MTS is not a panacea, especially at times when you want to invoke a dedicated process for your program. For Pro*C programs and I/O-intensive SQL*Forms applications — or any processes that have little idle time — you may derive better performance using a dedicated process.

In general, the MTS offers benefits such as reduced memory use, fewer processes per user, and automatic load balancing. However, it is often very confusing to tell whether the MTS is turned on — much less working properly.

Remember the following rules of thumb when initially starting the MTS:

- The MTS is governed by the init.ora parameters. If no MTS params are present in init.ora, the MTS is disabled.

- The MTS is used when the MTS params are in the init.ora and requests are made by service name (such as **@myplace**). In other words, you must retrieve the **ROWID** of all version 1.0 connect strings (such as **t:unix1:myplace**).

- Each user of the MTS requires 1 K of storage, so plan to increase your **shared_pool_size**.

- The **v$queue** and **v$dispatcher** system tables indicate if the number of MTS dispatchers is too low. Even though the number of dispatchers is specified in the init.ora file, you can change it online in SQL*DBA with the **ALTER SYSTEM** command:

```
SQLDBA> ALTER SYSTEM SET MTS_DISPATCHERS = 'TCPIP,4';
```

- If you encounter problems with the MTS, you can quickly regress to dedicated servers by issuing an **ALTER SYSTEM** command. The following command turns off the MTS by setting the number of MTS servers to zero:

```
SQLDBA> ALTER SYSTEM SET MTS_SERVERS=0;
```

- In order to use **OPS$**, you must set two init.ora values to **true** (they default to **false**):

```
remote_os_authent = true
remote_os_roles = true
```

- When both SQL*Net 1.0 and 2.0 are installed, the user may connect to the server either via a dedicated server or via the MTS. However, you cannot stop and restart the listener when connecting via the MTS. You must connect to SQL*DBA with a dedicated server.

- In some cases, the instance must be bounced if the listener is stopped, or it will restart in dedicated mode. Whenever an instance is to be bounced, stop the listener, shut down the instance, restart the listener, and start up the instance. The listener reads the MTS parameters only if it is running before startup of the instance. Therefore, bouncing the listener will disable the MTS.

MANAGING THE LISTENER PROCESS

The listener is a software program that runs on each remote node and "listens" for any incoming database requests. When a request is detected, the listener may direct the request to:

- A dedicated server

- A multithreaded server

- An existing process or prespawned shadow

Note that the configuration of an Oracle listener is a direct result of the parameters that are specified in the startup deck for the Oracle database. This parameter file is called init.ora, and will contain the following parameters to define the multithreaded server and listener:

```
# ----------------------
# Multi-threaded Server
# ----------------------

MTS_DISPATCHERS = "tcp,3"
```

```
MTS_LISTENER_ADDRESS = "(ADDRESS=(PROTOCOL=tcp) (HOST=seagull)
(PORT=1521))"

MTS_MAX_DISPATCHERS = 5

MTS_MAX_SERVERS = 20

# -------------------------
# Distributed systems options
# -------------------------

DISTRIBUTED_LOCK_TIMEOUT = 60

DISTRIBUTED_RECOVERY_CONNECTION_HOLD_TIME = 200

DISTRIBUTED_TRANSACTIONS = 6
```

MISCELLANEOUS MANAGEMENT TIPS FOR SQL*NET

Just as the /etc/oratab file for SQL*Net version 1.0 is interpreted, the tnsnames.ora file is also interpreted. This means that you can change it at any time without fear of bouncing anything. However, changes to listener.ora require that the listener be reloaded with **LSNRCTL RELOAD**.

When a database is accessed remotely via a database link, SQL*Net uses the temporary tablespace on the destination database, regardless of the processor invoking the task or the original database location. The moral? SQL*Net will use the temporary tablespace on the destination database— not on the initiating database. In other words, applications on one processor that accessed another processor with a database link will use the temporary tablespaces on the terminal processor—not the processor that contains the link.

Always remember to change your $ORACLE_HOME/bin/oraenv file to unset **ORACLE_SID** and set **TWO_TASK=sid**.

Three logs appear in SQL*Net:

- listener log = /usr/oracle/network/log/listener.log

- sqlnet log = /usr/oracle/network/log/sqlnet.log

- trace log = destination set with the **trace_directory_listener** parameter of the /etc/listener.ora file

Three levels of tracing are found in SQL*Net:

- **LSNRCTL TRACE ADMIN**
- **LSNRCTL TRACE USER**
- **LSNRCTL TRACE OFF**

It is possible to run two listeners, one for version 1 and another listener for version 2. If a version connect string is sent, a version listener (**TCPCTL**) will be used. Conversely, if a TNS connect description is sent, the version listener (**LSNRCTL**) will be used. A connect description is the name of a database (such as **@mydata**), which maps to the tnsnames.ora on the sending side, and listener.ora on the receiving side.

It is essential to note that the functions of the **oracle_sid** and **two_task** variables have changed. To use the MTS while you are "local" to the database, you should unset the **oracle_sid** variable and set the **two_task** to the SID name (**EXPORT two_task=mydb**). If the **oracle_sid** is active, you will still be able to connect—although you will not be able to take advantage of the MTS. You must change all login scripts and ORACLE_HOME/bin/oraenv files to reflect this new functionality.

We now have three ways to establish distributed database communications with MTS. We can choose from a shared service name (**sqlplus /@ram2db**) or a dedicated service name (**sqlplus /@d_ram2db**—prefixing the SID with **d_** will direct the listener to spawn a dedicated process for your program). We can also use a (**two_task**) server connect string (**sqlplus /@t:host:sid**). This latter approach will bypass the MTS and use a dedicated process.

Managing Two-Phase Commits (2PCs)

When a distributed update (or delete) has finished processing, SQL*Net will coordinate **COMMIT** processing, which means that the entire transaction will roll back if any portion of the transaction fails. The first phase of this process is a prepare phase to each node, followed by the **COMMIT**, and then terminated by a forget phase.

If a distributed update is in the process of issuing the 2PC and a network connection breaks, Oracle will place an entry in the **dba_2pc_pending** table. The recovery background process (RECO) will then roll back or commit the good node to match the state of the disconnected node to ensure consistency. You can activate RECO via the **ALTER SYSTEM ENABLE DISTRIBUTED RECOVERY** command.

The **dba_2pc_pending** table contains an *advise* column that directs the database to either **COMMIT** or **ROLLBACK** the pending item. You can use the **ALTER SESSION ADVISE** syntax to direct the 2PC mechanism. For example, to force the completion of an **INSERT**, you could enter the following:

```
ALTER SESSION ADVISE COMMIT;
INSERT INTO payroll@london . . . ;
```

When a 2PC transaction fails, you can query the **dba_2pc_pending** table to check the state column. You can enter SQL*DBA and use the "recover in-doubt transaction" dialog box to force either a rollback or a commit of the pending transaction. If you do this, the row will disappear from **dba_p2c_pending** after the transaction has been resolved. If you force the transaction the wrong way (for example, rollback when other nodes committed), RECO will detect the problem, set the **MIXED** column to yes, and the row will remain in the **dba_2pc_pending** table.

Internally, Oracle examines the init.ora parameters to determine the rank that the commit processing will take. The **commit_point_strength** init.ora parameter determines which of the distributed databases is to be the commit point site. In a distributed update, the database with the largest value of **commit_point_strength** will be the commit point site. The commit point site is the database that must successfully complete before the transaction is updated at the other databases. Conversely, if a transaction fails at the commit point site, the entire transaction will be rolled back at all of the other databases. In general, the commit point site should be the database that contains the most critical data.

Listing 8.5 shows a script that will identify two-phase commit transactions that have failed to complete.

Listing 8.5 pending.sql reports on any pending distributed transactions.

```
SET PAGESIZE 999;
SET FEEDBACK OFF;
SET WRAP ON;
```

```
COLUMN local_tran_id   format a22 HEADING 'Local Txn Id'
COLUMN global_tran_id  format a50 HEADING 'Global Txn Id'
COLUMN state           format a16 HEADING 'State'
COLUMN mixed           format a5  HEADING 'Mixed'
COLUMN advice          format a5  HEADING 'Advice'

SELECT local_tran_id,global_tran_id,state,mixed,advice
FROM   dba_2pc_pending
ORDER  BY local_tran_id;
```

Establishing SQL*Net Sessions

On systems running SQL*Net version 2, the session script can be used to query the number of dedicated and shared servers on the system. For example, Listing 8.6 shows an SQL*Plus script to view all sessions.

Listing 8.6   session.sql displays all connected sessions.

```
SET ECHO OFF;
SET TERMOUT ON;
SET LINESIZE 80;
SET PAGESIZE 60;
SET NEWPAGE 0;
TTITLE "dbname Database|UNIX/Oracle Sessions";
SPOOL /tmp/session
SET HEADING OFF;
SELECT 'Sessions on database '||substr(name,1,8) FROM v$database;
SET HEADING ON;
SELECT
        substr(b.serial#,1,5) ser#,
        substr(b.machine,1,6) box,
        substr(b.username,1,10) username,
        substr(b.osuser,1,8) os_user,
        substr(b.program,1,30) program
FROM v$session b, v$process a
WHERE
b.paddr = a.addr
AND type='USER'
ORDER BY spid;
TTITLE OFF;
SET HEADING OFF;
SELECT 'To kill, enter SQLPLUS>  ALTER SYSTEM KILL SESSION',
''''||'SID, SER#'||''''||';' from dual;
SPOOL OFF;
```

```
[oracle]ram2: sqlx session

Wed Sep 14
                                                    Page    1
                                              ram2db Database
                                           Sessions for SQL*Net

SERVER      Oracle user  O/S       User    Machine Program

---------   -----------  --------  ------  ------------------------------

DEDICATED   SYS          oracle    ram2    sqldba@ram2 (Pipe Two-Task)

DEDICATED   OPS$REDDY    reddy     ram2    runform30@ram2 (Pipe Two-Task)

DEDICATED   GLINT        lkorneke  ram2    sqlplus@ram2 (Pipe Two-Task)

DEDICATED   OPS$ORACLE   oracle    clt2    sqlplus@clt2 (TNS interface)

DEDICATED   OPS$JOKE     joke      ram2    ?  @ram2 (TCP Two-Task)

DEDICATED   OPS$WWRIGHT  wwright   ram2    runmenu50@ram2 (Pipe Two-Task)

DEDICATED   OPS$ORACLE   oracle    ensc    sqlplus@ensc (TCP Two-Task)

DEDICATED   SECTION125   OraUser           C:\PB3\PBSYS030.DLL

DEDICATED   OPS$ORACLE   oracle    ram2    sqlplus@ram2 (Pipe Two-Task)

DEDICATED   OPS$JSTARR   jstarr    ram2    sqlforms30@ram2 (Pipe Two-Task)

DEDICATED   OPS$WWRIGHT  wwright   ram2    RUN_USEX@ram2 (Pipe Two-Task)


12 rows selected.
```

Here we see each of the four types of SQL*Net connections:

- Pipe Two-Task—Used for internal tasks (SQLPLUS /).

- TNS Interface—Used when connection is made with a v2 service name (SQLPLUS /@ram2).

- TCP Two-Task—Used when connection is made with a v1 connect string (SQLPLUS /@t:ram2:ram2db).

- PC connection task—Denoted by the PC DLL name (C:\PB3\PBSYS030. DLL = initiated via PowerBuilder DLL).

While we can only gloss over the high points, sophisticated tools such as SQL*Net 2.0 require a great deal of knowledge and skill to use effectively. As systems continue to evolve into complex distributed networks, inter-database communications will become even more complex, requiring even more sophisticated tools. While object-orientation promises to make interdatabase communications simple, the DBA in the trenches will continue to struggle with implementing everyday distributed database communications.

Cross Database Connectivity With IBM Mainframes

A great deal of interest in database connectivity has resulted from the proliferation of companies that are choosing diverse database platforms. Database designers are working actively to develop bridges between the divergent database systems, and many tools are becoming available to assist with multidatabase connectivity.

We currently have three classes of methods for database connectivity:

- Transparency products that allow applications written for a database to run on another product

- Fourth generation languages that access multiple databases

- "Hook" products that allow exits to other databases

This very exciting area of technology is explored in detail in Chapter 9. Fortunately, we have some very simple ways to begin working with multiple databases. One start at database connectivity can be achieved in the batch environment. By embedding database commands from two databases into a single COBOL program, compile procedures can be developed to separately precompile each set of database statements, creating a single program which concurrently accesses two different databases. (See Figure 8.6.)

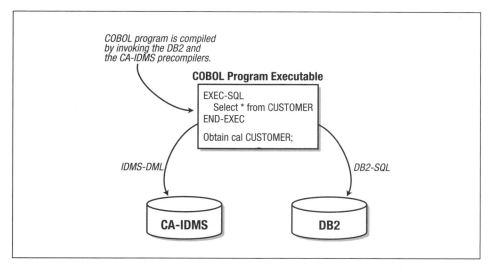

Figure 8.6 Interdatabase communications with mainframes.

In this example, a COBOL program was created to read DB2 tables and dynamically store them into an CA-IDMS database. The statements for DB2 and CA-IDMS remain as they would in a single database program, but a special compile procedure is set up to precompile each set of statements separately. The trick is to invoke the DB2 precompiler before the CA-IDMS pre-compiler. Because all DB2 commands are bracketed with **EXEC-SQL .... END-EXEC**, all DB2 commands will be processed before the CA-IDMS pre-compiler begins its job. Listing 8.7 shows some JCL that works well for compiling a COBOL program to simultaneously access DB2 and CA-IDMS.

Listing 8.7   A COBOL compiler.

```
//DB2IDMSC PROC  PROGRAM=,SYSTEM=PROD,DICT=LCPDICT
//****************************************************************
//*  THIS IS THE IDMS/DB2 COBOL COMPILER  (BATCH IDMS/DB2 COBOL)
//****************************************************************
//DB2 EXEC PGM=DSNHPC,PARM='HOST(COBOL),APOST,APOSTSQL,NOSOURCE,NOXREF'
//****************************************************************
//DBRMLIB  DD DSN=DB2.LCP.DBRMLIB(&PROGRAM),DISP=SHR
//SYSCIN   DD DSN=&&DSNHOUT,DISP=(MOD,PASS),UNIT=SYSDA,
//            SPACE=(800,(50,50))
//SYSLIB   DD DSN=DB2.LCP.DCLGNLIB,SUBSYS=LAM
```

```
//SYSPRINT DD  SYSOUT=*
//SYSTERM  DD  SYSOUT=*
//SYSUDUMP DD  SYSOUT=*
//SYSUT1   DD  SPACE=(800,(50,50),,,ROUND),UNIT=SYSDA
//SYSUT2   DD  SPACE=(800,(50,50),,,ROUND),UNIT=SYSDA
//******************************************************************
//DMLC EXEC  PGM=IDMSDMLC,REGION=1024K,PARM='DBNAME=&DICT',COND=(4,LT)
//******************************************************************
//STEPLIB  DD  DSN=LCP.IDMS.&SYSTEM..PRODLIB,DISP=SHR
//         DD  DSN=LCP.IDMS.&SYSTEM..CDMSLIB,DISP=SHR
//SYSLST   DD  DUMMY
//SYSPRINT DD  SYSOUT=*
//SYSCTL   DD  DSN=LCP.IDMS.&SYSTEM..SYSCTL,DISP=SHR
//SYSJRNL  DD  DUMMY
//SYSPCH   DD  DSN=&&WRK1WORK,UNIT=SYSDA,DISP=(NEW,PASS),
//             DCB=BLKSIZE=800,SPACE=(CYL,(5,1))
//SYSIPT   DD  DSN=&&DSNHOUT,DISP=(OLD,DELETE,DELETE)
//******************************************************************
//COMP     EXEC PGM=IKFCBL00,COND=(4,LT),
// PARM='&CPARM,&PAYPR,STA,LIB,DMAP,CLIST,APOST,NOSXREF,BUF=28672'
//******************************************************************
//STEPLIB  DD  DSN=SYS1.VSCOLIB,DISP=SHR
//SYSPRINT DD  SYSOUT=*
//SYSUDUMP DD  SYSOUT=*
//SYSLIN   DD  DSN=&&LOADSET,DISP=(MOD,PASS),UNIT=SYSDA,
//             SPACE=(800,(50,50),RLSE)
//SYSLIB   DD  DSN=ISD.COBOL.TEST.COPYLIB,DISP=SHR
//         DD  DSN=ISD.COBOL.COPYLIB,DISP=SHR
//SYSUT1   DD  SPACE=(800,(50,50),RLSE),UNIT=SYSDA
//SYSUT2   DD  SPACE=(800,(50,50),RLSE),UNIT=SYSDA
//SYSUT3   DD  SPACE=(800,(50,50),RLSE),UNIT=SYSDA
//SYSUT4   DD  SPACE=(800,(50,50),RLSE),UNIT=SYSDA
//SYSIN    DD  DSN=&&WRK1WORK,DISP=(OLD,DELETE,DELETE)
//******************************************************************
//LKED     EXEC PGM=IEWL,PARM='XREF,LIST,&LPARM',
//             COND=((12,LE,COMP),(4,LT,DB2))
//******************************************************************
//SYSPRINT DD  SYSOUT=*
//SYSUDUMP DD  SYSOUT=*
//SYSLIN   DD  DSN=&&LOADSET,DISP=(OLD,DELETE)
//         DD  DSN=LCP.IDMS.TEST.PROCLIB(IDMSCOB),DISP=SHR
//SYSUT1   DD  SPACE=(1024,(50,50)),UNIT=SYSDA
//SYSLIB   DD  DSN=SYS1.DB2.DSNLINK,DISP=SHR
//         DD  DSN=SYS1.VSCOLIB,DISP=SHR
//         DD  DSN=SYS1.VSCLLIB,DISP=SHR
//         DD  DSN=LCP.IDMS.&SYSTEM..CDMSLIB,DISP=SHR
```

```
//SYSLMOD  DD  DSN=LCP.IDMS.&SYSTEM..LINKLIB(&PROGRAM),DISP=SHR
//LIB      DD  DSN=LCP.IDMS.&SYSTEM..OBJLIB,DISP=SHR
//****************************************************************
//BIND  EXEC PGM=IKJEFT01,DYNAMNBR=20,COND=((8,LT),(4,LT,DB2))
//****************************************************************
//SYSTSIN  DD DSN=ISD.TEST.PARMCARD(PCRDB21),DISP=SHR
//DSNTRACE DD SYSOUT=*
//SYSUDUMP DD SYSOUT=*
//SYSPRINT DD SYSOUT=*
//SYSTSPRT DD SYSOUT=*
//SYSIN    DD DSN=LCP.IDMS.&SYSTEM..LINKLIB(&PROGRAM),DISP=SHR
```

The execution of the COBOL program is normally achieved by running it under the domain of the DB2 foreground processor. Listing 8.8 shows how the execution JCL for a DB2/IDMS COBOL program would appear.

Listing 8.8   The execution JCL for the COBOL program.

```
//GOFORIT  JOB (CARD)
//GOFORIT  EXEC PGM=IKJEFT01,DYNAMNBR=20
//****************************************************************
//SYSTSIN  DD *
   DSN SYSTEM    (DB2P)
   RUN PROG      (MYCOBOL) -
   LIB           ('MY.LINK.LIB')  -
   PLAN          (MYCOBOL)
//DSNTRACE DD SYSOUT=*
//SYSUDUMP DD SYSOUT=*
//SYSPRINT DD SYSOUT=*
//SYSTSPRT DD SYSOUT=*
//STEPLIB  DD  DSN=MY.IDMS.LIBRARIES,DISP=SHR
```

With this technique, batch programs on IBM mainframes can be created to share information between architectures. While many methods to accomplish database connectivity are available, it seems certain that shops are demanding tools to allow diverse databases to communicate with each other. Rather than gravitating toward some panacea database that handles everyone's data requirements, the industry is recognizing that many different database architectures are required to meet the needs of the organization. Consequently, we are going to continue seeing the evolution of methods that allow true connectivity, regardless of the hardware platforms or database architectures that must be crossed.

Summary

Now that we have addressed the Oracle connectivity issues relating to client/server systems, we need to take a look at techniques for linking a client/server application with a non-Oracle data server. It's time to look at Oracle open gateway architecture as well as numerous vendors and programmatic solutions.

Linking Oracle And Non-Oracle Databases

Now is the time to take a look at the different methods for linking together databases from many vendors. In general, there are three approaches to achieving these links:

- *Via manual consolidation*—Data is extracted from a variety of databases and loaded into a common repository, an approach commonly used with data warehouses. Red Brick Systems are an example of manual consolidation.

- *Via remote connection*—Many databases are monitored via a common console. In this scenario, status information is shipped from a variety of databases to a common console that is used to alert the operations staff to extraordinary conditions. Patrol by BMC Software is an example of this type of linking.

- *Via online applications*—An online application (usually running on a PC) accesses data from a variety of databases, presenting the data to the user as if the data was coming from a single source. EDA-SQL and UniFace are examples of this type of linking.

We will be exploring the following issues:

- History and evolution of linking multivendor databases

- The gateway products

- Data replication products

- Middleware solutions

- Remote measurement solutions

The History And Evolution Of Linking Multivendor Databases

You will find two schools of thought about having applications that span across multiple vendor databases. One group maintains that a single vendor should be able to provide a global, omniscient database that is capable of supporting all types of data requirements—from online transaction processing to decision support. Many vendors foster this belief by marketing their database products as suitable for every type of application, pointing out the nightmares that result when a multidatabase application attempts to make diverse databases communicate with each other in a seamless fashion. The opposing philosophy believes that the only way to successfully implement database technology is to use numerous databases, leveraging the strengths of each engine. As recently as five years ago, database vendors touted their products as a corporate panacea, appropriate for all types of data and application systems.

All of this began to change around the time when IBM conceded that its DB2 database was not appropriate for high-volume systems. Prior to this, DB2 was marketed as an all-purpose engine that was suitable for any application, regardless of the size or performance requirements. With time, it became clear that DB2 was not appropriate for systems that required thousands of transactions per second, so IBM began recommending IMS for very large, high-speed databases.

The whole multidatabase trend is a reaction to corporate acquisitions and weak development. Companies have had little or no strategic direction for databases, although it is doubtful that any company ever decided to go heterogeneous, either. Heterogeneous databases mean duplicating licenses and talent, and few companies have a large enough talent pool to support multiple databases. The difference between the engines is too minimal.

From this beginning, other vendors began to embrace the concept of "the right database for the right application." Systems that required flexibility and ad-hoc query were implemented with relational databases, while systems with complex data relationships and high performance requirements were implemented with network or hierarchical database architectures. New types of specialized database products began appearing on the scene: special word-searchable databases for textual data, databases designed especially for CAD/CAM systems, and so on. Database systems began their long march away from corporate repositories into specialized niche markets, some of which are shown in Table 9.1.

Originally, the desire for a central repository of data was driven by the need to impose some control over data redundancy and multiple updates to the same information placed on various file systems. From this situation evolved our centralized systems, using a single-vendor database. However, end-user computing—and to some degree, slow data transmission—helped to justify to the corporate world a move to client/server platforms. Unfortunately, there has been no standard model for client/server data management. In spite of all the open systems standards (OSF, POSIX, X-Windows, IEEE, and so on), nothing truly solid has emerged for databases. Furthermore, the standards that we do have—such as SQL—are implemented in very different ways. While real-world developers wait anxiously for standards to emerge, they simply make their own decisions on the best DBMS platform. Other departments in the corporate world have followed the same thinking, choosing their idea of the best DBMS, and so on. The results of this scattered approach are islands of information distributed among our LANs and WANs—not only distributed among different file systems on the same box,

Table 9.1   Samples of specialized database products.

Type of Database	Product
Text Databases	Oracle Book, Basis Plus, Folio, Fulcrum
High-Speed Databases	IDMS, IMS, Teradata
Object Databases	Objectivity/DB, Ontos, Versant
Warehouse Databases	Red Brick Warehouse, MetaCube, Fusion

but distributed across the country and around the world. Linking these databases has become a very complicated but critical chore.

External influences have also impacted the database configuration of shops. Corporate acquisition, mergers, and right-sizing efforts have all had the side effect of leaving a plethora of database engines within the newly reformed organization. Regardless of the wisdom of having multiple types of databases, most IS departments must link more than one database, and cross-database connectivity has become commonplace. Sentry Market Research estimates that the average corporation has approximately nine different databases. End users are demanding applications that integrate legacy data from mainframes with data in open systems, while MIS designers are faced with the incredible challenge of making these diverse systems function as a unified whole.

While linking nonrelational databases such as IMS and CA-IDMS into relational databases is considered challenging, it is a common misconception that relational databases are basically the same and therefore easy to link together.

Even linking databases that share the same architecture is difficult, especially with relational databases. The idea that relational databases are "plug-and-play" is pure fantasy. For example, the popular PowerBuilder application development tool was primarily designed for use with a Sybase relational database. To accommodate PowerBuilder, Oracle had to add an init.ora parameter to cache cursors for PowerBuilder, since the product doesn't give the user control over specific cursors resulting in many SQL reparses. Locking between Oracle and Sybase is also totally different. If you use Oracle and want to build a high-performance OLTP application, you should first lock all records (which doesn't exist in Sybase); set a transaction boundary to roll back everything except the locks in case of a transaction error; then perform array operations such as array inserts, deletes, updates, and selects (all of which are not supported by Sybase). Even the SQL syntax differs, and the procedural extensions to each database's SQL are never equal.

So, how do large IS shops deal with these problems? Should companies invest in training their employees for many different relational databases? The cost of this comprehensive training is difficult to justify.

To further illustrate the stumbling blocks, consider the cost of converting an application from one relational database to another. First, do you even have the talent to make it happen when the interfaces are so diverse? Even more confounding is the lack of clarity about the "truths" of the differences. Rarely is an RDBMS chosen over another on the basis of which RDBMS is best for the type of application.

The challenge of linking multivendor databases is not one of syntax—we can solve that through standard query languages, data dictionaries, and the like. The real challenge is one of semantics: How do we extract meaning from the data contained in the many different locations? I believe that this challenge can only be met by building executable business models that pull related information out of multiple databases as a side effect of their ongoing operations.

Even the major DBMS vendors are recognizing that extensions into other products are necessary for their survival. The crux of the situation is becoming evident: Most shops are not capable of moving their data into a single database.

The Gateway Products

In response to the realities of linking multivendor databases, just about every database vendor has created a tool that claims to allow seamless communications between its engine and other vendors' products.

For example, Oracle's philosophy emphasizes the need for a smooth transition path for non-Oracle databases by offering a three-phase program. Oracle recognizes that customers can't be expected to shift into Oracle overnight, so this gateway strategy allows for a smooth transition into an Oracle environment.

In phase one, Oracle applications provide gateways into non-Oracle databases, allowing Oracle applications to make calls (using Oracle SQL) to non-Oracle databases. The converter then translates the Oracle SQL into the native SQL for the foreign database. Now the developer can use the robust extensions found in Oracle SQL with a non-Oracle database, while the Oracle open gateway relies on "SQL compensation" to perform Oracle SQL functions against the non-Oracle database. This technology would allow an Oracle application to join a DB2 table with a Sybase table—all within the gateway product. Oracle believes in connectivity into all databases—not just relational databases. For this reason, Oracle bundle is packaged with Information Builders Incorporated, using its EDA-SQL product to help insulate the front-end application from the foreign data source. This takes the form of an access manager that handles the communications to and from the Oracle database, allowing Oracle to access nonrelational databases. (See Figure 9.1.)

While this approach seems noble, Oracle has experienced some problems with a few of its SQL extensions that do not have equivalents in other relational databases. For example, Oracle's **DECODE** function cannot be implemented in Informix, since the **DECODE** verb has no direct equivalent in Informix SQL. (See Figure 9.2.)

Phase two of Oracle's strategy allows a foreign application to access Oracle. For example, a CICS COBOL customer may require access to Oracle data. With phase two of the Oracle gateway, the non-Oracle application on the mainframe can access Oracle as if it was on a local host. However, some middleware vendors do not feel that the gateway approach is the best long-term solution for database connectivity. Unlike the gateway products that have a single interface, some products have separately tuned drivers for each target database. This movement away from general interfaces such as ODBC is primarily for performance reasons, and it is not uncommon for each product to have its own custom interface for each database that is supported.

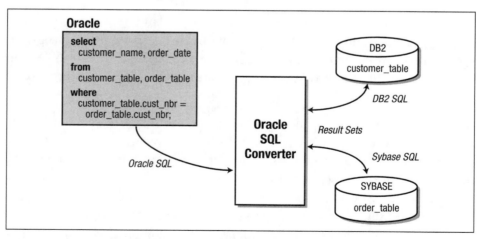

Figure 9.1   Oracle's transparent gateway—phase one.

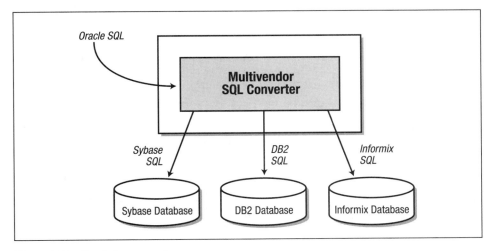

Figure 9.2   Oracle's open gateway.

Data Replication Products

Phase three of Oracle's strategy is heterogeneous replication. We now have a solution that allows us to replicate data from a variety of sources and import the table data into Oracle. The Oracle gateway also provides a mechanism to constantly update the replicated non-Oracle data. The gateway approach is commonly used with data warehouse applications, but it also allows updates to non-Oracle data to be quickly transported into a replicated Oracle database, as shown in Figure 9.3.

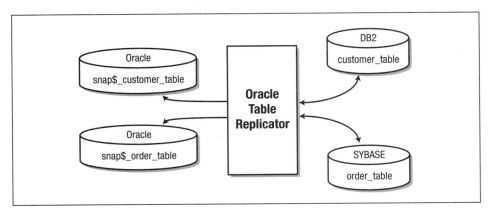

Figure 9.3   Foreign tables imported into Oracle.

The replication can work in the other direction as well—taking Oracle tables and propagating them into the foreign database where they behave as native tables within the foreign database, as shown in Figure 9.4.

The ability to replicate in both directions gives the database design an enormous flexibility in choosing the best approach to replication based on the needs of the client/server application. However, we need to be aware that these replication interfaces are complicated and often require manual intervention, especially when data is being transferred from one hardware architecture to another. For example, populating EBCDIC data from DB2 tables into the ASCII world of Oracle involves translating characters that are unknown to ASCII, such as the cent sign.

Middleware Solutions

Many of the new middleware packages allow the applications to be developed independently of the databases, providing drivers for more than 25 database products. Some products such as UniFace accomplish this with *data choreography* where the developer specifies the data with query by example. The developer does not have to write SQL, and UniFace takes care of all of the I/O and relationship management. A middleware product that is capable of enforcing business rules across database architectures is

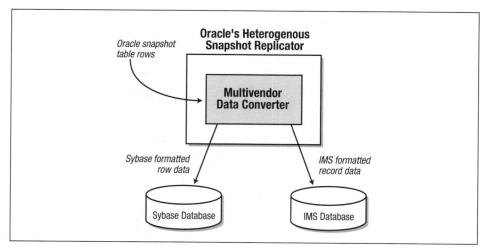

Figure 9.4   Oracle tables exported into foreign databases.

also needed. One important aspect of UniFace is the ability to enforce referential integrity across platforms. For example, a customer database may exist at corporate headquarters using Oracle, but the orders are taken in the field using a C/ISAM database. The tool will maintain the business rules between these tables, even though they are in different databases at different locations.

Some large IS shops have had great success using gateway technology to link multiplatform databases. For example, consider a company that supports IMS, DB2, and Oracle. After looking at various solutions to try to make these databases communicate, they may choose two different gateway products. One gateway might be Oracle's transparent gateway for communication from Oracle applications to DB2 and IMS, and the other gateway could be IBM's DDCS and Data Joiner to handle communications from DB2 into Oracle databases. Many companies use Oracle's transparent gateway, since it allows them to treat calls to DB2 as if DB2 was just another Oracle database. The gateway product takes care of the translation into DB2 SQL. The company will then have the capability to join two DB2 tables, each on a separate processor, from within an Oracle application. While these gateway solutions are definitely functional, the long-term goal for most companies is to avoid gateways altogether and move into a three-tiered architecture with a protocol layer such as CORBA or DCE.

It is interesting to note that demand for mainframe resources does not always decline after the company has made a commitment to embrace open systems. Having a single database may have offered definite advantages in the mainframe days, but most large IS shops are now both decentralized and distributed worldwide. To complicate matters, many of the remote locations have the authority to choose their own database—usually selecting whatever is in vogue at the time, or perhaps the cheapest database available. This approach can lead to a realtime support load problem. Interestingly, even after a large company completes its push into open systems, the largest share of costs may still be on the mainframe. Although new development is moving to open systems, companies are still seeing mainframe requirements growing at a rate of 15 to 20 percent per year—even though total dollar cost has dropped.

As we move further away from proprietary operating systems to open systems, it seems evident that the days of single-vendor environments are numbered. We are already witnessing the shift toward a plug-and-play RDBMS environment.

It is becoming clear that the differences between proprietary databases will become less of a problem as robust interfaces are developed. Very little theoretical reason can support remaining bound to the technology of a single database vendor. Within the next few years, we will be entering an era when cross-platform joins will be demanded. Vendors who do not provide the capability to do so will be seen as hampering the flow of information, therefore decreasing productivity. This doesn't mean that vendors will abandon their notable differences in favor of a standardized database environment. In fact, these differences are likely to intensify with the addition of new functionality, since each RDBMS will need to emphasize its strengths to establish superiority over the competition.

Some vendors have seen a market opportunity for a tool that could easily access multivendor databases, both for retrieval and updates. One such product is called Passport, an object-oriented tool that makes the development of three-tiered multivendor applications unbelievably easy. Passport started out as a front-end tool when Oracle and Ingres dominated the market. It wasn't long, however, before customers wanted to mix-and-match databases. For example, they might want one database for the tool set and another database for the SQL. Either case requires a tool that quickly allows the developer to switch databases on an as-needed basis.

Some of the new middleware products have the capability of leveraging on their object-oriented architecture to easily access multiple databases. For example, some middleware treats each database as an object with its own attributes and behaviors, making it trivial to swap out one database for another. These middleware products have an inherent distributed database model to manage two-phase commits across numerous midrange and PC databases, so that a single update screen can display data from many different databases. When update time comes, the tool uses synchronous communications to ensure that all databases are updated.

Remote Measurement

One trend in the marketplace is linking diverse databases with a common tool, an approach primarily used for measuring database and system performance. For example, the Patrol product by BMC Software can provide a common interface to numerous relational databases. Patrol uses a Knowledge Module on each database to collect information on each remote database, shipping exception information to the master console. We call this our fat-agent technology, since most of the processing is done on the agent. These agents contain all of the protocols needed to communicate with the master console, regardless of the agent's platform. Our knowledge modules also abstract the user interface, making it possible for the knowledge module to adapt to a Unix or MVS view of the data and providing a way to cover up to 5,000 databases from a single console. A complete overview can be found in Chapter 11, Oracle Application Monitoring.

Summary

Today we are seeing more heterogeneous database platforms than ever before. Data continues to reside on many platforms and within many different databases, and methods need to be created for building bridges between these islands of information. The immediate future for managing cross-database communications lies in emerging standards such as the OMG's CORBA specification and Microsoft's OLE 2.0 standard. It is only with these frameworks that true, seamless distributed systems will be practical.

10

Tuning Oracle Data Warehouse And OLAP Applications

As more companies begin to embrace the concept of creating a historical data repository for online analytical processing (OLAP) and decision support systems (DSS) applications, new client/server issues have emerged as developers struggled to create Oracle-based client/server applications that would perform acceptably. This chapter will review the data warehouse with a focus on creating fast Oracle applications. Topics for this chapter will include:

- The evolution of data warehouses and online analytical processing (OLAP)

- Tuning multidimensional databases

- Tuning relational database warehouses

- STAR schema design techniques

- Tuning techniques for relational warehouses

- Using middleware solutions to data warehousing

Data Warehousing And Multidimensional Databases

A great deal of interest has surfaced in the application of data warehousing and multidimensional databases to advanced systems. These systems, including expert systems and decision support systems, have been used to solve semistructured and even unstructured problems. Traditionally, these types of systems combine inference engines and relational databases in order to store the knowledge processing components. Unfortunately, very little work has been done with the application of warehouse databases for decision support and expert systems.

Expert Systems

Expert system is a term that is used very loosely in the computer community regarding anything from a spreadsheet program to any program which contains an IF statement. In general terms, an expert system is one that models the well-structured decision process of the human mind, applying that reasoning process to a real-world situation. Any decision-making process with quantifiable rules can have the rules stored in an *inference engine.* An inference engine is used to drive the information-gathering component of the system, eventually arriving at the solution to the problem.

It has been said that an expert system makes a decision "for" the user, while a decision support system makes a decision "with" the user. This distinction is essentially true, because an expert system makes no provision for human intuition in the decision-making process. Many real-world management decisions do not require human intuition. For example, one of the crucial jobs of a retail manager is the choice of what goods to order, the quantity, and the ordering time frame. These decisions can be represented by a model called economic order quantity (EOQ). If the EOQ equation knows the velocity at which the goods are leaving the retail store, the delivery time on reorders, the average time on the shelf, and the cost of the goods, the computer can confidently produce automatic daily reports specifying which goods to order and the appropriate quantity. Also, a DSS can presummarize data so that the manager can quickly take a high-level look at the relevant figures, as shown in Figure 10.1.

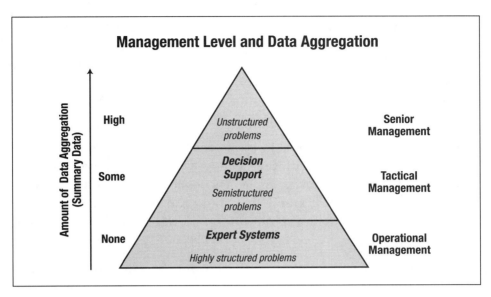

Figure 10.1 Defining different levels of aggregation.

Decision Support Systems And Data Warehouses

Decision support systems (DSS) are generally defined as the type of system that deals with the semistructured problem. In other words, the task has a structured component as well as a component that involves human intuition. The well-structured components are the decision rules that are stored as the problem-processing system. The intuitive, or creative component, is left to the user.

The following represent some examples of semistructured problems:

- Choosing a spouse
- Building a factory
- Choosing magazine artwork
- Building a new sports car
- Designing a Graphical User Interface (GUI) for an OODBMS

Decision support technology recognizes that many tasks require human intuition. For example, the process of choosing a stock portfolio is a task that has both structured and intuitive components. Certainly, rules are associated with choosing a stock portfolio, such as diversification of the stocks and choosing an acceptable level of risk. These factors can be easily quantified and stored in a database system, allowing the user of the system to create "what-if" scenarios. However, just because a system has well-structured components does not guarantee that the entire decision process is well-structured (see Figure 10.2).

One of the best ways to tell if a decision process is semistructured is to ask the question, "Do people with the same level of knowledge demonstrate different levels of skill?" For example, it is possible for many stock brokers to have the same level of knowledge about the stock market. However, these brokers clearly demonstrate different levels of "skill" when assembling stock portfolios.

Computer simulation is one area that is used heavily within the modeling components of decision support systems. In fact, one of the first object-oriented languages was SIMULA, which was used as a driver for these what-if scenarios, and was incorporated into decision support systems so that users could model a particular situation. The user would create a scenario with objects that were subjected to a set of predefined behaviors.

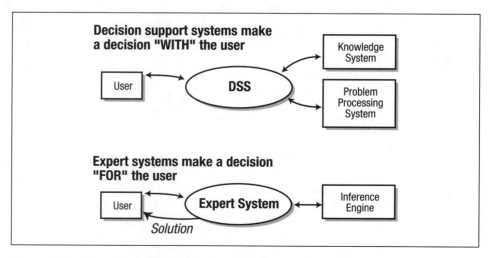

Figure 10.2   Comparing decision support with expert systems.

The general characteristics of a decision support system include:

- *A nonrecurring problem to be solved*—DSS technology is used primarily for novel and unique modeling situations that require the user to simulate the behavior of some real-world problem.

- *A DSS requires human intuition*—DSS makes the decision *with* the user, unlike expert systems that make the decision *for* the user.

- *A DSS requires knowledge of the problem being solved*—Unlike an expert system that provides the user with answers to well-structured questions, decision support systems require the user to thoroughly understand the problem being solved. For example, a financial decision support system, such as the DSSF product, would require the user to understand the concept of a stock Beta. Beta is the term used to measure the covariance of an individual stock against the behavior of the market as a whole. Without an understanding of the concepts, a user would be unable to effectively utilize a decision support system.

- *A DSS allows ad hoc data query*—As users gather information for their decision, they make repeated requests to the online database, with one query answer stimulating another query. Since the purpose of ad hoc query is to allow free-form query to decision information, response time is critical.

- *Decision support systems may produce more than one acceptable answer*—Unlike an expert system that usually produces a single, finite answer to a problem, a decision support system deals with problems that have a domain or range of acceptable solutions. For example, a user of DSSF may discover many "acceptable" stock portfolios that match the selection criteria of the user. Another good example is a manager who needs to place production machines onto an empty warehouse floor. The goal would be to maximize the throughput of work in process from raw materials to finished goods. Clearly, he could choose from a number of acceptable ways of placing the machines on the warehouse floor in order to achieve this goal. This is called the "state space" approach to problem solving: First a solution domain is specified, then the user works to create models to achieve the desired goal state.

- *A DSS uses external data sources*—For example, a DSS may require classification of customers by Standard Industry Code (SIC) or customer addresses by Standard Metropolitan Statistical Area (SMSA). Many warehouse managers load this external data into the central warehouse.

Decision support systems also allow the user to create what if scenarios. These futuristic glimpses are essentially modeling tools that allow the user to define an environment and simulate the behavior of that environment under changing conditions. For example, the user of a DSS for finance could create a hypothetical stock portfolio and then direct the DSS to model the behavior of that stock portfolio under different market conditions. Once these behaviors are specified, the user may vary the contents of the portfolio and view the results.

The type of output from decision support systems include:

- *Management Information Systems (MIS)*—Standard reports and forecasts of sales.

- *Hypothesis testing*—Did sales decrease in the eastern region last month because of changes in buying habits? This involves iterative questioning, with one answer leading to another question.

- *Model building*—Creating a sales model and validating its behavior against the historical data in the warehouse. Predictive modeling is often used to forecast behaviors based upon historical factors.

- *Discovery of unknown trends*— For example, why are sales up in the eastern region? Data mining tools answer questions in those instances where you may not even know what specific questions to ask.

The role of human intuition in this type of problem solving has stirred great debate. Decision support systems allow the user to control the decision-making process, applying his or her own decision-making rules and intuition to the process. However, the arguments for and against using artificial intelligence to manage the intuitive component of these systems has strong proponents on both sides.

Data Warehouses

Multidimensional databases are approaching the DSS market through two methods. The first approach is though "niche" servers that use a proprietary architecture to model multidimensional databases. Examples of niche servers include Arbor and IRI. The second approach is to provide multidimensional front ends that manage the mapping between the RDBMS and the dimensional representation of the data. Figure 10.3 offers an overview of the various multidimensional databases.

In general, the following definitions apply to data warehouses:

- *Subject oriented data*—Unlike an online transaction processing application that is focused on a finite business transaction, a data warehouse attempts to collect all that is known about a subject area (e.g., sales volume, interest earned) from all data sources within the organization.

- *Read-only during queries*— Data warehouses are loaded during off hours and are used for read-only requests during day hours.

- *Highly denormalized data structures*—Unlike an OLTP system with many "narrow" tables, data warehouses prejoin tables, creating "fat" tables with highly redundant columns.

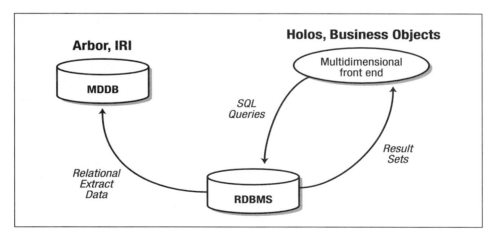

Figure 10.3 The major types of multidimensional databases.

- *Data is preaggregated*—Unlike OLTP, data warehouses precalculate totals to improve runtime performance. Note that preaggregation is anti-relational, meaning that the relational model advocates building aggregate object at runtime, only allowing for the storing of atomic data components.

- *Features interactive, ad hoc query*—Data warehouses must be flexible enough to handle spontaneous queries by the users. Consequently, a flexible design is imperative.

When we contrast the data warehouse with a transaction-oriented, online system, the differences become apparent. These differences are shown in Table 10.1.

Aside from the different uses for data warehouses, many developers are using relational databases to build their data warehouses and simulate multiple dimensions. Design techniques are being used for the simulations. This push toward STAR schema design has been somewhat successful, especially since designers do not have to buy a multidimensional database or invest in an expensive front-end tool. In general, using a relational database for OLAP is achieved by any combination of the following techniques:

- *Prejoining tables together*—This is an obtuse way of saying that a denormalized table is created from the normalized online database. A large prejoin of several tables is sometimes called a fact table in a STAR schema.

- *Presummarization*—This prepares the data for any drill-down requests that may come from the end user. Essentially, the different levels of aggregation are identified, and the aggregate tables are computed and populated when the data is loaded.

- *Massive denormalization*—The side effect of very inexpensive disks has been the rethinking of the merits of Third Normal Form. Today, redundancy is widely accepted, as seen by the popularity of replication tools, snapshot utilities, and non–First Normal Form databases. If you can precreate every possible result table at load time, your end user will enjoy excellent response time when making queries. The STAR schema is an example of massive denormalization.

- *Controlled periodic batch updating*—New detail data is rolled into the aggregate table on a periodic basis while the online system is down, with

Table 10.1   Differences between OLTP and data warehouse.

	OLTP	Data Warehouse
Normalization	High (3NF)	Low (1NF)
Table sizes	Small	Large
Number of rows/table	Small	Large
Size/duration of transactions	Small	Large
Number of online users	High (1,000s)	Low (< 100)
Updates	Frequent	Nightly
Full-table scans	Rarely	Frequently
Historical data	< 90 days	Years

all summarization recalculated as the new data is introduced into the database. While data loading is important, it is only one component of the tools for loading a warehouse. There are several categories of tools that are used to populate the warehouse, including:

- *Data extraction tools*—Different hardware and databases

- *Metadata repository*—Holds common definitions

- *Data cleaning tools*—Tools for ensuring uniform data quality

- *Data sequencing tools*—RI rules for the warehouse

- *Warehouse loading tools*—Tools for populating the data warehouse

As we know, most data warehouses are loaded in batch mode after the online system has been shut down. In this sense, a data warehouse is bi-modal, with a highly intensive loading window, and an intensive read-only window during the day. Because many data warehouses collect data from nonrelational databases such as IMS or CA-IDMS, no standard methods for extracting data are available for loading into a warehouse. However, we do have a few common techniques for extracting and loading data:

- *Log "sniffing"*—Apply the archived redo logs from the OLTP system to the data warehouse.

- *Using update, insert, and delete triggers*— Fire off a distributed update to the data warehouse.

- *Use snapshot logs to populate the data warehouse*— Update the replicated tables and change log files.

- *Run nightly extract/load programs*—Retrieve the operational data and load it into the warehouse.

There are several methods that can be used to aggregate data within OLAP servers, as shown in Figure 10.4. As you can see, this method extracts data from the relational engine, summarizing the data for display. Another popular method preaggregates the data and keeps the summarized data ready for retrieval.

Two major changes have occurred over the past several years that have driven the movement toward data warehousing:

- *Disk space became inexpensive*— One gigabyte of disk carried a price tag of $100,000 in 1988. Today, one gigabyte is less than $1,000. To support large data warehouses, it is not uncommon to require terabytes of disk storage.

- *The movement into open systems*— The migration away from centralized processors has led to data residing on a plethora of different computer and database architectures.

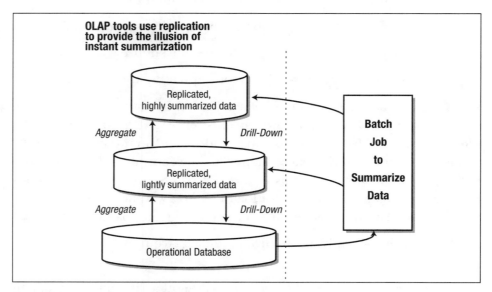

Figure 10.4 Aggregation and OLAP servers.

Since data is collected from a variety of sources, many warehouse installations find it necessary to create a metadata repository. But what is the role of a metadata repository? When data is consolidated from a variety of diverse systems, many intrasystem problems can arise. These issues include:

- *Homonyms*—Different columns with the same name

- *Synonyms*—The same column with different names

- *Unit incompatibilities*—Inches versus centimeters, dollars versus yen

- *Enterprise referential integrity*—Business rules that span operational systems

- *The warehouse design rules*—Determining how the tables will be built

  - Horizontal denormalization (fat tables)

  - Vertical denormalization (chunking tables based on time periods)

  - Using multidimensional front ends

There are other alternatives than using a "pure" multidimensional database (MDDB). One common approach is to insert a metadata serve between the OLTP relational database and the query tool, as shown in Figure 10.5.

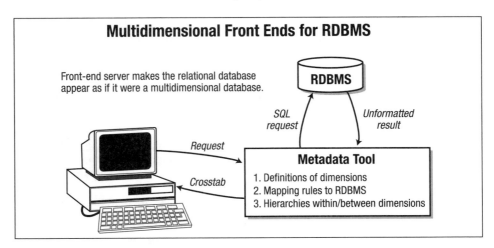

Figure 10.5 Using metadata repositories for multidimensional databases.

Examples of this approach include:

- DSS Agent by MicroStrategy
- MetaCube by Stanford Technology Group
- HOLOS by Holistic Systems

When embarking on a data warehousing project, many pitfalls can cripple the project. Characteristics of successful data warehouse projects generally include the following:

- *Clear business justification for the project*—Measurable benefits must be defined for the warehouse project (e.g., sales will increase by 10 percent, customer retention will increase by 15 percent). Warehouses are expensive, and the project must be able to measure the benefits.

- *Staff is properly trained*—Warehousing involves many new technologies, including SMP, MPP, and MDDB; the staff must be trained and comfortable with the new tools.

- *Ensuring data quality and consistency*—Since warehouses deal with historical data from a variety of sources, care must be taken to create a metadata manager that ensures common data definitions and records changes of historical data definitions.

- *Subject privacy is ensured*—Gathering data from many sources can lead to privacy violations. A good example is the hotel chain that targeted frequent hotel customers and sent a frequent-user coupon to their home addresses. Some spouses intercepted these mailings, leading to numerous divorces.

- *The warehouse starts small and evolves*—Some projects fail by defining too broad of a scope for the project. Successful projects consider their first effort a "prototype" and continue to evolve from that point.

- *Intimate end-user involvement*—Data warehouses cannot be developed in a vacuum. The system must be flexible to address changing end-user requirements, and the end users must understand the architecture so they are aware of the limitations of their warehouse.

- *Properly planning the infrastructure*—A new infrastructure must be designed to handle communications between data sources. Parallel computers must be evaluated and installed, and staff must be appropriately educated.

- *Proper data modeling and stress testing*—The data model must be validated and stress tested so that the finished system performs at acceptable levels. A model that works great at 10 gigabytes may not function as the warehouse grows to 100 gigabytes.

- *Choosing the wrong tools*—Many projects are led astray because of vendor hype. Unfortunately, many vendors inappropriately label their products as being for warehouse applications, or they exaggerate the functionality of their tools.

Data Aggregation And Drill-Down

One of the most fundamental principles of the multidimensional database is the idea of aggregation. As we know, managers at different levels require different levels of summarization to make intelligent decisions. To allow the manager to choose the level of aggregation, most warehouse offerings have a "drill-down" feature, allowing the user to adjust the level of detail, eventually reaching the original transaction data. For obvious performance reasons, the aggregations are precalculated and loaded into the warehouse during off hours.

Of the several types of aggregation, the most common is called a *roll-up aggregation*. An example of this type of aggregation would be taking daily sales totals and rolling them up into a monthly sales table—making this type relatively easy to compute and run. The more difficult type is the aggregation of boolean and comparative operators. For example, assume that a salesperson table contains a boolean column called "turkey." A salesperson is a turkey if his or her individual sales are below the group average for the day. A salesperson may be a turkey on 15 percent of the individual days; however, when the data is rolled up into a monthly summary, a salesperson may become a turkey—even though they only had a few (albeit very bad) sales days. Table 10.2 shows the differences between the presentation and display styles for OLAP and MDDB servers.

The base rule is simple: If the data looks like it would fit well into a spreadsheet, it is probably well-suited to an MDDB—or at least an MDDB representation.

Table 10.2   Differences between OLAP and MDDB.

	OLAP	MDDB
Presentation display	List	Crosstab
Extraction	Select	Compare
Series variable "dimensions"	Columns	User-defined

Relational Answers To MDDB

Dr. Ralph Kimball, founder of Red Brick Systems, popularized the term *STAR schema* to describe a denormalization process that simulates the structure of a multidimensional database. With a STAR schema, the designer can simulate the functions of a multidimensional database without having to purchase expensive third-party software. Kimball describes denormalization as the prejoining of tables, such that the runtime application does not have to join tables. At the heart of the STAR schema is a *fact table*, usually comprised entirely of key values and raw data. A fact table is generally very long and may have millions of rows.

Surrounding the fact table is a series of *dimension tables* that serve to add value to the base information in the fact table. For example, consider the E/R model for a sales database shown in Figure 10.6.

Here we see a standard Third Normal Form (3NF) database to represent the sales of items. No redundant information is given; therefore, salient data such as the total for an order would have to be computed from the atomic items that comprise the order. In this 3NF database, a list of line items would need to be created, multiplying the quantity ordered by the price for all items that belong in order 123.

In the following example, an intermediate table called **TEMP** is created to hold the result list:

```
CREATE TABLE TEMP AS
SELECT (quantity.QUANTITY_sold * ITEM.list_price) line_total
FROM QUANTITY, ITEM
WHERE
QUANTITY.order_nbr = 123
AND
QUANTITY.item_nbr = ITEM.item_nbr;
SELECT sum(line_total) FROM TEMP;
```

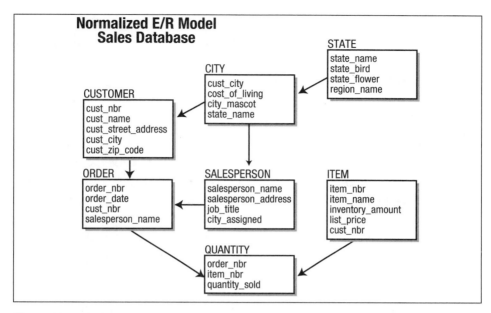

Figure 10.6   A sample fully normalized schema design.

Also note that the state-city table hierarchy in this example is very deliberate. In order to be truly in Third Normal Form, we do not allow any redundant information (except, of course, foreign keys). Given that this example has been fully normalized into five tables, a query that would appear very simple to the end user would have relatively complex SQL.

For example, the SQL to calculate the sum of all orders in the western region might look very complex, involving a five-way table join:

```
CREATE TABLE TEMP AS
SELECT (QUANTITY.quantity_sold * ITEM.list_price) line_total
FROM QUANTITY, ITEM, CUSTOMER, CITY, STATE
WHERE
QUANTITY.item_nbr = ITEM.item_nbr      /* join QUANTITY and ITEM */
AND
ITEM.cust_nbr = CUSTOMER.cust_nbr      /* join ITEM and CUSTOMER */
AND
CUSTOMER.cust_nbr = CITY.cust_nbr      /* join CUSTOMER and CITY */
AND
CITY.state_name = STATE.state_name     /* join CITY and STATE */
AND
STATE.region_name = 'WEST';
```

In the real world, of course, we would introduce enough redundancy to eliminate the city and state tables. The point is clear: A manager who wants to analyze a series of complete order totals would need to do a huge amount of realtime computation. Here we arrive at the basic tradeoff: If we want true freedom from redundant data, we must pay the price at query time.

Remember, the rules of database design have changed. Ten years ago, normalization theory emphasized the need to control redundancy and touted the benefits of a structure that was free of redundant data. Today, with disk prices at an all-time low, the attitude toward redundancy has changed radically. The relational vendors are offering a plethora of tools to allow snapshots and other methods for replicating data. Other vendors, such as UniSQL, are offering database products that allow for non–First Normal Form implementations. Today, it is perfectly acceptable to create First Normal Form implementations of normalized databases—prejoining the tables to avoid the high performance costs of runtime SQL joins.

The basic principle behind the STAR query schema is the introduction of highly redundant data for performance reasons. Let's evolve the 3NF database into a STAR schema by creating a fact table to hold the quantity for each item sold. Essentially, a fact table is a First Normal Form representation of the database, with a very high degree of redundancy being added into the tables. This un-normalized design, shown in Figure 10.7, greatly improves the simplicity of the design—but at the expense of redundant data.

At first glance, it is hard to believe that this representation contains the same data as the fully normalized database. The new fact table will contain one row for each item on each order, resulting in a tremendous amount of redundant key information. Of course, the STAR query schema is going to require far more disk space than the 3NF database from which it was created, and the STAR schema would most likely be a read-only database due to the widespread redundancy that has been introduced into the model. Also, the widespread redundancy would make updating difficult, if not downright impossible.

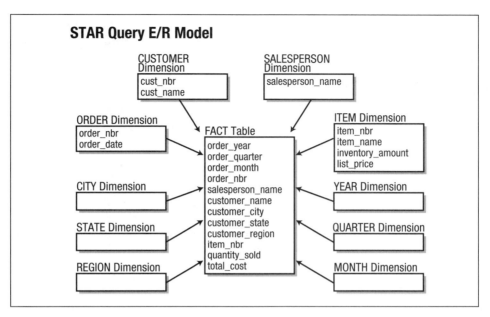

Figure 10.7   The completed STAR schema.

Also note the dimension tables surrounding the fact table. Some of the dimension tables contain data that can be added to queries with joins, while other dimensions such as **REGION** do not contain any data and only serve as indexes to the data.

Considering the huge disk space consumption and read-only restriction, what does this STAR schema really buy for us? The greatest benefit is the simplicity of data retrieval. Now that we have a STAR schema, we can formulate SQL queries to quickly get the information that we desire.

For example, getting the total cost for an order now becomes simple:

```
SELECT sum(total_cost) order_total
FROM FACT
WHERE
FACT.order_nbr = 123;
```

By doing some of the work up front, the realtime query become both faster and simpler.

Now, let's consider what would happen if the user of this schema wanted to analyze information by aggregate values. Assume our manager wants to know the breakdown of sales by region. The data is not organized by region, but the fact table can easily be queried to find the answer.

At this point, retrieving the sum of all orders for the western region becomes trivial, as shown in the following snippet:

```
SELECT sum(total_cost)
FROM FACT
WHERE
region = 'WEST';
```

In addition to making the query simpler in structure, all of the table joining has been eliminated, so we can easily get the extracted information from our STAR schema.

 *A value such as **region** would be an ideal candidate for the use of Oracle 7.3 bitmapped indexes. Columns that have less than three distinct values can see dramatic performance improvements by utilizing the bitmapped index technique. Bitmapped indexes are described later in this chapter.*

The natural consequence of this approach is that many IS shops will keep two copies of their production databases: one in Third Normal Form for online transaction processing, and another denormalized version of the database for decision support and data warehouse applications.

Populating STAR Schemas With Distributed SQL

Although it is evident at this point that having several copies of the same database can sometimes be desirable, problems arise with this dual approach when attempting to keep the STAR schema in sync with the operational database. Fortunately, Oracle provides several mechanisms to assist in this synchronization. Since it is safe to assume that the STAR schema will be used by executives for long-range trend analysis, it is probably not imperative that the STAR schema be completely up-to-date with the operational database. Consequently, we can develop an asynchronous method for updating the STAR schema.

If we make this assumption, then a single SQL statement can be used to extract the data from the operational database and populate the new rows into the STAR schema. In Listing 10.1, we assume that the STAR schema resides at our corporate headquarters in London. The table is called the **FACT_TABLE**.

Listing 10.1   Updating the STAR schema.

```
INSERT INTO FACT_TABLE@london
VALUES
(SELECT
    order_year,
    order_quarter,
    order_month,
    order_nbr,
    salerperson_name,
    customer_name,
    customer_city,
    customer_state,
    customer_region,
    item_nbr,
    quantity_sold,
    price*quantity_sold
FROM QUANTITY, ITEM, CUSTOMER, CITY, STATE
WHERE
QUANTITY.item_nbr = ITEM.item_nbr       /* join QUANTITY and ITEM */
AND
ITEM.cust_nbr = CUSTOMER.cust_nbr       /* join ITEM and CUSTOMER */
AND
CUSTOMER.city_name = CITY.city_name     /* join CUSTOMER and CITY */
AND
CITY.state_name = STATE.state_name      /* join CITY and STATE */
AND
order_date = SYSDATE                    /* get only today's transactions */
);
```

This is a very simple method for achieving the extraction, normalization, and insertion of the operational data into the STAR schema. By specifying the **SYSDATE** in the **WHERE** clause, we ensure that only the day's transactions are extracted and loaded into the STAR schema **FACT_TABLE**. Of course, we are still undertaking a very large five-way table join, but we would hope to run this extraction during off hours where the retrieval would not impact the production users.

But what about rows that have been deleted? While uncommon, we still need to account for the possibility that some orders may be canceled. We need a mechanism for updating the STAR schema to reflect these deletions.

The most obvious method for removing deleted orders from the STAR schema is to create a **DELETE** trigger on the **ORDER** table of the operational system. This delete trigger will fire off a remote delete from the trigger to delete all rows from the STAR schema that are no longer valid:

```
CREATE TRIGGER delete_orders
    AFTER DELETE ON ORDER
AS
(DELETE FROM FACT_TABLE@london
    WHERE
    order_nbr = :del_ord
);
```

We now have a mechanism for keeping our data warehouse in relative synchronization with the operational database.

What are we going to do as the **FACT_TABLE** expands beyond normal table capacity? Let's assume that our organization processes 20,000 orders daily, leading to 7.3 million rows per year. With Oracle's efficient indexing, a table this large can create unique performance problems, primarily because the index must spawn many levels to properly index 7.3 million rows. Whereas a typical query might involve three index reads, a query against a 7-million-row table might involve five index reads before the target row is fetched.

To alleviate this problem, many designers will partition the table into smaller subtables, using the data as the distinguishing factor. As such, we may have a table for each month, with a name such as **FACT_TABLE_1_96**, **FACT_TABLE_2_96**, and so on.

Whenever we need to address multiple tables in a single operation, we can use the SQL **UNION ALL** verb to merge the tables together:

```
SELECT * FROM FACT_TABLE_1_96
UNION ALL
SELECT * FROM FACT_TABLE_2_96
```

```
UNION_ALL
SELECT * FROM FACT_TABLE_3_96
ORDER BY order_year, order_month;
```

> *In addition to having the benefit of smaller table indexes, this type of table partitioning combined with the **UNION ALL** statement has the added benefit of allowing Oracle's parallel query engine to simultaneously perform full-table scans on each of the subtables. In this case, a separate process would be invoked to process each of the three table scans. Oracle query manager would then gather the result data and sort in according to the **ORDER BY** clause. In the above example, we could expect a 50 percent performance improvement over a query against a single **FACT_TABLE**.*

Aggregation, Roll-Ups, And STAR Schemas

We have now defined and populated a STAR schema that contains the **total_sales** for each order for each day. While it is now easy to see the total for each order, rarely do the users of a decision support require this level of detail. Most managers would be more interested in knowing the sum of sales or units sold—aggregated by month, quarter, region, and so on. Even with a STAR schema, these types of aggregation would be hard to compute at runtime with an acceptable response time. Essentially, we can either aggregate at runtime or preaggregate the data offline, making the totals available without realtime computation. One simple alternative to realtime aggregation is to write SQL to preaggregate the data according to the dimensions that the end user may want to see. In our example, let's assume that management would want to aggregate monthly sales by region, state, item type, and salesperson. Since we have four possible dimensions, we can generate a list of the following six aggregate tables to precreate. Assume that all of the tables would have a **month_year** field as their primary key:

- *Region by state*—This table would have **region_name**, **state_name**, and **monthly_sales** as columns.

- *Region by* **item_type**—This table would have **region_name**, **item_type**, and **monthly_ sales** as columns.

- *Region by salesperson*—This table would have **region_name**, **salesperson_name**, and **monthly_sales** as columns.

- *State by* **item_type**—This table would have **state_name**, **item_type**, and **monthly_sales** as columns.

- *State by salesperson*—This table would have **state_name**, **salesperson_name**, and **monthly_sales** as columns.

- **item_type** *by salesperson*—This table would have **item_type**, **salesperson_name**, and **monthly_sales** as columns.

The SQL to produce these table can be easily run as a batch task at end-of-month processing. For example, the SQL to create the **region_by_state** table might look like this:

```
INSERT INTO REGION_ITEM_TYPE
VALUES
(SELECT '3', '1996', region_name, item_type, total_cost)
FROM FACT_TABLE_3_96
GROUP BY region_name, item_type
);
```

The sample **REGION_ITEM_TYPE** table might look like the one shown in Table 10.3.

These aggregate tables can be built in the middle of the night if need be—right after the master fact tables have been populated with the day's sales. The next morning, the prior day's sales will have been rolled up into these summaries, giving management an accurate, fast, and easy-to-use tool for decision support.

Of course, these tables are two-dimensional, but they can easily be massaged by an application to provide a tabular representation of the variables. Table 10.4 presents this tabular form.

 This technique replicates the functionality of a multidimensional database where an end user can specify the axis of interest and the multidimensional database (MDDB) will build a tabular representation of the data.

Table 10.3   A sample REGION_ITEM_TYPE table.

DATE	REGION	TYPE	MONTHLY_SALES
3/96	WEST	Clothes	$113,999
3/96	WEST	Hardware	$56,335
3/96	WEST	Food	$23,574
3/96	EAST	Clothes	$45,234
3/96	EAST	Hardware	$66,182
3/96	EAST	Food	$835,342
3/96	SOUTH	Clothes	$1,223
3/96	SOUTH	Hardware	$56,392
3/96	SOUTH	Food	$9,281
3/96	NORTH	Clothes	$826,463
3/96	NORTH	Hardware	$77,261
3/96	NORTH	Food	$43,383

But what if management wants to look at quarterly summaries instead of monthly summaries? What about yearly summaries? Of course, this same technique can be used to roll up the monthly summary tables into quarterly summaries, yearly summaries, and so on, according to the demands of the end user.

History Of OLAP

Dr. E. F. (Ted) Codd first coined the term OLAP in a 1993 report that was sponsored by Arbor Software. In addition to coining the term, Codd also went on to create 12 rules for OLAP. Despite the claims of a new technology, some offerings such as IRI date to the early 1970s.

Table 10.4   REGION versus TYPE.

	Clothes	Food	Hardware
WEST	$113,999	$23,574	$56,335
EAST	$45,234	$835,342	$66,182
NORTH	$826,463	$43,383	$77,261
SOUTH	$1,223	$9,281	$56,392

N☉TE   *The Internet offers a popular forum that discusses OLAP issues. It is called **comp.database.olap**.*

SIMULATION OF CUBIC DATABASES (DIMENSIONALITY)

For an illustrative example, consider the sample customer table in Table 10.5. Assume that this table is physically stored in data order. We can imagine how this data might look as a cubic table by reviewing Figure 10.8.

Table 10.5   A sample customer table.

Customer Name	# Sales	YY-MM	City	State
Bob Papaj & Assoc.	300	91-01	NY	NY
Mark Reulbach Inc.	400	91-01	San Fran	CA
Rick Willoughby Co.	120	91-02	NY	NY
Kelvin Connor Co.	300	91-02	San Fran	CA
Jame Gaston Inc.	145	91-03	NY	NY
Linda O'Dell Assoc.	337	91-03	Fairport	NY
Rick Wahl & Assoc.	134	91-03	San Fran	CA

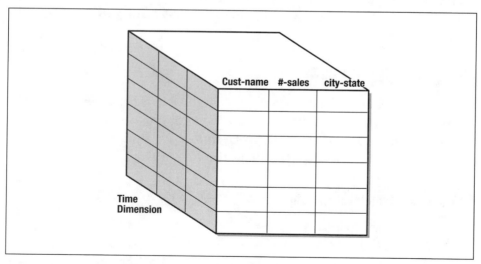

Figure 10.8   Cubic representation of relational data.

Of course, the cubic representation would require that the data be loaded into a multidimensional database or a spreadsheet that supported pivot tables. When considering an MDDB, two arguments emerge. The relational database vendors point out that MDDBs are proprietary—they feel that the more open relational databases should be used. The MDDB vendors point out some serious inadequacies with SQL that make it very difficult to use a relational database.

Keep in mind that dimensions may be hierarchical in nature, adding further confusion. A time dimension, for example, may be represented as a hierarchy with **year**, **quarter**, **month**, and **day**. Each of these "levels" in the dimension hierarchy may have its own values. In other words, a cubic representation with **time** as a dimension may be viewed in two ways:

- A series of cubes—one for **year**, another for **quarter**, and another with **full_date**

- A five-dimension table

MDDBs are most commonly used with data that is a natural fit for pivot tables, and it should come as no surprise that most MDDB sites are used with finance and marketing applications. Unfortunately, most multidimensional databases do not scale up well for warehouse applications. For example, the largest supported database for Essbase is about 20 gigabytes, whereas data warehouses with sizes measured in terabytes are not uncommon.

It is important to note that defining aggregation of a multidimensional database is no different than defining aggregate tables to a relational database. At load time, the database will still need to compute the aggregate values. MDDBs also employ the concept of sparse data. Since data is aggregated and presliced, some cells on a cube may not contain data. For example, consider a cube that tracks sales of items across a large company. The cells representing sales of thermal underwear would be null for Hawaii, while the sales of surfboards in Wyoming would also be null. Nearly all of the product offerings are able to maintain a mechanism for compressing out these types of null values.

Alternatives To Cubic Data Representation

Many traditional database designs can be used to simulate a data cube. One alternative to the cubic representation would be to leave the table in linear form, using SQL to join the table against itself to produce a result, as shown in Figure 10.9.

Let's take a look at a query that might require the self-joining of a table:

- Show all customers in Hawaii who purchased our product more than 500 times.

- Show all customers in L.A. who purchase less than 10 times/month.

- Show all large customers (buying more than 100 items per month) in Alaska whose usage has dropped more than 10 percent in 1990.

- Show all customers in New York whose usage in March of 1990 deviated more than 20 percent from their usage in March of 1991.

- Show all customers in California where the company name contains "Widget" and usage has dropped more than 20 percent in 1991.

In our example, we compare all user sites where usage of our product has experienced a negative usage variance of greater than 5 percent between October of 1990 compared to December of 1990. A subset of this data can easily be extracted such that only California sites with more than 100 uses

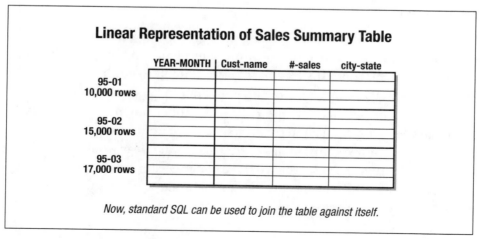

Figure 10.9　Joining a relational table against itself.

per month are displayed. For display, the user chose percentage variance, number of requests, site number, ZIP code, and city. Note the sort order of the report: It is sorted first by ZIP, followed by city, and then by percentage variance within city:

```
SELECT INTEGER
(((E.NUMBER_OF_SALES - S.NUMBER_OF_SALES) / S.NUMBER_OF_SALES) * 100) ,
E.CUSTOMER_NAME , E.CITY_NAME , E.ZIP , S.NUMBER_OF_SALES ,
E.NUMBER_OF_SALES

FROM DETAIL S , DETAIL E

WHERE
S.CUSTOMER_NAME = E.CUSTOMER_NAME
 AND
E.STATE_ABBR = 'CA'
 AND
E.DATE_YYMM = 9101
 AND
S.DATE_YYMM = 9201
 AND
E.NUMBER_OF_SALES < S.NUMBER_OF_SALES - (.05 * S.NUMBER_OF_SALES)

ORDER BY E.ZIP ASC , E.CITY_NAME ASC , 1 ;
```

Note that the variance analysis is done directly in the SQL statement. The above case displays California users whose usage has dropped by more than 5 percent (comparing January 1991 to January 1992).

But what if the user wants to compare one full year with another year? The table is structured for simple comparison of two specific month dates, but the SQL query could be modified slightly to aggregate the data, offering comparison of two ranges of dates.

The query shown in Listing 10.2 will aggregate all sales for an entire year and compare 1991 with 1992. Here we meet the request "show me all customers in California whose sales have dropped by more than 5 percent between 1991 and 1992."

Listing 10.2   Aggregating sales for an entire year.

```
SELECT INTEGER
((((E.NUMBER_OF_SALES - S.NUMBER_OF_SALES) / S.NUMBER_OF_SALES) * 100) ,
E.CUSTOMER_NAME , E.CITY_NAME , E.ZIP , S.NUMBER_OF_SALES ,
E.NUMBER_OF_SALES

FROM DETAIL S , DETAIL E

WHERE
S.CUSTOMER_NAME = E.CUSTOMER_NAME
 AND
E.STATE_ABBR = 'CA'
 AND
substr(E.DATE_YYMM,1,2) = '91'
 AND
substr(S.DATE_YYMM,1,2) = '92'
 AND
E.NUMBER_OF_SALES < S.NUMBER_OF_SALES - (.05 * S.NUMBER_OF_SALES)

ORDER BY E.ZIP ASC , E.CITY_NAME ASC , 1 ;
```

On the surface, it appears that SQL can be used against two-dimensional tables to handle three-dimensional time-series problems. It also appears that SQL can be used to roll up aggregations at runtime, alleviating the need to do a roll up at load time, as with a traditional database. While this implementation does not require any special multidimensional databases, two important issues remain to be resolved:

- *Performance*—Joining a table against itself—especially when comparing ranges of dates—may create many levels of nesting in the SQL optimization and poor response time.

- *Ability*—No end user would be capable of formulating this type of sophisticated SQL query.

If one strips away all of the marketing hype and industry jargon, we see that data warehouse and a multidimensional database can be easily simulated by precreating many redundant tables, each with precalculated roll-up information. In fact, the base issue is clear. Complex aggregation with either needs to be computed at runtime—or when the data is loaded.

Table 10.6   OLAP/MDDB product information.

Vendor	Tool	Description
Oracle	Express	Excel spreadsheet extension, true OO
Oracle	Oracle 7.3	STAR query hints, parallel query, bitmap indexes
MicroStrategy	DSS Agent	MDDB queries against RDBMS
D&B	Pilot Lightship	OLAP w/custom and spreadsheet GUI
IBI	Focus Fusion	MDDB engine
VMark	uniVerse	NT-based MDDB engine
Kenan	Acumate ES	MDDB with PC-OLAP GUI
Arbor	OLAP Builder	Extracts data from DW for Essbase
Arbor	Essbase	MDDB engine w/Excel spreadsheet GUI
Think Systems	FYI Planner	PC-GUI with MDDB and OLAP server

There are many different types of OLAP and MDDB products on the market today, as shown in Table 10.6. Each has its own relative advantages and disadvantages, and they are all fighting to achieve recognition for their strengths.

Data Mining And OLAP

The recent interest in data warehousing has created many new techniques and tools for getting useful information out of these behemoth databases. Data mining is one area that tends to hold a great deal of promise for users of data warehouses.

In traditional decision support systems, the user was charged with formulating the queries against the database and deciphering any trends that were present in the data. Unfortunately, this approach is only as good as the user of the system, and many statistically valid associations between data items can be missed. This is especially true in data warehouse systems where unobtrusive trends may be present. For example, the Psychology Department at the University of Minnesota—developers of the hugely popular Minnesota Multiphasic Personality Inventory (MMPI)—have discovered some startling patterns correlating a psychological diagnosis to seemingly unrelated, ordinary questions. The results provide unobtrusive measures for human personality. For example, they found that people with low self-esteem tend to prefer baths to showers. While no "reason" for this preference is obvious, the statistically valid correlation between self-concept and cleaning preferences remains.

These types of unobtrusive trends also plague the business world, and it is the goal of data mining software to identify these trends for the users of the warehouse. In addition to simply identifying trends, some data mining software goes one step further in an attempt to analyze other data and determine the underlying reasons for the trend.

While basic statistical tools are adequate for doing correlations between a small number of related variables, large databases with hundreds of data items are quickly bogged down in a mire of multivariate "chi-square" techniques that are hard to follow for even the most experienced statistician. As such, the new data mining tools are meant to accept only general hints from the users, and then go forth into the data probing for trends.

In other cases, data mining techniques are used to prove a hypothesis based on existing data. For example, a marketing person may speculate that those with an income between $50,000 and $80,000 are likely to buy his or her product. A quick verification of this hypothesis can be run, thereby either confirming or disproving the hypothesis.

Yet another class of tools uses a relatively straightforward exception detection mechanism to cruise the database looking for unexpected trends or unusual patterns. Many of the data mining tools use techniques borrowed from Artificial Intelligence (AI), including fuzzy logic, neural networks, fractals, and sundry other statistical techniques. Since many of these tools perform a huge amount of internal processing, many of them read selected information from the relational database into a proprietary, internal data representation for analysis. No widely used data mining tools are available that run directly against the relational database, although there are several promising start-up companies, as shown in Table 10.7.

Table 10.7   Data mining product information.

Vendor	Tool	Description
Thinking Machines	Darwin	Neural nets
MIT GmbH	DataEngine	Fuzzy logic
Reduct Systems	DataLogic	Fuzzy sets
IBM	Data Mining Toolkit	Fuzzy logic
Epsilon	Epsilon	Rule-based
Cross/Z	F-DBMS	Fractals
Info. Discovery	IDIS	Rule-based
Info. Harvester	InfoHarvester	Rule-based
Angoss Software	KnowledgeSEEKER	Rule-based
Software AG	NETMAP	Neural networks
NeuralWare	NeuralWorks	Neural nets
Nestor	PRISM	Neural nets
Cognitive Systems	ReMind	Inductive logic

While there is still a great deal of interest in data mining applications, no single vendor has stepped up to claim market leadership. It will probably be many years before all owners of a data warehouse have tools that will be able to fully exploit their data resources.

An Illustration Of STAR Schema Design

Let's assume that Moncato State Savings & Loan uses the E/R model shown in Figure 10.10 for its database. Using this E/R model, perform the following tasks. State any assumptions that you may have to make.

Part 1

1. Write an SQL query to display the **cust_name** for all customers who have had a transaction of more than $5,000 at the Boston branch.

2. Starting with this E/R model, denormalize the structure into a STAR schema.

3. How many "dimensions" are present in this system?

4. Rewrite the query from Question 1.

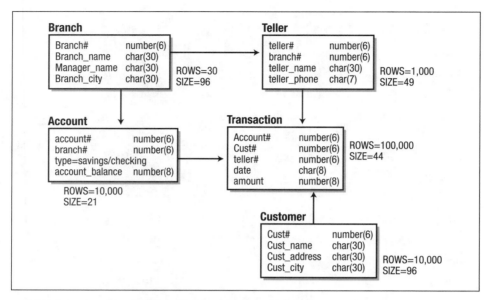

Figure 10.10 A non-STAR schema for Moncato State Savings & Loan.

PART 2

1. Using the size estimates, determine the space required for the original schema.

2. How much additional storage is required for your STAR schema?

3. Now, assuming that each day's transactions are "rolled-up" into the **account_balance** field, design a new STAR schema and give sizing estimates for a database that summarizes each day's transactions.

Using Oracle 7.3's Features With Data Warehouses

Please note that the new features of Oracle 7.2 and Oracle 7.3 will not be activated unless the following init.ora parameter has been used:

```
COMPATIBILITY=7.3.0.0.0
```

With Oracle version 7.3, several new features can dramatically improve performance of Oracle data warehouse and decision support systems.

Parallel Query For Data Warehouses

It is a common misconception that parallel processors (SMP or MPP) are necessary to use and benefit from parallel processing. Even on the same processor, multiple processes can be used to speed up queries. Data warehouses generally employ parallel technology to perform warehouse loading and query functions. These include:

- *Parallel backup/recovery*—Some parallel tools are capable of rates in excess of 40 GB/hour.

- *Parallel query (SMP and MPP)*—Multiple processes are used to retrieve table data.

- *Parallel loading*—Multiple processes are used to simultaneously load many tables.

- *Parallel indexing*—Multiple processes are used to create indexes.

For parallel query, the most powerful approach deals with the use of the SQL **UNION** verb in very large databases (VLDBs). In most very large Oracle data warehouses, it is common to logically partition a single table into many smaller tables in order to improve query throughput. For example, a sales table that is ordered by **date_of_sale** may be partitioned into **1997_SALES**, **1998_SALES**, and **1999_SALES** tables. This approach is often used in data warehouse applications where a single logical table might have millions of rows. While this splitting of a table according to a key value violates normalization, it can dramatically improve performance for individual queries. For large queries that may span many logical tables, the isolated tables can then easily be reassembled using Oracle's parallel query facility, as shown here:

```
CREATE VIEW all_sales AS
    SELECT * FROM 1997_SALES
    UNION ALL
    SELECT * FROM 1998_SALES
    UNION ALL
    SELECT * FROM 1999_SALES;
```

We can now query the **all_sales** view as if it were a single database table. Oracle parallel query will automatically recognize the **UNION ALL** parameter, firing off simultaneous queries against each of the three base tables.

For example, the following query will assemble the requested data from the three tables in parallel, with each query being separately optimized. The result set from each subquery is then merged by the query manager:

```
SELECT customer_name
FROM all_sales
WHERE
sales_amount > 5000;
```

For more details on using Oracle's parallel query facility, refer to Chapter 2, *Physical Performance Design For Oracle Databases.*

STAR Query Hints And STAR Joins With Oracle 7.3

As we have already discovered, the STAR schema design involves creating a main fact table that contains all of the primary keys in the related tables. This massive denormalization of the database structure means that just about any query against the STAR schema is going to involve the joining of many large tables—including a large "fact" table and many smaller reference tables. Oracle has provided a new feature with release 7.3 that detects STAR query joins and invokes a special procedure to improve performance of the query. Prior to release 7.3 of Oracle, this feature only worked with up to five tables, but this restriction has been eliminated. Also, release 7.3 no longer requires the use of STAR query hints. However, they are still allowed in the SQL syntax and are generally a good idea for documentation purposes. The STAR query requires that a single concatenated index resides in the fact table for all keys.

Essentially, Oracle follows a simple procedure for addressing these queries. Oracle will first service the queries against the smaller reference tables, combining the result set into a Cartesian product table in memory. Once the sum of the reference tables has been addressed, Oracle will perform a nested-loop join of the intermediate table against the fact table. This approach is far faster than the traditional method of joining the smallest reference table against the fact table, and then joining each of the other reference tables against the intermediate table.

Using Oracle's Bitmap Indexes

For data warehouse applications that must elicit as much performance as possible, some special situations can arise where Oracle bitmapped indexes may be useful. As we know, the sheer volume of rows in very large tables can make even a trivial query run for a long time. Oracle has introduced bitmapped indexes with release 7.3 in an attempt to improve index lookup performance for queries, especially decision support type queries that may have many conditions in the **WHERE** clause.

The bitmap approach to indexing is very different from the traditional B-tree style of indexes. In a traditional index, the index keys are sorted and carried in several tree nodes; in a bitmapped index, an array is created. This array has all possible index values as one axis, while the other axis contains all rows in the base table. For example, consider a bitmapped index on the **region** field of the **SALES** table, where the regions are **North**, **South**, **East**, and **West**. If the **SALES** table contains 1 million rows, the bitmapped index would create an array of 4×1 billion to store the possible key values.

Within this array, the index data is binary. If a value is true, it is assigned a binary "1"—a false reading is set to binary "0" (see Figure 10.11).

Here we can see how this query runs faster than a traditional query. The Oracle optimizer will notice that the items in the **WHERE** clause have bitmapped indexes, scan for non-zero values in the proper array column, and quickly return the Row ID of the columns. A fast merge of the result set will then quickly identify the rows that meet the query criteria.

While it may appear that the index is very large, Oracle has developed a compression method whereby all of the binary zeros are omitted from the bitmap. This makes it very compact.

While this may look reasonable at first glance, some drawbacks to bitmapped indexing have to be considered. The first and most obvious is that bitmapped indexes work best for columns that only have a small amount of possible values. For columns that have many values such as **state_name** or **city_name**, the index overhead would probably exceed any performance gains that might accrue from using bitmapped indexes.

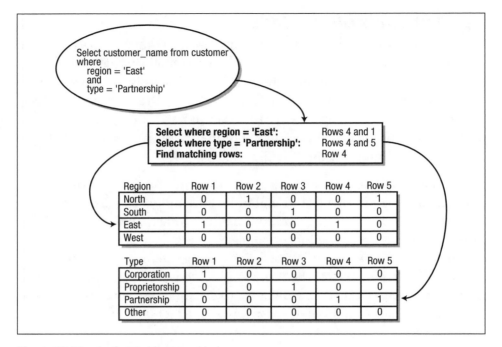

Figure 10.11　An Oracle bitmapped index.

However, for columns such as **sex**, **color**, and **size** that have a small number of finite values, bitmapped indexes will greatly improve query retrieval speeds. Bitmapped indexes are especially useful for decision support systems where many conditions are combined to a single **WHERE** clause.

Using Oracle 7.3 Hash-Joins

Oracle release 7.3 also provides another method for speeding up decision support and warehouse queries. This method is called the *hash-join*. A hash-join is a technique where Oracle bypasses the traditional sort-merge join technique and replaces it with an algorithm that performs a full-table scan, placing the rows into memory partitions. Partition pairs that do not fit into memory are placed in the **TEMP** tablespace. Oracle will then build a hash table on the smallest partition, using the larger partition to probe the newly created hash table. This technique alleviates the need for in-memory sorting and does not require that indexes exist on the target tables.

The following init.ora parameters must be set to use hash-joins:

- **optimizer_mode** parameter must be set to **COST**

- **hash_join_enabled=TRUE**

- **hash_multiblock_io_count=TRUE**

- **hash_area_size=SIZE**

To execute a hash-join, the hash-join hint must be used. Consider this example:

```
SELECT /* USE_HASH/ *
FROM CUSTOMER, ORDER
WHERE
CUSTOMER.cust_no = ORDER.cust_no
AND
credit_rating = 'GOOD';
```

Summary

Now that we have seen how data warehouse applications function in a client/server environment, we can move on for a closer look at networking issues and how Oracle servers can be monitored for performance.

Oracle Application Monitoring

Because Oracle is the world's leading relational database, many vendors will offer tools that claim to monitor Oracle and alert the DBA to performance problems. Even Oracle itself is entering the monitoring marketplace with an Oracle Expert tool that was released in the second quarter of 1996.

These tools fall into a couple of broad categories. First are the reactive tools that diagnose a problem after it has been reported. The second group of tools is able to proactively monitor the database and search for trouble before it ever impacts the user.

An example of the reactive class is the AdHawk tool by Eventus Software. AdHawk allows the DBA to rapidly view database locks and SQL in graphical format, quickly pinpointing the cause of a specific performance problem. This tool is especially useful for situations where only a few users are plagued with poor performance, while other users on the database are not experiencing problems.

The second, proactive category consists of tools that constantly monitor the database and create "alerts" for unusual conditions. These tools allow the developer to set predefined thresholds, which trigger an alert when the threshold has been exceeded. These alerts may take a number of different forms, including a report, a telephone call, or a pager. Some of the more sophisticated tools, such as BMC's Patrol, allow the developer to program corrective actions directly into the rule base and automatically take corrective action when the alert occurs. For example, if a table's next extent is 10 megabytes but only 8 megabytes of free space exist in the tablespace, the alert will alter the table's next extent size to 5 megabytes and alert the DBA on call. This automatic action buys valuable time for the DBA to investigate the problem before a stoppage occurs. Table 11.1 offers a compact glimpse of the various monitoring tools on today's market, complete with vendor.

Proactive Vs. Reactive Measuring Techniques

When deciding how to monitor your servers, the first conscious choice you will need to make is whether to adopt a proactive or a reactive system. It is unfair to place a judgment on either one of these methods, since each has a legitimate place in Oracle monitoring. Let's review each one in greater detail.

A proactive system is one that makes forecasts based upon statistical information and decides that intervention is necessary in order to prevent a

Table 11.1　Representative Oracle monitoring tools.

Tool	Vendor
DBAnalyzer	Database Solutions
iVIEW Performance Logger	Independence Technologies
Patrol	BMC software
EcoTOOLS	Compuware
DBVision	Platinum Technology
AdHawk	Eventus Software
R*SQLab	R*Tech Systems

performance problem. For example, a proactive system could detect that a table will reach its maximum allocation of extents tomorrow, thereby hanging the system unless the DBA compresses the table extents.

A reactive system is used *after* performance problems have been noticed. These types of systems give detailed information about the current status of the Oracle instance and allow the DBA to quickly see—and hopefully correct—the problem.

Creating An Oracle-Based Monitor

Now that we have covered the basics, we can take a look at designing an expert system for monitoring Oracle performance. We will need to address the following issues:

- What data will we collect, and how will we collect it?

- How do we create a centralized repository for performance information?

- How will the centralized database be accessed?

- How do we automate the exception reporting?

As we already know, the **V$** tables are of limited value, since they keep running statistics for the total time that the Oracle instance has been running.

Instead, we can alter the existing statistics report to collect information, storing it into a database that we define especially for this purpose. Once we have the data in all of our local hosts, we can transfer the performance and tuning data into a single Oracle database. This database will be the foundation for the creation of automated exception reporting, as well as alerts.

Gathering The Oracle Performance Statistics

The fastest and simplest way to check the status of a database is to interrogate the **V$** tables. While this provides only a crude measure of the overall health, it is usually one of the first techniques that is used. The script in Listing 11.1 is a collection of the most useful **V$** scripts, all packaged into a single collection.

Listing 11.1 snapshot.sql—a full snapshot of the V$ tables.

```
REM    Remember, you must first run $ORACLE_HOME/rdbms/admin/catblock.sql
REM    before this script will work. . .
SET LINESIZE 75;
SET PAGESIZE 9999;
SET PAUSE OFF;
SET ECHO OFF;
SET TERMOUT ON;
SET SHOWMODE OFF;
SET FEEDBACK OFF;
SET NEWPAGE 1;
SET VERIFY OFF;


--spool /tmp/snap;


PROMPT **********************************************************
PROMPT  Hit Ratio Section
PROMPT **********************************************************
PROMPT
PROMPT           ==========================
PROMPT           BUFFER HIT RATIO
PROMPT           ==========================
PROMPT (SHOULD BE > 70, ELSE INCREASE db_block_buffers IN init.ora)

--SELECT trunc((1-(sum(decode(name,'physical reads',value,0))/
--                (sum(decode(name,'db block gets',value,0))+
--                (sum(decode(name,'consistent gets',value,0)))))
--              )* 100) "Buffer Hit Ratio"
--FROM v$sysstat;


COLUMN "logical_reads" FORMAT 99,999,999,999
COLUMN "phys_reads"    FORMAT 999,999,999
COLUMN "phy_writes"    FORMAT 999,999,999
SELECT a.value + b.value  "logical_reads",
       c.value            "phys_reads",
       d.value            "phy_writes",
       ROUND(100 * ((a.value+b.value)-c.value) / (a.value+b.value))
         "BUFFER HIT RATIO"
FROM v$sysstat a, v$sysstat b, v$sysstat c, v$sysstat d
WHERE
   a.statistic# = 37
AND
   b.statistic# = 38
AND
   c.statistic# = 39
```

```
AND
    d.statistic# = 40;

PROMPT
PROMPT
PROMPT              ===========================
PROMPT              DATA DICT HIT RATIO
PROMPT              ===========================
PROMPT (SHOULD BE HIGHER THAN 90 ELSE INCREASE shared_pool_size IN
    init.ora)
PROMPT

COLUMN "Data Dict. Gets"           FORMAT 999,999,999
COLUMN "Data Dict. cache misses"   FORMAT 999,999,999
SELECT sum(gets) "Data Dict. Gets",
       sum(getmisses) "Data Dict. cache misses",
       trunc((1-(sum(getmisses)/sum(gets)))*100)
       "DATA DICT CACHE HIT RATIO"
FROM v$rowcache;

PROMPT
PROMPT              ===========================
PROMPT              LIBRARY CACHE MISS RATIO
PROMPT              ===========================
PROMPT (IF > 1 THEN INCREASE THE shared_pool_size IN init.ora)
PROMPT
COLUMN "LIBRARY CACHE MISS RATIO"       FORMAT 99.9999
COLUMN "executions"                     FORMAT 999,999,999
COLUMN "Cache misses while executing"   FORMAT 999,999,999
SELECT sum(pins) "executions", sum(reloads) "Cache misses while
       executing",
       (((sum(reloads)/sum(pins)))) "LIBRARY CACHE MISS RATIO"
FROM v$librarycache;

PROMPT
PROMPT              ===========================
PROMPT              LIBRARY CACHE SECTION
PROMPT              ===========================
PROMPT HIT RATIO SHOULD BE > 70, AND PIN RATIO > 70 ...
PROMPT

COLUMN "reloads" FORMAT 999,999,999
SELECT namespace, trunc(gethitratio * 100) "Hit ratio",
       trunc(pinhitratio * 100) "pin hit ratio", RELOADS "reloads"
FROM v$librarycache;
PROMPT
PROMPT
```

```
PROMPT             ===========================
PROMPT             REDO LOG BUFFER
PROMPT             ===========================
PROMPT (SHOULD BE NEAR 0, ELSE INCREASE SIZE OF LOG_BUFFER IN init.ora)
PROMPT
SET HEADING OFF
COLUMN VALUE FORMAT 999,999,999
SELECT substr(name,1,30),
       value
FROM v$sysstat WHERE NAME = 'redo log space requests';

SET HEADING ON
PROMPT
PROMPT
PROMPT *********************************************************
PROMPT free memory should be > 1,000
PROMPT *********************************************************
PROMPT

COLUMN BYTES FORMAT 999,999,999
SELECT NAME, BYTES FROM v$sgastat WHERE NAME = 'free memory';

PROMPT
PROMPT *********************************************************
PROMPT  SQL SUMMARY SECTION
PROMPT *********************************************************
PROMPT
COLUMN "Tot SQL run since startup"    FORMAT 999,999,999
COLUMN "SQL executing now"            FORMAT 999,999,999
SELECT sum(executions) "Tot SQL run since startup",
       sum(users_executing) "SQL executing now"
       from v$sqlarea;


prompt
prompt
prompt *********************************************************
prompt  Lock Section
prompt *********************************************************
prompt
prompt             ===========================
PROMPT             SYSTEM-WIDE LOCKS - all requests for locks or latches
PROMPT             ===========================
PROMPT
SELECT substr(username,1,12)  "User",
       substr(lock_type,1,18) "Lock Type",
```

```
        substr(mode_held,1,18) "Mode Held"
FROM sys.dba_lock a, v$session b
WHERE lock_type not in ('Media Recovery','Redo Thread')
AND a.session_id = b.sid;
PROMPT
PROMPT          =========================
PROMPT          DDL LOCKS - These are usually triggers or other DDL
PROMPT          =========================
PROMPT
SELECT substr(username,1,12) "User",
       substr(owner,1,8) "Owner",
       substr(name,1,15)  "Name",
       substr(a.type,1,20)  "Type",
       substr(mode_held,1,11) "Mode held"
FROM sys.dba_ddl_locks a, v$session b
WHERE a.session_id = b.sid;

PROMPT
PROMPT          =========================
PROMPT          DML LOCKS - These are table and row locks...
PROMPT          =========================
PROMPT
SELECT substr(username,1,12) "User",
       substr(owner,1,8) "Owner",
       substr(name,1,20)  "Name",
       substr(mode_held,1,21) "Mode held"
FROM sys.dba_dml_locks a, v$session b
WHERE a.session_id = b.sid;

PROMPT
PROMPT
PROMPT ************************************************************
PROMPT  LATCH SECTION
PROMPT ************************************************************
PROMPT If miss_ratio or IMMEDIATE_MISS_RATIO > 1 then  latch
PROMPT Contention exists, decrease LOG_SMALL_ENTRY_MAX_SIZE in init.ora
PROMPT
COLUMN "miss_ratio"             FORMAT .99
COLUMN "immediate_miss_ratio" FORMAT .99
SELECT substr(l.name,1,30) name,
       (misses/(gets+.001))*100 "miss_ratio",
       (immediate_misses/(immediate_gets+.001))*100
       "immediate_miss_ratio"
FROM v$latch l, v$latchname ln
WHERE l.latch# = ln.latch#
AND (
```

```
(misses/(gets+.001))*100 > .2
OR
(immediate_misses/(immediate_gets+.001))*100 > .2
)
ORDER BY l.name;


PROMPT
PROMPT
PROMPT ***************************************************************
PROMPT   ROLLBACK SEGMENT SECTION
PROMPT ***************************************************************
PROMPT If any count below is > 1% of the total number of requests for
  data
PROMPT then more rollback segments are needed
PROMPT If free list > 1% then increase freelist in init.ora

--COLUMN COUNT FORMAT 999,999,999
SELECT CLASS, COUNT
FROM v$waitstat
WHERE CLASS IN ('free list','system undo header','system undo block',
                'undo header','undo block')
GROUP BY class,count;

COLUMN "Tot # of Requests for Data" FORMAT 999,999,999
SELECT sum(value) "Tot # of Requests for Data" FROM v$sysstat
WHERE
NAME IN ('db block gets', 'consistent gets');

PROMPT
PROMPT            ============================
PROMPT            ROLLBACK SEGMENT CONTENTION
PROMPT            ============================
PROMPT
PROMPT            If any ratio is > .01 then more rollback segments are
needed

COLUMN "Ratio" FORMAT 99.99999
SELECT name, waits, gets, waits/gets "Ratio"
FROM v$rollstat a, v$rollname b
WHERE a.usn = b.usn;


COLUMN "total_waits"    FORMAT 999,999,999
COLUMN "total_timeouts" FORMAT 999,999,999
PROMPT
PROMPT
SET FEEDBACK ON;
```

```
PROMPT ************************************************************
PROMPT  SESSION EVENT SECTION
PROMPT ************************************************************
PROMPT IF AVERAGE-WAIT > 0 THEN CONTENTION EXISTS
PROMPT
SELECT substr(event,1,30) event,
       total_waits, total_timeouts, average_wait
FROM v$session_event
WHERE average_wait > 0 ;
--OR total_timeouts > 0;


PROMPT
PROMPT
PROMPT ************************************************************
PROMPT QUEUE SECTION
PROMPT ************************************************************
PROMPT Average wait for queues should be near zero ...
PROMPT
COLUMN "totalq"   FORMAT 999,999,999
COLUMN "# queued" FORMAT 999,999,999
SELECT paddr, type "Queue type", queued "# queued", wait, totalq,
DECODE(totalq,0,0,wait/totalq) "AVG WAIT" FROM v$queue;


SET FEEDBACK ON;
PROMPT
PROMPT
PROMPT ************************************************************
PROMPT  MULTI-THREADED SERVER SECTION
PROMPT ************************************************************
PROMPT
PROMPT     If the following number is > 1
PROMPT     Then increase MTS_MAX_SERVERS parm in init.ora
PROMPT
SELECT DECODE( totalq, 0, 'No Requests',
               wait/totalq || ' hundredths of seconds')
               "Avg wait per request queue"
FROM v$queue
WHERE TYPE = 'COMMON';

PROMPT
PROMPT If the following number increases, consider adding dispatcher
  processes
PROMPT
SELECT DECODE( sum(totalq), 0, 'No Responses',
               sum(wait)/sum(totalq) || ' hundredths of seconds')
```

```
                "Avg wait per response queue"
FROM v$queue q, v$dispatcher d
WHERE q.type = 'DISPATCHER'
AND q.paddr = d.paddr;


SET FEEDBACK OFF;
PROMPT
PROMPT
PROMPT            ==========================
PROMPT            DISPATCHER USAGE
PROMPT            ==========================
PROMPT (If Time Busy > 50, then change MTS_MAX_DISPATCHERS in init.ora)
COLUMN "Time Busy" FORMAT 999,999.999
COLUMN busy        FORMAT 999,999,999
COLUMN idle        FORMAT 999,999,999
SELECT name, status, idle, busy,
       (busy/(busy+idle))*100 "Time Busy"
FROM v$dispatcher;


PROMPT
PROMPT
SELECT COUNT(*) "Shared Server Processes"
FROM v$shared_server
WHERE STATUS = 'QUIT';


PROMPT
PROMPT
PROMPT high-water mark for the multi-threaded server
PROMPT

SELECT * FROM v$mts;

PROMPT
PROMPT ****************************************************************
PROMPT file i/o should be evenly distributed across drives.
PROMPT

SELECT
       substr(a.file#,1,2) "#",
       substr(a.name,1,30) "Name",
       a.status,
       a.bytes,
       b.phyrds,
       b.phywrts
FROM v$datafile a, v$filestat b
WHERE a.file# = b.file#;
```

```
SELECT substr(name,1,55) system_statistic, VALUE
FROM v$sysstat
ORDER BY name;

SPOOL OFF;
```

Listing 11.2 shows you the output of the snapshot script.

Listing 11.2 The output of snapshot.sql.

```
SQL> @snapshot


***********************************************************************
Hit Ratio Section
***********************************************************************


==========================
BUFFER HIT RATIO
==========================
(should be > 70, else increase db_block_buffers in init.ora)

 logical_reads    phys_reads     phy_writes    BUFFER HIT RATIO
 --------------   ------------   ------------   ----------------
    46,961,377     2,194,393        154,145             95


==========================
DATA DICT HIT RATIO
==========================
(should be higher than 90 else increase shared_pool_size in init.ora)


Data Dict. Gets  Data Dict. cache misses  DATA DICT CACHE HIT RATIO
 --------------   -----------------------  -------------------------
        380,780                   13,797                         96


==========================
LIBRARY CACHE MISS RATIO
==========================
(If > 1 then increase the shared_pool_size in init.ora)


  executions  Cache misses while executing  LIBRARY CACHE MISS RATIO
 ------------  ----------------------------  ------------------------
      380,971                         2,437                     .0064
```

```
=============================
Library Cache Section
=============================
hit ratio should be > 70, and pin ratio > 70 ...


NAMESPACE             Hit ratio      pin hit ratio   reloads
--------------        -----------    -------------   ------------
SQL AREA                  95              97          1,253
TABLE/PROCEDURE           88              93          1,174
BODY                      98              97             10
TRIGGER                   50              50              0
INDEX                      3              31              0
CLUSTER                   44              33              0
OBJECT                   100             100              0
PIPE                     100             100              0



=========================
REDO LOG BUFFER
=========================
(should be near 0, else increase size of LOG_BUFFER in init.ora)


redo log space requests                29



****************************************************************
Free memory should be > 1,000
****************************************************************


NAME                         BYTES
-------------------------    -------------
free memory                  54,820

****************************************************************
SQL Summary Section
****************************************************************


Tot SQL run since startup  SQL executing now
-------------------------  -----------------
              60,390                2
```

```
**********************************************************************
Lock Section
**********************************************************************


========================
SYSTEM-WIDE LOCKS - all requests for locks or latches
========================


User            Lock Type            Mode Held
------------    -------------------  -------------------
OPS$G449488     DML                  Exclusive
DATAPUMP        PL/SQL User Lock     Share


========================
DDL LOCKS - These are usually triggers or other DDL
========================


User            Owner      Name              Type              Mode held
------------    -------    ----------------  ---------------   ---------
OPS$G241107     GENESIS    VALID_DOMAIN_VA   Table/Procedure   Null
OPS$G499058     GENESIS    REB0004_PKG       Body              Null
OPS$G499058     GENESIS    REB0004_PKG       Table/Procedure   Null
OPS$G241107     SYS        DBMS_STANDARD     Body              Null
OPS$G499058     GENESIS    INSERT_REBPGMCH   Table/Procedure   Null
OPS$G499058     GENESIS    INSERT_REBPGMCH   Table/Procedure   Null


========================
DML LOCKS - These are table and row locks
========================



**********************************************************************
Latch Section
**********************************************************************
if miss_ratio or immediate_miss_ratio > 1 then  latch
contention exists, decrease LOG_SMALL_ENTRY_MAX_SIZE in init.ora


NAME                              miss_ratio  immediate_miss_ratio
------------------------------    ----------  --------------------
cache buffers lru chain             ####                       .59
redo copy                           ####                       .01
```

```
******************************************************************
Rollback Segment Section
******************************************************************
if any count below is > 1% of the total number of requests for data
then more rollback segments are needed
if free list > 1% then increase FREELIST in init.ora

CLASS                   COUNT
-------------------     ----------
free list                   0
system undo block           0
system undo header          0
undo block                  0
undo header                 6


Tot # of Requests for Data
--------------------------
            46,961,805


=========================
ROLLBACK SEGMENT CONTENTION
=========================


If any ratio is > .01 then more rollback segments are needed

NAME                                 WAITS        GETS     Ratio
-------------------------------  ----------  ----------  --------
SYSTEM                                    0        1431   0.00000
ROLB1                                     0       10808   0.00000
ROLB2                                     0       11225   0.00000
ROLB3                                     0       11832   0.00000
ROLB4                                     0        9976   0.00000



******************************************************************
Session Event Section
******************************************************************
if average-wait > 0 then contention exists


no rows selected



******************************************************************
Queue Section
******************************************************************
average wait for queues should be near zero ...
```

```
no rows selected


*******************************************************************
Multi-threaded Server Section
*******************************************************************


==========================
Dispatcher Usage
==========================
```

Creating A Performance Repository With Oracle Utilities

The basic premise of this approach is to demonstrate how the DBA can automate the tedious analysis tasks within Oracle databases and be automatically alerted in extraordinary conditions. While many products exist that perform this function, the DBA can benefit from an understanding of the internal workings of the Oracle SGA as well as from insights into the complex interactions that contribute to response time.

In general terms, Oracle tuning can be divided into two areas: disk tuning and memory tuning. Since many shops now use RAID or LVM to stripe data files across disks, disk tuning has become a moot issue for most Oracle DBAs.

Tuning of memory is another story. Since an Oracle instance resides in the real memory of the CPU, the allocation of memory pages and the configuration of the SGA is a primary concern for understanding performance. SGA tuning for Oracle involves two areas: the parameters in the init.ora file, and parameters that are used when an individual table is created. The init.ora file is used at startup time by Oracle to allocate the memory region for the instance, and the parameters in the init.ora control this allocation. Other parameters used at table creation time (such as **freelist** and **pctused**) can influence performance, but we will focus on the system-wide tuning parameters.

When tuning Oracle, two init.ora parameters become more important than all of the others combined:

- **db_block_buffers**—The number of buffers allocated for caching database blocks in memory

- **shared_pool_size**—The amount of memory allocated for caching SQL, stored procedures, and other nondata objects

These two parameters define the size of the in-memory region that Oracle consumes on startup and determine the amount of storage available to cache data blocks, SQL, and stored procedures.

> **NOTE** *It is a good idea to set your **db_block_size** as large as possible for your system. For example, HP-9000 computers read 8 K blocks; hence, **db_block_size** should be set to 8 K.*

Keep in mind that many of these tuning issues will change when Oracle 7.3 allows for dynamic modification of the SGA. It will not be necessary to bounce the instance to change the amount of **db_block_size**, and utilities will soon appear to detect extraordinary conditions and dynamically reconfigure the SGA.

PREPARING THE SGA FOR PACKAGES AND STORED PROCEDURES

Oracle's shared pool is very important, especially if the system relies heavily on stored procedures and packages. This is because the code in the stored procedures is loaded into memory. The shared pool consists of the following subpools:

- Dictionary cache
- Library cache
- Shared SQL areas
- Private SQL area (exists during cursor open-cursor close; contains persistent and runtime areas)

Both the data buffer and the shared pool utilize a least-recently-used algorithm to determine which objects are paged out of the shared pool. As this paging occurs, *fragments* or discontiguous chunks of memory are created within the memory areas.

Imagine the shared pool as being similar to a tablespace. Just as ORA-1547 error appears when insufficient contiguous free space occurs in the tablespace; similarly, you will encounter an ORA-4031 error when contiguous free space is not available in the shared pool of the SGA.

This means that a large procedure that initially fit into memory may not fit into contiguous memory when it is reloaded after being paged out.

For example, consider a problem that occurs when the body of a package has been paged out of the instance's SGA because of other more recent/frequent activity. Fragmentation occurs, and the server cannot find enough contiguous memory to reload the package body, resulting in an ORA-4031 error.

To effectively measure memory, a standard method is recommended. It is a good idea to regularly run the estat-bstat utility (usually located in ~/rdbms/admin/utlbstat.sql and utlestat.sql) for measuring SGA consumption over a range of time.

Many new Oracle DBAs rely on the **V$** tables to gather tuning statistics—often with misleading results. As we know, the **V$** tables are in-memory tables that gather statistics from the startup of the instance and do not provide any "point in time" measures of system resources. As such, basic measures such as the buffer hit ratio may be misleading. For example, assume that an instance has been running for one week. Computing the buffer hit ratio for an instance using the **V$** tables may yield a value of 95 percent. However, this is a running average and will not show the current buffer hit ratio of 60 percent.

Using Oracle utlbstat And Outlets Utilities

The standard utilities for creating a performance report are known as estat-bstat, found in $ORACLE_HOME/rdbms/admin. The names of the utilities are utlbstat.sql (begin statistics) and utlestat.sql (end statistics). You must enter SQL*DBA to run the reports:

```
$ > cd $ORACLE_HOME/rdbms/admin
$ sqldba mode=line
SQLDBA > connect internal
connected.
SQLDBA > @utlbstat
...
5 rows processed
SQLDBA > @utlestat
```

The utlbstat utility samples the database and stores the results in a temporary table. When utlbstat is run and the database is sampled again, a report is made by comparing the differences in values between the begin snapshot and the end snapshot. The output is spooled to a file called report.txt. Although the report is very ugly and hard to read, the salient data is included. Listing 11.3 presents a sample of how the statistics report might appear.

Listing 11.3 The output from the bstat-estat Oracle utility.

```
oracle@myhost:mtty-61>more report.txt
SQLDBA>
SQLDBA> set charwidth 12
SQLDBA> set numwidth 10
SQLDBA> Rem Select Library cache statistics...The pin hit rate should be
  SQLDBA> Remhigh.
SQLDBA> select namespace library,
   2>        gets,
   3>        round(decode(gethits,0,1,gethits)/decode(gets,0,1,gets),3)
   4>          gethitratio,
   5>        pins,
   6>        round(decode(pinhits,0,1,pinhits)/decode(pins,0,1,pins),3)
   7>          pinhitratio,
   8>        reloads, invalidations
   9> from stats$lib;
```

LIBRARY	GETS	GETHITRATI	PINS	PINHITRATI	RELOADS	INVALIDATI
BODY	9	1	9	1	0	0
CLUSTER	0	1	0	1	0	0
INDEX	8	.125	12	.333	0	0
OBJECT	0	1	0	1	0	0
PIPE	0	1	0	1	0	0
SQL AREA	490	.935	1675	.937	21	20
TABLE/PROCED	111	.865	281	.911	8	0
TRIGGER	0	1	0	1	0	0

```
8 rows selected.

SQLDBA>
SQLDBA> set charwidth 27;
SQLDBA> set numwidth 12;
SQLDBA> Rem The total is the total value of the statistic between the time
SQLDBA> Rem bstat was run and the time estat was run...Note that the estat
SQLDBA> Rem script logs on as "internal" so the per_logon statistics will
SQLDBA> Rem always be based on at least one logon.
SQLDBA> select n1.name "Statistic",
   2>        n1.change "Total",
   3>        round(n1.change/trans.change,2) "Per Transaction",
```

```
4>          round(n1.change/logs.change,2)  "Per Logon"
5> from stats$stats n1, stats$stats trans, stats$stats logs
6> where trans.name='user commits'
7> and  logs.name='logons cumulative'
8> and  n1.change != 0
9> order by n1.name;
```

Statistic	Total	Per Transact	Per Logon
CR blocks created	45	15	9
DBWR buffers scanned	49630	16543.33	9926
DBWR checkpoints	13	4.33	2.6
DBWR free buffers found	49389	16463	9877.8
DBWR lru scans	1515	505	303
DBWR make free requests	1513	504.33	302.6
DBWR summed scan depth	49634	16544.67	9926.8
DBWR timeouts	38	12.67	7.6
background timeouts	114	38	22.8
calls to kcmgas	136	45.33	27.2
calls to kcmgcs	16	5.33	3.2
calls to kcmgrs	1134	378	226.8
cleanouts and rollbacks - c	4	1.33	.8
cleanouts only - consistent	90	30	18
cluster key scan block gets	266	88.67	53.2
cluster key scans	114	38	22.8
consistent changes	48	16	9.6
consistent gets	111477	37159	22295.4
cursor authentications	90	30	18
data blocks consistent read	48	16	9.6
db block changes	1292	430.67	258.4
db block gets	1286	428.67	257.2
deferred (CURRENT) block cl	112	37.33	22.4
enqueue releases	2277	759	455.4
enqueue requests	2282	760.67	456.4
enqueue timeouts	4	1.33	.8
execute count	605	201.67	121
free buffer inspected	146	48.67	29.2
free buffer requested	28628	9542.67	5725.6
immediate (CR) block cleano	94	31.33	18.8
immediate (CURRENT) block c	13	4.33	2.6
logons cumulative	5	1.67	1
messages received	1610	536.67	322
messages sent	1610	536.67	322
no work - consistent read g	109953	36651	21990.6
opened cursors cumulative	387	129	77.4
parse count	502	167.33	100.4
physical reads	28505	9501.67	5701

```
physical writes                    213         71        42.6
recursive calls                   6838    2279.33      1367.6
redo blocks written                607     202.33       121.4
redo entries                       769     256.33       153.8
redo size                       282490   94163.33       56498
redo small copies                  723        241       144.6
redo synch writes                   33         11         6.6
redo wastage                     23060    7686.67        4612
redo writes                         94      31.33        18.8
rollbacks only - consistent         44      14.67         8.8
session logical reads           112714   37571.33     22542.8
session pga memory              629940     209980      125988
session pga memory max          629940     209980      125988
session uga memory               14248    4749.33      2849.6
session uga memory max          228624      76208     45724.8
sorts (memory)                      23       7.67         4.6
sorts (rows)                      5957    1985.67      1191.4
table fetch by rowid             36144      12048      7228.8
table fetch continued row        31679   10559.67      6335.8
table scan blocks gotten          5884    1961.33      1176.8
table scan rows gotten          123829   41276.33     24765.8
table scans (long tables)           11       3.67         2.2
table scans (short tables)          19       6.33         3.8
user calls                         188      62.67        37.6
user commits                         3          1          .6
write requests                     100      33.33          20
64 rows selected.
SQLDBA>
SQLDBA> set charwidth 27;
SQLDBA> set numwidth 12;
SQLDBA> Rem System wide wait events.
SQLDBA> select  n1.event "Event Name",
    2>          n1.event_count "Count",
    3>          n1.time_waited "Total Time",
    4>          (n1.time_waited/n1.event_count) "Average Time"
    5> from stats$event n1
    6> where n1.event_count > 0
    7> order by n1.time_waited desc;
```

```
Event Name                    Count     Total Time   Average Time
----------------------------  ------------ ------------ ------------
smon timer                        2            0            0
buffer busy waits                 3            0            0
control file sequential rea       8            0            0
rdbms ipc reply                  12            0            0
```

```
log file sync               39          0          0
pmon timer                  57          0          0
latch free                  73          0          0
log file parallel write     93          0          0
db file parallel write      96          0          0
client message             190          0          0
db file scattered read     635          0          0
rdbms ipc message         1600          0          0
db file sequential read  25071          0          0
13 rows selected.
SQLDBA>
```

The output of utlbstat and utlestat can offer some very valuable performance information. Listing 11.3 shows the basic statistics for the database during the period between your bstat and the estat. While all of the information can be important, we can view several critical performance statistics here:

- **BUFFER BUSY WAITS**—A high value indicates that either more buffer blocks or rollback segments are needed.

- **DRWR CHECKPOINTS**—A high value indicates a need to increase the init.ora **log_checkpoint_interval**.

- **DBWR FREE LOW**—A high value indicates a need to increase the init.ora parameter **free_buffer_requested**.

- **REDO LOG SPACE REQUESTS**—This should be zero. If not, increase the size of your redo logs.

- **SORTS (DISK)**—Since sorts to disk are time-consuming, consider increasing your init.ora parm **sort_area_size**.

 This parameter takes effect for each user who accesses Oracle. Check your "high water mark" in your alert.log to ensure that your host has enough memory to support your choice. The formula is:

total_memory = oracle_high_water_mark * sort_area_size

- **TABLE SCANS (LONG TABLES)**—This should only happen in cases where reading most of the table rows would be required to answer the query.

The benefit to running bstat-estat is the ability to measure changes over a period of time. It is relatively simple to write a script that invokes bstat (begin statistics) at a specified time and runs the estat (end statistics) utility at a later time. Some sites compute bstat-estat statistics each hour so that hourly variations can be easily detected.

Running the utilities is very simple. Within a script, go to $ORACLE_HOME/rdbms/admin, enter SQL*DBA, and invoke the utlbstat.sql script. The report will be generated when utlestat.sql is invoked. The standard estat utility creates a report called report.txt that is dumped into the $ORACLE_HOME directory.

Once the report.txt file is created, there are two ways to extract the information. A command script in perl, awk, or Korn shell can be written to interrogate the report, extract the information, and write it into Oracle tables. The estat utility can also be altered to dump the data into Oracle tables while it creates the report.txt file.

Here is a sample Unix script that can be invoked from a cron process. In this case, the script called perf would be addressed as "**perf bstat**" and "**perf estat**," as shown in Listing 11.4.

Note that the regular estat utility has been replaced by a customized version called specialestat, and this customized estat utility is run in lieu of the one in $ORACLE_HOME/rdbms/admin. The specialestat is identical to the ultestat, except that it does not delete the temporary tables that are used to create report.txt. In this way, the temporary tables can be interrogated and loaded into special performance tracking tables. Following specialestat, the tracker utility is then invoked to capture the estat information into permanent tables, dropping the temporary tables.

Listing 11.4 A Unix script to gather performance information.

```
if [ $# != 1 ]
then
    echo "usage: $0 { bstat | estat }"
    exit 1
fi

if [ "${1}" != bstat -a "${1}" != estat ]
then
    echo "usage: $0 { bstat | estat }"
```

```
    exit 1
fi

SQLPATH=/usr/perfmon

if [ "${1}" = bstat ]
then
    #  Begin collection
    sqldba << !
        connect internal
        @${ORACLE_HOME}/rdbms/admin/utlbstat
        exit
!

else
    #  End data collection
    sqldba << !
        connect internal
        @${SQLPATH}/specialestat
        exit
!
    sqlplus / @${SQLPATH}/tracker ${ORACLE_SID}
fi

exit 0
```

After the data has been transferred into permanent tables, the statistical information can be analyzed and graphed to show performance trends. Predictions can be extrapolated from the data using linear forecasting methods, and problems such as full tablespaces can be predicted with relative accuracy. Listing 11.5 presents the script that will load the performance tables.

Listing 11.5   tracker.DDL—an SQL script to gather performance statistics.

```
INSERT INTO track_stats
(   oracle_sid,   collection_started)
SELECT   '&1',min(stats_gather_times)
FROM    sys.stats$dates;

UPDATE track_stats
SET    collection_ended =
        (SELECT  max(stats_gather_times)
          FROM    sys.stats$dates),
```

```
      run_date = to_date(substr(collection_started,1,12),
               'DD-MON-YY HH24'),
   consistent_gets =
     (SELECT   change
      FROM     sys.stats$stats
      WHERE    name = 'consistent gets'),
   block_gets =
     (SELECT   change
      FROM     sys.stats$stats
      WHERE    name = 'db block gets'),
   physical_reads =
     (SELECT   change
      FROM     sys.stats$stats
      WHERE    name = 'physical reads'),
   buffer_busy_waits =
     (SELECT   change
      FROM     sys.stats$stats
      WHERE    name = 'buffer busy waits'),
   buffer_free_needed =
     (SELECT   change
      FROM     sys.stats$stats
      WHERE    name = 'free buffer requested'),
   free_buffer_waits =
     (SELECT   change
      FROM     sys.stats$stats
      WHERE    name = 'free buffer waits'),
   free_buffer_scans =
     (SELECT   change
      FROM     sys.stats$stats
      WHERE    name = 'free buffer scans'),
   enqueue_timeouts =
     (SELECT   change
      FROM     sys.stats$stats
      WHERE    name = 'enqueue timeouts'),
   redo_space_wait =
     (SELECT   change
      FROM     sys.stats$stats
      WHERE    name = 'redo log space wait time'),
   write_wait_time =
     (SELECT   change
      FROM     sys.stats$stats
      WHERE    name = 'write wait time'),
   write_complete_waits =
     (SELECT   change
      FROM     sys.stats$stats
      WHERE    name = 'write complete waits'),
   rollback_header_gets =
```

```
             (SELECT  sum(trans_tbl_gets)
                FROM    sys.stats$roll),
          rollback_header_waits =
             (SELECT  sum(trans_tbl_waits)
                FROM    sys.stats$roll)
WHERE  collection_ended is null;


INSERT INTO LATCHES
(ls_latch_name, ls_latch_gets, ls_latch_misses,
 ls_latch_sleeps, ls_latch_immed_gets, ls_latch_immed_misses)
SELECT  name, gets, misses, sleeps, immed_gets, immed_miss
FROM    sys.stats$latches;

UPDATE LATCHES SET
    ls_collection_started =
        (SELECT  min(stats_gather_times)
           FROM    sys.stats$dates)
WHERE ls_oracle_sid IS NULL;

UPDATE LATCHES SET
    run_date = to_date(substr(ls_collection_started,1,12),'DD-MON-YY HH24')
WHERE ls_oracle_sid IS NULL;

UPDATE LATCHES
SET ls_oracle_sid =
        (SELECT  '&1'
           FROM    sys.dual),
    ls_collection_ended =
        (SELECT  max(stats_gather_times)
           FROM    sys.stats$dates)
WHERE ls_oracle_sid IS NULL;
```

Generally speaking, a "sum of the least squares" technique will suffice for forecasting, but single or double exponential smoothing techniques might yield more accurate predictions under certain circumstances.

What Oracle Statistics Do We Want To Collect?

A need has already been identified for collecting database statistics from all of the Oracle instances. In short, we desire a proactive performance and tuning system that will:

- Predict future resource needs (DASD, memory, CPU) based on historical consumption rates.

- Allow ad-hoc query to determine where tuning resources are needed.

- Provide an empirical measure of the benefits from adding resources to a database—both human and hardware (e.g., a 20 MB memory increase improved buffer hit ratio by 13 percent).

Building The Oracle Performance Database

Now the question arises: How do we extract this information and place it into our Oracle database? We start by determining which data items we want to track, and then designing a table structure that fills our requirements (see Figure 11.1).

The philosophy for this performance and tuning repository is to collect virtually all of the information from the bstat-estat reports and the **V$** and **DBA** tables. The original information is collected on each remote agent

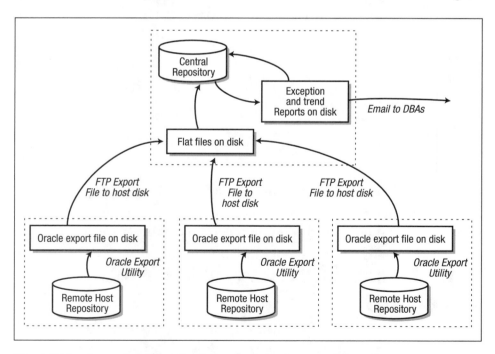

Figure 11.1 A sample schema for storing Oracle performance information.

and stored in local tables. For example, on Saturday at 8:00 AM, a crontab job could start a task to invoke the export and compress utilities that will extract the information into a flat file. Following extraction, the data is transferred to a central host via anonymous FTP, where the extract files will be loaded into the master Oracle tables on the central host. Each remote host will then have its performance and tuning tables re-created.

At a predetermined time on Saturday, a crontab will verify that all remote agents have delivered their daily extract files and notify the DBA of any agents who have failed.

The next step is to translate the model into some physical Oracle tables. Now that the empty database has been created, we will need to alter the utlestat.sql program to insert the information into our new tables whenever it is invoked. Here is an example of how the hit ratios can be captured:

```
INSERT INTO oracle.pt_instance (buffer_hit_ratio)
(
SELECT
ROUND(decode(gets-misses,0,1,gets-misses)/decode(gets,0,1,gets),3)
     hit_ratio,
     SLEEPS,
     ROUND(sleeps/decode(misses,0,1,misses),3) "SLEEPS/MISS"
   FROM stats$latches
   WHERE gets != 0
   AND name = 'buffer cache lru'
);
```

Once all of the modifications have been completed, this new version of utlestat.sql will replace the older version. Whenever it is invoked, it will add rows to our performance and tuning database.

To make the utility run, it is suggested that a cron job be set to start utlbstat.sql at a predetermined time, followed by utlestat.sql several hours later. This way you will receive a daily, consistent record of the status of your Oracle database at the same time each day. Of course, if you wanted to measure trends during the processing day, you could run this every hour, with 15 minutes between bstat and estat.

In a distributed environment, it is necessary to transfer all of the local table data into a large, centralized Oracle database that will hold performance and tuning information for all of the Oracles. This can be easily accomplished by running a cron job from the main repository. This cron will execute the necessary SQL to select all rows from the remote table, inserting them into the main table. Finally, it will either truncate the tables or delete all rows from the remote table:

```
INSERT INTO MAIN.pt_instance
(
SELECT * FROM ORACLE.pt_instance@bankok
);
DELETE FROM ORACLE.pt_instance@bankok;
```

We can now run reports and alert scripts against the centralized repository to predict when problems will be encountered. Here is an example of a query that will list any tables that have extended more than three times on the previous day (see Listing 11.6).

Listing 11.6 A sample table report.

```
COLUMN c0   HEADING "SID";
COLUMN c1   HEADING "Owner";
COLUMN c2   HEADING "ts";
COLUMN c3   HEADING "Table";
COLUMN c4   HEADING "Size (KB)" FORMAT 999,999;
COLUMN c5   HEADING "Next (K)"  FORMAT 99,999;
COLUMN c6   HEADING "Old Ext"   FORMAT 999;
COLUMN c7   HEADING "New Ext"   FORMAT 999;

SET LINESIZE 150;
SET PAGESIZE 60;

BREAK ON c0 SKIP 2 ON c1 SKIP 1
TTITLE " Table Report| > 50 Extents or new extents";
SPOOL /tmp/rpt10
SELECT
DISTINCT
        b.sid                     c0,
        substr(b.owner,1,6)       c1,
        substr(b.tablespace_name,1,10) c2,
        substr(b.table_name,1,20) c3,
        (b.blocks_alloc*2048)/1024 c4,
        c.next_extent/1024        c5,
```

```
           a.extents                    c6,
           b.extents                    c7
FROM       perf a,
           perf b,
           dba_tables c
WHERE
           rtrim(c.table_name) = rtrim(b.table_name)
AND
           a.sid = b.sid
AND
           rtrim(a.tablespace_name) <> 'SYSTEM'
AND
           a.tablespace_name = b.tablespace_name
AND
           a.table_name = b.table_name
AND
           to_char(b.run_date) = to_char(round(sysdate,'DAY')-7)
           -- start with closest SUNDAY minus one week
AND
           to_char(a.run_date) = to_char(b.run_date-7)
           -- compare to one week prior
AND
(
           a.extents < b.extents
           -- where extents has increased
OR
           b.extents > 50
)
--AND
--         b.extents - a.extents > 1
ORDER BY b.sid;
SPOOL OFF;
```

Notice that this query joins the **PERF** table with itself, comparing the table data for one week against the table data for the prior week. Reports like these are the basis for automated exception reporting, since they can be used to detect out-of-the-ordinary conditions and alert the developer before performance becomes a problem.

SYSTEM ARCHITECTURE

The system architecture shown in Figure 11.2 has been designed to have "agents" on each remote Oracle host to perform the daily data collection, which is accomplished with two cron tasks (bstat-estat). Each remote host

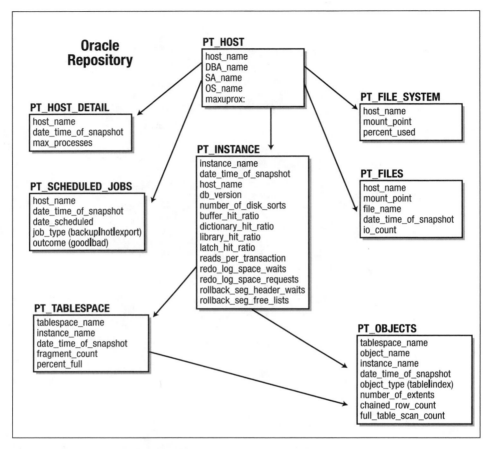

Figure 11.2　A sample performance and tuning architecture.

will have a small copy of the performance and tuning database to hold one week's worth of data. Each Saturday, the hosts will execute two cron jobs to:

- Export_p_and_t_tables (C shell script)—This will export and compress the Oracle performance and tuning and FTP the file to central:/$DBA/ DBAX/p_and_t.

- Create_p_add_t_tables (C shell)—This will drop and re-create the local database tables.

WEEKLY PROCESSING

After all remote sites have FTPed their export files, a cron will fire on the central database to:

- Import_p_and_t_tables (C shell) (For example, runs each Saturday at 1:00 PM)—It will loop through all entries in $DBA/DBAX/p_and_t/ hostfile (the list of SIDs) and then load the export file into the main performance and tuning database.

- Run the script $DBA/DBAX/p_and_t/reports/extract_reports.csh (For example, runs each Saturday at 2:00 PM)—It will loop through all entries in $DBA/DBAX/p_and_t/hostfile (the list of SIDs), and then for each entry execute p_and_t_rpt**.sql (where ** = 01–11), spooling the reports to SERVER.SID.p_and_t_rpt** in directory $DBA/ DBAX/p_and_t/reports.

- Run the script $DBA/DBAX/p_and_t/reports/mail_reports.csh (For example, runs each Saturday at 3:00 PM)—Loops through all entries in $DBA/p_and_t/hostfile (the list of SIDs). For each entry, it will get the email address of the primary DBA for the host (in $DBA/p_and_t/ hostfile) and then email reports SERVER.SID_rpt** to the address specified in hostfile. The reports will remain on Central as well, for reference.

Local Oracle Processing

On each remote host, a directory will exist to hold all of the code required to collect the data. The central database will exist on Central:DBAX, but each remote host will have a small, local copy of the master database to temporarily hold the performance and tuning data until the weekly upload.

Each remote host will have the following:

- Scripts (chmod +x)

  - bstat—A C shell script to start the bstat utility.

  - estat—A C shell script to run the estat utility.

  - export_p_and_t_tables—A C shell script to export and FTP the file.

  - create_stat—A C shell script to drop and re-create the local tables.

- Parm Files (chmod 440)

  - pass_system—A protected file containing the Oracle **SYSTEM** password.

  - pass_oracle_central—A protected file with the Unix Oracle password for Central.

- SQL Files

    - p_and_t_collect_b_e_stats.sql—Retrieves performance and tuning data from the BSTAT-ESTAT tables.

    - p_and_t_collect_object_stats.sql—Retrieves performance and tuning table data from DBA tables.

    - p_and_t_collect_ts_stats.sql—Retrieves performance and tuning tablespace data from DBA tables.

    - create_p_and_t_tables.sql—SQL to drop and re-create the local p_and_t tables with **SYSTEM** owner.

    - add_server_name.sql—SQL to add the server name to the local p_and_t tables.

    - p_and_t_utlbstat.sql—Customized bstat.

    - p_and_t_utlestat.sql—Customized estat utility to retain the TEMP tables.

- Other Files

    - create_failed—Error message file for create_stat.

    - export_failed—Error message file from export_p_and_t_tables.

    - export_p_and_t_tables.par—A parfile for the export job.

    - Any other files in $DBA/PROD_SID/p_and_t—Output (i.e., log files) from running the jobs.

cron Run Schedules

The bstat script is run each weekday at 8:00 AM, followed by the estat at 4:00 PM. Here is the crontab listing:

```
#
# Below are the cron entries for the performance & tuning database
#
00 08 * * 1-5 /u03/home/oracle/admin/tranp/p_and_t/bstat 2>&1
00 16 * * 1-5 /u03/home/oracle/admin/tranp/p_and_t/estat 2>&1
#
00 08 * * 6   /u03/home/oracle/admin/tranp/p_and_t/export_p_and_t_tables
2>&1
30 08 * * 6   /u03/home/oracle/admin/tranp/p_and_t/create_p_and_t_tables
2>&1
```

On the central server, weekly processes are executed to:

- Uncompress and load the incoming data
- Extract the weekly performance and tuning reports
- Mail the reports to the DBAs

Here is the crontab listing:

```
#
#
00 13 * * 1 /u01/dba/oracle/admin/DBAX/p_and_t/import_p_and_t_tables 2>&1
#
00 14 * * 1 /u01/dba/oracle/admin/DBAX/p_and_t/reports/
extract_reports.csh 2>&1
00 15 * * 1 /u01/dba/oracle/admin/DBAX/p_and_t/reports/mail_reports.csh
2>&1
```

Performance Reports

This system consists of 10 reports that provide detailed performance information about each Oracle component. Tables 11.2 through 11.12 show samples of each report.

Table 11.2 MY_SID instance hit and enqueue report data for the last seven days (07/08/96 10:06).

B/Estat Execution	Logical Reads	Physical Reads	Enqueue Waits	Hit Ratio
96/07/01 MON 08:00-09:30	127,460,970	29,344,200	192	.77
96/07/02 TUE 09:18-09:30	1,571,052	1,187,076	0	.24
96/07/03 WED 08:00-09:30	18,588	366	0	.98
96/07/04 THU 08:00-09:30	12,548	320	0	.97
96/07/05 FRI 08:00-09:30	12,372	244	0	.98
Average	25,815,106	6,106,441	38	.79
Minimum	12,372	244	0	.24
Maximum	127,460,970	29,344,200	192	.98

Table 11.3 **Excerpts from MY_SID sort stats report for the last 21 days (07/08/96 10:06).**

B/Estat Execution	Sorts (Memory)	Sorts (Disk)	Sorts (Rows)
96/06/28 FRI 09:23-09:24	42	0	636
96/06/28 FRI 09:28-16:00	600	0	13,302
96/07/01 MON 08:00-09:30	3,630	282	11,025,378
96/07/02 TUE 09:18-09:30	42	0	660
96/07/03 WED 08:00-09:30	42	0	660
96/07/04 THU 08:00-09:30	44	0	440
96/07/05 FRI 08:00-09:30	28	0	440
Average	633	40	1,577,359
Minimum	28	0	440
Maximum	3,630	282	11,025,378

Table 11.4 **Excerpts from MY_SID user call stats report for the last 21 days (07/08/96 10:06).**

B/Estat Execution	User Calls	User Commits	User Rollbacks	Recursive Calls	Call Ratio
96/06/28 FRI 09:23-09:24	270	12	0	156	.58
96/06/28 FRI 09:28-16:00	14,934	54	0	211,998	14.20
96/07/01 MON 08:00-09:30	24,468	2,970	0	2,956,938	120.85
96/07/02 TUE 09:18-09:30	270	30	0	14,868	55.07
96/07/03 WED 08:00-09:30	270	12	0	12,738	47.18
96/07/04 THU 08:00-09:30	180	8	0	8,528	47.38
96/07/05 FRI 08:00-09:30	180	8	0	8,372	46.51
Average	5,796	442	0	459,085	47.39
Minimum	180	8	0	156	.58
Maximum	24,468	2,970	0	2,956,938	120.85

Table 11.5   Excerpts from MY_SID fetch and scan stats report for the last 21 days (07/08/96 10:06).

B/Estat Execution	Fetch By ROWID	Fetch CtRow	Scans Long	Scans Short	Scans Rows	Scan Ratio
96/07/01 11:03-11:06	720	0	0	18	18	.00
96/07/01 11:28-16:00	3,222,765	207	144	947,241	120,345,201	.00
96/07/02 08:00-16:00	109,052,170	55	240	570,605	355,301,755	.00
96/07/03 08:00-16:00	2,456,540	164	764	25,000	310,878,908	.03
96/07/04 08:00-16:00	160	0	0	472	18,312	.00
96/07/05 08:00-16:00	19,796	0	0	532	92,844	.00
Average	22,458,692	71	191	257,311	131,106,173	.01
Minimum	160	0	0	18	18	.00
Maximum	109,052,170	207	764	947,241	355,301,755	.03

Table 11.6   Excerpts from MY_SID average write queue and redo wait report for the last 21 days (07/08/96 10:06).

B/Estat Execution	Summed Dirty Que Length	Write Requests	Avg Write Que Length	Redo Special Requests
96/06/26 WED 16:19-16:20	0	128	.00	0
96/06/27 THU 08:05-12:05	5,572	16,856	.33	28
96/06/28 FRI 09:28-16:00	18	378	.05	0
96/07/01 MON 08:00-09:30	35,784	122,334	.29	138
96/07/01 MON 08:00-12:00	41,909	38,976	1.08	126
96/07/02 TUE 08:00-12:00	2,016	22,950	.09	126
96/07/02 TUE 08:00-16:00	116,455	28,080	4.15	40
96/07/03 WED 08:00-12:00	437	2,207	.20	3
96/07/03 WED 08:00-16:00	87,396	74,064	1.18	80
96/07/04 THU 08:00-09:30	0	32	.00	0
96/07/05 FRI 08:00-16:00	0	184	.00	0
Average	30,612	18,540	.96	32
Minimum	0	32	.00	0
Maximum	116,455	122,334	4.15	138

Table 11.7   Excerpts from MY_SID instance B/E file stats totals by data file for last 31 days (07/08/96 10:06).

Data File	Total Reads	Total Read Time	Total Writes	Total Write Time
/Datadisks/d01/ORACLE/my_ sid/mptv.dbf	6,870,264	0	100,596	0
/Datadisks/d02/ORACLE/my_ sid/index.dbf	282,408	0	66,876	0
Average	806,251	0	54,535	0
Minimum	0	0	0	0
Maximum	6,870,264	0	255,474	0
sum	7,256,258	0	490,816	0

Table 11.8   Excerpts from OIDB instance B/E file totals by file system for last 7 days stats (07/09/96 09:22).

File System	Total Reads	Total Writes
/Datadisks/d01/ORACLE	373,144	45,823
/Datadisks/d02/ORACLE	22,120	67,729
/Datadisks/d03/ORACLE	449,608	9,107
/Datadisks/d04/ORACLE	1,119,456	11,920
/Datadisks/d05/ORACLE	272,716	9,703
/Datadisks/d06/ORACLE	1,051,170	37,835
/Datadisks/d09/ORACLE	746	1,186
Average	644,920	158,627
Minimum	0	0
Maximum	2,876,425	1,444,968
sum	9,673,799	2,379,401

Table 11.9 Excerpts from MY_SID instance B-E rollback stats last 21 days (07/08/96). Transaction table wait ratio > .05 Add rollbacks.

B/Estat Execution	Gets	Waits	Ratio	Undo Bytes
96/06/28 FRI 09:23-09:24	28	0	.00	9,576
96/06/28 FRI 09:28-16:00	2,975	0	.00	99,988
96/07/01 MON 08:00-07:36	94,101	0	.00	124,102,104
96/07/02 TUE 09:18-09:30	266	0	.00	501,942
96/07/03 WED 08:00-09:30	658	0	.00	9,632
96/07/04 THU 08:00-09:30	470	0	.00	6,880
96/07/05 FRI 08:00-09:30	470	0	.00	6,880

Table 11.10 Excerpts from MY_SID instance B-E lib stats last 40 days (07/08/96). Reparse ratio > .01 Increase SHARED_POOL_SIZE.

B/Estat Execution	Pins	Reloads	Reparse Ratio
96/06/28 FRI 09:23-09:24	728	21	.0288
96/06/28 FRI 09:28-16:00	36,330	742	.0204
96/07/01 MON 08:00-07:36	1,123,808	315	.0003
96/07/02 TUE 09:18-09:30	7,315	70	.0096
96/07/03 WED 08:00-09:30	994	0	.0000
96/07/04 THU 08:00-09:30	700	0	.0000
96/07/05 FRI 08:00-09:30	660	0	.0000
Average	167,219	164	.0084

Table 11.11 Excerpts from Table/Index extents (07/08/96 13:40). TRANP table report > 80 Extents or new extents data for the last 7 days.

SID	Owner	TS	Table	Size (KB)	Next (K)	Old Ext	New Ext
TRANP	HOCK	USERS_01	LOBHOCK11	7,606	352	67	69
RPT		USERS_01	USER_TABLES_RPT	660	0	12	15

	Table 11.12 Excerpts from Tablespace report (07/12/96). OIDB instance data file storage in Oracle megabytes (1,048,576 bytes).					
Date	Tablespace	Tablesp Pieces	Tablesp Mbytes	Free Mbytes	Free Mbytes	Percent Free
03-JUL-96	INDEXG	5	600	20	17	3
03-JUL-96	GSA_DATA	4	600	61	57	10
03-JUL-96	INDEXH	1	200	21	21	10
03-JUL-96	INDEXE	3	400	42	38	10
03-JUL-96	PROSPECTING01	1	900	99	99	11
03-JUL-96	PERSON	1	200	30	30	15
03-JUL-96	PROSPECTING02	7	750	165	82	22
03-JUL-96	ADDRESS	1	200	49	49	24
03-JUL-96	INDEXB	2	400	114	62	29
03-JUL-96	RESPONSIBILITY	1	150	45	45	30
03-JUL-96	TOOLS	2	10	3	3	32
03-JUL-96	ORGANIZATION	1	300	121	121	40

TABLESPACE AND TABLE DATA GATHERING

While the estat-bstat utilities are great for measuring memory usage, the DBA may still want to capture information about Oracle tables and tablespaces. For example, an alert report can easily be generated that shows all tables and indexes that have extended more than twice in the past 24 hours. A tablespace alert report could be written to display all tablespaces that have free space less than 10 percent of the tablespace size.

A routine can easily be written to interrogate all tablespaces and dump the information into a statistical table (Listing 11.7), and this tablespace information can be tracked to predict the rate of growth and the time when it will become necessary to add a data file to the tablespace.

Listing 11.7 A tablespace data gathering script.

```
INSERT INTO tablespace_stat VALUES (
SELECT   dfs.tablespace_name,
         round(sum(dfs.bytes)/1048576,2),
         round(max(dfs.bytes)/1048576,2)
FROM     sys.dba_free_space dfs
```

```
GROUP BY dfs.tablespace_name
ORDER BY dfs.tablespace_name);
```

Tables are usually tracked to provide information on unexpected growth. A high growth rate can indicate that the table was undersized on the **next** parameter, or it can indicate an upturn in end-user processing. In either case, the DBA wants to be informed whenever any table extends more than twice within any 24 hour period.

Gathering the table extent information is a simple matter, as shown in Listing 11.8. This script can be attached to a cron process to gather the extent information at a specified time interval.

Listing 11.8 A table data gathering script.

```
INSERT INTO tab_stat VALUES(
SELECT   ds.tablespace_name,
         dt.owner,
         dt.table_name,
         ds.bytes/1024,
         ds.extents,
         dt.max_extents,
         dt.initial_extent/1024,
         dt.next_extent/1024,
         dt.pct_increase,
         dt.pct_free,
         dt.pct_used
FROM     sys.dba_segments ds,
         sys.dba_tables dt
WHERE    ds.tablespace_name = dt.tablespace_name
AND    ds.owner = dt.owner
AND    ds.segment_name = dt.table_name
ORDER BY 1,2,3);
```

Once these tables have been populated, it is a relatively simple matter to write some SQL to generate alert reports for the DBA.

A tablespace alert report may be defined by the DBA, but would usually contain a list of tablespaces where the largest fragment is less than 10 percent of the size of the tablespace. Regardless, the data that is created from table analysis routines can be used to generate variance reports that alert the DBA to possible problems in the databases. (See Listing 11.9.) Note the clever method of joining the extents table against itself to show growth in extents.

Listing 11.9   A table extents report.

```
BREAK ON c0 SKIP 2 ON c1 SKIP 1
TTITLE " Table Report| > 50 Extents or new extents";
SPOOL /tmp/rpt10
SELECT
DISTINCT
         b.sid                            c0,
         substr(b.owner,1,6)              c1,
         substr(b.tablespace_name,1,10)   c2,
         substr(b.table_name,1,20)        c3,
         (b.blocks_alloc*2048)/1024       c4,
         c.next_extent/1024               c5,
         a.extents                        c6,
         b.extents                        c7
FROM     tab_stat         a,
         tab_stat         b,
         dba_tables       c
WHERE
         rtrim(c.table_name) = rtrim(b.table_name)
AND
         a.sid = b.sid
AND
         rtrim(a.tablespace_name) <> 'SYSTEM'
AND
         a.tablespace_name = b.tablespace_name
AND
         a.table_name = b.table_name
AND
         to_char(a.run_date) = to_char(b.run_date-7)
         -- compare to one week prior
AND
(
         a.extents < b.extents
         -- where extents has increased
OR
         b.extents > 50
)
ORDER BY b.sid;
```

While the marketplace is full of fancy tools for measuring Oracle performance, the basic Oracle DBA can benefit from extending the basic Oracle performance tools to create a proactive, customized framework for Oracle tuning. Today's Oracle DBA must automate as many functions as possible in order to maximize productivity.

Online Menu For The Performance System

Once a mechanism has been put in place to deliver the statistics to a centralized Oracle database, a menu-based system can be created to allow reports to be generated against the data. Here is a sample menu for such a system:

> Performance Reports for Oracle
>
> MAIN MENU
>
> 1. SGA waits & buffer hit ratio report
>
> 2. Cache hit ratio report
>
> 3. Data Dictionary report
>
> 4. File report
>
> 5. Tablespace report
>
> 6. Table report
>
> 7. Index report
>
> 8. SGA—hit ratio/wait count alert
>
> 9. Tablespace—fragment/free space alert
>
> 10. Table—Increased extents alert
>
> 11. Index—Increased extents alert
>
> 12. Audit
>
> 14. Exit
>
> Enter choice ==>

This menu is driven by a Korn shell script, as shown in Listing 11.10.

Listing 11.10   A Korn shell script to extract Oracle performance data.

```
trap "exit 0" 1 2 3 4 5 6 7 8 10 15


USER_NAME='id -un'
```

```
#if [ "$USER_NAME" != "root" -a "$USER_NAME" != "oracle" ]
if [ "$USER_NAME" != "root" ]
then
  echo
  echo "You must be ROOT to execute this script."
  echo
  return 0
fi

# Set PATH
        PATH=/bin:/u01/bin:/etc:/u01/contrib/bin:/u01/oracle/bin:/u01/
          oracle/etc:/u01/lib:/u01/lib/acct:/u01/backup/bin
        export PATH

# Set up Oracle environment

        ORACLE_HOME=/u01/oracle
        ORAKITPATH=/u01/oracle/resource
        FORMS30PATH=/u01/oracle/resource
        MENU5PATH=/u01/oracle/resource
        export ORACLE_HOME ORACLE_SID ORAKITPATH FORMS30PATH MENU5PATH
        PATH=$PATH:${ORACLE_HOME}/bin:
        export PATH
        ORAENV_ASK=NO

TWO_TASK=perfdb
export TWO_TASK
unset ORACLE_SID

get_sid()
{
echo
echo "Enter the database name: \c"
read DBNAME1
END1=${DBNAME1}
export END1
}


get_parms()
{

#************************************************************************
# Prompt for database name
#************************************************************************
echo
```

```
echo "Enter the database name: \c"
read DBNAME1


case $DBNAME1 in

  ""             ) END1="\" \""
     ;;

  *              ) END1="\" and
upper(rtrim(brndb.sid))=upper('"${DBNAME1}"')\""
     ;;
esac

export END1
} #  End of get_parms()

get_date()
{
#******************************************************************
# Prompt for start date
#******************************************************************
echo
echo "Enter a start date:(mm/dd/yy) (or press enter for none) \c"
read DATE1

if [ $DATE1 ]
then
   END2="\" and run_date >=to_date('$DATE1','MM/DD/YY')\""
else
   END2="\" and run_date >=to_date('01/01/01','MM/DD/YY')\""
fi

export END2

#******************************************************************
# Prompt for end date
#******************************************************************
echo
echo "Enter an end date:(mm/dd/yy) (or press enter for none) \c"
read DATE2

if [ $DATE2 ]
then
   END3="\" and run_date <=to_date('$DATE2','MM/DD/YY')\""
else
```

```
    END3="\" and run_date <=to_date('12/31/99','MM/DD/YY')\""
fi

export END3

}   # end of get_date...

get_extents()
{
#*********************************************************************
# Prompt for number of extents
#*********************************************************************
echo
echo "Where number of extents is greater than (default 0):\c"
read EXT1

if [ $EXT1 ]
then
   END4="\" and extents > $EXT1\""
else
   END4="\" and extents > 0\""
fi

export END4
}   # end of get_extents...


three_mess()
{
echo " "
echo "Data for this report is collected directly from the remote host."
echo " "
echo "Therefore, you may not want to run this against a database"
echo "unless you are prepared to wait awhile."
echo " "
}


#*********************************************************************
#  Main routine loop
#*********************************************************************
while true ; do
  clear

  echo "                    PER Reports for Oracle"
  echo
  echo "    1. SGA waits & Buffer hit ratio report"
```

```
echo "    2. Cache hit ratio report"
echo "    3. Data Dictionary report"
echo "    4. File report"
echo "    5. Tablespace report"
echo "    6. Table report"
echo "    7. Index report"
echo
echo "    8. SGA        - hit ratio/wait count alert "
echo "    9. Tablespace - fragment/free space alert"
echo "   10. Table      - Increased extents alert"
echo "   11. Index      - Increased extents alert"
echo
echo "   12. Audit      - Check a database for security violations"
echo
echo "   14. EXIT"
echo
echo $MESS1
echo

echo "Enter choice ==> \c:"
read PICK


case $PICK in

  "1") PREFIX=ps
       one_mess;
       get_parms;
       get_date;
       /u01/oracle/per/perf/rpt1.sh
       MESS1="Report has been spooled to  /tmp/rpt1.lst"
       ;;
  "2") PREFIX=ds
       one_mess;
       get_parms;
       get_date;
       /u01/oracle/per/perf/rpt2.sh
       MESS1="Report has been spooled to  /tmp/rpt2.lst"
       ;;
  "3") PREFIX=ls
       one_mess;
       get_parms;
       get_date;
       /u01/oracle/per/perf/rpt3.sh
       MESS1="Report has been spooled to  /tmp/rpt3.lst"
       ;;
  "4") PREFIX=fs
```

```
              one_mess;
              get_parms;
              get_date;
              /u01/oracle/per/perf/rpt4.sh
              MESS1="Report has been spooled to  /tmp/rpt4.lst"
              ;;
      "5") get_parms;
              get_date;
              /u01/oracle/per/perf/rpt5.sh
              MESS1="Report has been spooled to  /tmp/rpt5.lst"
              ;;
      "6") get_parms;
              get_date;
              get_extents;
              /u01/oracle/per/perf/rpt6.sh
              MESS1="Report has been spooled to  /tmp/rpt6.lst"
              ;;
      "7") get_parms;
              get_date;
              get_extents;
              /u01/oracle/per/perf/rpt7.sh
              MESS1="Report has been spooled to  /tmp/rpt7.lst"
              ;;
      "8") nohup /u01/oracle/per/perf/rpt8.sh > /tmp/rpt8.lst 2>&1 &
              MESS1="Report will be spooled to  /tmp/rpt8.lst"
              ;;
      "9") nohup /u01/oracle/per/perf/rpt9.sh > /tmp/rpt9.lst 2>&1 &
              MESS1="Report will be spooled to  /tmp/rpt9.lst"
              ;;
     "10") nohup /u01/oracle/per/perf/rpt10.sh > /tmp/rpt10.lst 2>&1 &
              MESS1="Report will be spooled to  /tmp/rpt10.lst"
              ;;
     "11") nohup /u01/oracle/per/perf/rpt11.sh > /tmp/rpt11.lst 2>&1 &
              MESS1="Report will be spooled to  /tmp/rpt11.lst"
              ;;
     "12") three_mess;
              get_sid;
              /u01/oracle/per/perf/rpt12.sh
              MESS1="Report has been spooled to  /tmp/rpt12.lst"
              ;;
     "14") echo bye
              break
              ;;
esac
```

This Korn shell script provides complete access to all of the reports in the database. Note that reports 1 through 7 can be parameterized, and the system will ask you to specify the database name and the date ranges.

Running The Oracle Reports And Alerts

The following parameters are required to run the script:

1. Database name (default is *all* databases)

2. Start date (default is 2000 BC)

3. End date (default is today)

Reports 6 and 7 (table and index reports) also prompt you to enter the number of extents that are used in the table or index query. The user will also be prompted for the following:

```
Enter the database name: (or press enter for all databases) cusdb
Enter a start date:(mm/dd/yy) (or press enter for none) 06/01/95
Enter an end date:(mm/dd/yy) (or press enter for none)
Where number of extents is greater than (default 0):30
```

Also note that reports 8 through 11 are the alert reports, whose criteria is described later in this chapter. The alert reports do not prompt for additional information.

A Closer Look—BMC's Patrol

In the fiercely competitive marketplace of system monitoring tools, vendors are striving to create products that take care of the routine and mundane administrative tasks, freeing the DBA and system administrator to do more high-level work. With the advent of open systems and geographically diverse networks of distributed databases, a centralized tool for monitoring system performance has become indispensable. Patrol (by BMC Software) is one such product that claims to meet this need. You can find out more about Patrol by looking on this book's Cd-ROM.

Marketed as an alert monitor, Patrol positions itself against products such as DBVision (by Platinum Software) and a host of other SNMP-compliant monitors. The goal of this type of tool is to provide an intelligent agent that will constantly monitor the database and operating environment, detecting extraordinary conditions (called events). Once detected, the event can trigger an intelligent script to automatically correct the problem while telephoning the beeper number of the on-call DBA. While this may sound like a lofty goal, Patrol has been very successful in creating a framework that removed much of the tedious monitoring from the DBA's and SA's job. Patrol is friendly enough that a naive operator can monitor dozens of hosts, drilling down quickly to identify the nature of any problems.

Patrol offers the ability to manage many different types of relational databases from a single console and currently supports a host of relational databases including Oracle, Sybase, Informix, DB2 version 2, OpenVMS, and CA-Ingres. In addition, Patrol offers special submodules for monitoring vendor application packages such as Oracle Financials. This ability to provide a common monitor for many diverse databases is one of the features of Patrol that appeals to large, multivendor database sites.

For such a sophisticated product, the installation of Patrol is relatively straightforward and consists of two steps: the installation of the "console" (the host that monitors the databases), and the installation of "agent" software on each agent that will be monitored. The installation guide is compact, yet well-written, and describes the procedures for loading the Patrol installer that is run to install the specific product components.

The front end for the console is Motif-based, offering an excellent GUI environment with a very intuitive drill-down capability. In fact, Patrol is so intuitive that an experienced DBA can instantly use the console to view a problem without any prior training. The main screen consists of one icon for each host, and the host will turn red to indicate that an event has been triggered within the knowledge module (see Figure 11.3).

Clicking on the host icon will drill down into a set of database icons—one for each database on the host—and will also have icons for other components on the host, including file systems and disk devices. A drill-down from the database icon will show numerous database statistics. Despite these superior display capabilities, Patrol's real value comes from its management of the user-defined rules that tell Patrol when something is amiss. Figure 11.4 displays the drill-down screen.

Patrol's Knowledge Module

Anyone who has ever used an alert monitor in a production environment knows that the effective use of a tool depends upon its ability to identify

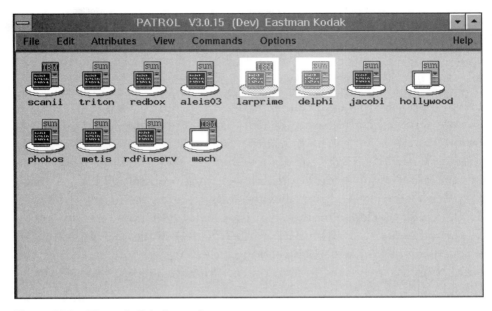

Figure 11.3   The main Patrol console screen.

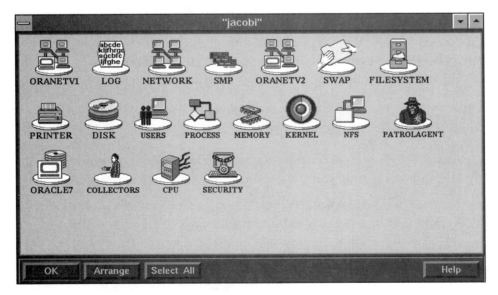

Figure 11.4   The drill-down Patrol screen.

salient problems while avoiding false alerts (precision). At the same time, no real problems can be missed (recall). This balancing act between precision and recall requires a very flexible set of customizable rule bases—an area in which Patrol is very effective.

Patrol supports a dynamic knowledge base that allows DBAs to continually customize specific events within their system. For example, a DBA might be interested in knowing when a file system is nearly full. However, file systems that are dedicated to database files will always be full—falsely alerting the DBA about a condition that does not require any intervention. Patrol collects these decision rules and calls them *knowledge modules* or KMs. To Patrol, a knowledge module consists of a set of parameters with meaningful names such as **BufferBusyRate** and **CacheHitRatio**. (See Figure 11.5.) A knowledge module can be versioned, customized, and stored on the main console (the global KM) or on each remote agent (the local KM).

The Patrol architecture provides a mechanism whereby the global knowledge module is referenced first, followed by any additional rules that are specific to an agent. This feature is especially useful for databases that have unique characteristics. For example, the value of **LongTableScanRatio** should stay below 80 percent for online transaction processing systems, but a **LongTableScanRatio** of 60 percent is perfectly acceptable for a batch-oriented reporting database that relies on full-table scans.

These parameters contain the following attributes:

- *Poll Time*—A parameter may be scheduled to "fire" on a schedule.

- *Automated Recovery*—Specific actions can be programmed to notify the DBA and trigger actions to automatically correct the problem.

- *Output Range*—The values that trigger an alert condition. For example, by default, the value of **MaximumExtents** will trigger a warning when a table reaches 90 percent of available extents, and an alarm when reaching 95 percent of available extents.

- *Manual Recovery*—This is a knowledge base that advises the DBA as to an appropriate corrective action. For example, the value of **LibraryCacheHitRatio** for Oracle correctly advises the DBA that increasing the value of **shared_pool_size** may relieve the problem. This feature of Patrol is especially nice for the newbie DBA who is not intimately familiar with corrective actions for database problems (see Figure 11.6).

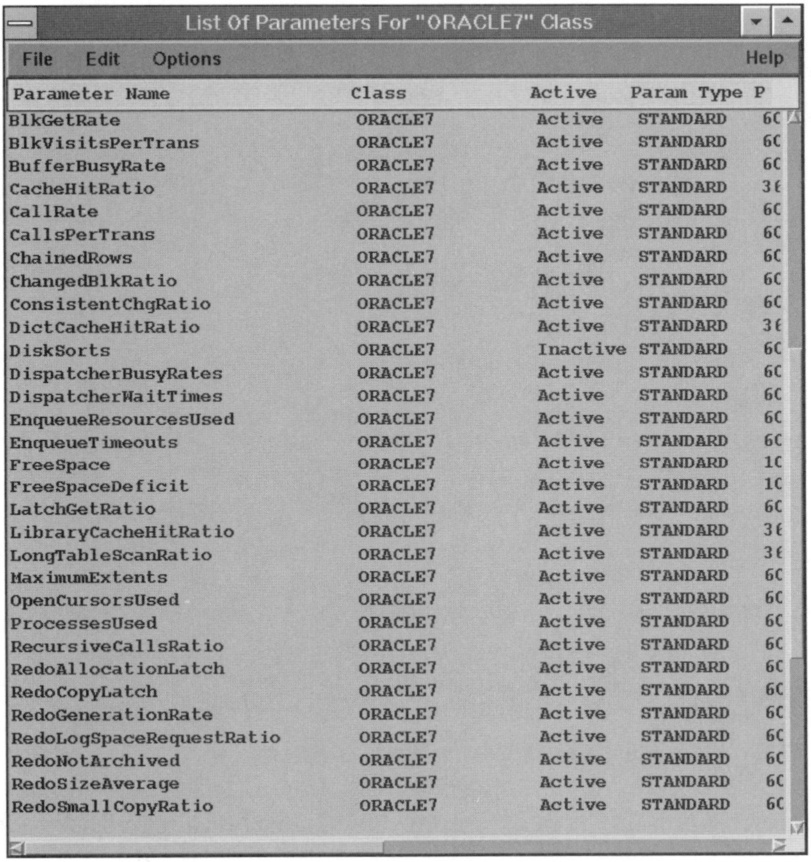

List Of Parameters For "ORACLE7" Class

File Edit Options Help

Parameter Name	Class	Active	Param Type	P
BlkGetRate	ORACLE7	Active	STANDARD	6C
BlkVisitsPerTrans	ORACLE7	Active	STANDARD	6C
BufferBusyRate	ORACLE7	Active	STANDARD	6C
CacheHitRatio	ORACLE7	Active	STANDARD	3€
CallRate	ORACLE7	Active	STANDARD	6C
CallsPerTrans	ORACLE7	Active	STANDARD	6C
ChainedRows	ORACLE7	Active	STANDARD	6C
ChangedBlkRatio	ORACLE7	Active	STANDARD	6C
ConsistentChgRatio	ORACLE7	Active	STANDARD	6C
DictCacheHitRatio	ORACLE7	Active	STANDARD	3€
DiskSorts	ORACLE7	Inactive	STANDARD	6C
DispatcherBusyRates	ORACLE7	Active	STANDARD	6C
DispatcherWaitTimes	ORACLE7	Active	STANDARD	6C
EnqueueResourcesUsed	ORACLE7	Active	STANDARD	6C
EnqueueTimeouts	ORACLE7	Active	STANDARD	6C
FreeSpace	ORACLE7	Active	STANDARD	1C
FreeSpaceDeficit	ORACLE7	Active	STANDARD	1C
LatchGetRatio	ORACLE7	Active	STANDARD	6C
LibraryCacheHitRatio	ORACLE7	Active	STANDARD	3€
LongTableScanRatio	ORACLE7	Active	STANDARD	3€
MaximumExtents	ORACLE7	Active	STANDARD	6C
OpenCursorsUsed	ORACLE7	Active	STANDARD	6C
ProcessesUsed	ORACLE7	Active	STANDARD	6C
RecursiveCallsRatio	ORACLE7	Active	STANDARD	6C
RedoAllocationLatch	ORACLE7	Active	STANDARD	6C
RedoCopyLatch	ORACLE7	Active	STANDARD	6C
RedoGenerationRate	ORACLE7	Active	STANDARD	6C
RedoLogSpaceRequestRatio	ORACLE7	Active	STANDARD	6C
RedoNotArchived	ORACLE7	Active	STANDARD	6C
RedoSizeAverage	ORACLE7	Active	STANDARD	6C
RedoSmallCopyRatio	ORACLE7	Active	STANDARD	6C

Figure 11.5 A Patrol Oracle parameter list.

Each of these parameters can be manually adjusted to reflect specific conditions that exist at specific sites. This customization is achieved by changing the Output Range Values and the polling times. For example, a transaction-oriented system could be customized to stop polling in the evenings when batch reporting occurs.

It is important to note that Patrol measures system-wide statistics, and not just the behaviors of each database on the host. Patrol currently supports Unix-level measurement on Bull, DC-OSX, DG, HP, SCO, Sequent, SGI, Solaris, Sun4, and SVR4. With the Unix knowledge module, a system administrator would be able to use Patrol to measure "swap" memory usage, paging within the Unix buffer cache, and just about every possible kernel component. Unfortunately, Patrol does not offer a "recovery" section for

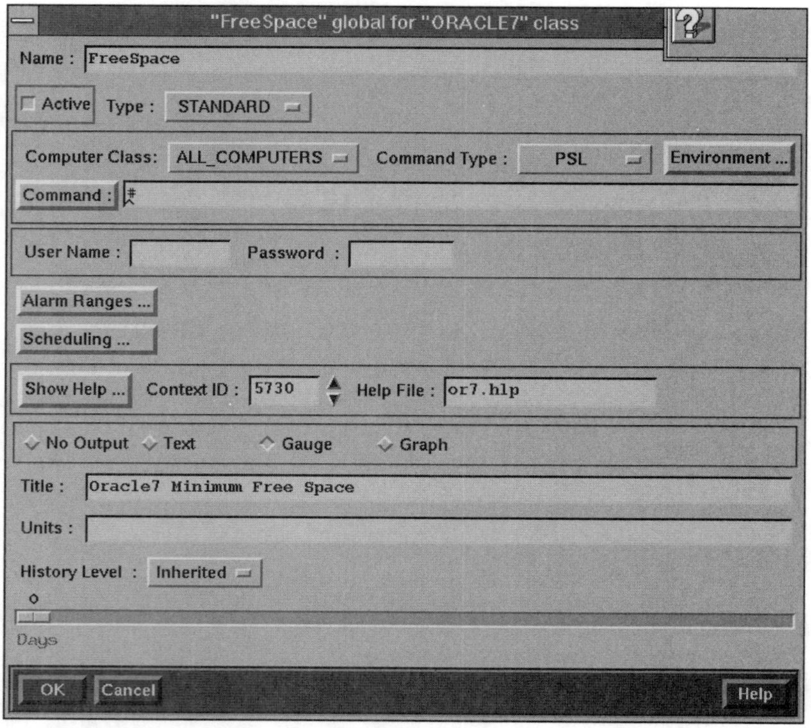

Figure 11.6 A Patrol Oracle parameter maintenance screen.

the Unix component. It may assume that system administrators would be offended by a tool that suggests possible remedies for the problems.

Customized events can also be incorporated into Patrol's knowledge modules. A customized event might be a backup process that is run every Tuesday morning at 1:00 AM. Patrol can be customized to check for the successful completion of the backup, and trigger an alert if a problem is encountered.

Patrol Reports

Patrol comes with a set of menu options that allows the manager to view salient information about the system. One interesting menu option is Patrol's "CPU Hog Percentage" and "all Problem users," which can be programmed to detect and alert for runaway processes on the host. For example, any process that consumes more than 30 percent of the overall CPU may be a runaway process, and Patrol can be programmed to detect these conditions (see Figure 11.7).

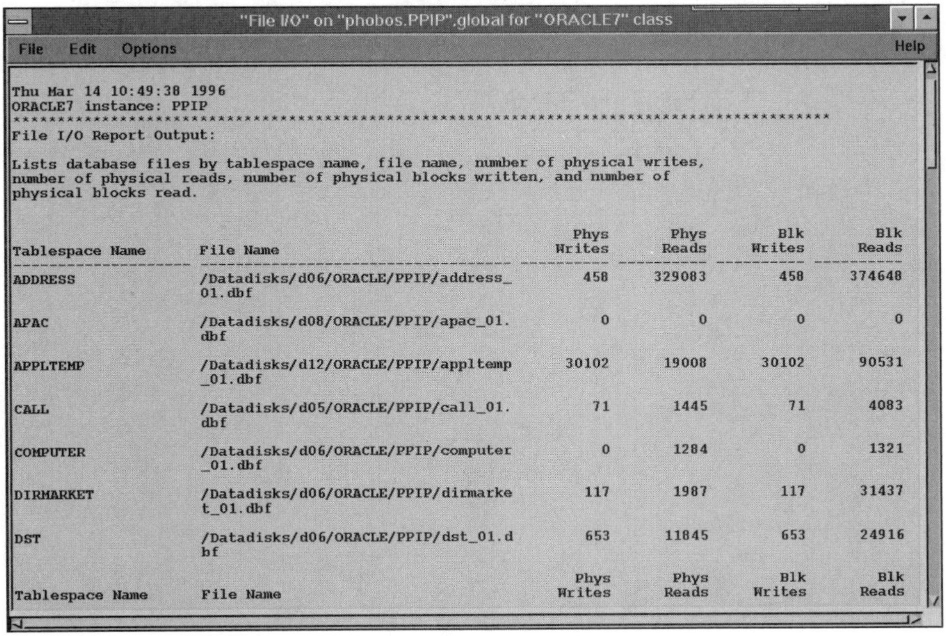

"File I/O" on "phobos.PPIP".global for "ORACLE7" class

File Edit Options Help

Thu Mar 14 10:49:38 1996
ORACLE7 instance: PPIP
****
File I/O Report Output:

Lists database files by tablespace name, file name, number of physical writes, number of physical reads, number of physical blocks written, and number of physical blocks read.

Tablespace Name	File Name	Phys Writes	Phys Reads	Blk Writes	Blk Reads
ADDRESS	/Datadisks/d06/ORACLE/PPIP/address_01.dbf	458	329083	458	374648
APAC	/Datadisks/d08/ORACLE/PPIP/apac_01.dbf	0	0	0	0
APPLTEMP	/Datadisks/d12/ORACLE/PPIP/appltemp_01.dbf	30102	19008	30102	90531
CALL	/Datadisks/d05/ORACLE/PPIP/call_01.dbf	71	1445	71	4083
COMPUTER	/Datadisks/d06/ORACLE/PPIP/computer_01.dbf	0	1284	0	1321
DIRMARKET	/Datadisks/d06/ORACLE/PPIP/dirmarket_01.dbf	117	1987	117	31437
DST	/Datadisks/d06/ORACLE/PPIP/dst_01.dbf	653	11845	653	24916
Tablespace Name	File Name	Phys Writes	Phys Reads	Blk Writes	Blk Reads

Figure 11.7 A Patrol Oracle report.

Overall, the report facility of Patrol is very robust and comprehensive, replacing the need to have additional database reports for all but the most specific queries.

Patrol Exception Handling

Patrol also provides preset automated recovery actions. For example, the Oracle component allows Patrol to automatically resize a table's **NEXT EXTENT SIZE**, thereby averting a possible downtime. To illustrate this feature, assume a customer table that has been defined to grow in chunks of five megabytes (for example, **NEXT**=5MB). If the tablespace that contained the table only had 3MB available, Patrol would automatically downsize the table to **NEXT**=3M, allowing the table to extend one more time and buying time for the DBA to be notified. In this way, the DBA can add a data file to the tablespace without disruption of the system (see Figure 11.8).

Patrol offers extensions into its base system using a proprietary language called Patrol Script Language (PSL). PSL is used to extend upon the base functionality of the software and automatically handle sophisticated recovery, where

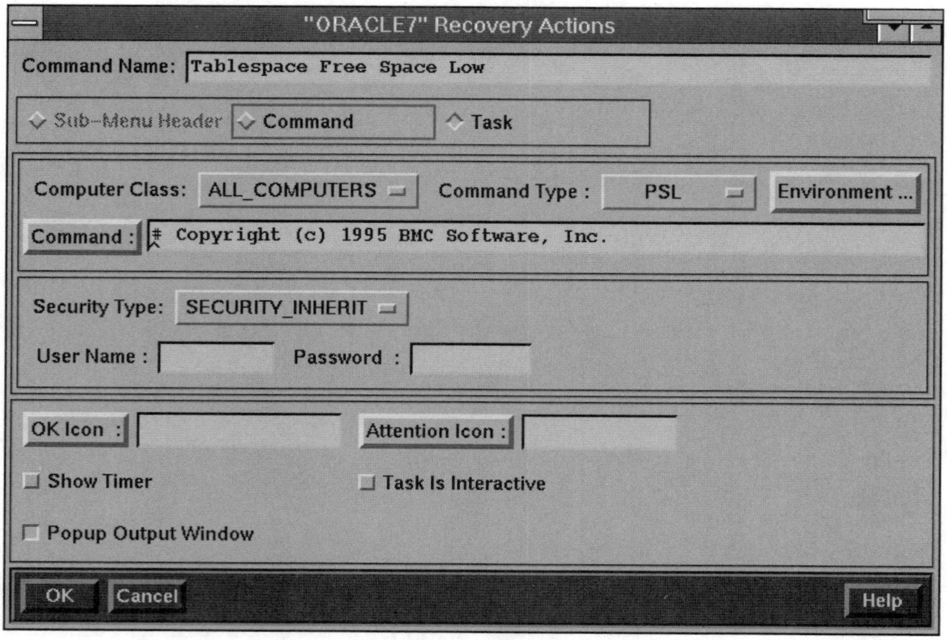

Figure 11.8   A Patrol recovery action.

numerous conditions must be checked. Internally, PSL is a large library of more than 100 prewritten functions. These functions, in turn, are called from within a small framework of 10 commands. The functions also include calls to SNMP modules for interfacing with other SNMP-compliant tools.

In short, Patrol offers a very robust and comprehensive system and database monitoring tool. Like any powerful monitor, Patrol is not plug-and-play—it requires a significant investment in up-front customization. However, once the framework is in place, Patrol delivers its promise to continually monitor, alert, and correct problems. The result? The elimination of many tedious and time-consuming chores for the systems and DBA staffs.

Summary

Now that we have investigated database performance monitoring techniques, we can wrap up the text with a look at the future of relational database tuning, with a focus on object orientation, and a discussion about how objects will change the way that databases are implemented and tuned.

The Future Of Database Management—Object Technology

Many organizations recognize the importance of standards in the emerging area of object-oriented systems development. In the spring of 1992, the Object Management Group (OMG), a nonprofit corporation dedicated to developing object standards, published the *Common Object Request Broker Architecture* (CORBA) standard for object-oriented development. CORBA was developed jointly by Sun, Hewlett-Packard, Digital Equipment Corporation, NCR, and HyperDesk Corporation. CORBA creates a standard protocol for an object to place requests and receive responses from other objects. It is interesting to note that these competing vendors—all with vested interests in proprietary software—have agreed to adhere to the CORBA standard in the development of new object-oriented systems.

Most of the major distributed operating systems state that they adhere to the CORBA. Consequently, an understanding of the foundation architecture for distributed systems is critical. The following text is selected from the *Object Management Architecture Guide* (1993) and is reproduced with the permission of the Object Management Group.

Chris Stone, President and CEO of the Object Management Group, states:

> *The OMG's goal is to get everybody to agree on a messaging format and how objects talk to each other; get them to agree to the language and a model of how to structure the data; get them to agree to some common interfaces; get them to agree on how to do security and containment.... The real significance of the CORBA specification is for application developers who want to build new client/server applications that will work across disparate platforms.*

Twin business pressures of decentralization and globalization prompted technology to come to the rescue in the form of the personal computer and desktop computing. All information of a business, however, was distributed throughout the many computing resources of the business.

Software provides these major hurdles: time to develop software, maintenance and enhancement of software, the limits on program complexity for profitable software sales, and time required to learn and use the software. These hurdles herald the major issues facing corporate information systems today: the quality, cost, and lack of interoperability of software. Hardware costs are plummeting, but software costs are rising.

The Object Management Group formed to help reduce complexity, lower costs, and hasten the introduction of new software applications. OMG has plans to accomplish this through the introduction of an architectural framework with supporting detailed interface specifications. These specifications drive the industry towards interoperable, reusable, portable software components based on standard object-oriented interfaces.

The mission of OMG is as follows:

- OMG is dedicated to maximizing the portability, reusability, and interoperability of software. OMG is the leading worldwide organization dedicated to producing the framework and specifications for commercially available object-oriented environments.

- The Object Management Group provides a Reference Architecture with terms and definitions upon which all specifications are based. OMG will create industry standards for commercially available object-oriented systems by focusing on Distributed Applications, Distributed Services, and Common Facilities.

- OMG provides an open forum for industry discussion, education, and promotion of OMG-endorsed object technology. OMG coordinates its activities with related organizations and acts as a technology/marketing center for object-oriented software.

- OMG defines the object management paradigm as the ability to encapsulate data and methods for software development. This models the "real world" through representation of program components called "objects." This representation results in faster application development, easier maintenance, reduced program complexity and reusable components. A central benefit of an object-oriented system is its ability to grow in functionality through the extension of existing components and the addition of new objects to the system.

OMG envisions a day when users of software start up applications as they start up their cars, with no more concern about the underlying structure of the objects they manipulate than the driver has about the molecular construction of gasoline.

The members of the Object Management Groups, Inc. (OMG) have a shared goal of developing and using integrated software systems. These systems are built using a methodology that supports modular production of software; encouraging reuse of code; allowing useful integration across lines of developers, operating systems, and hardware; and enhancing long-range maintenance of that code. Members of OMG believe that the object-oriented approach to software construction best supports their goals.

Object orientation, both at the programming language and applications environment levels, provides a terrific boost in programmer productivity, and greatly lends itself to the production of integrated software systems. Not necessarily promoting faster programming, object technology allows constructing more with less code. This is partly due to the naturalness of the approach, and to its rigorous requirement for interface specification. Only a set of standard interfaces for interoperable software components is missing.

The Benefits Of Object Management

As mentioned in the previous section, the technological approach of object technology (or object-orientated technology) was chosen by OMG member companies—not for their own sake, but to attain a set of end-user goals. End users benefit in four ways from the object-oriented approach to application construction.

An object-oriented user interface offers many advantages over more traditional user interfaces. In an object-oriented interface, *applications objects* (computer-simulated representations of real-world objects) are presented to end users as objects that can be manipulated in a manner similar to real-world objects. Examples of such object-oriented interfaces can be seen in systems such as Xerox Star, Apple Macintosh, NeXT Computer's NEXTSTEP, OSF Motif, HP NewWave, and to a limited degree, Microsoft Windows. CAD systems represent another good example of design components that can be manipulated in a way similar to that of real components. The end result is a reduced learning curve with a common look and feel to multiple applications. After all, "seeing and pointing" is much easier than "remembering and typing."

A more indirect end-user benefit of object-oriented applications, provided that they cooperate according to some standard, is that independently developed general-purpose applications are combined in a user-specific way. OMG's central purpose is to create a standard that allows interoperability between independently developed applications across heterogeneous networks of computers. This means that multiple software programs appear as one to the user of information, regardless of where the programs reside.

Common functionality in different applications—storage, retrieval, mailing, printing, creation, and deletion of objects, or help and computer-based training—is realized by common shared objects leading to a uniform and consistent user interface. Sharing of information drastically reduces documentation redundancy. Consistent access across multiple applications allows increased focus on application creation, as opposed to application education.

Transition to object-oriented application technology does not make existing applications obsolete. Existing applications can be embedded (with different levels of integration) in an object-oriented environment.

Pragmatic migration of existing applications gives a user control over computing resources, as well as how quickly these resources change. Likewise, application developers benefit from object technology and object-oriented standards. These benefits fall into the two general categories of modular architecture and reuse of existing components.

Encapsulation of object data applications are built in a truly modular fashion, preventing unintended interference. In addition, it is possible to build applications in an incremental way, preserving correctness during the development process.

Reusing existing components, specifically when the OMG standard is in effect, standardizes interaction between independently developed applications (and application components). Cost and lead time can be saved by using existing object class implementations.

In developing standards, OMG keeps these benefits of object orientation in mind, together with a set of overall goals:

- *Heterogeneity*—Integration of applications and facilities are available across heterogeneous networks of systems, independent of networking transports and operating systems.

- *Customization options*—Common facilities are customizable to meet specific end-user or organizational requirements and preferences.

- *Management and control*—Examines issues such as security, recovery, interruptability, auditing, and performance.

- *Internationalization*—OMG is an international group, and its standards reflect built-in support for internationalization of software.

- *Technical standards*—Standards that meet user goals are the central focus of the OMG.

The Object Management Architecture Components

The Object Request Broker (ORB) component of the Object Management Architecture (OMA) is the communications heart of the standard, referred to commercially as CORBA. It provides an infrastructure that allows objects to communicate independently of specific implementation platforms and techniques for addressed objects. The Object Request

Broker component guarantees portability and interoperability of objects over a network of heterogeneous systems.

The Object Services component standardizes the life cycle management of objects. Functions create objects (the Object Factory), control access to objects, keep track of relocated objects, and control relationships among species of objects (class management). The Object Services component provides the generic environment in which single objects perform their tasks. Standardization of Object Services leads to consistency over different applications and improved productivity for the developer.

The Common Facilities component provides a set of generic applications functions configured to the individual requirements of a specific configuration. Examples are printing, database, and email facilities. Standardization leads to uniformity in generic operations and allows end users to manipulate their configurations as opposed to configuring individual applications.

The Application Objects part of the architecture represents those application objects performing specific tasks for users. One application is typically built from a large number of basic object classes—partly specific for the application, partly from the set of Common Facilities. New classes of application objects are built by modification of existing classes through generalization or specialization of existing classes (inheritance) as provided by Object Services. This multiobject class approach to application development leads to improved productivity for the developer, and enhances the ability of end users to combine and configure their applications.

The OMG Object Model

This model defines a common object's semantics, specifying the externally visible characteristics of objects in a standard and implementation-independent way. The common semantics characterize objects existing in an OMG-compliant system, which performs operations and maintains states for objects.

An interface describes the externally visible characteristics of objects, consisting of operation signatures. The external view of both object behavior and object state (information needed to alter the outcome of a subsequent operation) are modeled in terms of operation signatures.

Objects are grouped into types, and individual objects are instances of their respective types. A type determines which operations are applied to its instances. Types participate in subtype/supertype relationships that affect the set of operations applicable to their instances.

Types also have implementations. An implementation of an object type is typically a set of data structures constituting a stored representation and a set of methods or procedures that provide the code to implement each of the operations' defined type.

Implementation details are encapsulated by operations and are never directly exposed in the external interface. For example, the stored representation is only observable or changeable through an operation request. Formally, the OMG Object Model states nothing regarding implementations of a type. It only claims their existence and the possibility that a given type can have multiple implementations (note that systems are not required to support multiple implementations).

The OMG Object Model defines a core set of requirements that must be supported in any system that complies with the Object Model standard. This set of required capabilities is termed the Core Object Model. The core serves as the basis for portability and interoperability of object systems across all technologies, as well as across implementations within technology domains.

While the Core Object Model serves as the common ground, the OMG Object Model also allows for extensions to the core to enable even greater commonality within different technology domains. The Object Model defines the concept of components that are compatible extensions to the core Object Model, but are not required to be supported by all systems. For example, relationships are defined as components. The OMG Object Model Components guide contains descriptions of components that are accepted as a standard.

The Object Model also defines a mechanism, referred to as *profiles*, for technology domains to group pertinent components. Profiles are groups of components combining as a useful set of extensions for particular domains.

The Object Management Architecture

An OMA-compliant application consists of a set of interworking classes and instances interacting via the ORB (as defined in a later section). Compliance, therefore, means conformance to the OMA and the protocol definitions. Using ORB, objects make and receive requests and responses. The Object Management Architecture consists of the following components:

- Object Services (OS) is a collection of services with object interfaces providing basic functions to realize and maintain objects.

- Common Facilities (CF) is a collection of classes and object interfaces providing general purpose capabilities, useful in many applications.

- Application Objects (AO) are specific to particular end-user applications.

In general terms, the Application Objects and Common Facilities have an application orientation, but the ORB and Object Services are oriented more with the system or infrastructure aspects of distributed object management. However, Common Facilities provides higher-level services, such as transactions and versioning, that use primitives provided within Object Services.

The three categories reflect a partitioning in terms of functions—from those basic to most applications or sufficiently common to broad classes of standardized applications, to those that are too application-specific or special-purpose to be standardized today. Therefore, the ORB, Object Services, and Common Facilities are focal to OMG standardization efforts.

Object Services, Common Facilities, and Application Objects intercommunicate using the Object Request Broker. Objects may also use non-object interfaces to external services, but these are outside the scope of the OMA. Although not explicitly stated in the Reference Model, objects may (or may not) communicate with the Object Services via object interfaces. For example, the addition of a new class is a request to an object providing this service. If this were done manually, it would be performed by editing a class definition script or a C++ include file.

Application Objects and Common Facilities use and provide functions and services via object interfaces. In general, objects issue as well as process requests for services, and Application Objects provide services for other applications or facilities. For example, an application-specific service such as printer rendering is cast as an application object invoked by a Common Facility like print queue. Common Facilities objects use services provided elsewhere.

Note that applications need only provide or use OMA-compliant interfaces to participate in the Object Management Architecture. Applications do not have to be constructed using the object-oriented paradigm, which also applies to the provision of Object Services. For example, existing relational or object-oriented database management systems provide some or all of the Object Services. Existing applications, external tools, and system support software are embedded as objects participating in the Object Management Architecture, using class interface front ends, also known as *adapters* or *wrappers*.

The Reference Model does not impose any restrictions on how applications and common facilities are structured and implemented. Objects of a given application class deal with the presentation of information, interaction with the user, semantics, functionality, the persistent storage of data, or a combination of the above.

The OMA assumes that underlying services provided by a platform's operating system and lower-level basic services (such as network computing facilities) are available and usable by OMA implementations. Specifically, the Object Management Architecture does not address user interface support. The interfaces between applications and windowing systems or other display support are the subjects of standardization efforts outside the OMG. Eventually, however, Common Facilities may provide standard user interface classes. In addition, the Reference Model does not deal explicitly with the choice of possible binding mechanisms such as compile time, load time, and run time.

Object Request Broker

The ORB provides mechanisms by which objects transparently make and receive requests and responses. In so doing, the ORB provides interoperability between applications on different machines in heterogeneous distributed environments and seamlessly interconnects multiple object systems.

The OMG Object Model defines an object request and its associated result (response) as the fundamental interaction mechanism. A request names an operation and includes zero or more parameter values, any of which may be object names identifying specific objects. The ORB arranges processing of the request. This entails identifying and calling some method to perform the operation using the parameters. After the operation terminates, the ORB conveys results to the requester.

The ORB itself may not maintain all the information needed to carry out its functions. The ORB may generate requests of its own to Object Services or use them in the process of conveying a request. For example, to find the specific method executed for a given request, the ORB uses a class dictionary service or searches runtime method libraries.

In order to satisfy the OMG Technical Objectives, the ORB is expected to address—at least to some degree—all of the following areas:

- *Name services*—The Object name-mapping services map the object names in the naming domain of the requester into equivalent names in the domain of the method to be executed. The OMG Object Model does not require object names to be unique or universal. Object location services, involving simple attribute lookups on objects, use the object names in the request to locate the method to perform the requested operation. In practice, different object systems or domains have locally preferred object naming schemes.

- *Request dispatch*—This function determines the invocation method. The OMG Object Model does not require a request to be delivered to any particular object. As far as the requester is concerned, it does not matter whether the request first goes to a method that operates on the variables of objects passed as parameters, or whether it goes to any particular object in the parameter list.

- *Parameter encoding*—These facilities convey the local representation of parameter values in the requester's environment to equivalent representations in the recipient's environment. To accomplish this, parameter encodings may employ standards or de facto standards: for example, OSF/DCE, ONC/NFS/XDR, NCA/SCS/NDR, ANSI.

- *Delivery*—Requests and results are delivered to the proper location characterized by a particular node, address, space, thread, or entry point. These facilities use standard transport protocol: for example, TCP/UDP/IP, ISO/TPN.

- *Synchronization*—Synchronization primarily deals with handling the parallelism of the objects making and processing a request, and the rendezvousing of the requester with the response to the request. Possible synchronization models include: asynchronous (request with no response), synchronous (request and await reply), and deferred synchronous (proceed after sending request and claim reply later).

- *Activation*—Activation is the housekeeping process that is necessary before invoking a method. Activation and deactivation (passivation) of persistent objects obtains the object state for use when the object is accessed and saves the state when it no longer needs to be accessed. For objects holding persistent information in non-object storage facilities such as files and databases, explicit requests are made to objects for activation and deactivation.

- *Exception handling*—Object location failures and attempted request delivery failures will report to either the requester or recipient in ways that distinguish them from other types of errors. Needed actions recover session resources and resynchronize the requester and the recipient. The ORB coordinates recovery housekeeping activities.

- *Security mechanisms*—The ORB provides security enforcement mechanisms supporting higher-level security control and policies. These mechanisms ensure secure conveyance of requests among objects. Authentication mechanisms ensure identities of requesting and receiving objects, threads, address spaces, nodes, and communication routes. Protection mechanisms ensure integrity of conveyed data and ensure that the data is accessible only to authorized parties. Access enforcement mechanisms control access and licensing policies.

OMG is very active in establishing standard interfaces for object-oriented distributed systems. OMB's CORBA is widely accepted. Vendors are developing distributed object technology tools that promise to revolutionize the software market in the 1990s. IBM, Hewlett-Packard, DEC, and many others recognize the huge market potential for object-oriented distributed systems.

Summary

This book has hopefully provided a simple and straightforward approach to the design and implementation of Oracle high-speed information systems. While many of the techniques are specific to the Oracle database, the principles apply to all areas of database management and all commercial database offerings. Hopefully, I've provided the knowledge and information that is required to pragmatically tune your Oracle databases.

A

Useful SQL Scripts

This chapter is a collection of useful SQL scripts that can be run from Oracle's SQL*Plus to interrogate your Oracle database.

alllocks.sql

This script interrogates all of the **dba_lock** tables to quickly identify locking contention.

```
rem alllocks.sql - shows all locks in the database.
rem written by Don Burleson

set linesize 132
set pagesize 60

spool /tmp/alllocks

column owner                     format a10;
column name                      format a15;
column mode_held                 format a10;
column mode_requested            format a10;
column type                      format a15;
column lock_id1                  format a10;
column lock_id2                  format a10;
```

```
prompt Note that $ORACLE_HOME/rdbma/admin/catblock.sql
prompt must be run before this script functions . . .

prompt Querying dba_waiters . . .
select
 waiting_session,
 holding_session,
 lock_type,
 mode_held,
 mode_requested,
 lock_id1,
 lock_id2
from sys.dba_waiters;

prompt Querying dba_blockers . . .
select
 holding_session
from sys.dba_blockers;

prompt Querying dba_dml_locks . . .
select
 session_id,
 owner,
 name,
 mode_held,
 mode_requested
from sys.dba_dml_locks;

prompt Querying dba_ddl_locks . . .
select
 session_id,
 owner,
 name,
 type,
 mode_held,
 mode_requested
from sys.dba_ddl_locks;

prompt Querying dba_locks . . .
select
 session_id,
 lock_type,
 mode_held,
 mode_requested,
```

```
 lock_id1,
 lock_id2
from sys.dba_locks;
```

Here is the output from alllocks.sql:

```
SQL> @alllocks
Note that $ORACLE_HOME/rdbma/admin/catblock.sql
must be run before this script functions . . .
Querying dba_waiters . . .


no rows selected

Querying dba_blockers . . .


no rows selected

Querying dba_dml_locks . . .

SESSION_ID  OWNER   NAME              MODE_HELD        MODE_REQUE
----------- ------- ----------------- ---------------- ----------
        19  RPT     RPT_EXCEPTIONS    Row-X (SX)       None

Querying dba_ddl_locks . . .

SESSION_ID  OWNER  NAME             TYPE             MODE_HELD  MODE_REQUE
----------- ------ ---------------- ---------------- ---------- ----------
        13  RPT    SHP_PRE_INS_UPD  Table/Procedure  Null       None
                   _PROC
        13  SYS    STANDARD         Body             Null       None
        14  SYS    STANDARD         Body             Null       None
        13  SYS    DBMS_STANDARD    Table/Procedure  Null       None
        14  SYS    DBMS_STANDARD    Table/Procedure  Null       None
        13  SYS    DBMS_STANDARD    Body             Null       None
        14  SYS    DBMS_STANDARD    Body             Null       None
        13  SYS    STANDARD         Table/Procedure  Null       None
        14  SYS    STANDARD         Table/Procedure  Null       None

9 rows selected.

Querying dba_locks . . .
```

```
SESSION_ID LOCK_TYPE        MODE_HELD  MODE_REQUE  LOCK_ID1   LOCK_ID2
---------- ---------------- ---------- ----------  ---------- ----------
         2 Media Recovery   Share      None             32           0
         2 Media Recovery   Share      None             31           0
         2 Media Recovery   Share      None             30           0
         2 Media Recovery   Share      None             29           0
         2 Media Recovery   Share      None             28           0
         2 Media Recovery   Share      None             27           0
         2 Media Recovery   Share      None             26           0
         2 Media Recovery   Share      None             25           0
         2 Media Recovery   Share      None             24           0
         2 Media Recovery   Share      None             23           0
         2 Media Recovery   Share      None             22           0
         2 Media Recovery   Share      None             21           0
         2 Media Recovery   Share      None             20           0
         2 Media Recovery   Share      None             19           0
         2 Media Recovery   Share      None             18           0
         2 Media Recovery   Share      None             17           0
         2 Media Recovery   Share      None             16           0
         2 Media Recovery   Share      None             15           0
         2 Media Recovery   Share      None             14           0
         2 Media Recovery   Share      None             13           0
         2 Media Recovery   Share      None             12           0
         2 Media Recovery   Share      None             11           0
         2 Media Recovery   Share      None             10           0
         2 Media Recovery   Share      None              9           0
         2 Media Recovery   Share      None              8           0
         2 Media Recovery   Share      None              7           0
         2 Media Recovery   Share      None              6           0
         2 Media Recovery   Share      None              5           0
         2 Media Recovery   Share      None              4           0
         2 Media Recovery   Share      None              3           0
         2 Media Recovery   Share      None              2           0
         2 Media Recovery   Share      None              1           0
         3 Redo Thread      Exclusive  None              1           0
        14 PS               Null       None              0           0
        14 PS               Null       None              0           1
        19 DML              Row-X (SX) None           1457           0

36 rows selected.
```

audit.sql

This script, audit.sql, is used to check an Oracle instance for unauthorized role privileges. In many shops, this type of script is run on a weekly basis to ensure that nobody has unauthorized privileges.

```
rem audit.sql a script to check for bad privileges
set linesize 80;
set pagesize 999;
set verify off;

set heading off;
PROMPT
**********************************************************************
select 'AUDIT OF &&1 ', to_char(sysdate,'mm-dd-yy hh:mm') from dual;
PROMPT
**********************************************************************
PROMPT
set heading on;

PROMPT
**********************************************************************
PROMPT Searching &&1 for any system privileges
PROMPT that are granted WITH ADMIN OPTION...
PROMPT
**********************************************************************
column c1 heading "Grantee";
column c2 heading "Privilege";
column c3 heading "Admin?";
select    substr(grantee,1,20)     c1,
          substr(privilege,1,30)   c2,
          substr(admin_option,1,5) c3
from      sys.dba_sys_privs
where     admin_option = 'YES'
and       grantee not in
          ('DB_USER','DB_ADMIN','DBA','OPS$ORACLE','SYSTEM','SYS')
order by grantee;

PROMPT
**********************************************************************
PROMPT Searching &&1 for any end-users with system privileges...
PROMPT
**********************************************************************
column c1 heading "Grantee";
column c2 heading "Privilege";
column c3 heading "Admin?";
select    substr(grantee,1,20)     c1,
          substr(privilege,1,30)   c2,
          substr(admin_option,1,5) c3
from      sys.dba_sys_privs
where
          grantee not in ('DBA','SYSTEM','SYS','COMMON','OPS$ORACLE',
```

```
                'RESOURCE','CONNECT','OPS$TPSOPR','IMP_FULL_DATABASE',
                'DB_USER','DB_ADMIN','DB_OWNER','EXP_FULL_DATABASE',
                'OPS$ADMOPR')
order by grantee;

PROMPT
**********************************************************************
PROMPT Searching &&1 for any non-DBA roles
PROMPT that are granted WITH ADMIN OPTION...
PROMPT
**********************************************************************
column c1 heading "Role";
column c2 heading "Privilege";
column c3 heading "Admin?";
select   substr(role,1,20)        c1,
         substr(privilege,1,30)   c2,
         substr(admin_option,1,5) c3
from     sys.role_sys_privs
where    admin_option = 'YES'
and      role not in ('DBA','DB_ADMIN')
order by role;

select   substr(grantee,1,20)     c1,
         substr(granted_role,1,22) c2,
         substr(admin_option,1,3) c3,
         substr(default_role,1,12) c4
from     sys.dba_role_privs
where    admin_option = 'YES'
and granted_role not in ('RESOURCE','DB_USER','DB_OWNER','CONNECT')
and grantee not in
   ('DB_ADMIN','DBA','SYS','SYSTEM','ORACLE','OPS$ORACLE','OPS$ADMOPR')
order by granted_role;

PROMPT
**********************************************************************
PROMPT Searching &&1 for any table privileges
PROMPT that can be granted to others...
PROMPT
**********************************************************************
column c1 heading "Grantee";
column c2 heading "Owner";
column c3 heading "Table";
column c4 heading "Grantor";
column c5 heading "Privilege";
column c6 heading "Grantable?";
select   substr(grantee,1,12)     c1,
```

```
          substr(owner,1,12)       c2,
          substr(table_name,1,15)  c3,
          substr(grantor,1,12)     c4,
          substr(privilege,1,9)    c5,
          substr(grantable,1,3)    c6
from      sys.dba_tab_privs
where     grantable = 'YES'
and owner not in ('SYS','SYSTEM','GL','APPLSYS','BOM','ENG',
                  'PO','AP','PER','WIP','LOGGER')
order by table_name;

PROMPT
********************************************************************
PROMPT Searching &&1 for DBA and RESOURCE Roles (To other than
ops$oracle)...
PROMPT
********************************************************************
column c1 heading "Grantee";
column c2 heading "Role";
column c3 heading "Admin?";
column c4 heading "Default Role";
select    substr(grantee,1,20)      c1,
          substr(granted_role,1,22) c2,
          substr(admin_option,1,3)  c3,
          substr(default_role,1,12) c4
from      sys.dba_role_privs
where     granted_role in ('RESOURCE','DB_OWNER','DBA','DB_ADMIN')
and grantee not in ('SYS','SYSTEM','OPS$ORACLE')
order by granted_role;

--select to_char(sysdate,'hhmmss') from dual;

create table temp1 as
  select distinct username from dba_users
  where substr(username,1,4) = 'OPS$';

create table temp2 as
  select distinct grantee from dba_role_privs
  where granted_role not in ('DB_USER');

PROMPT
********************************************************************
PROMPT Searching &&1 for any users
PROMPT that have no meaningful roles (orphan users)...
PROMPT
********************************************************************
```

```
select substr(username,5,20) username from temp1
where username not in
(select grantee from temp2);

drop table temp1;
drop table temp2;

PROMPT
PROMPT **********************************************************************
PROMPT Searching &&1 for all tables granted to PUBLIC . . .
PROMPT
PROMPT **********************************************************************
column c0 format a10 heading "Owner";
column c1 heading "Table";
column c2 format a10 heading "Grantor";
select distinct owner c0,
                table_name c1,
                grantor    c2
from sys.dba_tab_privs a
where grantee = 'PUBLIC'
and
owner not in ('OPS$ORACLE','SYS','SYSTEM')
and not exists
   (select * from dba_sequences b
    where a.table_name = b.sequence_name)
and privilege not in ('EXECUTE')
order by owner, table_name
;

PROMPT
PROMPT **********************************************************************
PROMPT Searching &&1 for all objects owned by ops$ users . . .
PROMPT
PROMPT **********************************************************************

select substr(owner,1,10),
       substr(object_type,1,20),
       substr(object_name,1,40)
from dba_objects
where owner like 'OPS$%'
and owner not in ('OPS$ORACLE')
and object_type not in ('SYNONYM')
;

spool off;
```

Here is the listing from this script:

```
SQL> @audit my_sid
********************************************************************

AUDIT OF my_sid
03-08-96 08:03


********************************************************************

********************************************************************
Searching my_sid for any system privileges
that are granted WITH ADMIN OPTION...
********************************************************************


no rows selected

********************************************************************
Searching my_sid for any end-users with system privileges...
********************************************************************
```

Grantee	Privilege	Adm
ORACLE	ALTER USER	NO
ORACLE	CREATE USER	NO
ORACLE	RESTRICTED SESSION	NO
ORACLEDEV	CREATE DATABASE LINK	NO
ORACLEDEV	CREATE PROCEDURE	NO
ORACLEDEV	CREATE PUBLIC DATABASE LINK	NO
ORACLEDEV	CREATE PUBLIC SYNONYM	NO
ORACLEDEV	CREATE SEQUENCE	NO
ORACLEDEV	CREATE TABLE	NO
ORACLEDEV	CREATE TRIGGER	NO
ORACLEDEV	CREATE VIEW	NO
ORACLEDEV	DROP PUBLIC SYNONYM	NO
ORACLEDEV	FORCE TRANSACTION	NO
ORACLEDEV	SELECT ANY TABLE	NO
ORACLEUSR	CREATE SESSION	NO
ORADBA	UNLIMITED TABLESPACE	NO
PATROL	CREATE PROCEDURE	NO
PATROL	CREATE SEQUENCE	NO
PATROL	CREATE SESSION	NO
PATROL	CREATE SYNONYM	NO
PATROL	CREATE TABLE	NO

```
PATROL                    CREATE VIEW                           NO
PATROL                    SELECT ANY TABLE                      NO

23 rows selected.

**********************************************************************
Searching my_sid for any non-DBA roles
that are granted WITH ADMIN OPTION...
**********************************************************************

no rows selected

no rows selected

**********************************************************************
Searching my_sid for any table privileges
that can be granted to others...
**********************************************************************

no rows selected

**********************************************************************
Searching my_sid for DBA and RESOURCE Roles (To other than ops$oracle)...
**********************************************************************

Grantee                Role                    Adm Def
--------------------   ----------------------  --  ---
ORADBA                 DBA                     NO  YES
ORADBA                 RESOURCE                NO  YES

Table created.

Table created.

**********************************************************************
Searching my_sid for any users
that have no meaningful roles (orphan users)...
**********************************************************************

no rows selected

Table dropped.

Table dropped.
```

```
*********************************************************************
Searching my_sid for all tables granted to PUBLIC . . .
*********************************************************************

Owner       Table                               Grantor
----------  ----------------------------------  ----------
ORACLE      ERR4                                ORACLE
ORACLE      ORGSEG                              ORACLE
ORACLE      PERSEG                              ORACLE
ORACLE      PLAN_TABLE                          ORACLE


*********************************************************************
Searching my_sid for all objects owned by ops$ users . . .
*********************************************************************


no rows selected


************************************************************
```

allprivs.sql

This script accepts the user ID as a parameter, and then lists all of the privileges that the user possesses in Oracle. It includes all table, system, and role privileges.

```
rem allprivs.sql <userid> -Lists all table, system and role privs. (ops$
rem is NOT added)
set pause off;
--set echo off;
--set termout off;
set linesize 75;
set pagesize 999;
set newpage 0;
--set feedback off;
--set heading off;
set verify off;

select  'grant '||privilege||' on '||table_name||' to &&1;'
from dba_tab_privs
where grantee = upper('&&1')
and table_name not like 'MENU_%'
;
```

```
select  'grant '||privilege||' to &&1;'
from dba_sys_privs
where grantee = upper('&&1')
;

select  'grant '||granted_role||' to &&1;'
from dba_role_privs
where grantee = upper('&&1')
;

spool off;
```

Here is the listing from this script:

```
@allprivs oradba

grant UNLIMITED TABLESPACE to oradba;

grant CONNECT to oradba;
grant DBA to oradba;
grant ORACLEDEV to oradba;
grant RESOURCE to oradba;
```

bitmap.sql

This script identifies low cardinality indexes for 7.3 bitmapped indexes.

```
rem  Written by Don Burleson

prompt Be patient.  This can take awhile . . .

set pause off;
set echo off;
set termout off;
set linesize 300;
set pagesize 999;
set newpage 0;
set feedback off;
set heading off;
set verify off;

rem  First create the syntax to determine the cardinality . . .
```

```
spool idx1.sql;

select 'set termout off;' from dual;
select 'spool idx2.lst;' from dual;
select 'column card format 9,999,999;' from dual;

select 'select distinct count(distinct '
     ||a.column_name
     ||') card, '
     ||''' is the cardinality of '
     ||'Index '
     ||a.index_name
     ||' on column '
     ||a.column_name
     ||' of table '
     ||a.table_owner
     ||'.'
     ||a.table_name
     ||''' from '
     ||index_owner||'.'||a.table_name
     ||';'
from dba_ind_columns a, dba_indexes b
where
  a.index_name = b.index_name
and
  tablespace_name not in ('SYS','SYSTEM')
;

select 'spool off;' from dual;
spool off;

set termout on;

@idx1

!sort idx2.lst
```

Here is the listing from bitmap.sql:

```
3  is the cardinality of Index GEO_LOC_PK on column GEO_LOC_TY_CD of
   table RPT.GEM_LCC
4  is the cardinality of Index REGION_IDX on column REHION of table
   RPT.CUSTOMER
7  is the cardinality of Index GM_LCK on column GEO_LC_TCD of table
   RPT.GEM_LCC
```

8	is the cardinality of Index USR_IDX on column USR_CD of table RPT.CUSTOMER
50	is the cardinality of Index STATE_IDX on column STATE_ABBR of table RPT.CUSTOMER
3117	is the cardinality of Index ZIP_IDX on column ZIP_CD of table RPT.GEM_LCC
71,513	is the cardinality of Index GEO_LOC_PK on column GEO_LOC_CD of table RPT.GEM_LCC
83,459	is the cardinality of Index GEO_KEY_PK on column GEO_LOC_TY_CD of table RPT.GEM_LCC

coalesce.sql

This script modifies all tables that have (pctincrease = 0) to (pctincrease = 1).

```
rem coalesce.sql - changes all tablespaces with PCTINCREASE not equal to
rem one.
rem written by Don Burleson

set linesize 132;
set pagesize 999;
set feedback off;
set verify off;
set heading off;
set termout off;

spool coalesce;

select
    'alter tablespace '
    ||tablespace_name||
    ' storage ( pctincrease 1 );'
from dba_tablespaces
where
    tablespace_name not in ('RBS','SYSTEM','TEMP','TOOLS','USER')
and
    pct_increase = 0;

spool off;

set feedback on;
set verify on;
set heading on;
set termout on;

@coalesce.lst
```

dbusers.sql

This is a large report that lists all users in the Oracle database. For each user, it lists all of the user's privileges. This is a useful report to run weekly, dumping the output into a file where it can be easily searched.

```
remdbusers.sql - Lists all users, role privileges, default and temp
remtablespaces
set pause off;
set linesize 78;
set pagesize 56;
set newpage 0;

column c1 heading "User"        format a20;
column c2 heading "Privilege";
column c3 heading "Default TS" format a10;
column c4 heading "Temp TS"    format a10;
ttitle "dbname Database|User Profiles";

select   substr(dba_users.username,1,20) c1,
         dba_role_privs.granted_role c2,
         substr(dba_users.default_tablespace,1,15) c3,
         substr(dba_users.temporary_tablespace,1,15) c4
from     sys.dba_role_privs, sys.dba_users
where    sys.dba_role_privs.grantee = sys.dba_users.username
order by 1,2;
```

Here is the listing from this script:

```
SQL> @dbusers
SQL>

Fri Mar  8                                            page    1
                          dbname Database
                          User Profiles


User                    Privilege                        Default TS Temp TS
----------------------- -------------------------------- ---------- ----------
EMANS                   ORACLEUSR                            TEMP       TEMP
GENERAL                 ORACLEUSR                            USERS      TEMP
KRAMER                  ORACLEUSR                            TEMP       TEMP
L114339                 ORACLEUSR                    •       TEMP       TEMP
L118358                 ORACLEUSR                            TEMP       TEMP
L119069                 ORACLEDEV                            TEMP       TEMP
L119069                 ORACLEUSR                            TEMP       TEMP
```

L122739	ORACLEUSR	TEMP	TEMP
L123577	CONNECT	USERS	TEMP
L123577	ORACLEUSR	USERS	TEMP
L125033	ORACLEUSR	TEMP	TEMP
L570974	ORACLEUSR	TEMP	TEMP
L575696	ORACLEUSR	TEMP	TEMP
L575706	ORACLEUSR	TEMP	TEMP
L579080	ORACLEUSR	TEMP	TEMP
L589886	ORACLEUSR	TEMP	TEMP
L609306	ORACLEUSR	TEMP	TEMP

dbroles.sql

This script produces a report of all users who have system privileges within
Oracle. This script is a useful security check to detect anyone who may
have unwanted privileges.

```
rem dbroles.sql - Lists all roles that are defined to the database
set heading off;
set pause off;
set echo on;
set termout on;
set linesize 75;
set showmode on;
set feedback on;
set newpage 1;
set verify off;
set pagesize 9999;

select distinct 'grant db_owner',
                ' to ',
                substr(grantee,1,20),
                ';'
from dba_role_privs where
granted_role = 'RESOURCE';

select distinct 'grant unlimited tablespace',
                ' to ',
                substr(grantee,1,20),
                ';'
from dba_role_privs where
granted_role = 'RESOURCE';

select distinct 'revoke resource',
                ' from ',
```

```
                      substr(grantee,1,20),
                      ';'
from dba_role_privs where
granted_role = 'RESOURCE';

spool dbadmin.sql

select distinct 'grant db_admin',
                ' to ',
                substr(grantee,1,20),
                ';'
from dba_role_privs where
granted_role = 'DBA';

select distinct 'revoke dba',
                ' from ',
                substr(grantee,1,20),
                ';'
from dba_role_privs where
granted_role = 'DBA' and
grantee not in ('SYS','SYSTEM');

select distinct 'grant unlimited tablespace',
                ' to ',
                substr(grantee,1,20),
                ';'
from dba_role_privs where
granted_role = 'DBA';
```

Here is the listing from this script:

```
@dbroles

Fri Mar  8                                                        page    1
                              dbname Database
                              User Profiles

grant db_owner   to  ORADBA               ;
grant db_owner   to  SYS                  ;

grant unlimited tablespace  to  ORADBA          ;
grant unlimited tablespace  to  SYS             ;

revoke resource  from  ORADBA             ;
revoke resource  from  SYS                ;
```

```
grant db_admin  to  ORADBA              ;
grant db_admin  to  SYS                 ;
grant db_admin  to  SYSTEM              ;

revoke dba  from  ORADBA              ;

grant unlimited tablespace  to  ORADBA              ;
grant unlimited tablespace  to  SYS                 ;
grant unlimited tablespace  to  SYSTEM              ;
```

files.sql

This script produces a report of all files that are defined to Oracle. For each file the tablespace name is given along with the size of the data file.

```
rem files.sql - shows all datafiles by tablespace and size

set pause off;
set linesize 60;
set pagesize 60;
set newpage 0;
column c1 heading "Tablespace";
column c2 heading "File name";
column c3 heading "Size (MB)";
ttitle "dbname Database|Data files by Tablespace";

select   substr(tablespace_name,1,10) c1,
         substr(file_name,1,30) c2,
         round(sum(bytes)/1048576,2) c3
from     sys.dba_data_files
group by tablespace_name,file_name
order by tablespace_name;
```

Here is the listing from this script:

```
Fri Mar  8                                    page    1
                    dbname Database
                Data files by Tablespace

Tablespace File name                         Size (MB)
---------- ------------------------------- ----------
INDX       /Datadisks/d02/ORACLE/my_sid/ind     200
MPTV       /Datadisks/d01/ORACLE/my_sid/mpt     500
PATROL     /Datadisks/d02/ORACLE/my_sid/pat      10
```

```
ROLB         /Datadisks/d03/ORACLE/my_sid/rol         40
SYSTEM       /Datadisks/d09/ORACLE/my_sid/sys         15
TEMP         /Datadisks/d02/ORACLE/my_sid/tem         80
TEMP         /Datadisks/d02/ORACLE/my_sid/tem        180
TOOLS        /Datadisks/d03/ORACLE/my_sid/too         15
USERS        /Datadisks/d02/ORACLE/my_sid/use         10
```

getprivs.sql

This script accepts a user ID as input and produces a report showing all system and role privileges that are granted to this user.

```
rem getprivs.sql <user id> - Lists all privileges assigned to the
rem specified user

set pause off;
--set echo off;
--set termout off;
set linesize 75;
set pagesize 999;
set newpage 0;
set feedback off;
set heading off;
set verify off;

select  'grant '||privilege||' to '||grantee||';'
from dba_sys_privs
where grantee = upper('&&1')
;

select  'grant '||granted_role||' to '||grantee||';'
from dba_role_privs
where grantee = upper('&&1')
;

select
    'grant '||privilege||' on '||owner||'.'||table_name
    ||' to '||grantee||';'
from dba_tab_privs
where grantee = upper('&&1')
order by owner
;

  select
```

```
          'grant '||privilege||' ('||column_name
          ||') on '||owner||'.'||table_name
          ||' to '||grantee||';'
from dba_col_privs
where grantee = upper('&&1')
;
```

Here is the listing from this script:

```
Fri Mar  8                                                     page    1
                            dbname Database
                       Data files by Tablespace

grant UNLIMITED TABLESPACE to ORADBA;

grant CONNECT to ORADBA;
grant DBA to ORADBA;
grant ORACLEDEV to ORADBA;
grant RESOURCE to ORADBA;
```

getrole.sql

This report accepts a user ID and produces a report that shows all role
privileges that have been granted to this user.

```
rem getrole.sql <user id> - Lists all roles assigned to the user

rem keyed script
set pause off;
--set echo off;
--set termout off;
set linesize 75;
set pagesize 999;
set newpage 0;
set feedback off;
set heading off;
set verify off;

select  '&&1 has system privilege: '||privilege
from dba_sys_privs
where grantee = upper('&&1')
;

select  '&&1 has role: '||granted_role
```

```
from dba_role_privs
where grantee = upper('&&1')
;
```

Here is the listing from this script:

```
SQL>  @getrole oradba

oradba has role: CONNECT
oradba has role: DBA
oradba has role: ORACLEDEV
oradba has role: RESOURCE
```

index.sql

This report tells all relevant information about an index.

```
rem index.sql - Shows the details for indexes

set pagesize 999;
set linesize 100;

column c1 heading 'Index'      format a19;
column c3 heading 'S'          format a1;
column c4 heading 'Level'      format 999;
column c5 heading 'Leaf Blks'  format 999,999;
column c6 heading 'dist. Keys' format 99,999,999;
column c7 heading 'Bks/Key'    format 99,999;
column c8 heading 'Clust Ftr'  format 9,999,999;
column c9 heading 'Lf/Key'     format 99,999;

spool index.lst;

select
  owner||'.'||index_name     c1,
  substr(status,1,1)         c3,
  blevel                     c4,
  leaf_blocks                c5,
  distinct_keys              c6,
  avg_data_blocks_per_key    c7,
  clustering_factor          c8,
  avg_leaf_blocks_per_key    c9
from dba_indexes
where
```

```
    owner not in ('SYS','SYSTEM')
order by blevel desc, leaf_blocks desc;
```

Here is the output of index.sql:

```
                                Leaf    dist.      Bks/    Clust      Lf/
Index                 S Level   Blks    Keys       Key     Ftr        Key
------------------    - -----   ------  ----------  ------  ---------- ------
RPT.LOB_SHPMT_PK      V   2     25,816  3,511,938        1    455,343       1
RPT.SHP_EK_CUST_INV   V   2     23,977  2,544,132        1  1,764,915       1
RPT.SHP_FK_GLO_DEST   V   2     23,944     22,186      112  2,493,095       1
RPT.LSH_FK_SHP        V   2     22,650  1,661,576        1    339,031       1
RPT.SHP_FK_ORL_ORIG   V   2     21,449        404      806    325,675      53
RPT.LSA_FK_LSH        V   2     21,181  2,347,812        1    996,641       1
RPT.LSH_FK_LOB        V   2     19,989        187    4,796    896,870     106
RPT.SHPMT_PK          V   2     19,716  3,098,063        1  1,674,264       1
RPT.SHP_FK_CAR        V   2     18,513        689      390    268,859      26
RPT.SHP_EK_ROLE_TY_   V   2     17,847         10   24,613    246,134   1,784
RPT.SHP_FK_SPT        V   2     16,442          4   46,872    187,489   4,110
RPT.INV_EK_INV_NUM    V   2     16,407  2,014,268        1    518,206       1
RPT.SHP_FK_ORL_DEST   V   2     15,863        385      692    266,656      41
RPT.SHP_FK_SRC        V   2     15,827         10   17,469    174,694   1,582
RPT.INV_LINE_ITEM_P   V   2     14,731  2,362,216        1    102,226       1
```

idxexts.sql

This report produces a report of all indexes that have more than five extents. This report is useful for determining which indexes may benefit from being dropped and re-created, since index fragmentation can impede performance.

```
rem idxexts.sql - Lists all indexes where extents are > 5

set pause off;
set echo off;
set linesize 150;
set pagesize 60;
column c1  heading "Tablespace";
column c2  heading "Owner";
column c3  heading "Index";
column c4  heading "Size (KB)";
column c5  heading "Alloc. Ext";
column c6  heading "Max Ext";
```

```
column c7  heading "Init Ext (KB)";
column c8  heading "Next Ext (KB)";
column c9  heading "Pct Inc";
column c10 heading "Pct Free";
break on c1 skip 2 on c2 skip 2
ttitle "dbname Database|Fragmented Indexes";

select  substr(ds.tablespace_name,1,10) c1,
        substr(di.owner||'.'||di.table_name,1,30) c2,
        substr(di.index_name,1,20) c3,
        ds.bytes/1024 c4,
        ds.extents c5,
        di.max_extents c6,
        di.initial_extent/1024 c7,
        di.next_extent/1024 c8,
        di.pct_increase c9,
        di.pct_free c10
from    sys.dba_segments ds,
        sys.dba_indexes di
where   ds.tablespace_name = di.tablespace_name
  and   ds.owner = di.owner
  and   ds.segment_name = di.index_name
  and   ds.extents > 3
order by 1,2;
```

Here is the listing from this script:

```
SQL> @idxexts

Fri Mar  8                                              page    1
                        dbname Database
                        Fragmented Indexes

INDX    ORACLE.DETSALE   DETSALE_PK      9420    5   249  8616  200 0   10
                         DETSALE_UK     10600   22   249  6400  200 0   10
                         DETSALE_INDEX4  5100    4   249  4500  200 0   20
```

keep.sql

This is a very useful script for pinning packages in the SGA. Pinning packages in the SGA improves performance for frequently used packages. The syntax is spooled to the exec.sql file, where the script executes after the file has been created. You may want to review the contents of exec.sql, and only pin those packages that are frequently called by the application.

```
rem keep.sql - pins all packages in the SGA

SET PAGESIZE 999
SET HEAD OFF
SET FEEDBACK OFF

SPOOL keep_exec.sql

SELECT 'execute dbms_shared_pool.keep('''||name||''');' sql_stmt
FROM v$db_object_cache
WHERE type='PACKAGE'
/
SPOOL OFF
```

Here is the listing from this script:

```
@exec

package kept
package kept
```

linkv1.sql

This script produces a list of all public and private database links that are using SQL*Net version 1 connect strings. This is a useful report to run when you convert to SQL*Net version 2, and it can easily be modified to create the drop-and-create syntax for new version 2 database links.

```
rem linkv1.sql - find a SQL*Net v 1 database links

column c2 heading "Owner";
column c3 heading "User";
column c5 heading "Connect";

set pagesize 60;


ttitle "SQL*Net v 1|Installations"

select
  substr(db_link,1,15) c1,
  substr(owner,1,10) c2,
  substr(username,1,19) c3,
```

```
    substr(host,1,15) c5
from dba_db_links
where
      host like 't:%'
order by db_link;
```

Here is the listing from this script:

```
@linkv1

DB LINK     OWNER     USER        CONNECT
--------    -------   ---------   -----------
mdb_link    ORADBA    OPS$JONES   t:mdb:mdb01
lis_link    ORAPRM1   MFISHER     t:lis:lis01
```

objects.sql

This script lists all trigger and stored procedure names in the database showing the creator of the object.

```
rem objects.sql - Lists all triggers and procedures in the database.
rem
set pause off;
set echo off;
set termout on;
set linesize 80;
set pagesize 999;
column object_name format a10;
column object_type format a12;
column object_name format a30;

break on owner skip 0;
ttitle "Objects in Database";

select  owner,
        object_type,
        object_name
from dba_objects
where
--owner not in ('SYS','SYSTEM')
--and
object_type in ('PACKAGE','TRIGGER','PROCEDURE')
order by 1,2,3;
```

Here is the listing from this script:

```
SQL> @objects

Fri Mar  8                                                        page   1
                        Objects in Database

ORACLE                       PROCEDURE    MERGE_MF
                             PROCEDURE    REMOVE_LINK
                             TRIGGER      ORG_SEGMENT
PATROL                       PACKAGE      P$COLL
                             PACKAGE      P$EXCLUSION
                             PACKAGE      P$MONITOR
                             PACKAGE      P$PREF
                             PACKAGE      P$RECOVERY
SYS                          PACKAGE      DBMS_ALERT
                             PACKAGE      DBMS_DDL
                             PACKAGE      DBMS_DEFER_IMPORT_INTERNAL
                             PACKAGE      DBMS_DEFER_SYS
```

paramete.sql

This script shows all of the Oracle initialization parameters as defined in the init.ora and config.ora files. Identical to the SQL*DBA **SHOW PARAMETERS** command, this report is useful because it does not require access to SQL*DBA.

```
rem paramete.sql - Lists values of the v$parameter table.

set pagesize 999;

column c1 heading "Name";
column c3 heading "Value";
column c4 heading "Default?"

select substr(name,1,35)  c1,
       substr(value,1,30) c3,
       isdefault          c4
 from v$parameter
order by substr(name,1,20)
;
```

Here is the listing from this script:

```
SQL> @paramete


Fri Mar  8                                                      page    1
                            Objects in Database


Name                                Value                        Default?
----------------------------------  ---------------------------  --------
async_read                          TRUE                         TRUE
async_write                         TRUE                         TRUE
audit_file_dest                     /opt/oracle/admin/my_sid/audit  FALSE
audit_trail                         TRUE                         FALSE
background_core_dump                full                         TRUE
background_dump_dest                /opt/oracle/admin/my_sid/bdump  FALSE
blank_trimming                      FALSE                        TRUE
cache_size_threshold                40                           FALSE
ccf_io_size                         134217728                    TRUE
checkpoint_process                  FALSE                        TRUE
cleanup_rollback_entries            20                           TRUE
close_cached_open_cursors           FALSE                        TRUE
commit_point_strength               1                            TRUE
compatible                                                       TRUE
compatible_no_recovery                                           TRUE
control_files                       /Datadisks/d09/ORACLE/my_sid/con  FALSE
core_dump_dest                      /opt/oracle/admin/my_sid/cdump  FALSE
cursor_space_for_time               FALSE                        TRUE
db_block_buffers                    400                          FALSE
db_block_checkpoint_batch           8                            TRUE
db_block_lru_extended_statistics    0                            TRUE
db_block_lru_statistics             FALSE                        TRUE
db_block_size                       4096                         FALSE
db_domain                           WORLD                        TRUE
db_file_multiblock_read_count       16                           FALSE
db_file_simultaneous_writes         4                            TRUE
db_files                            30                           TRUE
db_name                             my_sid                       FALSE
db_writers                          1                            TRUE
dblink_encrypt_login                FALSE                        TRUE
discrete_transactions_enabled       FALSE                        TRUE
distributed_lock_timeout            60                           TRUE
distributed_recovery_connection_hol 200                          TRUE
distributed_transactions            19                           FALSE
dml_locks                           100                          FALSE
enqueue_resources                   177                          FALSE
event                                                            TRUE
fixed_date                                                       TRUE
gc_db_locks                         400                          FALSE
```

gc_files_to_locks		TRUE
gc_lck_procs	1	TRUE
gc_rollback_locks	20	TRUE
gc_rollback_segments	20	TRUE
gc_save_rollback_locks	20	TRUE
gc_segments	10	TRUE
gc_tablespaces	5	TRUE
global_names	FALSE	TRUE
ifile	/opt/oracle/admin/my_sid/pfile/c	FALSE
instance_number	0	TRUE
job_queue_interval	60	TRUE
job_queue_keep_connections	FALSE	TRUE
job_queue_processes	0	TRUE
license_max_sessions	0	TRUE
license_max_users	0	TRUE
license_sessions_warning	0	TRUE
log_archive_buffer_size	64	TRUE
log_archive_buffers	4	TRUE
log_archive_dest	/opt/oracle/admin/my_sid/arch/mp	FALSE
log_archive_format	%t_%s.dbf	TRUE
log_archive_start	TRUE	FALSE
log_buffer	32768	TRUE
log_checkpoint_interval	10000	FALSE
log_checkpoint_timeout	0	TRUE
log_checkpoints_to_alert	FALSE	TRUE
log_files	255	TRUE
log_simultaneous_copies	2	FALSE
log_small_entry_max_size	800	TRUE
max_commit_propagation_delay	90000	TRUE
max_dump_file_size	500	TRUE
max_enabled_roles	20	TRUE
max_rollback_segments	30	TRUE
max_transaction_branches	8	TRUE
mts_dispatchers		TRUE
mts_listener_address	(address=(protocol=ipc)(key=%s	TRUE
mts_max_dispatchers	0	FALSE
mts_max_servers	0	FALSE
mts_servers	0	FALSE
mts_service	my_sid	FALSE
nls_currency		TRUE
nls_date_format		TRUE
nls_date_language		TRUE
nls_iso_currency		TRUE
nls_language	AMERICAN	TRUE
nls_numeric_characters		TRUE

nls_sort		TRUE
nls_territory	AMERICA	TRUE
open_cursors	100	FALSE
open_links	4	TRUE
optimizer_comp_weight	0	TRUE
optimizer_mode	CHOOSE	FALSE
os_authent_prefix		TRUE
os_roles	FALSE	TRUE
parallel_default_max_scans	0	TRUE
parallel_default_max_instances	0	TRUE
parallel_default_scansize	100	TRUE
parallel_max_servers	5	TRUE
parallel_min_servers	0	TRUE
parallel_server_idle_time	5	TRUE
post_wait_device	/devices/pseudo/pw@0:pw	TRUE
pre_page_sga	FALSE	TRUE
processes	60	FALSE
recovery_parallelism	0	TRUE
reduce_alarm	FALSE	TRUE
remote_login_passwordfile	NONE	FALSE
remote_os_authent	FALSE	TRUE
remote_os_roles	FALSE	TRUE
resource_limit	FALSE	TRUE
rollback_segments	rolb1, rolb2, rolb3, rolb4	FALSE
row_cache_cursors	10	TRUE
row_locking	default	TRUE
sequence_cache_entries	10	TRUE
sequence_cache_hash_buckets	7	TRUE
serializable	FALSE	TRUE
session_cached_cursors	0	TRUE
sessions	71	FALSE
shadow_core_dump	full	TRUE
shared_pool_reserved_size	0	TRUE
shared_pool_reserved_min_alloc	5000	TRUE
shared_pool_size	6000000	FALSE
single_process	FALSE	TRUE
snapshot_refresh_interval	60	TRUE
snapshot_refresh_keep_connections	FALSE	TRUE
snapshot_refresh_processes	0	TRUE
sort_area_retained_size	65536	FALSE
sort_area_size	65536	TRUE
sort_mts_buffer_for_fetch_size	0	TRUE
sort_read_fac	5	TRUE
sort_spacemap_size	512	TRUE
spin_count	2000	TRUE

sql92_security	FALSE	TRUE
sql_trace	FALSE	TRUE
temporary_table_locks	71	FALSE
thread	0	TRUE
timed_statistics	FALSE	TRUE
transactions	78	FALSE
transactions_per_rollback_segment	34	FALSE
use_ism	TRUE	TRUE
use_post_wait_driver	FALSE	TRUE
use_readv	FALSE	TRUE
user_dump_dest	/opt/oracle/admin/my_sid/udump	FALSE

140 rows selected.

profile.sql

This script shows all sign-on profiles that have been defined to Oracle. For each profile, the resource and the resource limit is shown.

```
rem profile.sql - Lists all profiles in the database.

rem sqlx script
set echo off;
set pagesize 60;

ttitle "dbname Database|Profiles";

break on c0 skip 2;

column c0 heading "Profile";
column c1 heading "Resource";
column c2 heading "Limit";

select
    substr(profile,1,10) c0,
    substr(resource_name,1,30) c1,
    substr(limit,1,10) c2
from dba_profiles
group by
    substr(profile,1,10),
    substr(resource_name,1,30),
    substr(limit,1,10)
order by 1;
```

Here is the listing from this script:

```
SQL> @profile

Fri Mar  8                                                          page    1
                              dbname Database
                                 Profiles

Profile    Resource                      Limit
-------    -------------------------     ---------
DEFAULT    COMPOSITE_LIMIT               UNLIMITED
           CONNECT_TIME                  UNLIMITED
           CPU_PER_CALL                  UNLIMITED
           CPU_PER_SESSION               UNLIMITED
           IDLE_TIME                     UNLIMITED
           LOGICAL_READS_PER_CALL        UNLIMITED
           LOGICAL_READS_PER_SESSION     UNLIMITED
           PRIVATE_SGA                   UNLIMITED
           SESSIONS_PER_USER             UNLIMITED

ADHOC      COMPOSITE_LIMIT               DEFAULT
           CONNECT_TIME                  4800
           CPU_PER_CALL                  UNLIMITED
           CPU_PER_SESSION               UNLIMITED
           IDLE_TIME                     120
           LOGICAL_READS_PER_CALL        UNLIMITED
           LOGICAL_READS_PER_SESSION     UNLIMITED
           PRIVATE_SGA                   51200
           SESSIONS_PER_USER             5
```

quotas.sql

This script lists all quotas defined to Oracle. A quota is assigned on a tablespace-by-tablespace basis to each user, and is used to prevent a single user from consuming an entire shared tablespace. For example, user **FRED** could be prevented from using more then 500 K in the **TEMP** tablespace with the command: **ALTER USER FRED QUOTA 500K ON TEMP**.

```
rem quotas.sql - Lists all quotas.

set pause off;
set echo off;
set linesize 79;
```

```
set pagesize 56;
set newpage 0;

column c1 heading "Table|Space";
column c2 heading "User Name";
column c3 heading "Bytes|Used (KB)";
column c4 heading "Bytes|Allowed (KB)";
ttitle "dbname Database|Quotas";


select    substr(tablespace_name,1,10) c1,
          substr(username,1,15) c2,
          (bytes/1024) c3,
          (max_bytes/1024) c4
from      sys.dba_ts_quotas
order by  tablespace_name, username;
```

Here is the listing from this script:

```
SQL> @quotas

Fri Mar  8                                                        page    1
                             dbname Database
                                 Quotas

Table              Bytes       Bytes
Space    User Name Used (KB)   Allowed (KB)
-------- --------- ---------   ------------
INDX     ORACLE       115976   -.00097656
MPTV     ORACLE       259688   -.00097656
TEMP     PATROL            0   -.00097656
USERS    ORACLE            0   -.00097656
USERS    PATROL         1092   -.00097656
```

rbsegs.sql

This script shows all of Oracle's rollback segments and their status. This report can be very useful for determining if a long-running SQL statement is using all rollback segment resources. This can result in the **SNAPSHOT TOO OLD** or **ROLLBACK SEGMENT FAILED TO EXTEND** Oracle error messages.

```
rem rbsegs.sql - shows size and status of rollback segments

select substr(segment_name,1,10) RBS,
```

```
              substr(tablespace_name,1,10) tablespace,
              bytes/1048576 Meg,
              extents
from dba_segments where segment_type = 'ROLLBACK';

select 'offline rollback segments' from dual;

select segment_name, status
from dba_rollback_segs
where
segment_name not like ('SYS%');
```

Here is the listing from this script:

```
SQL> @rbsegs

RBS         TABLESPACE         MEG    EXTENTS
----------  ----------  ----------  ----------
SYSTEM      SYSTEM         .17578125          3
ROLB1       ROLB          7.32421875          3
ROLB2       ROLB          7.32421875          3
ROLB3       ROLB          7.32421875          3
ROLB4       ROLB           3.046875           3


'OFFLINEROLLBACKSEGMENTS'
-----------------------
offline rollback segments


SEGMENT_NAME                    STATUS
------------------------------  ----------------
ROLB1                           ONLINE
ROLB2                           ONLINE
ROLB3                           ONLINE
ROLB4                           ONLINE
```

rbslock.sql

This is a very useful script for seeing who is assigned to a rollback segment. If a rollback segment is extending dramatically, the DBA will want to find out which user is running the task, and this script identifies the user.

```
remrbslock.sql - shows all users assigned to a rollback segment.

set pause off;
set echo off;
set termout off;
set linesize 45;
set pagesize 60;
set newpage 0;

column c1 heading "RBS" format a10
column c2 heading "User" format a15;
ttitle "dbname Database|Rollback Segment Access";

select    r.name c1,
          username c2
from      v$transaction t,
          v$rollname r,
          v$session s
where     t.addr = s.taddr
and       t.xidusn = r.usn
order by 1,2;
```

Here is the listing from this script:

```
@rbslock

RBS         User
----        ------------------
RB01        DMARTIN
RB02        JFISHER
```

role.sql

This script accepts a role name and produces a report that shows all privileges that comprise the role, and all users who have been granted the roles.

```
rem role.sql <role_name> - Shows all privs with the role and all
rem users w role.

set pause off;
set echo off;
set termout on;
```

```
set linesize 80;
set pagesize 999;

column c1  heading "Role";
column c2  format a40 heading "Table Name";
column c3  heading "Priv.";
break on c1 skip 0 on c2 skip 0 on c3 skip 0

ttitle "Role &&1 in Database dbname";
select  substr(granted_role,1,29) c1
from sys.role_role_privs
where  role = (upper('&&1'))
;

select  substr(role,1,30) c1,
        ltrim(rtrim(owner))||'.'||substr(table_name,1,29) c2,
        substr(privilege,1,6) c3
from sys.role_tab_privs
where  role = (upper('&&1'))
order by 1,2,3;

column c1  heading "Role";
column c2  heading "Grantee";
ttitle "Users with &&1 role";
select  substr(granted_role,1,10) c1,
        substr(grantee,1,20) c2
from dba_role_privs
where  granted_role = (upper('&&1'))
order by 1,2;
```

Here is the listing from this script:

```
SQL > @role dba

Fri Mar  8                                           page    1
                     Role dba in Database dbname

Role
----------
EXP_FULL_DATABASE

IMP_FULL_DATABASE
```

```
                        Users with dba role

Role        Grantee
----------  ----------
DBA         ORADBA
            SYS
            SYSTEM
```

roles.sql

This report shows all roles within Oracle. It also shows all system and table privileges that comprise each role, and finally all users who have been granted the role. Be forewarned that this can be a very large report if the Oracle instance has many roles.

```
rem roles.sql - Shows all roles within database and all users (huge report)

set pause off;
set echo off;
set linesize 80;
set pagesize 60;

column c1  heading "Role";
column c2  format a40 heading "Table Name";
column c3  heading "Priv.";
break on c1 skip 0 on c2 skip 0

ttitle "Roles in Database dbname";
select  substr(role,1,30) c1,
        substr(granted_role,1,30)
from sys.role_role_privs;

ttitle "Roles in Database dbname";
select  substr(role,1,30) c1,
        ltrim(rtrim(owner))||'.'||substr(table_name,1,30) c2,
        substr(privilege,1,6) c3
from sys.role_tab_privs
where   owner not in ('SYS','SYSTEM')
order by 1,2,3;
column c1  heading "Role";
column c2  heading "Grantee";

ttitle "Roles Granted to Users in Database dbname";
select  substr(granted_role,1,30) c1,
        substr(grantee,1,20) c2
```

```
from dba_role_privs
where   granted_role not in ('DBA','RESOURCE','CONNECT','SYS','SYSTEM',
        'EXP_FULL_DATABASE','IMP_FULL_DATABASE','MONITORER')
order by 1,2;
```

Here is the listing from this script:

```
SQL> @roles
Fri Mar  8                                                          page 1
                          Roles in Database

Role       SUBSTR(GRANTED_ROLE,1,30)
---------- ------------------------------
DBA        EXP_FULL_DATABASE
           IMP_FULL_DATABASE
2 rows selected.

Fri Mar  8                                                          page 1
                          Roles in Database

Role       Table Name                               Priv.
---------- ---------------------------------------- ------
ORACLEUSR  ORACLE.BRANCH                            DELETE
                                                    INSERT
                                                    SELECT
                                                    UPDATE
           ORACLE.CAT_MGC                           DELETE
                                                    INSERT
                                                    SELECT
                                                    UPDATE
           ORACLE.CHOICELIST                        DELETE
                                                    INSERT
                                                    SELECT
                                                    UPDATE
           ORACLE.CISUPDATES                        DELETE
                                                    INSERT
                                                    SELECT
                                                    UPDATE
           ORACLE.CUSTMAST                          DELETE
                                                    INSERT
                                                    SELECT
                                                    UPDATE
           ORACLE.CUSTTYPE                          SELECT
           ORACLE.ERR3                              DELETE
                                                    INSERT
```

```
Fri Mar  8                                                      page 1
                  Roles Granted to Users in Database dbname

Role       Grantee
---------- ----------------------------------------
ORACLEDEV  L119069
           L250526
           L623063
           L650637
           ORACLE
           ORADBA
           SYSTEM
ORACLEUSR  EMANS
           GENERAL
           KRAMER
           L12273
```

sqltext.sql

This script gives all of the SQL that currently resides in the SGA shared pool. This script could be extended to extract this SQL to run through the explain plan utility, to see where full-table scans exist.

```
rem sqltext.sql - Shows all SQL in the SGA shared pool.
rem Written by Don Burleson

set pagesize 9999;
set linesize 79;
set newpage 0;
set verify off;

break on address skip 2;

column address format 9;

select
      address,
      sql_text
from
      v$sqltext
order by
      address, piece;
```

Here is the output from sqltext.sql:

```
D09AFC4C    select decode(object_type, 'TABLE', 2,  'VIEW', 2, 'PACKAGE',
              3,'PACKAGE BODY', 3, 'PROCEDURE', 4, 'FUNCTION', 5,  0) from
              all_objects where object_name = upper('V_$SQLTEXT')  and
              object_type in ('TABLE', 'VIEW', 'PACKAGE', 'PACKAGE BODY',
              'PROCEDURE','FUNCTION') and owner = upper('SYS')

D09B653C    select owner, table_name, table_owner, db_link from
              all_synonyms where synonym_name = upper('V_$SQLTEXT') and
              owner = upper( 'SYS')

D09BC5AC    select owner, table_name, table_owner, db_link from
              all_synonyms where synonym_name = upper('v$sqltext') and
              (owner = 'PUBLIC'or owner = USER)

D09C2D58    select decode(object_type, 'TABLE', 2,  'VIEW', 2, 'PACKAGE',
              3,'PACKAGE BODY', 3, 'PROCEDURE', 4, 'FUNCTION', 5,  0)
              from user _objects where object_name = upper('v$sqltext')
              and object_type in ('TABLE', 'VIEW', 'PACKAGE', 'PACKAGE
              BODY',  'PROCEDURE','FUNCTION')

D09CFF4C    UPDATE SHPMT SET
              AMT_SUM_ILI=:b1,PMT_WGHT_SUM_ILI=:b2,CUST_PMT_W
              GHT_SUM_ILI=:b3 WHERE SHPMT_ID = :b4  AND SHPMT_SYS_SRC_CD
              = :b5
```

tblsize.sql

This script gives the amount of storage that a table consumes within its tablespace. Be aware that a table may consume far less than its initial extent. For example, a **CUSTOMER** table that is allocated with **INITIAL** 50 MB, may only consume 2 MB of real storage, even though 50 MB have been allocated for the table.

```
remtblsize.sql - gives the size of a table

select tablespace_name, sum(bytes/1048576) MEG
from dba_segments
group by tablespace_name;
```

Here is the listing from this script:

```
SQL> @tblsize
```

```
Fri Mar  8                                              page    1

TABLESPACE_NAME                        MEG
-------------------------------- ----------
INDX                             113.265625
MPTV                             253.609375
ROLB                             25.0195313
SYSTEM                           11.3789063
TOOLS                            6.34765625
USERS                            1.06640625
```

tsfrag.sql

This script provides a map of all tables within a tablespace.

```
rem tsfrag.sql - shows a tablespace map.
rem written by Don Burleson

set linesize 132;
set pages 999;

rem set feedback off;
rem set verify off;
rem set heading off;
rem set termout off;

break on file_id skip page;
break on free skip 1;
compute sum of KB on free;

spool tsfrag;

column owner           format a10;
column segment_name    format a10;
column tablespace_name format a14;
column file_id         format 99 heading ID;
column end             format 999999;
column KB              format 9999999;
column begin           format 999999;
column blocks          format 999999;

select
   tablespace_name,
   file_id,
```

```
   owner,
   segment_name,
   block_id begin,
   blocks,
   block_id+blocks-1 end,
   bytes/1024 KB,
   '' free
from sys.dba_extents
where tablespace_name not in ('RBS','SYSTEM','TEMP','TOOLS','USER')
union
select
   tablespace_name,
   file_id,
   '' owner,
   '' segment_name,
   block_id begin,
   blocks,
   block_id+blocks+1 end,
   bytes/1023 KB,
   'F' free
from sys.dba_free_space
where tablespace_name not in ('RBS','SYSTEM','TEMP','TOOLS','USER')
order by 1, 2, 5
;

/

spool off;
!cat tsfrag.lst
```

tsfree.sql

This report shows the amount of fragmentation within a tablespace for all tablespaces in the database. This report is useful for determining when the tablespaces should be exported and rebuilt, since tablespace fragmentation can impede performance.

```
set verify off;
clear breaks;
clear computes;
set pagesize 66;
set linesize 79;
set newpage 0;
```

```
--set echo off;
--set show off;
--set term off;
--set verify off;

column temp_col new_value spool_file noprint;

column today new_value datevar noprint;
column TABLESPACE_NAME          FORMAT A15     HEADING 'Tablespace';
COLUMN PIECES                   FORMAT 9,999   HEADING 'Tablespace|Pieces';
COLUMN FILE_MBYTES              FORMAT 99,999  HEADING 'Tablespace|Mbytes';
COLUMN FREE_MBYTES             FORMAT 99,999  HEADING 'Free|Mbytes';
COLUMN CONTIGUOUS_FREE_MBYTES FORMAT 99,999  HEADING
'Contiguous|Free|Mbytes';
COLUMN PCT_FREE                 FORMAT 999     HEADING 'Percent|FREE';
COLUMN PCT_CONTIGUOUS_FREE      FORMAT 999     HEADING
'Percent|FREE|Contiguous';

ttitle left datevar right sql.pno -
        center ' Instance Data File Storage' SKIP 1 -
        center ' in ORACLE Megabytes (1048576 bytes)' -
        skip skip;

BREAK ON REPORT
COMPUTE SUM OF FILE_MBYTES ON REPORT

select to_char(sysdate,'mm/dd/yy') today,
        TABLESPACE_NAME,
        PIECES,
        (D.BYTES/1048576) FILE_MBYTES,
        (F.FREE_BYTES/1048576) FREE_MBYTES,
        ((F.FREE_BLOCKS / D.BLOCKS) * 100) PCT_FREE,
        (F.LARGEST_BYTES/1048576) CONTIGUOUS_FREE_MBYTES,
        ((F.LARGEST_BLKS / D.BLOCKS) * 100) PCT_CONTIGUOUS_FREE
from SYS.DBA_DATA_FILES D, SYS.FREE_SPACE F
where D.STATUS = 'AVAILABLE' AND
        D.FILE_ID= F.FILE_ID AND
        D.TABLESPACE_NAME = F.TABLESPACE
order by TABLESPACE_NAME;

set verify on;
```

Here is the listing from this script:

```
SQL> @tsfree

03/08/96                      Instance Data File Storage
1
                         in ORACLE Megabytes (1048576 bytes)


                                               Contiguous  Percent
               Tablespace  Tablespace  Free    Percent     Free      FREE
Tablespace     Pieces      Mbytes      Mbytes  FREE        Mbytes    Contiguous
------------   ----------  ----------  ------  -------     ---------- ----------
INDX                  902         200      87       43             42         21
MPTV                   20         500     246       49            180         36
PATROL                 33          10      10      100              9         95
ROLB                   10          40      15       37              2          6
SYSTEM                 23          15       4       29              4         27
TEMP                  315          80      80      100              0          0
TEMP                    1         180     180      100            180        100
TOOLS                   1          15       9       58              9         58
USERS                  11          10       9       89              6         64
                                   ----------
                                        1,050


9 rows selected.
```

Abiteoul, S.; Kanellkis, P.; and E. Waller. "Method Schemas." *Communications of the ACM*, 1990.

Accredited Standards Committee X3/SPARC/DBSSG/ OODBTG—Final Report of the Object-Oriented Database Task Group, September 1991.

Ahad, R. and D. Dedo. "OpenODB from Hewlett-Packard: A Commercial Object-Oriented Database System." *Journal of Object-Oriented Programming*, Vol. 4, Issue 9, Feb. 1992.

Alagic, S. *Object-Oriented Database Programming*, New York: Springer Verlag Publishers, 1988.

Ahmed, S.; Wong, A.; Sriram, D.; and R. Logcher. "A Comparison of Object-Oriented Database Management Systems for Engineering Applications." *MIT Technical Report*, IESL-90-03, 1990.

Atkinson M.P. et al. "The Object-Oriented Database Systems Manifesto." *Deductive and Object-Oriented Databases*, Elsevere Science Publishers, 1990.

Atwood, T. and J. Orenstein. "Notes Toward a Standard Object-Oriented DDL and DML." *Computer Standards & Interfaces*, Vol. 13, 1991.

Babcock, C. "Object Lessons." *Computerworld*, May 3, 1993.

Banciinon, F. *Building an Object-Oriented Database System: The Story of O2.* San Mateo, CA: Morgan Kaufman Publishers, 1992.

Banerjee, J. "Data Model Issues for Object-Oriented Applications." *ACM Transactions on Office Information Systems*, 5(1):3–26, 1987.

Bradley, J. "An Object-Relationship Diagrammatic Technique for Object-Oriented Database Definitions." *Journal of Database Administration*, Vol. 3, Issue 2, Spring 1992.

Brathwaite, K. *Object-Oriented Database Design: Concepts and Applications.* San Diego, CA: Academic Press, 1993.

Bratsberg, S.E. "FOOD: Supporting Explicit Relations in a Fully Object-Oriented Database." *Proceedings of the IFIP TC2/WG 2.6 Working Conference*, 1991.

Brown, A.W. *Object-Oriented Databases and Their Applications to Software Engineering.* New York: McGraw-Hill, 1991.

Burleson, D.; Kassicieh, S.; and R. Lievano. "Design and Implementation of a Decision Support System for Academic Scheduling." *Information and Management*, Volume II, Number 2, September 1986.

Burleson, D. "SQL Generators." *Database Programming & Design*, July 1993.

Burleson, D. "Performance & Tuning Strategies for the Very Large Database." *Database Programming & Design*, October 1989.

Burleson, D. and S. Kassicieh. "A Decision Support System for Scheduling." *Proceedings of the International Conference*, Chicago, IL: Operations Research Society of America, 1983.

Cattell, R.G.G. *Object Data Management: Object-Oriented and Extended Relational Database Systems.* Reading, MA: Addison-Wesley, 1991.

Cattel, R.G.G. and T. Rogers. "Combining Object-Oriented and Relational Models of Data." International Workshop on Object-Oriented Database Systems, Proceedings, Wash. DC: IEEE Computer Society Press, 1986.

Chung, Y. and G. Fischer. "Illustration of Object-Oriented Databases for the Structure of a Bill of Materials." *Computers in Industry*, Vol. 19, June 1992.

Codd, E.F. *The Relational Model for Database Management.* Version 2, Addison-Wesley, 1990.

Comaford, C. "At Long Last, a True Query Tool for End Users." *PC Week,* March 1993.

Date, C. J. *An Introduction to Database Systems.* Addison-Wesley, 1990.

De Troyer, O.; Keustermans, J.; and R. Meersman. "How Helpful Is Object-Oriented Language for an Object-Oriented Database Model?" International Workshop on Object-Oriented Database Systems, Proceedings, Wash. DC: IEEE Computer Society Press, 1986.

"Deductive and Object-Oriented Databases: Proceedings of the First International Conference on Deductive and Object-Oriented Database." Elsevier Science Publishing Co., 1990.

"Deductive and Object-Oriented Databases: Proceedings of the Second International Conference on Deductive and Object-Oriented Database." Elsevier Science Publishing Co., 1991.

Dittrich, K. "Object-Oriented Database Systems: The Notions and the Issues." International Workshop on Object-Oriented Database Systems, Proceedings, Wash. DC: IEEE Computer Society Press, 1986.

Dittrich K. R., Dayal U., and Buchmann A. P. *On Object-Oriented Database Systems.* Springer Verlag Publishers, 1991.

Gorman, K. and J. Choobineh. "An Overview of the Object-Oriented Entity Relationship Model (OOERM). *Proceedings of the Twenty-Third Annual Hawaii International Conference on Information Systems,* (Vol. 3), pp. 336–345.

Goutas, S.; Soupos, P.; and D. Christodoulakis. "Formalization of Object-Oriented Database Model with Rules." *Information and Software Technology,* Vol. 33, Dec. 1991.

Gray, P. *Object-Oriented Databases: A Semantic Data Model Approach.* Englewood Cliffs, NJ: Prentice Hall, 1992.

"Implementing Persistent Object Bases: Principles and Practice." International Workshop on Persistent Object Systems, Morgan Kaufman Publishers, 1991.

Kersten, M. and F. Schippers. "Towards an Object-Centered Database Language." International Workshop on Object-Oriented Database Systems, Proceedings, Wash. DC: IEEE Computer Society Press, 1986.

Kim, W. "Issues of Object-Oriented Database Schemas." Ph.D. diss., University of Texas at Austin, 1988.

Kim, W. *Introduction to Object-Oriented Databases*. The MIT Press, 1990.

Kim, W. "Research Directions in Object-Oriented Database Systems." Communications of the ACM, 1990.

Liu, L. and E. Horowitz. *Object Database Support for CASE*. Englewood Cliffs, NJ: Prentice Hall, 1991.

Loomis, M. "Integrating Objects with Relational Technology." *Object Magazine*, July/August 1991.

Loomis, M. "Object and Relational Technology. Can They Cooperate?" *Object Magazine*, July/August 1991.

Loomis, M.; Atwood, T.; Cattel, R.; Duhi, J.; Ferran, G.; and D. Wade. "The ODMG Object Model." *Journal of Object-Oriented Programming*, June 1993.

Lyngbaek, P. and W. Kent. "A Data Modeling Methodology for the Design and Implementation of Information Systems." International Workshop on Object-Oriented Database Systems, Proceedings, Wash. DC: IEEE Computer Society Press, 1986.

Magedson. "Building OT from the Bottom Up." *Object Magazine*, July/August 1991.

Martin, J. and J. Odell. *Object-Oriented Analysis and Design.*, Englewood Cliffs, NJ: Prentice Hall, 1992.

McFadden, F. and J. Hoffer. *Database Management*. Menlo Park, CA: Benjamin Cummings Publishing Company, 1987.

McFadden, F. "Conceptual Design of Object-Oriented Databases." *Journal of Object-Oriented Programming*, Vol. 4, September 1991.

Meyer, B. *Object-Oriented Software Construction*. Englewood Cliffs, NJ: Prentice Hall, 1988.

Morgan, J. "Ingres for DB2 Users." *Relational Database Journal*, May-July 1993.

Rowe, L. "A Shared Object Hierarchy." International Workshop on Object-Oriented Database Systems, Proceedings, Wash. DC: IEEE Computer Society Press, 1986.

Ruben, K. and A. Goldberg. "Object Behavior Analysis." *Communications of the ACM*, September 1992.

Schek, H. and M. Scholl. "Evolution of Data Models." International Workshop on Object-Oriented Database Systems, Proceedings, Wash. DC: IEEE Computer Society Press, 1990.

Scholl, M.; Laasch, C.; and M. Tresch. "Updateable Views in Object-Oriented Databases." International Workshop on Object-Oriented Database Systems, Proceedings, Wash. DC: IEEE Computer Society Press, 1990.

Soloviev, V. "An Overview of Three Commercial Object-Oriented Database Management Systems: ONTOS, ObjectStore, and O/sub 2/." *SIGMOD Record*, Vol. 21, March 1992.

Stone, C. "The Rise of Object Databases: Can the Object Management Group Get Database Vendors to Agree on Object Standards?" *DBMS*, July 1992.

Thalhiem, B. "Extending the Entity-Relationship Model for a High-Level, Theory-Based Database Design." International Workshop on Object-Oriented Database Systems, Proceedings, Wash. DC: IEEE Computer Society Press, 1990.

Unland, R. and G. Schlageter. "Object-Oriented Database Systems: Concepts and Perspectives." International Workshop on Object-Oriented Database Systems, Proceedings, Wash. DC: IEEE Computer Society Press, 1990.

Varma, S. "Object-Oriented Databases: Where Are We Now?" *Database Programming & Design*, May 1993.

Vasan, R. "Relational Databases and Objects: A Hybrid Solution." *Object Magazine*, July/August 1991.

Yourdon, E. "The Marriage of Relational and Object-Oriented Design." *Relational Journal*, Vol. 3, Issue 6, January 1992.

Index